IRS AUDIT PROTECTION AND SURVIVAL GUIDE

BED AND BREAKFASTS

Other industries and professions in the IRS Audit Protection and Survival Guide Series

Attorneys
Bars and Restaurants
Trucking Industry

IRS AUDIT PROTECTION AND SURVIVAL GUIDE

BED AND BREAKFASTS

Gerald F. Bernard

Daniel J. Baran

John Wiley & Sons, Inc.

NEW YORK • CHICHESTER • BRISBANE • TORONTO • SINGAPORE • WEINHEIM

Library of Congress Cataloging in Publication Data:
Baran, Daniel J.
    IRS audit protection and survival guide: Bed and breakfasts /
    Gerald F. Bernard, Daniel J. Baran.
        p.   cm.
    Includes index.
    ISBN 0-471-16634-0 (cloth : alk. paper)
    1. Bed and breakfast accommodations—United States—Finance.
    2. Bed and breakfast accommodations—United States—Auditing.
    I. Daniel J. Baran.   II. Title.
    TX911.3.F5B37   1996
    647.9473'03'0681—dc20   96-17989
                                                                       CIP

Book design by Anne Scatto / PIXEL PRESS

Printed in the United States of America

10 9 8 7 6 5 4 3 2 1

CONTENTS

CHAPTER 3 • IMPORTANT PLANNING WHEN FORMING A BED AND BREAKFAST BUSINESS 38

CHAPTER 4 • TARGETING EMPLOYEE AND INDEPENDENT CONTRACTOR ISSUES 47

CHAPTER 5 • WHAT HAPPENS WHEN THERE IS A LOSS 56

CHAPTER 6 • SPECIAL CIRCUMSTANCES   68

CHAPTER 7 • PLAN AHEAD WHEN CHOOSING A BUSINESS ENTITY   74

CHAPTER 8 • THE AUDIT PROCESS AND IMPORTANT STEPS OF SELF-PROTECTION   88

CHAPTER 9 • APPEALS AND TAX COLLECTION   103

CHAPTER 10 • CONCLUSION   109

ACKNOWLEDGMENTS

The authors are indebted to research assistant Lynella Grant, JD, whose research techniques and dedication contributed immensely to the development of the technical issues discussed in this book. Many thanks for the initial coaching by authors/publishers Steven Walker, President of Camelback Design Group and Carl Young, Vice President of Documedia Technology, Inc. who provided numerous suggestions on the format of this book. We also appreciate the contributions of Pat Hardy for her review and recommendations regarding book content. Our appreciation also goes to journalist Gerry Mueller for his review and editing of the manuscript as well as to Yale Goldberg, Certified Tax Specialist of Frazer, Ryan, Goldberg, and Hunter, LLP for sharing his technical expertise relating to employment tax issues.

The coaching, assistance, and patience of Wiley editor Sheck Cho and his assistant Tim Burgard helped greatly in making the creation of this book an enjoyable experience.

ACKNOWLEDGMENTS

PREFACE

The IRS Knows More about the Bed and Breakfast Business than You Do

CAUTION—THE BED AND BREAKFAST INDUSTRY IS UNDER
ASSAULT BY AN IRS ARMY OF HIGHLY TRAINED SPECIALISTS

Traditionally, the Internal Revenue Service (IRS) has trained its auditors to be generalists dealing with a variety of issues in many unrelated businesses. Now, however, it has entered a new age, using trained specialists to impose tougher and more intensive audits.

The new IRS Market Segment Specialization Program (MSSP), originally launched in 1994, uses a specialized approach to assure greater adherence to federal statutes for specific industries such as Bed and Breakfast (B&B). The MSSP is part of the nationwide Compliance 2000 initiative to modernize the Internal Revenue Service with the technical advancements necessary to move into the twenty-first century. This new program changes the way tax audits have been conducted for the past 50 years. Failure to prepare for this specialized IRS attack will cost the Bed and Breakfast industry millions of dollars a year.

The objectives of the MSSP include: conducting tax audits using examiners who have specialized skills and knowledge; sharing of MSSP knowledge; involving representatives of key market segments to address noncompliance.

The new MSSP auditors are thoroughly trained in operating procedures, issues, and particular laws specific to the B&B industry. Auditors expert in Bed and Breakfast issues will probe in greater depth than was ever before possible. They are trained in the latest technological research tools and compare industry statistics to the company's prior years' tax returns. These MSSP auditors can quickly identify areas of noncompliance and assess additional taxes, interest, and penalties.

Computers provide the means to track, compile, and retrieve the massive data to manage the economy of today's civilization. Just as businesses must compete for resources and market shares, the IRS must also compete to ensure an equal compliance with the tax laws by all members of society. The IRS approached this goal in a businesslike manner, and articulated this new policy in terms of increasing its market share by competing for dollars. IRS agents are supplied with portable computers that enable them to tap the vast IRS database and many other information sources. Agents will carry online access to tax return data for as many as five prior years. The enhanced training of auditors under the MSSP program is a clear message from the IRS that it intends to use sophisticated equipment to keep pace with the changing business environment. The new MSSP auditor will be well-armed, well-taught, and well-informed.

This *IRS Audit Protection and Survival Guide* explains the issues in the Internal Revenue Service MSSP audit guide for the Bed and Breakfast industry. Coauthors Daniel J. Baran, CPA, and Gerald F. Bernard, CPA, provide insights from their over forty combined years of experience advising other CPAs, attorneys, and businesses on complex compliance and tax controversy issues. In addition, Gerald F. Bernard, a former IRS agent, offers unique and practical guidance for surviving an IRS audit.

The authors explain which issues auditors will be examining, which they have been taught to question, and what outside information is available to the IRS auditors as they conduct the audit. Wise use of the *Audit Protection Guide* will preclude the need to use it as an *Audit Survival Guide.* Don't make the mistake of letting the Internal Revenue Service know more about your business than you do. *Your Bed and Breakfast's survival depends on total preparation for the impending IRS attack.*

IRS AUDIT PROTECTION AND SURVIVAL GUIDE

BED AND BREAKFASTS

CHAPTER 1

Bed and Breakfasts and Internal Revenue Service Market Segments

THE NEW INTERNAL REVENUE SERVICE AUDIT MISSION

The Internal Revenue Service (IRS) is in the process of implementing its Compliance 2000 modernization program and is embarking on a mission that will change the way income tax audits have been conducted for the last 50 years. It is a mission armed with an arsenal of specialty teams of auditors trained in newly developed audit techniques. Such audit techniques are being carefully tailored to each industry. The auditors' training concentrates on industry operating procedures, issues, and applicable laws specifically relating to the business, group, industry, or profession. Such training allows the auditors to examine an issue in more depth than ever before possible.

TRADITIONAL AUDIT TECHNIQUES

Traditionally, the IRS has trained its auditors to be generalists dealing with a variety of issues in many unrelated businesses. Since its inception in 1932, it has used several different methods of choosing tax returns for audits. Such methods have included:

- Taxpayer Compliance Measurement Program (TCMP): Taxpayers are randomly chosen for gathering of statistical information. All items of income and expense are examined for compliance. The IRS designed the programs to be conducted in three-year cycles to keep pace with the innovative accounting techniques developed by taxpayers and their advisors.

- Discriminant Function Scoring (DIF): For each examination class, different items on the return are scored. Returns are chosen when amounts reported are outside norms established under the TCMP. The total DIF score for a return is the sum of the scores of the individual items. The higher the score, the greater the probability of tax change. Most of the individual, partnership, and corporate returns that are examined each year are DIF-selected returns.

- Identifying differences in amounts reported by taxpayers and amounts reported by third parties such as wages on W-2s and interest on 1099s.

- Identifying differences in amounts reported by other government agencies and the amounts reported by the taxpayer.

- Reviewing information supplied by informers.

INDUSTRY SPECIALIZATION AND MARKET SEGMENT SPECIALIZATION PROGRAMS

The IRS has recognized the need to change its traditional approach by addressing significant issues that materially affect a tax return or group of returns being examined. To qualify as significant, an issue needs to have a material effect on proposed adjustments, apply to many taxpayers, or relate to a widespread difference in the interpretation of law.

John J. Monaco, executive director of IRS coordinated examination programs, IRS, said the programs were started because the IRS recognized that its examination personnel could not hope to be familiar with the many accounting and business practices particular to all the different industries. The IRS also realized the need for greater communication and coordination among the various IRS regions and individual examiners working similar cases. As a result, the Industry Specialization Program was initiated to promote better identification and development of issues under examination and to ensure uniform treatment of issues in the examination cycle.[1]

The IRS refers to targeted industries, including the Bed and Breakfast business, as market segments. A market segment can be an industry such as Bed and Breakfast or construction, a profession such as medicine or sales, or an issue such as tip income or independent contractors. The mission of the MSSP is to use teams of experienced IRS auditors to develop training programs focusing on a specific market segment. The objectives of the MSSP program include:

- Conducting tax audits using examiners who have specialized knowledge of the particular market segment

- Sharing MSSP knowledge through educational efforts with the taxpayer community

- Involving representatives of key market segments to address noncompliance both from tax administration and taxpayer perspectives

The emphasis of the MSSP is the Audit Technique Guide (ATG) for specific market segments. The ATG is used for extensive training of auditors in a specific market segment. Training is conducted on a regional and national basis, developing industry experts with the ability to use the newest research tools, including CD-ROM, the Internet, archives of public records, and comparative industry statistics.

As of April 1996, the new program covers more than 40 industries and specific issues (Exhibit 1-1). The MSSP is currently in its developmental phase and there is little feedback available regarding its effectiveness. The data that does exist is closely guarded.

The MSSP will be a long-term and evolving process. Eventually, all 20,000 IRS auditors will be trained in these new techniques and will become industry experts. Keep in mind that the IRS auditor has access to closely guarded statistics that are not publicly available, in addition to reference sources that business owners and their advisors have. These guarded statistics were developed from tax returns and compiled by entity type, geographic area, standard industrial code (code that represents a group of similar companies), number of employees, total sales, total assets, and many other factors.

The following information from other Bed and Breakfasts is of great value to the IRS when examining the results of a taxpayer's operation:

- Average sales, in quantity and dollars, for the type of business in a particular city based on business size

- Percentages of money received from customers that come from cash, check, or credit card

- Typical gross profit on sales of goods for any particular industry

- Average pay rate and total payroll for any type of business in any particular locality

The IRS will have many statistics available before beginning an audit. Research technicians in the IRS District Offices Research and Analysis (DORA) will prepare a comparative analysis for the auditor using the information reported on

EXHIBIT 1-1 MARKET SEGMENT SPECIALIZATION PROGRAM (MSSP) GUIDES

Air Charters

Alaskan Commercial Fishing: Catcher Vessels—Part I

Alaskan Commercial Fishing: Processors and Brokers—Part II

Architects

Attorneys

Auto Body and Repair Industry

Bars and Restaurants

Beauty and Barber Shops

Bed and Breakfasts

Entertainment—Music Industry

Entertainment—Foreign Athletes and Entertainers

Entertainment—Important 1040 Issues

Farmers

Food Service Industry

Gas Retailers

Grain Farmers

Health Care Industry

Ministers

Mobile Food Vendors

Mortuaries

Passive Activity Losses

Pizza Restaurant

Rehabilitation Tax Credit

Reforestation Industry

Resolution Trust Corporation: Cancellation of Indebtedness

Taxi Cabs

The Port Project

The Wine Industry

Trucking Industry

the tax return with statistics available from other sources, including:

- Income statistics published in industry periodicals

- Industry statistics from national member organizations

- State and local public information

- Shared information from exchange agreements with certain states

- Service bureaus that provide statistics such as Dun & Bradstreet and TRW

THE FINANCIAL STATUS AUDIT— ECONOMIC REALITY ISSUES

Under the Compliance 2000 program, the IRS has designed another new audit program as a wake-up call for tax preparers and their clients. With the modernization of the IRS well under way, the economic reality audit has become the IRS audit method of choice. Also described as a lifestyle check, the economic reality audit may affect all taxpayers, but it is primarily focused on those that have small business activities with cash-skimming potential, such as repair services, beauty shops, retail stores, and gas stations. Lifestyle checks will also be imposed upon larger companies and their owners.

Under Compliance 2000, the IRS is serious about its goal to increase compliance from the current estimated 83 percent level to 90 percent in order to curtail the underground economy. Increased computerization makes it possible for auditors to prepare comparisons of prior returns by the taxpayer (and other taxpayers in the same or similar industries). Interviews are conducted with key business contacts of the taxpayer, current and prior employees, and others who have information about buying habits and business practices. Such methods provide very powerful tools to the auditor even before the audit begins.

The Compliance 2000 program includes plans to retrain all of its auditors to use economic reality techniques and industry specialty techniques. Auditors will be trained to review a taxpayer's lifestyle and determine if the amount of income reported is equal to the taxpayer's standard of living.

The economic reality type of audit is not new to the IRS, but prior to now was only conducted when a civil audit generated evidence of unreported income or the possibility of criminal activity. Now the IRS is placing the economic reality issues at the beginning of every audit to determine the depth of its investigative process.

Many tax practitioners, accounting groups, and attorneys are concerned that these new investigative procedures will lead to entrapment of the taxpayer, and as a result these groups have raised possible Fifth Amendment issues and questions of due process. The tax practitioner is worried about alleged, unseen criminal issues. If a civil fraud or criminal issue could be raised in the audit, both the taxpayer and the representative would have to consider retaining an attorney to review the potential risks. The attorney-client communication privilege is extremely important if this criminal exposure exists. See Chapter 8 for additional information on this topic.

THE BED AND BREAKFAST AS A TARGET

The U.S. Bed and Breakfast industry has roots reaching back to Colonial times when the early settlers brought with them the European tradition of the innkeeper's hospitality. The U.S. Bed and Breakfast industry has been gaining greater popularity in recent times. The eighteenth edition of *Bed & Breakfast U.S.A.*[3] lists more than 11,000 host homes. In the *Bed and Breakfast U.S.A.* editions, a "bed and breakfast" is defined as "an owner-occupied residence with breakfast included at a fair rate, where the visitor is made to feel more like a welcome guest than a paying customer."

There are some very good reasons why Bed and Breakfasts have been targeted by the Internal Revenue Service. One of these reasons is the abundant information about Bed and Breakfasts that is readily available to the IRS from state, county, and local regulatory agencies. Direct access to this comparative information makes the Bed and Breakfast operation an appealing audit target. An example of the kind of information available is a sample from the survey of the Professional Association of Innkeepers International (PAII) for 1994.[4] It is based on data collected from its members. The figures provide a wide array of statistics about Bed and Breakfast operations, which can provide useful industry norms. See Appendix B for excerpts from this survey.

Another reason for the IRS selecting the Bed and Breakfast industry is the inherently close relationship of business and personal expenses. Proper allocation of these expenses is complicated. Errors in computing proper deductions are common. In addition, the tax laws concerning the reporting of profits and losses are complex. Some issues have yet to be resolved by the courts, which have been unable to agree on certain specific interpretations.

REGULATORY AGENCIES

The volume of information filed with federal and state regulatory agencies by Bed and Breakfast companies give the IRS auditor extensive information to examine. Most Bed and Breakfasts are controlled by strict filing requirements. As a result, there is a wealth of information maintained by a multitude of regulatory agencies. Most of these agencies require that periodic reports be filed by Bed and Breakfasts. These filing requirements range from sales tax reports to food handling permits. All of the reports filed by Bed and Breakfasts are available to the Internal Revenue Service upon their request.

This means that a good portion of the IRS auditor's fieldwork can be performed before the taxpayer even knows his or her income tax return is under scrutiny. Using the abundant data kept on file by these regulatory agencies, the IRS can compare the information in those files to the income tax returns filed by the Bed and Breakfast owner. It is simple for an IRS auditor to determine if discrepancies exist among the information reported to the various agencies.

PRE-AUDIT EVALUATION

Information is power. Before meeting with the taxpayer, the auditor reviews a wide variety of information that will be useful for the audit. The following is an excerpt from the MSSP manual:

Pre-Audit—minimum review to include:
   a. Copies of any prior State or Federal audit reports,
   b. Copies of annual County Bed tax returns,
   c. Cash T and Bank Deposit Analysis,
   d. Extraordinary expenses and issues identified in the pre-contact analysis should be reviewed. Also, compare Schedule C and Schedule A for interest and tax allocations,
   e. Special attention should be given to personal usage of food and structure, and potential remodel of future retirement homes,
   f. Order transcripts for prior and subsequent years. Be sure to obtain payroll transcripts.
   g. Order IRP documents to identify "other" sources of income.

h. County Records have license applications which may be very informative. The Planning, Building and Health Departments as well as the Tax Assessor will have information.

i. Be aware of the tax ramifications of Real Estate transactions especially when business and personal aspects are present.

j. Do the taxpayers advertise in the phone book? Look for ads describing establishment and services available. Are credit cards accepted?[5]

The auditor is going into the audit well informed. The IRS is looking for evidence that there is a business, and has a profit motive. Agents will explore the following factors:

1. Manner in which the taxpayer carries on the activity.

2. The expertise of the taxpayer or his advisors.

3. The time and effort expended by the taxpayer in carrying on the activity.

4. Expectation that assets used in the activity may appreciate in value.

5. The success of the taxpayers in carrying on other similar or dissimilar activities.

6. The taxpayer's history of income or losses with respect to the activity.

7. The amount of occasional profits, if any, which are earned.

8. The financial status of the taxpayer.[6]

The business owner cannot afford to ignore the IRS or the issues that pertain to that market segment. By being armed and informed with information about the audit process, the taxpayer is less vulnerable to a well-prepared auditor.

ENDNOTES

1. IRS Press release.

2. *IRS Form 9846 (4-96) Department of Treasury—Internal Revenue Service.*

3. Rundback, Betty & Ackerman, Peggy, *1995 Bed and Breakfast U.S.A.* (New York: Plume, 1995).

4. Professional Association of Innkeepers International (PAII), *Bed and Breakfast/Country Inns Industry Study of Operations, Marketing and Finances* (Santa Barbara, CA: PAII, 1994).

5. *Market Segment Specialization Program (MSSP)* [training manual], "Bed and Breakfasts," Department of the Treasury, Internal Revenue Service, 1995, p. 2.

6. Ibid., p. 14.

CHAPTER 2

Prime Audit Issues for a Bed and Breakfast

SOURCES OF INCOME

The auditor is looking for money made from sources related to operating a Bed and Breakfast (B&B). The taxpayer needs to be able to show how much was earned and where it came from, and that requires good record keeping.

 WARNING: The primary objective of the IRS Market Segment Specialization Program (MSSP) audit techniques is to determine if income has been underreported.

By comparing the tax return to information on file with state and local agencies, the IRS can locate unreported income. For example, the IRS can compare the income reported for sales tax purposes with the income reported for federal tax purposes. In addition to receiving income data supplied by regulatory agencies, auditors are trained to canvas the registration bureaus and reservation agents servicing the B&B industry.

WARNING: Pocketing cash without reporting the income may result in criminal prosecution. See Chapter 8 for a discussion on the Criminal Investigation Division.

IRS auditors trained with these new audit techniques will be able to quickly identify the important issues commonly associated with the operation of B&Bs, and will be able to spot critical issues, such as unreported income or improper expenses. The auditor will also consider the particular type of tax forms used to report the B&B activity.

It is expected that the IRS will distinguish between "host homes" and professional inns. In this context, host homes would typically have four or less rooms available for guests. The IRS will be looking for returns with high renovation expenses and low income, which may occur more commonly with host homes.

The following list is a sample of the questions the IRS can be expected to ask in an audit:

Date opened for business? Has the business ever been closed?

Is this a seasonal activity?

Number of days open during the year?

Do you have a minimum number of days required for a stay?

Are one-day events acceptable (i.e. weddings, parties, etc.)? Are there additional charges for one-day events?

Can clients use their own caterers or must they go through you?

What is the charge for this service?

Which meals are included in rates: Regular or Continental Breakfast? Lunch? Dinner?

What types of credit cards are accepted?

Is there an extra fee if guests have pets?

Do you keep personal pets / livestock on the property?

Age of children accepted? Do you allow children to stay free of charge if under a certain age?

Do you have a liquor license?

Do you provide complimentary wine? If you charge for wine, how much?

Do you charge for canceled reservations?

How much do you charge for deposits? How much of the deposit is refundable?

Are you licensed with the city or county?

What was the source of the money used for the down payment of the B&B?

Have you ever been audited? (Please provide copies of any audit reports received.)

Are any items sold at the B&B (i.e. gifts, maps, wine, books, etc.)?

Do you charge a fee for making reservations? If so, how much?

Do you receive tips or other gratuities?

Do you engage in bartering for goods or services?[1]

INCOME FROM LODGING

Bed & Breakfast U.S.A.[2] lists over 100 reservation agencies that serve the B&B industry. The IRS uses these sources to determine the number of reservations booked by a particular B&B, along with its room rates and range of services offered. Armed with this information, it is a simple matter for them to determine whether a B&B's income has been fully reported.

Associations such as the Professional Association of Innkeepers International (PAII) conduct periodic surveys and publish the results. See an example of some of the PAII data in Appendix B.

Innkeepers from across the country provided information in one survey covering financial areas such as gross revenue, fixed and variable expenses, and other cost factors of their investments. The survey data was presented by room size, geography, and years in business. Such valuable public information provides the IRS with important statistical data. The information is summarized by geographic location as well as room size and amenities provided.

These surveys usually contain detailed expense information and bottom line profit-or-loss data for each group surveyed. These surveys are used by innkeepers in evaluating their own operations. By analyzing such information, the IRS can develop general guidelines as to the amount of income that should be generated by a B&B activity in a particular location. IRC Section 61 provides the definition of what constitutes income; it casts a broad net by describing gross income as all income from whatever source derived, including (but not limited to) 15 specific items. See Appendix C for the full text of *IRC Section 61*.

DEPOSITS

In the day-to-day operation of a B&B, the operator services guests who are present and communicates with future guests. In most cases, a deposit is taken at the time a reservation is made. Policies vary concerning the refund of deposits. *How to Open and Operate a Bed & Breakfast* instructs the operator how to handle deposits:

Explain the prices and ask for a deposit to be sent in advance. Some hosts ask for an amount equal to that of one night's stay;

others ask for a percentage of the total projected amount (usually 25 percent). . . . [There will be] cancellations as well as no-shows. Generally, hosts will refund if a cancellation is made seven days prior to the original planned date of arrival. A service charge is deducted from the refund (hosts charge anywhere from $5.00 to $10.00). The charge compensates for time and effort to process the reservation. Hosts generally do not refund the deposit for cancellations made at the last minute or for no-shows who later contact them.[3]

Rental income is the payment received for the occupation of property. There is no dispute about whether rental income must be reported as income when received. There has been an ongoing controversy about whether deposits should be treated the same way.

The hotly debated issue is "when do deposits become income to the receiver?" Should the deposits be treated as earnings at the time they are received or at the time the service (rental) occurs? The issue was decided by the U.S. Supreme Court in *Comr.* v. *Indianapolis Power & Light Company* 90-1 USTC Para. 50,007 (S. Ct. 1990). This case clearly articulated the rule regarding taxability of deposits. In arriving at its decision, the Supreme Court stated, "Our decision is also consistent with the Tax Court's long-standing treatment of lease deposits—perhaps the closest analogy to the present situation. The Tax Court has traditionally distinguished between a sum designated as prepayment of rent—which is taxable upon receipt—and a sum deposited to secure the tenant's performance of a lease agreement."

The court laid to rest a number of competing tests and ruled that deposits were not taxable income to the recipient when made. The determinative test was the amount of dominion and control the parties had over the funds. It was the customer's element of choice, the court decided, that distinguishes an advance payment from a loan. It supported the position that since the deposits may have to be refunded, they are not considered to be income until the services are rendered.

PLANNING TIP: The B&B proprietor need not report refundable deposits as income at the time of receipt.

Any portion of a nonrefundable deposit must be reported as income when received. A refundable deposit will become taxable as income at the time the deposit is forfeited by the customer. A record of refundable deposits should be maintained. The best policy is to keep a record of all pending reservation deposits and indicate when they are earned. In this way, it is possible at any point in time to determine how much is owed (held) as deposits. It is not necessary to segregate the deposits from other bank deposits.

INCOME FROM SPECIAL SERVICES

The IRS is fully aware of the seemingly unlikely places in which additional income is sometimes excluded from the B&B owner's tax return. The IRS auditor knows that many B&Bs offer additional services such as weddings and anniversary and banquet parties. These services are usually accompanied by catering fees and typically generate gratuities and tips (see next section). The IRS auditor may make anonymous inquiries about the extra services provided by the targeted B&B to determine if there is any additional, unreported income.

Other services and products subject to investigation include gifts and crafts marketed by the B&B. In addition, the IRS will check if the B&B provides package lunches or canned jellies or fruits. In those states with a sales tax on such items, the IRS will be able to obtain copies of the B&B owner's sales tax reports to learn what income is being reported from such sales. In most cases, the information obtained by the IRS is shared with state taxing agencies.

The IRS knows that transportation, guide, and ticket services can also result in extra income. Referral rebates, commissions, kickbacks, and bartering income will also be included on their list of inquiries. They know that B&Bs can supplement their income with pet fees, rental of recreational equipment, and wine corking fees. In addition, the IRS auditor may make an anonymous inquiry as to whether or not the B&B commonly charges cancellation fees. The inquiry will alert the auditor to look for reporting of this type of income.

TIP INCOME

Tips or gratuities paid to the business owner are to be treated like other income and should be reported as business income. Expect the IRS auditor to look for unreported tip income. If tip income is received, the auditor will expect to see cash deposited or otherwise accounted for as income in the record-keeping system.

INSURANCE COVERAGE

When a B&B is audited, the IRS will look for all sources of income as a routine procedure. One of the first items asked for is a copy of any insurance policies. The insurance coverage in a policy can provide a direct connection to other sources of income. For example, a B&B operator may own bicycles or other recreational equipment available to guests either as a complimentary service or for an additional fee. Generally, the owner will want insurance coverage on the equipment while it is being used by guests. If these items are covered for rental use, the IRS will be looking for income from such rental activity.

Insurance is also an issue for auditors in other ways, such as whether it is calculated appropriately as an expense. It is wise for the operator to discuss the operation with an insurance supplier because of the special requirements of B&Bs. Adequate insurance for the unique business requirements of a

B&B can also be located through the various B&B organizations, such as PAII.

WARNING: Homeowner's insurance policies need special riders to cover paying guests. Coverage is often denied or incomplete, so care should be exercised by the B&B owner.

CAVEAT ON UNREPORTED INCOME

There can be serious legal consequences if a B&B operator has neglected to report taxable income (see Chapter 8). If the B&B owner discovers an omission of income before receiving any notice of an imminent tax audit, it is generally advisable to file an amended return to report the correct amount of income. However, if the taxpayer has underreported income and has been notified of an imminent audit, it is important to immediately consult a tax attorney specializing in IRS compliance matters.

WARNING: Once the taxpayer has been notified of an audit, the correction of an error, such as the omission of income, is no longer as simple as filing an amended return. There may be far more serious issues at stake than merely paying the tax and interest on the additional income. Penalties could range from civil to criminal in nature.

If there has been more than a 25 percent omission of income, the IRS has up to six years to assess the additional tax, penalties, and interest. If a criminal intent can be proven, there is no statute of limitations, and the IRS can assess tax, penalties, and interest no matter how far back the tax year. More complete information on how to handle an IRS audit is included in Chapters 8 and 9.

ALLOCATION OF OPERATING COSTS (EXPENSES)

IRS agents are always looking for personal expenses that have been included with the deductible costs of operating a B&B. Personal expenses are not deductible, so a good record-keeping system is essential.

Expenses can be divided into two categories: direct and indirect. Direct expenses are costs that are incurred solely for the benefit of the customers, and would not have arisen without the B&B business. Examples of direct costs would be linen service for the rooms rented, depreciation of the furniture in the rooms rented, and food served to guests. Those items that qualify as direct expenses can be fully expensed.

Indirect expenses can only be written off proportionally to the business use of the premises. The auditor will look carefully at any expense that could provide benefits to the owner.

> **WARNING:** Unless the expense can be shown to be solely for the benefit of the guests, it should be apportioned according to the proper percentage calculated for the business.

Bed and Breakfasts can expect inquiries into the allocation of indirect expenses such as utilities, cable TV service, telephone expenses, repairs, and maintenance, as well as interest, taxes, and insurance payments. Repairs done to areas other than the specific room(s) held for rent will not be allowed. The IRS may attempt to apply this rule to costs incurred for the exterior and outside grounds as well. Expenses associated with common areas of the house used by both family members and B&B guests are also nondeductible.

The percentage of the home dedicated to the B&B activities is measured by the square footage of the guest rooms in relation to the square footage of the entire home. Only the guest rooms can be counted in determining the business percentage. The common areas—such as hallways, kitchens, and dining rooms—are not included as B&B rooms. The resulting percentage determines how much of the house is depreciable.

 WARNING: The calculated figures described above may not be the same percentage allowed to determine certain operating costs such as utilities, cable TV, or telephones.

These types of costs should be allocated based on actual use by guests or by guest days compared to total use by everyone. For example, utilities would be more accurately allocated by using a combination of square footage and the number of days guests occupied the rooms. For example:

Utilities cost for 1 year:		$3000
Square footage of guest rooms:	200	
Square footage of house:	2000	
Ratio:	10%	× .10
		$300
Guest days:	100	
Total days:	365	
Ratio:	27%	× .27
Deductible utilities costs		= $81

Agents are instructed to specifically inquire about the method used to allocate these expenses. Note in particular Item 4 in Exhibit 2-1, which is from the MSSP training manual given to IRS auditors.

FOOD COSTS

Food costs are a major area of auditor inquiry. IRS agents are instructed to check with the local regulatory authorities to see which meals the B&B is authorized to serve. Deductions are not allowed for the costs of providing guests meals that the

EXHIBIT 2-1   BUSINESS VS. PERSONAL EXPENSES

Personal expenses are deducted as business expenses on the schedule C's. These expenses are found in almost every category beginning with cost of goods sold to advertising and other expenses. Some areas of non-compliance are found to be:

1. Bank Charges—deduction of total monthly charges on both business and personal accounts, or when there is one account and all personal income and expenses are run through it.

2. Interest, Taxes, and Insurance—the business percentage is too high and may include items not related to the bed and breakfast activity.

3. Food—deduction includes the family's portion. Record keeping may be poor to nonexistent. The register receipts from the store are the only record that has been kept. No allocation for the specific food used for the guest is made. If no records have been kept and no reasonable allocation has been made, an audit technique would be to first check with the county and find out what type of meal can be served—continental or traditional breakfast. Determine an average cost (not Fair Market Value) of a meal and multiply it by the number of guests. When checking with the county be sure to ask if food can be served at other times during the day, and if so, what limitations exist. If food and drink are allowable at different times and the taxpayer does not have appropriate records, use the average cost times the number of guests to get a reasonable deduction. If the taxpayer goes beyond what is allowed by county rules and regulations, then no deduction will be allowed for the extra expense. Food purchased for the guests but consumed by the family is not deductible.

4. Utilities—deductions are disproportionately higher than the actual expense allowable. The percentage used to determine the business portion for depreciation is not always the same to be used for utilities. For example, if the business portion of the inn is 40% but the utilities directly relating to the business portion may only be 20%. Cable television is another expense where allocations can differ or may not be deductible. If there is only one television available for family and guest, no allocation can be made between business use

EXHIBIT 2-1 BUSINESS VS. PERSONAL EXPENSES
(continued)

and personal use. In these cases, no direct business relationship can be shown, and therefore, no deduction is allowable.

5. Telephone—deductions are taken for the full or percentage of basic rate plus the toll calls. If there is no separate business line going into the home/inn then there is no deduction for the basic rate (not even a percentage). Only the direct business toll calls may be deducted.

6. Repairs and Maintenance—deductions are taken for repairs and maintenance for the interior and exterior of the home. The business use percentage may be applied to the total expense. Deductions for repairs and maintenance to areas other than the specific rooms held for business are not deductible. Repairs to the exterior and grounds are not deductible. Personal and capital expenditures are often included as repairs and maintenance expenses.

7. Common Area—space used by the family and guests is common area. This may include kitchen, dining room, living room, den, etc. No deduction is allowable for this space. This is different from the provisions for day care services addressed by IRC §280A(c)(4).

There are other areas in which personal expenses have been misrepresented as business expenses. The above are the most commonly found.[4]

B&B has not been authorized or licensed to serve. The IRS also uses such information to help it calculate the average cost of meals served to guests. Note that any food purchased for guests but consumed by family members is not deductible.

The Bed and Breakfast operator should know how to document the average cost of the meals served to guests. A simple way to calculate the average cost of meals is to express each item of the meal in terms of a "serving." Most packaging labels show the number of servings per container. A record of any calculations should be saved in a "food cost" file. Local prices of items can be documented with copies of cash register receipts or even grocery store advertisements describing the typical food served at mealtimes. Keep copies of the menu list and guest order forms used to make breakfast selections. When it is impractical to segregate cooking supplies and condiments, reasonable estimates of the per-serving cost should be made. When grocery shopping, consider segregating personal and guest items at the checkout counter for receipts purposes.

The time spent by the owner should not be considered as a cost factor of preparing meals. In a sole proprietorship, time spent by the owner in any capacity is never considered as a cost factor for tax purposes. The value of an owner's services is never a deductible cost because the owner does not receive a paycheck for the services.

 WARNING: Proprietors should never pay themselves a salary.

Such a practice could result in taxable income to the owner and may not be deductible if the B&B business has a loss subject to limitations under the provisions of *IRC Section 280A* (see Chapter 5). Therefore, no deduction or income is ever recognized for the value of the services rendered by a proprietor or the proprietor's spouse to the business. However, the cost of remuneration paid to staff is deductible.

AUTOMOBILES AND COMPUTERS (LISTED PROPERTY)

The use and deduction of automobiles and computers always seem to receive special attention by the IRS. Both items are likely to be obtained for personal use, and therefore have a potential for misallocation of proper business percentages.

The first step in determining the business use of an auto is to keep a record of the total miles. Determining that figure can be easily accomplished by making a note of the odometer reading at the end of each year. If that step is missed, auto repair or oil change records often reflect the odometer reading. As a last resort, determine the average annual miles driven by dividing the current odometer reading by the number of years the car has been owned.

The next step is to determine the percentage of business miles driven—the hardest part of record keeping. The ideal method is a daily log complete with odometer readings at the beginning and end of each stop. If the auto is used in any routine manner, such as typical rounds, the total business miles can be verified by keeping a log for a few months. Otherwise, a reconstruction will be necessary by referring to appointment books, schedules such as "to do" lists, receipts, and invoices. This is a very cumbersome task, especially when preparing for an unexpected audit. Auto usage can be documented by reference to activities such as attendance at chamber of commerce meetings, trips to the bank and post office, and distribution of advertising.

The IRS is looking for reasonableness. For example, if there are four kids and only one family car, 80 percent or more business use may be difficult to establish by using indirect methods. The amount of credence the IRS gives to such indirect documentation will be directly related to the quality and accuracy of other records.

Computer usage is difficult to establish. The volume of business records and computer software loaded will determine how closely the IRS will scrutinize the business deductions for a computer. A computer becomes integral to the B&B by its use in handling reservations, maintaining routine bookkeeping, and preparing menus, notices, and promotional literature. Computers are also proving useful in marketing B&Bs. Increasingly, many guests are turning to the Internet and online methods to locate and book their stays. The ability to send and receive faxes is an attractive feature that many guests are willing to pay extra for. It is no longer incongruous to see a modern fax machine sitting on the antique credenza in the hallway.

Both cars and computers used in the home are considered "listed" property. Listed property is any property that lends itself to personal use or enjoyment. Besides cars and computers, video cameras, stereos, TVs, cellular phones, and tape recorders are examples of listed property.

 **WARNING:** The single most important tax attribute of listed property is the recapture rule. When listed property is depreciated as a business asset (see information on depreciation later in this chapter), the IRS requires a recapture of depreciation in any year the property's business use percentage drops below 50 percent.

The recapture amount is the depreciation claimed up to the date the property dropped below 50 percent business use, decreased by how much should have been claimed with straight-line depreciation from the time the property was first placed into use. For example, a $2,000 computer was depreciated by $1,400 using the accelerated method. The straight-line method would have resulted in only $1,000 in depreciation. If the computer is used less than 50 percent for business, the owner must recapture the excess depreciation by recognizing income of $400.

 PLANNING TIP: To avoid this depreciation pitfall, listed property subject to conversion of less than 50 percent business use should be depreciated at straight line beginning in the first year.

Deductions for automobiles can be calculated using the standard mileage allowance or actual expenses. In order to use the mileage method, a special rule requires that it be used in the first year the vehicle is placed in service. When the actual-expense method is used in the first year, the mileage method cannot be used in later years.

After using the mileage method in the first year, the tax-payer may change from year to year between actual expenses or the mileage method. However, straight-line depreciation must be used with the actual-expense method. Otherwise, the right to use the mileage method in subsequent years is for-feited. This special rule discourages depreciation deductions in the first year, and encourages the straight-line method of depreciation for subsequent years.

 PLANNING TIP: If the accelerated method of depreci-ation is chosen for an automobile, a taxpayer can-not use the mileage method in subsequent years for that automobile.

When an automobile is used more than 50 percent for business, and the actual-expense method is elected in the year an automobile is placed in service, then an accelerated-depreciation method (MACRS or Modified Accelerated Cost Recovery System) can be used. The actual-expense method may be advantageous for autos used more than 50 percent for business, and not kept for more than three or four years. The mileage method will work better for autos with high business mileage, kept in service for more than three or four years. This is due to the fact the mileage rate will apply to the total business miles driven over the life of the auto-mobile, resulting in potentially greater deductions than actual expenses.

The mileage rate usually changes each year, and for 1996 is 31 cents per mile. The mileage rate includes all costs of auto-mobile operations, including insurance and depreciation. However, annual registration taxes and interest expenses can be claimed as business expenses in addition to the mileage rate, in the respective business proportions. The interest expense deduction does not apply to employees who drive their autos as part of their job.

Depreciation deductions are subtracted from the cost (basis) of the property to determine the adjusted basis. In the case of the mileage method, part of the annual mileage allowance is considered a depreciation factor, which means the cost of the auto must be reduced when the standard mileage deduction is claimed. For example, in 1995 the standard mileage rate of .30¢ consists of .18¢ for operating costs and .12¢ for depreciation. The rates for the current and prior years can be found in IRS Publication 917.

DEPRECIATION OF THE REAL PROPERTY— THE HOME

The IRS expects to find errors in almost all depreciation calculations. Often, depreciation is either applied to property that is not used in the business, or it is incorrectly calculated. Depreciation is a systematic method of expensing the cost of property that has a useful life of more than one year. The period of depreciation is referred to as the recovery period. The recovery period is established by statute for all depreciable property.

Most personal property falls into a five- or seven-year recovery period. Real property falls into two categories: (1) Residential property (defined as a dwelling unit), which is assigned a useful life of 27.5 years, and (2) nonresidential real property, which has a useful life of 39 years. By statute, nonresidential real property acquired after 1986 but before May 13, 1993, assigned useful life is 31.5 years. Since May 14, 1993, nonresidential real estate is depreciated over 39 years.

The Internal Revenue regulations distinguish real property used as a dwelling from that used for transients. The effect is to require a longer life for calculation of depreciation for real property used for transient stays. Most B&B owners use a 27.5-year life for B&Bs, assuming the B&B is residential real estate because it seems logical. However, the definition of residential property is limited to dwelling units occupied for periods of 30 days or more, according to Treasury Regulation 1.48-(h)(2)(ii).

WARNING: Bed and Breakfasts do not qualify as a dwelling unit (most stays being less than 30 days); therefore, they are considered to be nonresidential real property requiring a 39-year life.[5] IRS agents expect confusion on the recovery period to be one of the most frequent adjustments for B&B audits.

To calculate depreciation, the basis of the home must be determined. Depreciation is calculated on the lesser of (1) the cost basis of the house, or (2) the fair market value of the house at the time the B&B is first placed into service. The cost basis of the home must be determined by taking into consideration all of the required statutory adjustments. For example, the purchase of the home may have resulted in the deferral of a gain from the sale of the former home. In such a case, the cost of the new home must be reduced by the deferred gain to determine the adjusted cost basis. Capital improvements are an example of adjustments increasing the cost basis. Since land is never depreciable, a reasonable value for the land on which the house is situated must be subtracted from the cost basis.

WARNING: Since the cost basis of the home is a historical number, it is usually much lower than the current worth of the home. As a result the depreciable basis of the house may be considerably lower than the market value. (See Chapters 3 and 6 for information on converting a home to a B&B.)

The next step in calculating depreciation is to determine the percentage of the home that can be depreciated. The square footage of guest rooms is divided by the total square footage of the home. This percentage is multiplied by the cost basis. The resulting number is the depreciable basis of the home.

The following example reflects the calculation of adjusted basis and the depreciation for a B&B:

CALCULATING DEPRECIATION

Facts:

8/01/85	Taxpayer Jones purchases first home for $45,000 (makes no improvements to home and uses the home exclusively as a residence).
10/21/87	Jones sells first home for $85,000.
10/22/87	Jones purchases second home for $115,000.
4/18/94	Jones adds a large addition to the house for $50,000.
4/19/95	Jones converts the home to a Bed and Breakfast.

Using the above facts, the basis in the second home may be computed as follows:

STEP 1

Calculate basis:

Purchase price of second home	$115,000
Add: Improvements	50,000
Subtract: Deferred gain from first home	
(85,000 – 45,000)	(40,000)
Adjusted basis in second home on 4/19/95	$125,000

STEP 2

Calculate the percentage of business use of the home:

Total square footage of home	2000
Square footage of rooms rented	500
Percentage of business use: (500:2000)	25%

STEP 3

Calculate depreciable basis of bed and breakfast:

Adjusted basis on 4/19/95	$125,000
Reduce cost basis for fair value of land	(25,000)
Adjusted basis of home, net land	$100,000
Multiplied by: Percentage of business use	.25
Depreciable basis for Bed and Breakfast	25,000

STEP 4

Annual Depreciation:

Depreciable basis of Bed and Breakfast	$25,000
Divided by 39[A]	÷ 39
Annual Depreciation Allowable	$641.02[B]

A. Number of years to depreciate nonresidential real estate.
B. Annual depreciation in the first year of operation of the Bed and Breakfast, and the last year will be prorated.

   Personal property used exclusively in the guest rooms of the B&B can be depreciated. Bedroom furniture will generally have a recovery period of seven years. Decorations and artifacts in the guest rooms can also be depreciated. Antiques—when used for decoration or functional purposes in the guest rooms—can be depreciated if it can be established that they have a useful life. The same rule concerning the adjusted cost basis of real property applies to personal property. That is, the starting point for depreciation is the lower of the original cost or the value at the time the property is first used for business.

PLANNING TIP: The starting point for depreciation is the lower of the adjusted cost basis, or market value at the time the property is first placed into service.

A gain is likely to occur in the year property is sold because the cost basis has been reduced by depreciation. Assume property cost $1,000 when it was purchased and placed into service. The depreciation claimed on the property is subtracted from the cost. If $800 was depreciated, the adjusted cost (or basis) of the property is $200. If the property is sold for $500, the gain is $300 ($500 – $300). This gain will be subject to tax and must be reported. The gain cannot be deferred, as when a principal residence is sold and replaced within a two-year period. This income is not reported on the Schedule C, which is used for determining the profits or loss of a business, and it is not subject to self-employment tax.

A loss on the sale of the B&B portion of the home is fully deductible, but the personal portion of the home is not. The loss from the sale of property cannot be deducted on Schedule C and is not allowed as a deduction for the purposes of determining self-employment tax. The gain or loss is reported on Form 4797.

The annual allowable depreciation for personal property using the accelerated method is included in Appendix B. Personal property such as automobiles, computers, and office equipment has a recovery period of five years. Furniture and fixtures have a seven-year recovery period.

The information in Exhibit 2-2 is taken from the MSSP training program for Bed and Breakfasts. These examples reflect some of the techniques the IRS is using to train their auditors in the area of depreciation:

IRC SECTION 179—PROPERTY

Some assets can be expensed without regard for their useful life. *IRC Section 179* allows a certain amount of the cost of selected property to be deducted in the year the property is acquired. *IRC Section 179* is included in Appendix C, and explains which assets qualify as "Section 179 property."

Because a B&B is considered to be a business, as opposed to a rental activity, depreciable personal property is eligible for the benefits of *IRC Section 179*. In 1995, the maximum allowance was $17,500. Therefore, the first $17,500 of newly acquired personal property could be 100 percent depreciated in the current period. The provisions of *IRC Section 179* are limited to property acquired during the year for the business.

 WARNING: Furniture or other personal property converted from personal to business use will not qualify for the expense allowance of *Section 179*.

When qualified purchases are made during the year for the B&B, a provision may limit the benefit of *Section 179*. A deduction under *IRC Section 179* cannot be used to create or increase a loss from the business operations. Under such circumstances, the election to expense can still be made, but the unusable portion of the expense is suspended and carried into future years until there is sufficient profit to absorb the deduction.

 **PLANNING TIP: The election to use *IRC Section 179*, even when the Bed and Breakfast hasn't any net income, could still provide a tax benefit in subsequent years.**

For example, in 1995, $17,000 in assets were purchased, but net income before the purchase was zero. In 1996, net income before depreciation was $20,000. By electing *IRC Section 179* for the assets purchased in 1995, the deduction is suspended until 1996 since there is no income in 1995. The 1996 taxable income is $3,000 as a result of the election in 1995. Not electing *IRC Section 179* in 1995 results in 1996 taxable income of $13,408 since the $20,000 income is only reduced by the annual depreciation allowed on the $17,000 of $2,429 in 1995 and $4,163 in 1996.

1995	*With* Sec 179 Election	*Without* Sec 179 Election
Income Before Depreciation	-0-	-0-
Depreciation: Section 179	$17,000	
Annual Allowance 7 Year Property		$2,429
Carryover to 1996	$17,000	$2,429
1996 Income Before Depreciation	$20,000	$20,000
Depreciation: Carryover from 1995	−17,000	−2,429
Annual Allowance 7 Year Property	-0-	−4,123
1996 Taxable Income	$3,000	$13,408

When the election under *IRC Section 179* is not made (or is not available), the personal property can be depreciated either ratably over the recovery period (straight line) or under an accelerated manner. However, special rules apply to the year in which the property is placed into or taken out of service.

To simplify the calculation process, the IRS provides tables for determining the annual depreciation allowances for the first and subsequent years. When personal property is disposed of before it is fully depreciated, generally one-half of the full year's depreciation is allowable as a deduction, irrespective of the date of disposition. A disposition by sale must be reported and the gain or loss determined. The amount of gain or loss is the difference between the amount received for the property and the property's adjusted basis. The property's cost basis must be reduced by the depreciation allowed or allowable on the property in determining the adjusted basis. The "allowable" rule means you must claim the depreciation or lose the benefit.

 WARNING: Whether or not the depreciation is taken as a deduction, the property's cost basis must be reduced by the amount that was allowable as depreciation.

START-UP EXPENSES

Deductions for expenses incurred in getting a B&B ready to rent are not deductible. Expenses incurred prior to opening the business are called "start-up" expenses. These costs cannot be deducted until the business opens its doors to the first customer.

IRC Section 195 requires all preproduction costs be capitalized until the business starts. The start of the business could be when the appropriate permits or licenses are issued. Even with such permits, the expenses still might require capitalization if the rooms are not suitable for occupancy. Mandatory insurance coverage or zoning restrictions may further delay the opening of the business.

 PLANNING TIP: The first day in business can be established by a record of advertising or marketing. In some cases it can be as simple as a "Vacancy" sign hung up on the first day.

Once the starting point is established, the capitalized expenses can be deducted over a 60-month period. These deductions are referred to as amortization. The expenses capitalized during the start-up period are all-inclusive. Repairs, maintenance, improvements (which will be subject to depreciation as real property if they are considered major improvements), car expenses, utilities, legal and accounting consultations, and research costs are examples of expenditures that must be capitalized and amortized under *IRC Section 195*. The text of *IRC Section 195* can be found in Appendix C.

THE PROFIT MOTIVE

The IRS agent will try to determine if a small business is being operated with the intention of making a profit, or if its expenses are being used to offset the taxable income of its owner. The handling of any single item of expense is of less concern to the IRS than the owner's intent to make a profit. The IRS wants to know—Did the operator go into the activity in order to derive income, or for the ability to write off a loss?

As part of the initial interview conducted during the audit process, the IRS agent will ask questions about the planning given to the enterprise. The steps taken by the entrepreneur before embarking into an activity reveal the mindset of the owner and help the agent determine if there was an intent to make a profit. A failure to convince the IRS of a sincere profit motive can result in a disallowance of any tax benefits from such a loss under *IRC Section 183*. See Chapter 5 for more information on the hobby loss rules of *IRC Section 183*.

ENDNOTES

1. Market Segment Specialization Program (MSSP) [training manual], "Bed and Breakfasts," Department of the Treasury, Internal Revenue Service, 1995.

2. Rundbach, Betty, and Peggy Ackerman, *1995 Bed and Breakfast U.S.A.* (New York: Plume, 1995).

3. Stankus, Jan, *How to Open and Operate a Bed and Breakfast* (Old Saybrook, Conn.: Globe Pequot Press, 1995), pp. 147–148.

4. *Market Segment Specialization Program (MSSP)* [training manual], "Bed and Breakfasts," Department of the Treasury, Internal Revenue Service, 1995.

5. Ibid.

6. Ibid.

CHAPTER 3

Important Planning when Forming a Bed and Breakfast Business

CONVERTING A HOME INTO A BED AND BREAKFAST BUSINESS

The primary asset of a Bed and Breakfast is the residence where the host and guests stay. Much of an MSSP audit will relate to the way the expenses related to the residence have been handled.

 PLANNING TIP: Before converting a home into a B&B activity, the homeowner should give careful consideration to the influence of two important factors: the cost basis and business form.

The cost basis of the home should be carefully analyzed. "Basis" is a term used in tax calculations, as defined by the Internal Revenue Code, and is generally defined as the initial cost of the residence, plus improvements, less depreciation which has been claimed on the property. Generally, a home that has been used solely as a principal residence has had no basis adjustment for depreciation. Additional adjustments may be required to arrive at the proper cost basis, such as reducing the cost of the current residence by any nonrecognized gain from the sale of prior homes. Nonrecognized gain occurs when prior gains have been deferred through the purchase of another home. These adjustments, sometimes referred to as "roll-over gains," can cause the cost basis to be very different from purchase price or market value. The basis of the home is important in calculating depreciation. In a B&B, that portion of the residence which is converted into business property can be depreciated for tax purposes. See Chapter 2 for more information on how to calculate depreciation.

> **WARNING: Two negative tax effects are caused by converting a low-basis, high-market-value home to business use: (1) low-basis property will not benefit from the increased depreciation that would be available if the full market value could be used; (2) the gain attributable to the appreciation that occurred before the B&B conversion will be taxable upon a sale.**

Converting a home that has greatly appreciated in value to business use causes taxation without any corresponding tax benefit.

Some relief for property owners caught in this unfortunate tax trap may result from terminating the B&B activity prior to sale. See Chapter 6 for more discussion on selling a personal residence.

FORM OF BUSINESS

The form of business the taxpayer selects to conduct and report for the B&B activities involves many important choices. A business can be a sole proprietorship, partnership, C corporation, S corporation, or LLC (Limited Liability Company). Each form of business has different tax implications. By definition, a sole-proprietorship is owned by one person. However, a married couple can be treated as a sole-proprietorship, since they can file together as a joint tax return. Any other combination of multiple owners requires the formation of a business entity: a partnership, C corporation, S corporation, or an LLC (see Chapter 7 for discussion on using separate entities).

Most B&B owners will report their rental activity as sole-proprietorships. Sole proprietors do not distinguish between the B&B earnings and any of their other earnings. A sole-proprietorship is the most common and simple form of conducting a B&B operation because of the many complexities associated with forming a separate entity. For example, a corporation requires annual reports and many corporate formalities that take the form of meetings and minutes. The sole-proprietorship is simple to create, inexpensive to maintain, and requires less complicated record keeping than other types of business entities. A separate income tax return is not required, and the reporting period is the calendar year, January 1 to December 31. No transfer of ownership of the residence needs to be made.

SOLE-PROPRIETORSHIPS

In most cases, forming a sole-proprietorship is simply a matter of printing letterhead and business cards and opening a business account. The IRS and most state laws do not require any special applications to establish a new proprietorship. The owner's Social Security number will be used for federal and state income tax reporting, and a separate federal Employer Identification Number (EIN) would be required if one expects to hire employees (see Chapter 4).

Although the state and local laws vary, most jurisdictions will require some form of registration to operate a B&B. Sales tax licenses and permits for food handling may also be necessary, and compliance with zoning regulations is critical. In addition, the B&B operator may want to protect any business name selected by registering a tradename and/or trademark with the proper state, county, or federal agencies.

Since the sole-proprietorship is the simplest form of business to start, discussions that follow treat the business as a sole-proprietorship.

PLANNING TIP: There are some valid reasons for establishing a separate entity, as well as complications that result from doing so.

Such issues are explored in Chapter 7 and should be evaluated very carefully prior to forming the business. However, it is always possible to convert an established sole-proprietorship into another type of operation.

KEEPING BUSINESS RECORDS

PLANNING TIP: A separate checking account should be the heart of every accounting system for the B&B. Only B&B transactions should be entered into this account.

Most business owners will attempt to keep a record of transactions by entering a description in the check register at the time the check is written. It is important that a deduction does not get overlooked when it comes time to prepare the tax reports. When the activities of the business are recorded through the checking account, a record is created that will be the basis of the accounting system. When sufficient descriptions, including accurate dates and amounts, are associated with the banking activities, the checkbook register can be used to produce a usable and meaningful set of books.

PLANNING TIP: In order to properly report income, benefit from all available deductions, and protect the business from an IRS MSSP audit, the business owner must keep complete and accurate accounting records.

To keep accurate records, a few rules must be followed. The first rule requires that all activity be funneled through the checking account. All business proceeds must be deposited intact. A deposit should never be a "less cash" transaction—that is, all checks (and cash) should be deposited in full. When money is to be taken out of a business, a check should be written. When there are numerous cash transactions paid with out-of-pocket cash, receipts for those transactions can be kept in an envelope until it is time to make out a reimbursement check from the business checking account. If a receipt is not available, a written memo about the purchase should be made as soon as possible, preferably at the time of purchase. Even though it is a self-prepared record, the timeliness of the memo helps it carry weight as documentation. The more contemporaneous the record, the better.

When the company is ready to make a reimbursement for cash expenditures, a company check is written for the total amount of the receipts. Total receipts should be totaled by category, such as supplies (designate whether shop, office, manufacturing, etc.), small tools, meals, entertainment, gas, repairs, etc. Affix an adding machine tape to the category of receipts. The total of each category is then written on the outside of the envelope for convenient reference. Write the check payable to the owner or other person that incurred the out-of-pocket expense. Cross-reference the check with the check date and the check register numbers.

The second rule to insure complete accounting records requires that each banking transaction is given a full and legible description.

PLANNING TIP: The key is to give the same attention to descriptions of deposits that is given to disbursements. *IRC Section 61* provides that all income is taxable.

WARNING: A deposit that cannot be explained can be taxed as additional income. Tracking the source of all deposits can prevent later headaches, anguish, and unnecessary taxation.

It is always a good policy to issue receipts for all moneys received by a business.

REPORTING FORMS FOR THE SOLE-PROPRIETORSHIP

If the B&B owner operates the activity as a sole proprietor, the IRS will expect the proprietor to report the income and deductions on the owner's Form 1040 (Individual Tax Return) using a Schedule C. The Schedule C is then filed with the Form 1040. It is due on or before April 15 of each year. A person can file more than one Schedule C with each Form 1040 if more than one business is conducted by the taxpayer. For example, the rental activities and catering activities may have separate Schedule Cs, although these activities can be reported on the same form.

The IRS considers a B&B a business activity in the "trade or business" category, instead of a rental activity. However, some B&B operators incorrectly report the activity on a Schedule E, which is the common form for reporting most rental activities.

PLANNING TIP: The Schedule C is considered the appropriate form for a B&B because the IRS distinguishes a B&B from the typical residential rental activity due to the range of services provided. For a sample Schedule C, see Appendix A, Exhibit A-8.

SELF-EMPLOYMENT TAX

Self-employment tax represents the Social Security and Medicare contributions (both employer's and employee's portions) made by self-employed individuals. The tax is paid on net profits of a business. Generally, rental of real estate is not subject to the tax. When significant services are rendered in connection with a rental activity, the net profit becomes subject to self-employment tax. Hotels, boarding houses, and tourist homes are examples of rental activity subject to self-employment tax. Bed and Breakfast activities are considered to be in the same category.

If there is a loss, no self-employment tax is reported or paid. When the B&B operator has a net loss from the activity, it could reduce the overall taxes of the B&B operator by decreasing income taxes and self-employment taxes from other self-employment activity.

 WARNING: The IRS has strict rules that may limit the amount of losses that can be taken from a B&B activity (see Chapter 5 for other issues resulting from an operating loss).

SCHEDULE SE AND THE SELF-EMPLOYMENT TAX RATES

When a B&B reports a net profit, the IRS expects to see Schedule SE with the Form 1040. The Schedule SE reflects the total net income from all self-employment activities and the resulting self-employment tax. This tax is then added to the income tax on Form 1040 and is considered part of the total tax liability for the year.

Self-employment tax is the most commonly overlooked tax on the Form 1040. Many people venturing into business for the first time rarely consider this substantial tax assessment in their budgets and estimates. It's common to have liability for this tax when the overall tax return reflects negative taxable income. Self-employment tax is calculated on the net profit from all activities considered self-employed-earnings of the taxpayer. As stated earlier, a loss from one business can offset the profit from another business of the taxpayer to offset both income and self-employment taxes.

The self-employment tax rates have continued to escalate over the years. In 1972, the rate was 7.5 percent on the first $9,000 of net earning from self-employment; in 1996 the self-employment tax rate was 15.3 percent. This rate is made up of two components applied in two separate manners. First, the Old-Age, Survivors, and Disability Insurance (OASDI) component is 12.4 percent and for 1996 is applied to the first $62,700 of net profit. The second component is the Medicare rate of 2.9 percent. This rate is applied to the net profit without limitation.

Self-employed individuals are paying double the Social Security rate imposed on employees. Employees pay one half of their Social Security Contribution (5.4 percent for OASDI and 1.45 percent for Medicare) and the employers pay the other one half of the contribution. Employers are allowed to deduct their matching portion of social security tax. Since self-employed individuals are paying both halves of the tax, a deduction is allowed for one half the self-employment tax paid by self-employed individuals. Such a deduction is allowed in reducing both the personal income tax and self-employment tax paid for the year. Because the deduction becomes a simultaneous equation, the tax form (Schedule SE) simplifies the process of determining the amount to deduct. The net earnings from self-employment are reduced by one half of the self-employment tax rate before calculating the self-employment tax. In 1996, for example, the combined tax rate of 15.3 percent is divided in half and the resulting 7.65 percent is multiplied by the net earnings. The results are then subtracted from the net earnings. The tax form simplifies this calculation by multiplying the net earnings by 92.35 percent before calculating the self-employment tax. One half of the resulting self-employment tax is deducted from gross income before arriving at adjusted gross income.

CHILDREN AS EMPLOYEES

When a proprietor has minor children (under age 18), a potential tax advantage exists, with significant tax benefits. Children can be compensated for their efforts in assisting in the business activity. Any reasonable compensation is considered a deduction by the proprietor in determining net profit or loss for the year. These deductions can result in a reduction of both the income tax and self-employment tax of the proprietor. The benefit is only available to proprietorships and a partnership of both the child's parents. The benefit is limited to children who are members of the immediate family.

The compensation paid to the child is not subject to Social Security tax, Medicare, or federal unemployment taxes. The child's wages are subject to federal (and state, if applicable) income taxes. However, each child can claim a standard deduction to the extent of the earned income. For example, the 1996 standard deduction allowance of $4,000 means there would be no taxes due on the first $4,000 of wages paid to a child in 1996 if he or she has no other taxable income.

To qualify, the amount of compensation must be reasonable and the hours and services should be documented. Keep a record of duties and chores and wages or time slips. The amounts paid should also be documented. This can be accomplished by having the child endorse a paycheck that is deposited into the child's bank account. When the only payroll activity involves a child of the proprietor, it is usually not necessary to file a formal Form W-2 or other payroll records, such as quarterly Form 941 reports. Technically, a Form W-2 should be issued, and quarterly payroll reports filed, but if the child does not owe any income tax, and does not otherwise have a filing requirement, the paperwork is usually ignored. If the child is required to file a return, sometimes a substitute Form W-2 is used in place of the formal Form W-2 when one has not been issued. A substitute Form W-2 is Form 4852. This form provides space for an explanation regarding the reason for a substitute W-2. All of the previously referenced forms are in Appendix A.

CHAPTER 4

Targeting Employee and Independent Contractor Issues

PAYROLL AND EMPLOYMENT ISSUES

Bed & Breakfast operators frequently hire extra help in providing B&B services. Employment tax laws may apply to cooks, gardeners, housekeepers, and members of the family who provide services in the B&B operations. Domestic workers, guides, and sometimes "inn sitters," who work your B&B while you are away, can be affected by the employment rules. The amount of control over a worker might result in a relationship that makes the B&B owner an employer subject to employment taxes and a vast array of paperwork. For example, a gardener working only at one place could be considered an employee, where a landscape company with many customers would be considered a contract service.

Although the B&B operator may treat these workers as casual labor or subcontractors, the IRS, as well as related state agencies, will be interested in recharacterizing the worker as an employee. A written agreement declaring the workers as an independent contractors is advisable, but it is not a safe harbor against the risk of having a government agency recharacterize the worker as an employee. Written agreements with workers are usually ignored by taxing agencies when a determination is made regarding a worker's status. Such factors as the amount of control held over the workers, and whether or not the workers make their services available to other establishments, weigh heavily in the employer-employee determination. The IRS uses 20 common-law tests to evaluate a worker's relationship and to determine if an employer/employee relationship is present. Exhibit 4-1 is a list of the 20 factors that have evolved through judicial rulings. Not all of them will apply to every situation, but the auditor will consider them in each particular audit.

To place these factors in perspective, the self-survey in Exhibit 4-2 would indicate whether a business may have a problem with the classification of independent contractors.

 WARNING: Reporting requirements exist even for independent contractors. When workers are hired, any compensation in excess of $600 per year must be reported to the IRS on a Form 1099 (see Appendix A, Exhibit A-1).

When workers are paid as independent contractors, a complete record should be kept in a permanent file. This record should contain information that will enable the worker to be contacted two to three years after the services have been provided or after the contract services have been terminated. The file should contain a permanent address, records of next of kin, and personal and professional references. The most important record, of course, is the worker's Social Security number.

 **PLANNING TIP: A Social Security number can be requested from the worker by using IRS Form W-9 (see Appendix A, Exhibit A-5, Request for Taxpayer Identification Number and Certification).**

EXHIBIT 4-1 TWENTY FACTORS TO DETERMINE EMPLOYEES VS. INDEPENDENT CONTRACTORS

1. Instructions
2. Training
3. Integration
4. Services rendered personally
5. Hiring, supervising, and paying assistants
6. Continuing relationship
7. Set hours of work
8. Full time required
9. Doing work on employer's premises
10. Order or sequence set
11. Right to discharge
12. Oral or written reports
13. Payment by hour, week, month
14. Payment of business and/or traveling expenses
15. Furnishing of tools and materials
16. Significant investment
17. Realization of profit or loss
18. Working for more than one firm
19. Making service available to general public
20. Right to terminate

Other reference numbers—such as a driver's license, sales tax number, and registration numbers of any associations to which the worker may belong—are helpful and should be kept on file.

If an audit of the B&B is conducted, it will involve records that may be two or more years old. If an independent contrac-

EXHIBIT 4-2   EMPLOYEE VS. INDEPENDENT CONTRACTOR CHECKLIST

Question	Indicates Employee (Yes)	Indicates Independent Contractor (No)
1. Does the taxpayer have the right to require when, where, and how the worker performs services?		
2. Does the taxpayer provide any training such as having someone work with the worker or requiring the worker to attend meetings or training?		
3. Does the worker's services integrate into the operations of the business?		
4. Are the services required to be rendered by the worker?		
5. Does the taxpayer hire, supervise, and pay assistants to obtain the goal or result?		
6. Does the worker have a continuing relationship with the taxpayer?		
7. Does the taxpayer set the hours?		
8. Does the person hired by the taxpayer work full-time?		
9. Does the person work on the taxpayer's premises?		
10. Does the worker perform services in an order or sequence dictated by the taxpayer?		

EXHIBIT 4-2   EMPLOYEE VS. INDEPENDENT CONTRACTOR CHECKLIST *(continued)*

Question	Indicates Employee (Yes)	Indicates Independent Contractor (No)
11. Is the worker required to submit oral or written reports?		
12. Is the person paid by the hour, week, or month instead of by the job?		
13. Does the taxpayer pay the worker's business expenses?		
14. Does the taxpayer furnish the tools and materials?		
15. Does the worker have a significant investment in the facilities used in performance of the services?		
16. Is the worker protected from suffering a loss as a result of the services he or she performs?		
17. Does the person work solely for the taxpayer?		
18. Is the person prevented from or does he or she refrain from offering his or her services to the general public?		
19. Can the taxpayer discharge the worker?		
20. Can the worker terminate his or her services?		

tor classification is challenged, the permanent file will be needed if it is necessary to contact the worker at a later date. The independent contractor status will have a better chance of being sustained when the worker is available to verify the nature of the services and to confirm that the remuneration has been reported to the government. Also, issuing a Form 1099 to the worker may reduce the amount of taxes attributable to a worker who may later be recharacterized as an employee.

Enforcement of the employer/employee rules was made much easier for the IRS with the passing of *IRC Section 3509*, effective December 31, 1982. The provisions are mandatory when its conditions are met. This code section addresses both situations where payments in question were reported on Form 1099 and situations where payments were not reported on Form 1099. The latter situations carry a stiffer penalty.

If the independent contractors are reclassified as employees, the employer will be liable for assessments of the income taxes and social security taxes that were not withheld. The liability for these taxes falls on the employer, not the employee. The tax assessment includes the employer's matching portion of Social Security. The rates applicable for both situations, where Form 1099s have and have not been filed, appear below:

Category	1099s Filed	1099s Not Filed
Income tax withholding paid	1.5% of Total paid	3.0% of Total paid
Employee's FICA/MED	20.0% of Rate	40.0% of Rate
Employer's FICA/MED	100% of Rate	100% of Rate

The "Total paid" is the actual amount paid to the worker. FICA is limited to the maximum wage base. In addition, the assessment will be treated the same as delinquent payments and therefore subject to interest and penalties.

The employee is not allowed to claim as a credit any of the amounts assessed against the employer for income tax. However, if the employee filed and paid self-employment tax, a claim may be made by the employee for the excess amount paid over the portion that should have been paid as an employee.

The provisions of *IRC Section 3509* are intended to apply only to independent contractors that are reclassified as employees. Under this section, the employer is precluded from recovering from the employee any amounts assessed against the employer for payment of payroll taxes, interest, and penalties.

The procedures described above do not apply to an individual that is being paid as both an employee and as an independent contractor by the same business. Nor does it apply to individuals who are statutory employees such as (1) full time insurance salesmen, (2) agent drivers or commission drivers engaged in distributing meat, vegetables, bakery, beverage (other than milk) products, or laundry or dry cleaning, (3) home workers, or (4) traveling or city salesmen. In these cases the employer is liable for the full amount of income tax withholding and Social Security. The income tax portion of these assessments may be abated if the reclassified worker has paid the proper amount of income tax and can produce a statement to that effect. It is important to note that this abatement process does not apply to assessments determined under *IRC Section 3509*, as outlined above.

WARNING: The effects of employee reclassification can be financially disastrous to any business. The statutes preclude recovery from the worker, which leaves the business to carry the full liability. Knowing these consequences ahead of time will help the business owner to make the correct decision about classifying any workers.

WITHHOLDING OF TAXES

Government agencies have a vested interest in maintaining a policy of rigid enforcement of employer-employee compliance. Failure to have a worker's taxes withheld at the workplace results in millions of dollars of lost tax revenue for the government. In turn, strict rules are placed on the employers. It is the employer's responsibility to properly withhold and remit the withholding to the government on a timely and accurate basis.

Penalties exist for late payment of payroll taxes by an employer. Furthermore, improper administration of the withholding rules can result in the employer being responsible for under-withheld taxes. When employees are hired, the IRS, and most state agencies, requires an Employer Identification Number (EIN) be assigned to the employer.

The federal EIN can be requested using form SS-4 (see Appendix A, Exhibit A-3). Soon after applying for the number, the IRS will send a package of forms and instructions. A booklet called *Circular E, Employer's Tax Guide,* is included in this package. The information in this guide should be carefully read and the booklet placed in a safe place, because it will be referred to frequently. Included in this booklet are the proper procedures for W-4s (see Appendix A, Exhibit A-4), determining withholding rates and times to make Federal Tax Deposits (FTDs) of the withheld taxes, including the matching employer's portion.

An employer should maintain a proper personnel file for each employee. Such a file should contain a signed W-4 (Employee's Withholding Allowance Certificate) and the related state withholding form if applicable.

WARNING: In addition to the IRS forms, the U.S. Department of Justice requires a Form I-9 (see Appendix A, Exhibit A-2). This form is administered by the Immigration and Naturalization Service and is required to be kept on file for either three years from date of hire or one year from date of termination of the employee, whichever is longer.

OTHER WORKER-RELATED ISSUES

Along with the hiring of employees comes additional responsibilities imposed by law and regulation. Hiring, compensation, and termination are all potential stumbling blocks for an employer. The Department of Labor (DOL) administers wages and hours regulations regarding overtime, minimum wage, and employment of minors. The workplace environment is, in itself, a world of red tape. Such concerns need to be addressed as a part of the cost of doing business. For example, anytime there is a worker on the premises, there is a risk of liability for injury suffered by the worker. A homeowner's policy generally will not cover all conditions. Insurance advisors should be consulted to determine if there is adequate coverage, or if coverage exists. Organizations such as the Professional Association of Innkeepers International (see resources in Appendix B) provide information on insurance coverage including workmen's compensation. The B&B operator always should seek professional advice before hiring any service providers.

CHAPTER 5

What Happens when There Is a Loss

WHEN THERE IS A LOSS

It is frustrating to work hard all year at a business and end up realizing a loss. Even worse things may be in store because of IRS rules that apply to some loss situations. The rules take the form of limiting the amount or duration of write-offs, or they put tight restrictions on costs that can be expensed. Many short-term room rentals are part-time operations with unsophisticated accounting procedures. Over time, some expense categories arising from use of a residence have been abused, so IRS regulations reflect the tightened rules. Congress has restricted the qualification for the write-off so the benefit to the homeowner is often minimal. *IRC Section 183*, called the hobby loss rules, and *IRC Section 280A*, called the vacation home rules, are triggered when the business loses money.

THE HOBBY LOSS RULES OF IRC SECTION 183

According to a 1988 national survey of innkeepers, Bed and Breakfasts with fewer than four guest rooms do not make money. Lack of earnings can be the result of seasonal rental activity, or because rooms are only available on a part-time basis. Losses may also result from incorrectly including the expenses of the entire household against the income from the B&B revenue. Bed and Breakfasts that report only minimal activity resulting in a small loss may feel immune from IRS focus.

However, reporting losses year after year might trigger an IRS audit. If no profits are realized, and the IRS can show that they are unlikely to occur in the future, the IRS can disallow the losses under *IRC Section 183*. The disallowance of losses that once resulted in tax benefits, such as the reduction of self-employment taxes due from profits earned from other activities, might be financially devastating now.

TAX TREATMENT OF HOBBY LOSSES

There is a widespread presumption that most businesses are profit motivated. Almost every new business takes time to become profitable. However, if no profit is made, yet the business continues to operate year after year, it might be perceived that the owner is in business for a reason other than making a profit.

Hobbies are activities that people do primarily for the enjoyment, not for their earnings. The IRS suspects that some businesses are really hobbies in disguise, using tax benefits permitted to owners. Therefore, when the business does not eventually make a profit, the taxpayer has the responsibility to justify that the business is indeed profit-motivated or the owner risks having the losses disallowed.

In such situations, the courts might ask these questions in applying the "Reasonable Businessman Test":

Would a businessperson who was in business to make money do business this way?

Is the business being operated in the same way that a reasonable businessman would operate it in order to make money?

The question is not whether the business made money, but whether it operated in a way that was consistent with good business practices, which would make money.

Hobby losses are not allowable deductions for tax purposes, and they do not carry over from year to year. The IRS requires income from hobby activity to be reported, but it limits the amount of deductions. Any mortgage interest and property taxes normally deductible and correctly apportioned are allowed as itemized deductions. Other deductions related to the Bed and Breakfast activity such as utilities, linens, and supplies can be deducted to the extent of income and only as itemized deductions. There is a cap on the amount that the business can deduct for tax purposes.

These other deductions are treated as miscellaneous itemized deductions, which means that they are subject to the standard limitation of two percent of adjusted gross income. That method of handling deductions could result in more income than deductions being reported. When the IRS determines that a B&B's business is a hobby, a one-year profit could result in additional taxes, while previous write-offs are disallowed.

WARNING TIP: Using *IRC Section 183*, the IRS can presume a Bed and Breakfast is a hobby if it does not show a profit in at least three out of five years.

STRATEGIES TO AVOID THE IRC SECTION 183 PITFALL

The hobby loss presumption of *IRC Section 183* can be overcome by careful planning and detailed record keeping. Good record keeping habits should start with a bank account used exclusively for the Bed and Breakfast. A separate account will help assure the deductibility of bank charges. One of the most important bookkeeping practices to avoid is the commingling of business funds with personal funds.

The IRS will inquire about the B&B operator's experience and business background to help determine if there is a likelihood for profit. The IRS will be interested in what kind of research was done prior to deciding to operate a Bed and Breakfast. Auditors raise questions about feasibility studies, market research, and adequacy of financing. The amount of time spent by the owners in the operation of the B&B is another big factor. Auditors also consider the uses of advertising or other marketing efforts by the Bed and Breakfast owner.

The IRS may consider factors that will be in the taxpayer's favor. Losses in the start-up phases can be justifiable. Management adjustments being made to increase income and reduce expenses may mitigate the reaction to repeated losses. The use of professional advisors and the potential for future profits are some other factors that may be helpful in overcoming the presumptive clause of the hobby loss rules.

The proprietors of new businesses are often advised to incorporate a business activity as a strategy to avoid pitfalls of *IRC Section 183*. This advice could cause problems for a new business. Although *IRC Section 183* does not specifically apply to corporations, it does apply to corporations with S elections in effect. But even regular C corporations can be subject to disallowance under *IRC Section 162*, which defines permissible business expenses. When any deduction does not meet the "ordinary and necessary" condition of *IRC Section 162*, it can be disallowed. When a disallowance is imposed on the corporation it can result in corporate tax, and the shareholders stand the risk of being taxed on benefits they received from the corporate activity.

In deciding whether to use a corporation for the operation of a Bed and Breakfast, consideration may be given to entering into a lease agreement with the corporation. However, there are restrictions against deducting expenses under such arrangements. In 1986, Congress added *IRC Section 280A(c)(6)* to disallow leases of personal residences to employers. It is a particularly strict provision. Normally under *IRC Section 280A*, expenses can be taken to the extent of the lease income earned. But in the case of a lease arrangement with an employer/corporation, the only deductions allowed by an employee/owner are those for interest and taxes, irrespective of the lease income earned. See Chapter 7 for more information on using corporations.

THE BED AND BREAKFAST PERSONAL USE TRAP OF IRC SECTION 280A

IRC Section 280A controls the recognition of losses from rental activities and the use of an office in the home. Under the vacation home rules of *IRC Section 280A*, the deductibility of Bed and Breakfast losses can be jeopardized if the guest rooms are used for personal purposes during the year. The text of *IRC Section 280A* appears in its entirety in Appendix C.

IRC Section 280A does not apply to hotels or inns, since these accommodations usually provide significant services and are considered a trade or business (see Chapter 3, section on "Self-Employment Tax"). It could be expected that Bed and Breakfasts will also escape *IRC Section 280A* because they have been defined as a hotel or inn accommodation. However, Bed and Breakfasts must meet a very strict requirement to be exempt from the loss limitation rules of *IRC Section 280A*. That section requires exclusive use of the portion of the residence held out for Bed and Breakfast purposes.

 **WARNING: Even a single day of personal use of a Bed and Breakfast room has been ruled sufficient to cause the Bed and Breakfast operation to lose the exemption from the vacation home rules.**

According to existing IRS regulations and case law, any personal use made of the guest room(s) will cause the Bed and Breakfast operation to be subjected to the loss limitation rules under *IRC Section 280A(f)(1)(B)*. The courts have supported this regulation. In *Byers v. Commissioner* 82T.C.919, 925 (1984), the Tax Court ruled that under *IRC Section 280A, any* personal use caused the rental to be subject to vacation home limitations.

There may be some relief from this harsh restriction under the IRS proposed regulations. Proposed regulation *IRC Section 1.280A-1(c)(2)* holds that a room must be regularly available for paying customers. Under this proposed regulation the strict ruling in *Byers* is relaxed. A single day of personal use of the Bed and Breakfast guest room by the owner would not cause the operation to lose its qualifications as an inn. As stated earlier, by qualifying as an inn the B&B is not subject to the loss limitation rules of *IRC Section 280A* imposed on vacation homes.

The IRS issued a private letter ruling (PLR 8009013) regarding the personal use of guest rooms. According to this ruling, personal use would not cause the losses to be limited as long as:

> *the property is regularly available for occupancy by paying customers on a transient basis and only if those with an interest in the property do not exercise any preferential rights with respect to the use of the property on behalf of themselves or others.*

The opportunity to avoid *IRC Section 280A* afforded to the B&B operator by the proposed regulations is only a slim one. Because it is still uncertain how the rules for exemption will be applied under the proposed regulations, caution is advised against reliance on them. In addition, it remains unclear under the proposed regulations how the personal use tests of *IRC Section 280A* are to be applied when a Bed and Breakfast is denied the hotel or inn exemption.

APPLYING THE LOSS LIMITATION RULES OF IRC SECTION 280A

IRC Section 280A applies to the treatment of losses from residential rentals, and denies the use of residential rental losses when excess personal use is made of the rental accommodation. *IRC Section 280A* establishes the amount of personal use that can be made of a vacation home before the rental losses are subject to limitation. Under *IRC Section 280A*, the number of days a rental unit can be used for personal purposes is limited to the greater of 14 days or 10 percent of the days rented at fair rental value. When the personal use exceeds this limit, the rental losses are subject to the rules of *IRC Section 280A*.

 **PLANNING TIP:** If a Bed and Breakfast room, or other residential rental, is rented for less than 15 days during the year, then *IRC Section 280A* has a very simple rule: The income is not reportable and the expenses are not deductible.

 **WARNING:** However, if the Bed and Breakfast room is rented for more than 14 days, and fails the personal use test, then the Bed and Breakfast operator will need to comply with the vacation home rules of *IRC Section 280A* to determine the deductibility of any losses.

DEFINING THE VACATION HOME UNDER IRC SECTION 280A

For purposes of applying the rules of *IRC Section 280A*, a vacation home is any dwelling unit that is used during the year for both rental and personal occupancy.

 **IMPORTANT:** To qualify as a dwelling unit, the accommodation must contain a sleeping facility, cooking facility, and a toilet facility.[1]

For example, a homeowner who converts the basement into an apartment with separate cooking, sleeping, and toilet facilities has two distinct dwelling units under one roof. In this case, personal use days are determined by the number of days the basement rental unit is used for personal purposes. The owner's use of the upstairs dwelling unit is not counted in determining personal use days.

However, Bed and Breakfast operators should not expect the same treatment because Bed and Breakfast guests are rarely, if ever, provided with separate cooking facilities; therefore, no area of the Bed and Breakfast operation would qualify as a separate dwelling unit. In determining if personal use has exceeded the 14 day or 10 percent limitation, specific rules apply to the calculation of the number of days rented. A strict application of these rules would appear to create a situation in which the Bed and Breakfast operation would always fail the 10 percent test.

DETERMINING PERSONAL USE DAYS FOR A BED AND BREAKFAST

Normally, under *IRC Section 280A*, days rented to unrelated persons for fair rental value count as rented days. However, a day doesn't count as a "rented day" if there is any personal use of the unit the same day. This disqualification occurs even if the guest room is rented to an unrelated person for that day. As a result, that day would not count as a rented day in calculating the 10 percent ratio. It quickly becomes apparent that, under *IRC Section 280A*, a Bed and Breakfast operator would always have more than ten percent personal use and always be subject to the loss limitation rules.

 **PLANNING TIP:** If Bed and Breakfasts do not qualify for the exemption from *IRC Section 280A* under the "hotel or inn" definition, then the Bed and Breakfast operator would always fall into the clutches of *IRC Section 280A*.

For purposes of *IRC Section 280A*, personal use includes any use made by related parties, even if they pay fair rental value. Personal use also includes any day the rent being charged is less than fair rental value. Reciprocal arrangements, where owners of rental units use each others' rentals, is also considered personal use.

ALLOWABLE DEDUCTIONS UNDER IRC SECTION 280A

When personal use exceeds the *IRC Section 280A* parameters, the loss limitation provision of *IRC Section 280A* applies. Special rules must be followed when determining the order and amount of allowable deductions. However, the rules for determining allowable expenses under *IRC Section 280A* for an owner of a separate dwelling unit are different from the rules that apply to a Bed and Breakfast operator.

The rules for an owner with a separate dwelling unit start with 100 percent of the expenses. The total expenses are then reduced, based on a ratio of days rented to all days occupied for any purpose, both personal and rental. The formula recognizes only the portion of expenses properly attributable to the rental days.

When a Bed and Breakfast operator falls under the *IRC Section 280A* rules, two different calculations must apply.

First, the expenses are prorated for the Bed and Breakfast percentage of use based on the size of the house compared to the size of the Bed and Breakfast rooms. Such allocations are based on the number of rental rooms to the total rooms or on rentable square footage to total square footage. The taxpayer cannot include as a Bed and Breakfast room any common area not used exclusively for Bed and Breakfast accommodations. This calculation for Bed and Breakfasts must always be made whether or not the *IRC Section 280A* rules apply. It is important to note that this is a different calculation from that described for rental property that qualifies as a separate dwelling unit. The calculation for these types of rental units is based on a size measurement instead of a measurement of number of days rented.

Second, the expenses, having been prorated by the ratio of square footage measurement, are then reduced again by the percentage of personal use days as discussed earlier. The personal use calculation is based on the ratio of rented days of the Bed and Breakfast rooms to the days the Bed and Breakfast rooms were used personally.

A Bed and Breakfast is not subject to the limitations of *IRC Section 280A* when it satisfies the exclusive use test, and thereby qualifies for the exclusion granted to hotels and inns. However, even if it is exempt from *IRC Section 280A*, the deductions attributable to the use of the Bed and Breakfast operation must still be carefully tabulated. Direct expenses such as food, linen service, and depreciation of the furnishings of the Bed and Breakfast rooms will normally be fully deductible. Indirect expenses such as mortgage interest, property taxes, and depreciation of the home should be allocated on a square footage basis. The same allocation rate may not apply to such things as utilities, cable services, and telephones.

WARNING: It would appear reasonable to include as indirect expenses the exterior maintenance costs such as lawn maintenance and roof repairs. However, the IRS audit training manual for the MSSP on Bed and Breakfasts specifically alerts the auditor to watch for these types of exterior maintenance costs that may be included in the deductions of a Bed and Breakfast.

PLANNING TIP: Although such costs are not allowable as deductions under *IRC Section 280A*, it appears that the IRS does not have sufficient authority to disallow exterior expenses when the Bed and Breakfast operations are exempt from *IRC Section 280A* under the "hotel or inn" definition.

DETERMINING THE HIERARCHY OF DEDUCTIONS

When *IRC Section 280A* applies, the allowable deductions are subtracted from income in a strictly controlled order. The order required by *IRC Section 280A* applies whether the rental operation is a separate dwelling unit or a Bed and Breakfast. When the *IRC Section 280A* expense limitation rules apply, the rental income is first reduced by a portion of the mortgage interest and taxes. If there is additional rental income remaining, then it is reduced by a portion of the insurance, utilities, and repair and maintenance costs. Depreciation is the final deduction allowed against any remaining income.

PLANNING TIP: If the applicable percentage of mortgage interest and taxes exceeds the rental income, a net rental loss is allowed. This is the only time the IRS would recognize a loss for tax purposes under *IRC Section 280A*.

However, if losses continue, the hobby loss rules may apply. If any residential interest or taxes remain after applying the applicable rental portion against the rental income, then the excess interest and taxes will be treated as an itemized deduction.

INTEREST AND TAX ALLOCATION CONTROVERSY

PLANNING TIP: When subject to the rules of 280A, there may be a tax savings alternative.

The portion of interest and taxes applied to rental income is under dispute in a controversy existing between the IRS and the Ninth and Tenth Circuit Courts of Appeal.[2] Under the IRS formula, the portion of interest and taxes applied to the rental income is larger than the courts' portion. At first, the method prescribed by the IRS may appear to favor the taxpayer since it could lead to an allowable loss, as mentioned above. However, the smaller calculation allowed by the Ninth and Tenth Districts generally favors the taxpayer. The courts' calculations permit more interest and taxes to be deducted as itemized deductions while the rental income is offset with other deductions. In such cases, deductions that would normally carry over into future years have little or no chance of being used.

The IRS requires a calculation of the interest and taxes to be applied to rental income by determining a ratio of total days rented to total days occupied by any occupant. The courts say the proper calculation should be the ratio of total days rented to the total days mortgage interest and taxes were accruing during the year. When the mortgage interest and taxes are prorated for the entire year, it will result in a smaller fraction and less interest and taxes going against rental income.

ENDNOTES

1. IRS Proposed Regulation Section 1.280A-1(c)(1): IN GENERAL. For purposes of this section and Sections 1.280A-2 and 1.280A-3, the term "dwelling unit" includes a house, apartment, condominium, mobile home, boat, or similar property, which provides basic living accommodations such as sleeping space, toilet, and cooking facilities. A single structure may contain more than one dwelling unit. For example, each apartment in an apartment building is a separate dwelling unit. Similarly, if the basement of a house contains basic living accommodations, the basement constitutes a separate dwelling unit. All structures and other property appurtenant to a dwelling unit which do not themselves constitute dwelling units are considered part of the unit. For example, an individual who rents to another person space in a garage which is appurtenant to a house which the individual owns and occupies may claim deductions with respect to that rental activity only to the extent allowed under section 280A, paragraph (b) of this section, and Section 1.280A-3.

2. *Bolton* v. *Comr.*, 77 T.C. 104 (1981), aff'd, 694 F.2d 556, 559 (9th Cir. 1982). Accord, McKinney v. Comr., 732 F.2d 414 (10th Cir. 1983).

CHAPTER 6

Special Circumstances

PLANNING ISSUES FOR BED AND BREAKFASTS

All businesses will face risk and uncertainty. These contingencies need to be considered when the business is being formed. Addressing these concerns early will influence what form of business will work best—proprietorship, partnership, S corporation, C corporation, or Limited Liability Company (LLC). Matters such as risk and insurance, asset exposure, capitalization, and continuity of business will impact the decisions. By the time any of these events occur, if they do, it is usually too late to develop a contingency plan or to protect the business. Some events have critical tax consequences as well, so the business impact could be compounded.

DEATH OF THE OWNER(S)

In a Bed and Breakfast operation the home represents the operator's residence and revenue source. Early in the business planning cycle it is important to consider what would happen if the owner(s) died. There are two major issues:

1. What happens to the real estate?

2. What happens to the business?

The language in the deed on the property determines what will happen to the home. If the property is owned 100 percent by the business owner, the title to the property will pass to whomever has been named in the will. If the property is owned as a tenant in common with another, the portion owned by the deceased B&B owner, again, passes according to the terms of the will. If the title to the home is held in joint tenancy, it passes directly, immediately, and totally to the surviving joint owner(s). If the surviving joint tenant is a co-owner of the B&B, business can continue as usual. Otherwise, continuation of the business is probably doubtful.

If the property has been conveyed to a corporation, partnership, or LLC (see Chapter 7), the entity will continue to own the property after the owner's death. If the entity is a partnership, the partnership agreement specifies what options exist for continuity of the business. The corporation theoretically can continue despite the owner's death, but there may be buy-sell agreements to arrange payment to the heirs. In reality, since the B&B is a service operation, the death of an owner may make the continuity of the entire enterprise unfeasible.

The other issue is, what becomes of the business, even if it is conveyed through a will? Probate is often slow and assets are likely to be sold to cover obligations of the estate. Service-intensive businesses present severe problems because they are perceived by personal representatives and heirs as potential losses, which could consume some other estate assets. The will should specify who is to receive the business and instruct that it be conveyed to that person as quickly as possible. Otherwise, it represents a risk to the estate, with little financial benefit to be derived. If the business ceases to be a going enterprise, there then is no value aside from the real estate.

Such issues argue for an entity or a trust arrangement, but they too can present other perils, as Chapter 7 demonstrates. Estate planning is beyond the scope of this book, but needs to be considered by anyone operating a business. At a minimum, the owner should have a will with provision for transfer of the business.

DIVORCE OF THE OWNER(S)

A B&B operation is unique in that the owner's personal life and the business life are so closely intertwined. In most cases, it is a family business with both spouses, and possibly children, actively involved. Under most of these circumstances, the B&B is operated as a sole-proprietorship. Therefore, a divorce cannot help but have a dramatic impact on the business and may even terminate it. The home usually is the largest single asset of the marriage, and if both parties own it, it may have to be sold, again ending the business. Even if it has been conveyed to an entity, the issue could develop into a tug-of-war to determine who gets the business or stock certificates.

 PLANNING TIP: One strategy is for the husband and wife to form a partnership and spell out how they would handle a divorce, as well as other issues customarily specified, in the partnership agreement.

By anticipating and agreeing to various courses of actions while everything is cordial, there will be the basis for handling potential problems when, or if, they occur. A partnership agreement can continue to bind the parties even after they divorce and could assure the continuity of the business. Likewise, the partnership agreement can have provisions which make it possible to pass the business to the other partner(s) without it passing through the will or probate.

PURCHASE OF HOME TO BE CONVERTED INTO A BED AND BREAKFAST

Two problems can arise when the new home being purchased is intended to be used as a B&B operation. Both problems arise only when a former home has been sold at a gain, and the gain is going to be deferred through the purchase of the new home under *IRC Section 1034*. This code section provides for the mandatory nonrecognition of gain when its provisions are met. The text of *IRC Section 1034* appears in Appendix C.

Problems can occur when a B&B is purchased with the proceeds from the sale of a former home used as a personal residence. A gain from the sale of a personal residence can be deferred when a new residence is purchased for at least the same amount as the sales price of the former home. However, a problem can occur when the new property is not used 100 percent as a personal residence. When a portion of the new property is used for business, such as a B&B, the price of the replacement home necessary to defer the gain on the sale of the former home cannot be measured by the full cost of the new home. Under *IRC Section 1034*, the price of the new home must be equal to or greater than the adjusted sales price of the former home. The adjusted sales price is the sales price less selling costs and qualified fix-up expenses. The price of the new home does not include any amount attributable to the portion of the home intended to be used as business property. For example, if 25 percent of the new home is to be used as a B&B, then only 75 percent of the price of the new home would be eligible to defer the gain from the former home.

A second problem arises when the decision is made to use the new home for a B&B after the purchase is made. The deferral of gain applies to the entire purchase price, and therefore causes the depreciable basis of the B&B portion of the home to be reduced by the respective portion of the gain as well. Such an adjustment causes the depreciation to be reduced, and the gain to be taxable when the property is sold. The problem can be avoided when the price of the new home is high enough to allow full deferral based on only the personal portion of the new home's purchase price. In such a case, the intent to use the new home for B&B activity must be documented as early as possible during the purchase process. Recognizing the B&B at the time of purchase will insure a full basis in the B&B portion of the new home. Then the B&B portion of the home can have a fair market value basis for depreciation purposes.

SALE OF A RESIDENCE USED AS A BED AND BREAKFAST

Additional problems exist when selling a personal residence while it is being used as a B&B. The sales price must be allocated between the personal and business portions of the residence. Any gain attributable to the B&B rooms will not qualify for deferral under *IRC Section 1034*, or for the one-time exclusion of $125,000 under *IRC Section 121*. *IRC Section 121* appears in Appendix C.

The B&B portion of the gain will be taxable whether or not a new home is purchased, and whether or not any portion of the new home is used as a B&B. There are some tax planning opportunities by using a tax-free exchange (beyond the scope of this book) for the portion of the sale allocable to B&B rooms when the new home will also serve as a B&B. A tax advisor should be consulted about such tax strategies.

 PLANNING TIP: However, the homeowner may want to consider terminating the B&B activity prior to offering the home for sale.

TERMINATION OF THE BUSINESS; CONVERSION TO 100 PERCENT PERSONAL USE

The benefits of *IRC Section 1034* may be reinstated when a B&B is terminated and the home is converted back to a personal residence. Prior business use of the property will not necessarily cause forfeiture of the benefits of *IRC Section 1034* if 100 percent of the property qualifies as a personal residence at the time of sale. The basis of the residence must be determined by properly reducing the basis by the allowed or allowable depreciation. In most cases, the resulting gain will still qualify for deferral under *IRC Section 1034*. Timing of the sale relative to the termination of the B&B activity is crucial. Generally, no business activity should occur in the year of sale.

Application of *IRC Section 121* (pertaining to the one-time exclusion of gain from sale of principal residence by individual who has attained age 55) is not as straightforward as *IRC Section 1034*, and requires careful and advanced planning. To qualify under *IRC Section 121*, the homeowner must have occupied the residence as a principal personal residence for at least three of the five years prior to sale. If a B&B has been in existence for more than two years, the homeowner must wait until the three-year period is satisfied before selling the property if the exclusion under *IRC Section 121* is to be elected. A sale of the home prior to requalification will result in a situation wherein the portion of the gain attributable to the B&B activity will not qualify for exclusion and may be taxable. If the B&B activity has been terminated, but the requalification has not been met, the gain may still qualify for deferral under *IRC Section 1034*.

DISASTER OR DESTRUCTION OF THE PROPERTY

It is tragic when property is destroyed due to a fire or other disaster. Fortunately, insurance will be able to restore the structure, assuming adequate and proper coverage has been obtained. However, restoring the business operation may not be as simple. First, all the reservations for the period of repairs will be lost. Furthermore, the period of business interruption can be indefinite, inhibiting additional reservations. Very likely, the business records and equipment have been destroyed or violated as well.

Every business should have a contingency plan for dealing with disasters. Also, even without a natural disaster, there could be a computer disaster in which all data are lost or inaccessible. Important documents and records should be duplicated and stored off the premises. Computer hard drives should be backed up, with the irreplaceable programs and data stored elsewhere as well. By considering the worst-case scenarios, the business should be able to take protective measures to survive unforeseeable disasters.

CHAPTER 7

Plan Ahead when Choosing a Business Entity

FORMATION OF SEPARATE BUSINESS ENTITIES

Prior to this chapter, all Bed and Breakfasts were treated as though they were sole proprietorships, since that is the easiest method of doing business. The B&B owner may consider one of the other business forms or entities available, such as a corporation, S corporation, partnership, or Limited Liability Company (LLC). Whenever there is more than one business owner (with the exception of a married couple) a business entity must be formed, although an individual can also operate as a business entity if no effort has been made to classify the business. If no formalities of forming an entity have been done, a business with more than one owner will be treated as a partnership with all owners as equal general partners. In the absence of a formalized entity, a partnership will arise, with or without a formal agreement. That means that the legal rights and obligations of a partnership, as well as its tax consequences, apply.

Each type of business structure has advantages and disadvantages. There are some significant tax risks that can follow from the choice of business structure.

WARNING: A deceptively simple choice can have major unexpected consequences that could eliminate the financial benefits of operating a business.

CHOICE OF TYPE OF BUSINESS ENTITY

A partnership is formed when two or more people join together to conduct a business. They each contribute cash, property, and/or labor, and share in the profits and losses of the business. Partnerships pay no tax, but the profits and losses "flow through" to the partners. The partners are personally liable for any business losses. Each partner's personal assets can be taken by creditors if the business cannot pay its bills. A two-member partnership terminates upon the death of a partner.

The terms of the partnership should be spelled out in a partnership agreement, but the terms of the agreement are too private. Disclosures do not need to be made to form or maintain a partnership. A partnership can be flexible and tailored to the specific needs of the partners and the business. A well-drafted partnership agreement can avoid or reduce many of the problems that are discussed later in this chapter. A husband and wife can form a partnership, which can specify how to handle such issues as the potential sale of the business, divorce, death, and avoiding probate.

Limited partnerships are an unsuitable form of ownership for most B&Bs. Registration and filing requirements can be strict and complicated. A limited partnership is really a form of financing a business, and the limited partner is not permitted to have any involvement in the management of the business. Limited partners are protected from creditors and can lose no more than the amount invested. However, general partners are still vulnerable for business debts even if they do not participate in the business activity.

Although Limited Liability Companies are recognized by most states, for federal tax purposes LLCs generally report business activities to the IRS as a partnership. The attributes of an LLC give its members the advantage of the limited liability of a corporation but without the management restrictions of a limited partnership. An LLC is filed with the state, but the procedure is very simple, inexpensive, and, in most states, annual reporting is usually not required. States differ regarding rules for LLC, and because they are treated by the IRS as partnerships, they may not be suitable for all kinds of businesses.

Corporations are formed at the state level and are somewhat more complex than sole proprietorships. Corporations require considerable paperwork, first to establish and later to keep functioning. Annual meetings, reports, fees, and public disclosures are required. Although these corporate formalities are often ignored by small businesses, they are necessary to maintain the division of business and personal exposure to liabilities, which is one of the primary benefits of the corporation. Also, taxes on earnings are paid twice, first at the corporate level, and then by the owners when profits in the form of dividends are distributed.

The double taxation of profits can be eliminated if the corporation elects to become an S corporation. After the corporation has been formed at the state level, the stockholders request S status from the IRS. See the IRC section on "Using the S Election for a Corporation," later in this chapter.

Careful analysis is required to decide whether to form the business as a corporation or a partnership. These forms of doing business are generally not feasible for small operators due to the legal costs of formation and the considerable tax complications. The administrative costs of formation, along with the annual filing requirements, will discourage most B&B operators from creating a separate entity. The use of a corporation will require some form of transfer of ownership or control to the operating entity. Transfer of ownership to a separate entity such as a corporation has more merit when the B&B has sufficient rooms to rent (usually five or more) resulting in a greater potential for profit.

ISSUES INVOLVING TRANSFER OF OWNERSHIP

The transfer of a personal residence to a separate entity should be carefully planned. Once a home is transferred to a separate entity, such as a corporation, the home becomes a business property and loses its status as a personal residence under the IRS code. As stated in the prior chapter, a transfer will result in the loss of the deferral benefits of *IRC Section 1034* and the $125,000 exclusion allowed by *IRC Section 121*. Any subsequent gain on the sale of the home would be subject to taxation.

Before a home is converted from residential to business status, the taxable gain factor needs careful analysis. If prior gains have been deferred under *IRC Section 1034*, the basis of the home may be so low it would not be feasible to transfer the home to a corporation. If the property is highly appreciated at the time of transfer, and the owner has a very low basis due to prior deferrals under *IRC Section 1034*, no benefit of depreciation will be available for the appreciated portion of the home's value. As mentioned earlier, this issue is exacerbated by the fact that the gain attributable to the appreciation will be taxable at the time of sale.

 WARNING: If the owners are nearing retirement, transferring a highly appreciated principal residence could jeopardize the use of the *IRC Section 121* exclusion of up to $125,000 in gain.

It is also advisable to check with the mortgage holder to be sure that any such transfer to another entity will not trigger a due-on-sale clause in the mortgage. In addition, zoning restrictions can be brutal and should be thoroughly researched.

In deliberating whether to use a corporation for the operation of a B&B, consideration is sometimes given to entering into a lease agreement with the corporation. In this scenario, ownership of the home is not transferred to the corporation, but control of the B&B operation is conveyed to the corporation by a lease agreement. A lease agreement will circumvent some of the problems associated with transfers of ownership, but it can create a few problems of its own. A lease will not solve the potential problem of low basis for depreciation purposes. Subjecting a home to a lease will remove the home from any benefits under *IRC Sections 1034 and 121*. If the home is leased to a C corporation, the owner may have limitations under the passive activity loss limitation rules of *IRC Section 469*. Whether leased to a C or S corporation, there are other restrictions that limit deduction of rental expenses under such arrangements. *IRC Section 280A(a)* limits deductions for dwelling units used as residences. The general rule of *IRC Section 280A(a)* appears as follows:

> *Except as otherwise provided in this section, in the case of a taxpayer who is an individual or an S corporation, no deduction otherwise allowable under this chapter shall be allowed with respect to the use of a dwelling unit which is used by the tax-payer during the taxable year as a residence.*

In 1986, Congress added *IRC Section 280A(c)(6)* to disallow most expenses for leases of personal residences to employers. This code section reads as follows:

> *280A(c)(6) Treatment Of Rental To Employer: Paragraphs (1) and (3) shall not apply to any item which is attributable to the rental of the dwelling unit (or any portion thereof) by the taxpayer to his employer during any period in which the taxpayer uses the dwelling unit (or portion) in performing services as an employee of the employer.*

Paragraphs 1 and 3 referred to in the above code section provide exceptions to the general rule of *IRC Section 280A(a)*, which denies deductions to the residences being leased. But *IRC Section 280(c)(6)* disallows these deductions when an employee lives in a dwelling unit leased by the corporate employer. *IRC Section 280A(c)(6)* is a particularly strict provision. Normally, under *IRC Section 280A*, expenses can be taken to the extent of the lease income earned.

WARNING: When an employer leases room in an employee's home, the only deductions allowed to the employee are interest and taxes, irrespective of the lease income earned.

The trap set by *IRC Section 280A(c)(6)* could be avoided if the residence contained separate "dwelling units." To qualify as a dwelling unit, the accommodation must have its own kitchen, sleeping, and toilet facilities. If the owner has such separate facilities available it may be difficult to justify the lease agreement with the corporation. In such a case, it would appear necessary to have a lease that applied only to the area held out for rent to guests. The trap may also be avoided if the corporate lessee is not considered an employer. The argument that the lessee corporation is not an employer is weakened by the fact that the lessor's personal use of the home is, admittedly, a form of fringe benefit. Whether this benefit is a dividend from the corporation, or remuneration in the form of compensation, is a matter of perspective. Under *IRC Section 280A(c)(6)*, the allowance of rental expenses, other than interest and taxes, will depend upon the IRS agent's perspective of the nature of the benefits being transferred to the lessors.

CORPORATIONS AND IRC SECTION 351

No gain is generally recognized when the owner of property transfers the property to a corporation for stock. The corporation, in turn, takes the property with the same cost basis as the transferor. The cost basis of property is the amount used to determine depreciation and gain or loss at the time of disposition. This is the general provision of *IRC Section 351*, which appears in Appendix C.

When substantially all the assets of a business are transferred to the corporation, and the transferor is in control of the corporation, the rules of *IRC Section 351* will apply. When the rules of *IRC Section 351* are satisfied, the application of its provisions are mandatory. Under the provisions of *IRC Section 351*, the incorporator's basis will carry over to the corporation and there will be no reportable gain to the transferor, nor to the transferee. The mandatory application of *IRC Section 351* states that a sale of property to a corporation by the incorporator could be disregarded and the basis to the corporation would remain the same as that of the incorporator.

 **WARNING: There is an exception to the general rule of nonrecognition of gain on a transfer of property to a corporation under *IRC Section 351*. When the mortgage balance is higher than the basis of the property, assumption of the mortgage by the corporation will result in a gain to the incorporator. Such a gain will be equal to the extent of the excess debt being assumed over the basis of the property.**

Mortgages in excess of basis can easily occur. When a second mortgage is taken on the property for uses other than improving or acquiring the property, the total debt secured by the home may exceed the basis of the home. Or, when several homes previously owned and sold have resulted in gains being deferred under *IRC Section 1034*, the basis of the current home may be considerably lower than the mortgage due on the current home. Since the prior gains are subtracted from the cost of the current home, these deferred gains reduce the basis of the current home.

As a result of the carryover basis rules of *IRC Section 351*, the corporation will calculate its depreciation, and any gain or loss on a future sale of the transferred property, by using the incorporator's cost basis. If the homeowner has a substantial amount of equity in the property, then a serious tax problem will arise in the future as a result of transferring that property to a corporation.

A solution to this problem would exist if the owner (either husband or wife) met the requirements of *IRC Section 121* and could elect to defer up to $125,000 in gain. If either the husband or wife is age 55 or older and has lived in the home as a primary residence for at least three of the five years prior to sale, then *IRC Section 121* may provide a remedy to the homeowner intending to incorporate a B&B activity.

PLANNING TIP: When gain can be excluded under *IRC Section 121*, the owner may want to consider selling the home on the market instead of selling it to their corporation. The homeowners could then exercise the one-time election to exclude up to $125,000 in gain and then acquire a new home with the full cost of the new home available for determining depreciation allowances. When a corporation is being formed to operate the B&B, the new home could then be transferred to the corporation with the benefits of the new, higher, basis. As an alternative, the sellers could also contribute the cash from the sale of the old home directly to the new corporation. The new home could then be purchased by the corporation with the same results.

WARNING: The homeowner, qualified under *IRC Section 121*, may consider selling the home directly to the corporation. However, even if *IRC Section 121* applies, the homeowner would still have to contend with the restrictions of *IRC Section 351* mentioned above.

It is possible to structure a sale intended to default out of the otherwise mandatory provisions of *IRC Section 351*. However, even if *IRC Section 351* could be avoided, another restriction applies to a sale of property to a corporation.

A sale of depreciable property to a corporation must contend with *IRC Section 1239*. *IRC Section 1239* causes gain that would have otherwise qualified for capital gain benefits to be taxed as ordinary income. It affects the sale of depreciable property to a related party, such as a corporation owned 80 percent or more by the seller. However, if the income exclusion provisions of *IRC Section 121* apply, then the limitations of *IRC Section 1239* could be avoided. Still, this would leave the homeowner to contend with the restrictions of *IRC Section 351*. In either case, without the benefits of *IRC Section 121*, the formation of a corporation using a low basis, high value property would not be feasible. The provisions of *IRC Section 1239* appear in Appendix C.

Relief to the recognition of gain may be available under the tax-free exchange rules of *IRC Section 1031*. Normally, *IRC Section 1031* would not apply to a personal residence since that provision only applies to business or investment property. There is no guarantee that conversion of a personal residence to a B&B would qualify the entire home as trade or business property. Even if the home would qualify for a tax-free exchange under *IRC Section 1031*, the carryover basis rules would prevent the depreciation of the full value of the house.

The use of a corporation further complicates matters when the B&B operators are ready to retire. A substantial gain could result to both the corporation and the stockholder if the corporation distributes appreciated property to the stockholder under a plan of liquidation.

CAPITALIZATION ISSUES OF FORMING A CORPORATION

A transfer of cash to the corporation instead of the property may allow for a more advantageous structure in capitalizing the corporation. The cash, as well as the value of any property transferred, will be treated as equity in the corporation and locked into the corporation until liquidation. To avoid locking all cash in equity, incorporators are tempted to treat a portion of the cash transferred to the corporation as a loan, allowing them to receive principal and interest on transferred funds. However, there are provisions in the Internal Revenue Code to prevent "thinly capitalized" corporations. *IRC Section 385* addresses the ratio of debt to equity for corporations. *IRC Section 1244* provides an incentive to fund corporations with equity as opposed to debt. Losses from failed investments in "small business corporations" pursuant to *IRC Section 1244* are entitled to ordinary loss deductions of up to $50,000 ($100,000 on joint returns). Losses from "debt" owed by failed corporations are treated as short-term capital losses, and may be applied to offset capital gains; otherwise, the capital loss deduction is limited to $3,000 per year. State laws must also be observed in determining the adequacy of a corporation's capital structure. Inadequately funded corporations run the risk of having the corporate shield disregarded by creditors seeking collection enforcement.

USING THE S ELECTION FOR A CORPORATION

When a corporation is formed, the incorporators should consider the use of an S election. Generally an S corporation does not pay any tax on its profits. Instead, the stockholders report the income of the corporation on their individual returns. The use of an S corporation would also resolve the problem of double taxation that would otherwise apply to a corporate liquidation of appreciated property. There are limitations to the availability of an S corporation and the election period is strictly controlled. The rules of *IRC Sections 351, 385*, and *1239* apply to S corporations just like they do to the standard C corporation.

WARNING: The capitalization provisions of *IRC Section 385* are even more important to follow when an S election has been made because certain debt of the corporation can be considered as a second class of stock. Such an occurrence would result in the termination of the corporation's S status since one of the rules for an S corporation restricts it to a single class of stock.

PLANNING TIP: An S corporation can have nonvoting stock.

The requirements for an S corporation are:

1. It must be a domestic corporation that is either organized in the United States or organized under federal or state law.

2. It must have only one class of stock.

3. It must have as shareholders only individuals, estates (including estates of individuals in bankruptcy), and certain trusts. Beginning in 1997, the ownership restriction is somewhat relaxed.

4. The 35 shareholder limit is increased to 75 beginning in 1997.

5. It must have no nonresident alien shareholders.

In order to form an S corporation, the corporation must make an election signed by all stockholders. The election is made on Form 2553.

An S corporation will not work in all situations, such as when the owner is not a U.S. citizen. If any of the original conditions change (such as having too much passive income or having a noncitizen become a co-owner), the S status can be lost. If the S status is unexpectedly lost, severe consequences could result. To be an effective election for the first taxable year of a corporation, the election must be made within 75 days of the earliest of the following three dates:

- The day the corporation first has assets

- The day the corporation starts business, or

- The day the corporation issues stock

The S corporation election form must be signed by every stockholder.

S CORPORATIONS AND THE EMPLOYMENT ISSUE

When an S corporation election is made, the owner that provides services to the corporation must take a reasonable salary. This rule is intended to prevent the conversion of earned income into dividends. Since dividends of an S corporation avoid the classic double taxation of subchapter C corporations, there is much temptation to simply pay an S corporation stockholder the corporate profits as a dividend. This dividend treatment avoids payroll taxes such as social security, Medicare, and unemployment.

However tempting this may appear, the IRS is prepared to challenge the S corporation stockholder/employee who does not treat a reasonable portion of the corporate profits as a salary. The need to pay a salary imposes a significant paperwork burden on the corporate employer, which is another reason the cost/benefit should be carefully analyzed before deciding to incorporate. But when the profits of the Bed and Breakfast are substantial, using an S corporation can avoid having all income subject to employment taxes.

FOOD AND LODGING FOR THE CONVENIENCE OF THE EMPLOYER

When a corporation is formed and the ownership of the home is transferred to the corporation, then the living arrangements of the B&B operators become a sensitive issue. When the corporation owns the home, the question arises as to whether or not the B&B operators would be required to pay the corporation fair rental value for their own personal use of the home. The B&B operators may try to make a case that their presence in the home is required as a condition of their employment, and for the convenience of their corporate employer, that operates the B&B. When this could be successfully argued, then the operators would not be required to pay fair rental value for their lodging or the food provided to them by their corporation. Furthermore, the corporation would be allowed to deduct the costs. The provisions of *IRC Section 119* appear in Appendix C.

Under *IRC Section 119*, the value of the lodging and food provided to the operators of the B&B by the employer corporation would not be considered income to them. According to *IRC Section 119*, when an employee's attendance is required for a 24-hour period as a condition of his or her employment, food and lodging can be provided to the employees at the corporation's expense. Such an arrangement would appear to have very favorable tax advantages as it would enable the operators to effectively write off all of their food and lodging costs through the corporation. But this lucrative loophole is tightly scrutinized by the IRS. As the old saying goes, "If it sounds too good to be true, it usually is." In fact, it is very difficult to qualify for the advantages of *IRC Section 119* to exclude the value of meals and lodging as income.

The IRS would first take a good look at the business purpose of such an arrangement. For example, the question would be asked if there was any possibility the corporation could show a profit under this arrangement. The auditor would also look for the reasonableness of the corporation providing free food and lodging to its owner/employees. If a B&B has guests on the weekend but is vacant during the week, the operators may not be able to justify the need for their presence during the idle weekdays. Under such circumstances, it would be advisable for the operators to repay the corporation for food and lodging costs during the idle periods.

THE DOUBLE TAXATION RISK OF CORPORATIONS

If the corporation failed to record a profit due to the costs of providing food and lodging to the operators, then the arrangement would fail the business purpose test discussed in Chapter 5.

WARNING: As a result, the IRS may disregard the corporation's existence and treat the activity as a hobby of the operators. Even when the corporation is not disregarded, the corporate deductions for food and lodging provided to the operators could be challenged. When such costs are disallowed as a deduction to the corporation, double taxation could result. First, there may be additional tax to the corporation, and second, the operators would be taxed on the value of the food and lodging received by them.

Initially it may appear that one side of this two-edged sword could be avoided by electing an S status for the corporation, as mentioned previously. The election under subchapter S of the Internal Revenue Code results in the corporation passing through its taxable income to the stockholders. Because an S corporation does not pay taxes on its income, no double taxation results when the IRS disallows any deductions.

WARNING: The benefits of *IRC Section 119* (meals or lodging furnished for the convenience of the employer) have been held not to apply to the owner/employees of an S corporation. Under *IRC Section 1372(a)*, a two percent or greater shareholder would be denied the benefits of the exclusion of *IRC Section 119*. *IRC Section 1372* appears in Appendix C.

The operator's presence as a condition of employment becomes more tenable when all the bedrooms, except for the operator's room, are dedicated to B&B guests. However, some seasonal adjustments would be necessary in situations where the B&B may be idle for several weeks at a time. But, as stated earlier, failure to show a profit may result in the IRS disregarding the form and looking to the substance of the arrangement of the corporation and its B&B activity.

CHAPTER 8

The Audit Process and Important Steps of Self-Protection

THE INTERNAL REVENUE SERVICE AND THE PUBLIC

The public perceives the tax system and the Internal Revenue Service as intimidating. Often the IRS has encouraged such fear to spur compliance. Complaints that the American tax system is too intrusive, costly, bureaucratic, unfair, and complicated have added to the mistrust of the IRS. Also, misinformation regarding tax matters is rampant, and everyone has, or knows someone who has, a tax horror story.

By establishing a voluntary system to report earnings, the IRS relies on taxpayers to provide honest and accurate information. Some have argued that the tax system violates the Fifth Amendment to the Constitution, which protects against self-incrimination. However, the Fifth Amendment offers protection in criminal matters only, while the IRS collection of taxes normally involves civil rather than criminal rights.

To protect the rights of taxpayers, due process is built into the tax collection system. In response to public concerns, there are now official ombudsmen and the Taxpayer's Bill of Rights to help citizens stuck in the tax maze. The IRS publication "Your Rights as a Taxpayer" appears in Appendix A, Exhibit A-7.

THE AUDIT SELECTION PROCESS

The IRS has been selecting most of the returns to be audited through a computer process referred to as the Discriminate Function (DIF) program. The DIF program screens tax returns for the "general program" audit system. All income-tax returns are categorized by the IRS into groups by similar size and type of incomes. The DIF program screens returns by measuring the various items of income and deduction reported and comparing that measurement against a norm developed for that particular category of return. The deviation from the norm is scored and the higher scores are assigned to a classifier for screening. Irregularities are likely to invite further scrutiny.

The selected returns are divided into two groups. One group consists of individuals without a business, and some with relatively uncomplicated businesses. The issues in this first group are marked on a checklist by the classifier and sent to office audit. The second group consists of business returns, whether owned by individuals, corporations, or partnerships. The classifier may include comments regarding any identified issues. These returns are sent to field audit. The "general program" audits make up the day-to-day routine of auditing for the IRS. In addition to the DIF program, tax returns are selected for audit as a result of a number of other factors, as discussed later in this chapter.

THE SELECTION PROCESS AND THE MSSP

With one exception, tax returns are never randomly selected for audit. The exception to this rule is the Taxpayer Compliance Measurement Program (TCMP). TCMP audits are tormenting experiences that require documentation of every income source and all deductions. TCMP audits are selected on a stratified random sample and are done in three-year cycles, one year for corporate returns, the next for partnership returns, and the next for individual returns. The TCMP audits have been used to supply the detailed taxpayer data required to fuel the DIF program used to select income tax returns for audit.

In a bold departure from this three-year cycle, the IRS was planning to combine the corporate, partnership, and individual TCMP audits for the 1994 filing year. However, just before the IRS began the selection process in October 1995, the program was terminated due to budget restrictions. The falling of the budget ax has at least temporarily spelled the end of the TCMP audit nightmare for taxpayers. According to "The Kiplinger Tax Letter," May 17, 1996, the IRS plans to bring back the TCMP audits on a limited basis after the November 1996 elections. Without updated TCMP results to feed into the computer, the DIF program will eventually dry up.

With the importance of DIF phasing out, the IRS will need a new cost-effective method for selecting returns to audit. Those returns selected for audit must have the optimum tax adjustment potential. The IRS must demonstrate to the Government Accounting Office (GAO), and to Congress, the ability to produce additional taxes in an acceptable cost-to-benefit ratio.

The IRS has not been idle. It has already been using some alternatives to DIF to identify and select returns. One such program is the Midwest Automated Compliance System (MACS). Named for the St. Paul service center that developed the system, MACS is a program that can be used to filter any number of tax return components. For example, the program can identify individuals who are 401(k) participants and who also take deductions for Keogh or other retirement contributions. MACS can also filter out tax returns filed with first names that appear to be male taxpayers and who are claiming earned-income credits.

In addition to MACS, the IRS uses statistical data to reveal trends of systematic noncompliance by taxpayers in local areas. The District Office Research and Analysis (DORA) program is currently functioning in all 33 IRS districts as part of the ongoing effort to replace the waning DIF program. DORA is used as an integral part of the Market Segment Specialization Program (MSSP) analysis system. DORA uses data from such sources as the Census Bureau and state-tax records, as well as commerce data and state sales tax information, to produce industry profiles based on demographic parameters. DORA programs can sort data by Principal Industry Activity (PIA) codes and Standard Industry Codes (SIC).

If the TCMP program is ever resurrected, it will, no doubt, come back as part of the MSSP. The information collected from within each market segment will provide the IRS with a valuable and confidential detailed database specific to each industry segment. Such information will better arm the IRS to detect returns based on deviations from industry norms, rather than stratified norms.

Remember, the Bed and Breakfast industry is targeted as one of the market segments.

DETERMINING THE SELECTION PROCESS

 **WARNING:** After a taxpayer receives an audit notice, it is very important to determine the process by which a return was selected for audit before providing any of the requested information to the IRS. The initial response to the audit notice will depend in part on what the audit notice discloses about the selection of the return. When uncertain about how or why any return was selected, it is essential to ask.

Knowing the reason the IRS selected the return indicates what it expects to find. Returns selected under the general program will have a DIF score, or will have been selected through one of the MSSP identification processes. Although the IRS will generally disclose whether a return has been DIF selected, the DIF score itself is never divulged. The IRS will always indicate in advance if the return was selected as part of a TCMP process.

In addition, an audit could result from an ongoing audit of a related business or investment, such as a partnership or a closely held corporation. An audit may be the consequence of using certain tax preparers. The IRS will disclose if the return was selected because of a related audit of another tax return. If the audit is related to another audit, the areas of concern and potential issues can generally be readily identified.

INFORMANTS AND THE REWARD SYSTEM

Returns can be selected for audit as a result of an information report received by the IRS. Information reports reach the IRS through a variety of sources. Sometimes they are filed by individuals who hardly know the taxpayer and are only seeking a reward. The information from these individuals ranges from hearsay or rumor, such as something they may have overheard in a restaurant, to fully documented evidence.

The IRS receives dozens of these information reports daily. Many are given a routine follow-up and filed away without further action. Some do not even receive more than a review before being filed away. Others are assigned to either a civil or criminal division for further action. When a reward has been claimed based on the information report, a file is created with the Informant's Claim Examiner (ICE) to monitor the case development and communicate the reward determination to the informant. Rewards are not claimed in all cases. Some informants may prefer to remain anonymous to the IRS. Others may want revenge against someone. It is not uncommon for irate customers, despondent spouses, former business partners or employees, or even neighbors and friends to submit information reports. Informants can receive a reward of up to 10 percent of the tax collected. The actual reward paid by the IRS for this information is based on the type of information received. The revenue agent assigned to the case makes a recommendation on the percentage to be rewarded, determined by the accuracy and detail of the information provided. The reward is based on the actual tax collected, and not the tax assessed.

When the return is selected as a result of an information report, it should, if possible, be noted from where the report came and the nature of the information it contains. An information report could be a serious matter requiring professional representation from an attorney or accountant.

FREEDOM OF INFORMATION ACT REQUESTS

Sometimes the Internal Revenue Service will explain why a return is being audited. If this information is being withheld, there is good cause to be concerned: In such cases it is safe to assume an information report has been filed. Filing a Freedom of Information Act (FOIA) request can generally gain access to the information withheld. Such information may be withheld by the IRS under certain circumstances, such as when fraud is suspected. When there is an informant, his or her identity is seldom released unless he or she is used for testimony against the taxpayer. For an example of FOIA request, see Appendix B, Exhibit B-7.

OFFICE AUDITS

When a tax return is selected to be audited, a classifier for the Office Audit Division determines the issues to be audited. The audit is usually limited to those issues identified in the notification letter sent to the taxpayer. When the required documentation is provided for those issues, the audit can usually be settled with a single visit. The process is usually simple and straightforward. However, an office auditor conducts several audits a day, and rarely has an opportunity to review the return to be examined prior to the time of the appointment.

Issues beyond those identified by the classifier are rarely questioned because of the time constraints placed on office auditors. However, the patience of an office auditor can wear thin very quickly due to workload pressures and time constraints. A little courtesy and patience on the part of the taxpayer could work favorably. When requested documentation is not provided on the first visit, it can result in a case being written up into an audit report referred to as a "30-day letter." Such a report reflects the initial adjustments being proposed by the IRS and sets a 30-day deadline to provide the documentation or make a written request for an appeal. (See Chapter 9, "The Appeals Process," for further information.)

FIELD AUDITS

Field audits are typically more complicated than office audits. Field auditors, known as revenue agents, receive more extensive training than office auditors and are generally required to have more than 20 hours of college accounting. When a revenue agent sends out a notification of audit, all of the issues that may be of concern to the revenue agent will not necessarily be identified. All books and records are usually required for a field audit. The revenue agent's fieldwork may require that several visits be made before the issues are developed (or resolved) and the case completed.

Most IRS districts require the revenue agent to interview the taxpayer and to conduct the audit at the taxpayer's place of business. This policy may be flexible under some circumstances. Generally, it is not in the taxpayer's best interest to be interviewed or to have the audit conducted at the taxpayer's place of business. For more information on minimizing the taxpayer's exposure during the audit, see the section in this chapter on "Using a Representative to Handle an Audit."

CRIMINAL INVESTIGATION DIVISION (CID)

The Criminal Investigation Division of the IRS, commonly referred to as CID, enforces the Internal Revenue Code. It is not involved in routine audits or tax disputes, but only pursues matters involving suspected criminal activity. The primary objective of CID agents is to indict taxpayers suspected of criminal tax fraud. Cases are referred to CID as a result of an informant's reports and/or by referral from the Office or Field Audit sections of the civil division.

Occasionally, CID engages in undercover work to ferret out tax cheats. An example of this is the Business Opportunity

Program (BOP). Under this program, CID agents pose as interested buyers of various businesses that are being advertised for sale. The CID agents attempt to gain the confidence of the business owner and hope to be told by the owner of the lucrative under-the-table cash business the owner conducts.

When an investigation occurs for suspected criminal violation of the Internal Revenue Code, the CID agents may not always read the taxpayer his or her legal rights. When the taxpayer is informed of his or her legal rights and that he or she is under criminal investigation, legal counsel becomes critical before any statements are made. However, a taxpayer may not know at the outset that he or she is suspected of a criminal violation. A routine audit of the tax return could escalate into a criminal case without the taxpayer's immediate knowledge. The question as to when an auditor must give up control of the case and refer it to CID is an ongoing controversy within the IRS. The CID wants to obtain all the information it can before the taxpayer is informed of his or her legal rights. However, if the civil division waits too long, the information CID obtains from the civil audit can become tainted and be denied as evidence in a criminal case. It is important to note that once records have been submitted to the IRS, such an action is generally considered to be a waiver of protection under the Fifth Amendment with regard to those records. In addition, information provided to an accountant is not protected under the privileged communication afforded to attorneys.

RESPONDING TO THE AUDIT NOTICE

Response to the audit notice is not necessary. However, such a course of action has its price, and is generally reserved for such dire circumstances as criminal exposure with a risk of self-incrimination. An attorney's representation is highly advisable if the taxpayer chooses not to respond. If there is no cooperation from a taxpayer in an audit, the IRS can disallow whatever deductions it wishes, and it usually does. In addition, the IRS can conduct the audit without the taxpayer's participation and can contact anyone able to provide relevant financial information. The IRS can gather information from the workplace, customers, relatives and neighbors, or from banks and credit card companies.

The IRS cannot disclose any specific information about the taxpayer. However, the courts have held consistently in favor of the IRS, ruling that it is not a violation of the taxpayer's rights to privacy for the IRS to disclose information necessary to enforce compliance to the Internal Revenue Code. This includes the fact that the taxpayer is being audited.

SCHEDULING THE AUDIT

Scheduling the appointment depends on whether the return has been selected by office audit or by field audit. The audit is scheduled for office audit when the issues are listed with instructions to call for an appointment to bring requested documentation into the office. The phone number listed on the notice is that of a scheduling clerk, so they are unable to discuss the specifics of the audit when the appointment is made. An office auditor is not assigned until the taxpayer arrives for the appointment. It is wise to schedule the appointment as far into the future as possible to provide sufficient time to locate and organize records.

Sometimes an audit is scheduled for an IRS office location that is not convenient. In those circumstances it is possible to request a transfer of the audit to a more convenient IRS office. The IRS is generally cooperative in transferring the audit, but once a case is underway, transfer to another office becomes more difficult.

When the audit notice does not list the issues, the audit will probably be a field audit. The letter will name a specific individual to be called to make an appointment. This person will usually be the revenue agent assigned to do the audit. The auditor will raise a series of questions regarding the return when the initial call is made. It is within the taxpayer's rights not to answer any questions at this time, so one can politely decline if unsure of appropriate responses.

TALKING TO THE INTERNAL REVENUE SERVICE

Always be polite when communicating with the IRS, because rudeness is not a wise course of action and can backfire. Keep good records with the date, time, name, and title of any IRS personnel contacted.

A taxpayer should follow these simple rules:

- Listen to the question and carefully consider the answer. If uncertain, say so, and delay the response until there is more information.

- Answer the question and then stop talking. If the IRS agent looks confused by an answer, do not continue to explain.

- Let the agent ask the questions, and wait for the agent to finish. Do not volunteer information.

REPETITIVE AUDITS

Sometimes a taxpayer deducts recurring items that cause the returns to repeatedly be selected for audit. When a taxpayer has been audited within the previous two years, he or she may qualify to have the audit terminated through the repetitive audit procedures. These procedures apply when the issues being examined are the same issues examined in the prior audit. The current audit will be terminated only if the prior issues were resolved without a disallowance.

USING A REPRESENTATIVE TO HANDLE AN AUDIT

The taxpayer may not want to face an IRS audit alone or may want a representative to insulate him or her from the IRS. Most IRS auditors relish the thought of meeting alone with a taxpayer. Appointment of a power of attorney to represent the taxpayer is accomplished by using Form 2848 (see Appendix A, Exhibit A-9).

Special rules apply to the audit when there is a representative appointed. Once there is a person designated as the taxpayer's power of attorney, the IRS is obligated to communicate with the taxpayer through this representative. The IRS is no longer allowed to contact the taxpayer directly. This arrangement provides insulation from the audit process, but it forces the taxpayer to rely exclusively on the chosen representative. Generally, the person who prepared the return is most likely to handle the audit. The taxpayer may elect someone other than his accountant: specifically authorized professionals, an immediate family member, a full-time employee, or a trustee or guardian.

The IRS recognizes certain groups of individuals as specifically authorized to practice before the IRS. These groups consist of attorneys, certified public accountants (CPAs), enrolled agents, and enrolled actuaries. Attorneys and CPAs must pass a rigorous exam and meet an experience requirement that varies from state to state. Enrolled agents are tax specialists, licensed by the IRS through either working for the IRS in a technical position for at least five years or by successfully completing a rigorous examination. Attorneys and CPAs are required to have continuing education in order to maintain their license to practice. A CPA must average 40 hours per year in most states; enrolled agents are required by the IRS to maintain continuing education with 72 hours of technical training within each three-year period.

RECORDS AND RECEIPTS

When gathering documentation for an audit, it is not uncommon to discover that some records may be missing. When all of the documentation is not available, it may be necessary to use alternative records or to reconstruct the missing documents. There are often many ways the taxpayer can find alternative sources for records that may be lost or destroyed. For example, if there are no receipts for business travel or entertainment, consider referring to appointment books, credit card statements, or other daily records that show daily business activity expenditures. Sales meeting records, convention schedules, and contracts can prove where travel occurred. Records and receipts provide documentation for purchases in addition to serving as travel documentation.

When the IRS challenges deductions, the burden of proof is on the taxpayer. The burden-of-proof rule ("innocent until proven guilty") does not apply to the IRS in a civil audit because no crime is being alleged. There has been much discussion about this issue, and some have suggested shifting the burden of proof to the IRS. Such a move could backfire and cause more problems to the taxpayers than they face under current conditions. If the IRS had to prove deductions were unallowable, the resulting investigation could be disastrous. The depth of the investigation would involve interviewing the taxpayer's business associates, vendors, customers, employees, competitors, family members, and neighbors. Information that the IRS uncovers could lead to criminal charges. Currently, when a deduction cannot be substantiated, the results are limited to paying the additional tax and interest. The frequency of penalties and even criminal indictments would certainly increase if the IRS had to carry the burden of proof standard on its shoulders.

F-1099 FILING REQUIREMENTS

Keep in mind that there is another IRS filing requirement for certain payments for services provided to a business. If the taxpayer pays an unincorporated business for services exceeding $600 in a single year (see Chapter 3 regarding the independent contractor issues), a Form 1099-Misc must be sent to the service provider and to the IRS. Most states will need a copy also. The Form 1099-Misc must show name, address, and tax identification number (EIN or Social Security number) of the service provider.

During an audit, the agent asks for file copies of any F-1099s provided. There is a minimum penalty of $50 per form, per year for failure to file the necessary F-1099s. When the failure to file the F-1099s is due to intentional disregard of rules and regulations, the penalty increases to the greater of $100 per form, or 10 percent of the amount unreported on the forms.

PREPARING RECORDS FOR AUDIT

When responding to the audit notice, there is always the temptation to dump a garbage bag full of receipts upon the auditor's desk. Never do this! Having the records organized before the audit will provide greater confidence, and will give the auditor a more comfortable feeling about the evaluation of your return. When good records are not available, it helps to start with those areas that have your best documentation: this may be of benefit later, when documentation may run a little thin.

When gathering documentation, a taxpayer may sometimes find receipts totaling more than the amount that was claimed on the return. These receipts should be kept until after the audit work is completed. Do not start the audit by informing the auditor that you expect a refund. Normally, the auditor should only be concerned with determining the correct amount of tax, whether or not the amount of tax paid was correct. But there is always a psychological factor that will cause auditors to examine in more detail, or otherwise be less accepting of some marginal documentation, if they feel there will be a refund due. If necessary, at the conclusion of the auditor's findings, the additional deductions can be disclosed. If they are nominal in amount and the auditor is not going to make any changes to the return, consider forgetting the issue.

WORKING WITH THE AUDITOR

When an agreement with the auditor cannot be reached, the next step for the taxpayer is to ask to speak to the auditor's supervisor. Such a step should not be done in a vengeful or vindictive manner. It is acceptable to ask to speak with the supervisor if the taxpayer wants a second opinion, or cannot understand the auditor's explanations. When communication with the auditor is difficult, the supervisor will occasionally grant a request for a change of auditors. The IRS may be reluctant to do so, however, and the supervisor will attempt to resolve the situation.

> **WARNING: Sometimes an irate taxpayer will contact a public official, such as an elected representative, regarding an IRS audit. Do not do this; the tactic almost always backfires. If there is a congressional inquiry regarding an IRS audit, then everyone in the department involved with the audit, from the top officials down to the auditor, shifts into formal mode. Many times in the course of an audit there will be give-and-take exchanges with the auditor. When the top brass starts looking over the auditor's shoulder, however, the examination may suddenly become a case "by the books."**

Technically, the auditor is not authorized to deal on any issues. In actual practice, negotiations occur on a routine basis in the course of closing agreed audits. However, if the audit has drawn the attention of the district director, then all of the rules are strictly by the book. Such a tactic should be reserved for only the most serious of circumstances.

STRUCTURE OF THE IRS AND STEPS TO COURT

The resulting audit report will reflect the amount the Internal Revenue Service claims is owed by or to the taxpayer. This audit report can be appealed to the Tax Court (see Chapter 9), at which time any available records will be presented as evidence for documentation of claims. The Tax Court can make its own determination of how much tax is due. If, for some reason, the IRS suspects any fraudulent acts, an audit report will not be issued. The IRS will eventually inform the taxpayer of his or her rights and proceed to develop a case. For purposes of this discussion, it will be assumed that the audit does not involve criminal tax fraud and a timely response to an audit notice is provided.

ENDNOTE

1. *Your Rights as a Taxpayer,* IRS, Publication 1, 1990.

CHAPTER 9

Appeals and Tax Collection

THE APPEALS PROCESS

When the taxpayer is unwilling to accept the auditor's report or is unable to get satisfaction from the supervisor, it is possible to appeal the issues to the next level, which is the Appellate Division. The Internal Revenue Service auditor will separate the agreed and unagreed issues and send a 30-day letter requesting response to the auditor's findings. The taxpayer can sign and return a Form 870, "Waiver of Restrictions on Assessment" (for a copy of Form 870, see Appendix A, Exhibit A-10) for the agreed issues. For the unagreed issues, the 30-day letter asks the taxpayer to:

1. Submit any additional evidence

2. Request further discussion with an examiner

3. Exercise his or her appeals rights

The 30-day letter informs the taxpayer that if he or she fails to do at least one of the foregoing, the case will be processed on the basis of the proposed adjustments within 30 days, and a notice of deficiency issued.

Within the 30 days, the taxpayer must request an appeal for the unagreed issues to an appellate hearing officer. An appellate officer is expected to be an impartial party to a dispute, but in most cases the appellate officers are former IRS auditors or agents. Nevertheless, the appeal process is recommended because there is only one other alternative. The next step, after utilizing or bypassing the Appellate Division, is to take the case to Tax Court.

Appellate division hearings are informal affairs usually conducted in the comfort of a private office. Appellate officers are allowed to negotiate issues based on what are referred to as "hazards of litigation." With a good case, the taxpayer can win most, if not all the issues. Either the taxpayer or his or her representative can meet with the appellate officer. (See the section in Chapter 8 on "Using a Representative to Handle an Audit.")

STATUTORY NOTICES OF DEFICIENCY

When an agreement cannot be reached with an appellate officer, the IRS issues a Statutory Notice of Deficiency. This is also referred to as a 90-day letter. Sometimes, at the conclusion of the initial audit process, the auditor will issue a 90-day letter instead of a 30-day letter. Generally, this is done when the three-year statutory period (the normal time limit for the IRS to make an assessment of tax) is about to expire. Once the 90-day letter is issued, the statutory period for making assessments will not expire. The Statutory Notice of Deficiency is a very important notice since 90 days after the notice is issued, the IRS can make the assessment of tax. The assessment of tax by the IRS can be postponed by filing a petition with the Tax Court. If a timely petition is not filed, the taxpayer will have to pay all of the tax, penalties, and interest and file a claim before the case can go into the Court of Claims or District Court. (For an example of a 90-day letter, see Appendix B, Exhibit B-8.)

TAX COURT ALTERNATIVES

After a Statutory Notice of Deficiency is issued, the taxpayer has two alternatives to avoid Tax Court and still challenge the issue(s): (1) A request can be made for the IRS to reconsider the issue, or (2) the taxpayer can file an Offer in Compromise (see Appendix A for a sample Offer in Compromise). These are final measures and taxpayers should not rely upon them for relief.

Under alternative one, the IRS can be asked to reconsider the audit issues. When new information becomes available, the IRS may grant a reconsideration and assign the file to an auditor. The auditor is likely to be the same one who handled the original audit, so some new arguments or documentation is important. This audit procedure is offered by the IRS as a courtesy to the taxpayer. The audit is generally a one-time opportunity for a resolution at the examination level. Without something convincing, the auditor may close the file, which could end the appeal rights.

WARNING: When involved in an audit reconsideration of a 90-day letter, the original 90-day period for petitioning the Tax Court will continue to tick away. When it does not appear that there will be a favorable resolution with the auditor, it will be necessary to file a timely Tax Court petition.

The other alternative to Tax Court, and paying the entire assessment when a 90-day letter is not responded to, is to file an Offer in Compromise. There are two types of Offers in Compromise; The first and most common is based on inability to pay. More is discussed about this issue later in this chapter. The second offer is based on "doubt as to liability." When an offer is filed based on doubt, it is assigned to an auditor for a technical determination. The auditor's findings can be appealed to the Appellate Division, but the decision at this level is final.

The preferred option is to file a timely Tax Court petition. Such petitions rarely get to court and usually result in another meeting with the same appellate officer. This time the case is controlled by the IRS attorney who will try the case if it is not settled in appeals. Pretrial settlements are common.

CONTROLLING THE INTEREST AND PENALTIES

There are over 150 civil penalties available to the IRS. These penalties cover everything from failure to file, failure to pay, and accuracy-related penalties to information returns, special penalties covering the activities of tax return preparers, tax shelter activities, and beyond. Separate and often multiple penalties apply to different types of prohibited behavior. Many times, penalties are imposed automatically as a procedural matter. In such cases, requests for abatement are usually successful. In most cases it is beneficial to try for an abatement. Interest can never be abated or waived. When a proposed assessment is going to be appealed, the interest and penalties will continue to accrue during the appeal process.

 **PLANNING TIP: When planning to fight an issue through Tax Court, a payment can be made under Revenue Procedure 82-51 to stop additional interest and penalties from accruing. The provision to post a payment in the form of a cash bond applies at any time during the audit.[1]**

A bond posted under Revenue Procedure 82-51 is a voluntary payment that is refundable upon request. A full refund will be given if no other taxes are owed. The IRS has the right to offset those taxes with the bond payment. No interest is credited on the money deposited in the form of a cash bond with the IRS. If the contested issue is lost, the cash bond will be applied to the taxes. The payment will be credited as of the day the bond was posted.

PAYMENT OF TAXES AND INSTALLMENT AGREEMENTS

When additional taxes are owed, and it is not possible to pay the full amount, in most cases the Internal Revenue Service will permit an installment payment agreement; however, it is usually not favorable for the taxpayer.

WARNING: The interest and failure to pay penalty will continue to accrue on the unpaid taxes even though there is a payment agreement. In 1995 and 1996, the combined rate has been averaging approximately 15 percent per year.

The amount of the monthly payment will be determined by the ability to pay and the amount of taxes owed. If more is owed than could be paid in a reasonable period of time (usually within 10 years), the taxpayer may be forced into a change of lifestyle. Generally the IRS is willing to work out a mutually agreeable arrangement, providing the terms are within prescribed guidelines. These guidelines are adjusted for geographic considerations and are used by the IRS in determining ability to pay.

To obtain a payment agreement, the IRS requires the taxpayer to file a financial statement and to stay current on filing and paying taxes. However, if there simply is not enough money left after reasonable operating expenses to pay anything towards the back taxes, it is possible to apply for an Offer in Compromise based on inability to pay.

The ugly side of the IRS comes into reality when the taxpayer does not show any attempt to cooperate. When there is no communication, the IRS can and will levy bank accounts, seize property, and garnish wages. It is never a pleasant situation when the IRS decides to get tough. When the situation has reduced itself to that level, it is generally because the taxpayer is looking for a fight. For the most part, the IRS will work with a taxpayer in making an arrangement to collect the taxes owed, and in the meantime let the taxpayer live a normal life.

OFFERS IN COMPROMISE AND BANKRUPTCY ISSUES

When it simply is not financially feasible to make full payment of the taxes, an Offer in Compromise should be considered. Offers in Compromise are not accepted without a thorough investigation by the IRS. They require a complete financial statement, along with current banking records. Expect the IRS to research all available records for property ownership or income sources before agreeing to compromise a tax debt. It is not simply a matter of negotiating a settlement. (For a sample Offer in Compromise, Form 656, see Appendix A, Exhibit A-11.)

In certain cases, tax liabilities can be discharged in bankruptcy. Different rules apply depending upon the type of bankruptcy that is filed. Chapter 7 differs from Chapter 13, for example. The normal 10-year period the IRS has to collect a tax debt is extended by the filing of a bankruptcy. When all of the qualifications are met, the bankruptcy laws can be used to set a fresh start financially, including the discharge of income taxes.

The use of bankruptcy laws to discharge taxes and the related interest and penalties requires careful planning. There are obviously many non–tax-related considerations as well to filing bankruptcy. Extreme caution should be exercised before attempting to utilize the possible benefits of bankruptcy law, and competent experts should be consulted when bankruptcy strategies are being considered. A detailed discussion of these complex issues are beyond the scope of this book.

ENDNOTE

1. Rev. Proc. 82-51 updated procedures found in Rev. Proc. 64-13, 1964-1 (Part 1) C.B. 674.

CHAPTER 10

Conclusion

It is instinctive to fear what we do not understand. Complicated tax laws defy understanding even by the court systems that are supposed to enforce them. Compliance with the tax laws becomes a source of frustration for us, and our wrath is taken out on the IRS. But the IRS is not to blame—it is our own fault. We are to blame.

We live in a complicated civilization. We demand complexity. The twentieth century has brought improvements to our lives through technologies that few of us understand. Most of us can no longer tune up our cars, and we can't explain how magnetic imaging works. But few would argue against newer cars and better medical diagnostics.

Complicated is not bad. Simple is not bad either, but simple is not fair. Fair and equitable tax laws are the result of addressing individual exceptions and details. Complicated tax laws reflect the advancement of civilization. The United States is the wealthiest country in history. Our successful economy is based on the concept of capitalism, which enhances and promotes entrepreneurial efforts. Our capitalistic system rewards individual efforts and encourages initiative and risk taking. This country's economic system is driven by the human desire to create and accumulate wealth.

The complexity brought about by more sophisticated production and management techniques results in a better society for all by recognizing individual needs and addressing the details of our human efforts to create wealth. Better technology and education fuels our progress and enables us to contend with the resulting complexity of our lives. But this progress comes at a price. The price we pay for these improvements is complicated and intrusive rules and regulations.

The IRS is continually striving to enforce compliance with the tax laws enacted by Congress. The departure by the IRS from the traditional systems of selecting income tax returns marks the beginning of new enforcement techniques. With the advent of advanced systems, the IRS is continuing its effort to keep up with technology and to gain greater compliance with revenue laws.

However, our tax laws should not be allowed to stifle the very efforts upon which they depend. Lawmakers should never be allowed to pass legislation that costs more in compliance efforts than it will raise in revenue. When Congress passes laws that are inconsistently complied with and impossible for the IRS to enforce, we must question the source of the laws, not the means of enforcement. When it becomes apparent that our elected officials have transcended principles of fairness and equity in an attempt to enhance revenue, we should question the lawmakers, not the administration of the laws by the IRS.

We must all take a greater role in the management of our country's resources. We can no longer afford to be apathetic about the legislative process demonstrated by our elected officials. Each voter has the responsibility to monitor his or her legislator's efforts and respond appropriately at election time. Bed and Breakfast owners and innkeepers can ensure their common interests are of concern to legislators by joining trade associations. Being informed about the issues and candidates and responding with communication, support, and the exercise of our rights at the polling booth will ensure a balance between our legislative process and our social and economic progress.

Lawmakers would lead us to believe that the IRS is the problem with our tax system. But the IRS merely enforces the law; our elected officials enact the law. Until we become concerned enough to get involved and speak up to Congress, we have nobody to blame but ourselves.

APPENDIX A

IRS Forms and Publications

Exhibit A-1   Form 1099 Miscellaneous Income, and Instructions

☐ CORRECTED (if checked)

PAYER'S name, street address, city, state, and ZIP code		**1** Rents $	OMB No. 1545-0115	
		2 Royalties $	**1995**	**Miscellaneous Income**
		3 Other income $	Form **1099-MISC**	
PAYER'S Federal identification number	RECIPIENT'S identification number	**4** Federal income tax withheld $	**5** Fishing boat proceeds $	**Copy B For Recipient**
RECIPIENT'S name		**6** Medical and health care payments $	**7** Nonemployee compensation $	This is important tax information and is being furnished to the Internal Revenue Service. If you are required to file a return, a negligence penalty or other sanction may be imposed on you if this income is taxable and the IRS determines that it has not been reported.
Street address (including apt. no.)		**8** Substitute payments in lieu of dividends or interest $	**9** Payer made direct sales of $5,000 or more of consumer products to a buyer (recipient) for resale ▶ ☐	
City, state, and ZIP code		**10** Crop insurance proceeds $	**11** State income tax withheld $	
Account number (optional)		**12** State/Payer's state number		

Form **1099-MISC** (Keep for your records.) Department of the Treasury - Internal Revenue Service

☐ CORRECTED (if checked)

PAYER'S name, street address, city, state, and ZIP code		**1** Rents $	OMB No. 1545-0115	
		2 Royalties $	**1995**	**Miscellaneous Income**
		3 Other income $	Form **1099-MISC**	
PAYER'S Federal identification number	RECIPIENT'S identification number	**4** Federal income tax withheld $	**5** Fishing boat proceeds $	**Copy B For Recipient**
RECIPIENT'S name		**6** Medical and health care payments $	**7** Nonemployee compensation $	This is important tax information and is being furnished to the Internal Revenue Service. If you are required to file a return, a negligence penalty or other sanction may be imposed on you if this income is taxable and the IRS determines that it has not been reported.
Street address (including apt. no.)		**8** Substitute payments in lieu of dividends or interest $	**9** Payer made direct sales of $5,000 or more of consumer products to a buyer (recipient) for resale ▶ ☐	
City, state, and ZIP code		**10** Crop insurance proceeds $	**11** State income tax withheld $	
Account number (optional)		**12** State/Payer's state number		

Form **1099-MISC** (Keep for your records.) Department of the Treasury - Internal Revenue Service

☐ CORRECTED (if checked)

PAYER'S name, street address, city, state, and ZIP code		**1** Rents $	OMB No. 1545-0115	
		2 Royalties $	**1995**	**Miscellaneous Income**
		3 Other income $	Form **1099-MISC**	
PAYER'S Federal identification number	RECIPIENT'S identification number	**4** Federal income tax withheld $	**5** Fishing boat proceeds $	**Copy B For Recipient**
RECIPIENT'S name		**6** Medical and health care payments $	**7** Nonemployee compensation $	This is important tax information and is being furnished to the Internal Revenue Service. If you are required to file a return, a negligence penalty or other sanction may be imposed on you if this income is taxable and the IRS determines that it has not been reported.
Street address (including apt. no.)		**8** Substitute payments in lieu of dividends or interest $	**9** Payer made direct sales of $5,000 or more of consumer products to a buyer (recipient) for resale ▶ ☐	
City, state, and ZIP code		**10** Crop insurance proceeds $	**11** State income tax withheld $	
Account number (optional)		**12** State/Payer's state number		

Form **1099-MISC** (Keep for your records.) Department of the Treasury - Internal Revenue Service

Exhibit A-1 *(continued)*

Instructions for Recipient

Amounts shown on this form may be subject to self-employment tax computed on **Schedule SE (Form 1040)**. See **Pub. 533**, Self-Employment Tax, for information on self-employment income. If no income or social security and Medicare taxes were withheld by the payer, you may have to make estimated tax payments if you are still receiving these payments. See **Form 1040-ES**, Estimated Tax for Individuals.

If you are an individual, report the taxable amounts shown on this form on your tax return, as explained below. (Others, such as fiduciaries or partnerships, report the amounts on the corresponding lines of your tax return.)

Boxes 1 and 2. — Report rents from real estate on Schedule E (Form 1040). If you provided significant services to the tenant, sold real estate as a business, or rented personal property as a business, report on Schedule C or C-EZ (Form 1040). For royalties on timber, coal, and iron ore, see **Pub. 544**, Sales and Other Dispositions of Assets.

Box 3. — Report on the "Other income" line on Form 1040 and identify the payment. If it is trade or business income, report this amount on Schedule C, C-EZ, or F (Form 1040). The amount shown may be payments you received as the beneficiary of a deceased employee, prizes, awards, taxable damages, or other taxable income.

Box 4. — Shows backup withholding. For example, persons not furnishing their taxpayer identification number to the payer become subject to backup withholding at a 31% rate on certain payments. See **Form W-9**, Request for Taxpayer Identification Number and Certification, for information on backup withholding. **Include this on your income tax return as tax withheld.**

Box 5. — An amount in this box means the fishing boat operator considers you self-employed. Report this amount on Schedule C or C-EZ (Form 1040). See **Pub. 595**, Tax Guide for Commercial Fishermen.

Box 6. — Report on Schedule C or C-EZ (Form 1040).

Box 7. — Generally, payments for services reported in this box are income from self-employment. Since you received this form, rather than Form W-2, the payer may have considered you self-employed and did not withhold social security or Medicare taxes. Report self-employment income on Schedule C, C-EZ, or F (Form 1040), and **compute the self-employment tax on Schedule SE (Form 1040).** However, if you are not self-employed, report this amount on Form 1040 on the "Wages, salaries, tips, etc." line. Call the IRS for information about how to report any social security and Medicare taxes.

If "EPP" is shown, this is excess golden parachute payments subject to a 20% excise tax. See your Form 1040 instructions for the "Total Tax" line. The unlabled amount is your total compensation.

Box 8. — Report as "Other income" on your tax return. This amount is substitute payments in lieu of dividends or tax-exempt interest received by your broker on your behalf after transfer of your securities for use in a short sale.

Box 9. — An entry in the checkbox means sales to you of consumer products on a buy-sell, deposit-commission, or any other basis for resale have amounted to $5,000 or more. The person filing this return does not have to show a dollar amount in this box. Any income from your sale of these products should generally be reported on Schedule C or C-EZ (Form 1040).

Box 10. — Report on the "Crop insurance proceeds..." line on Schedule F (Form 1040).

Instructions for Recipient

Amounts shown on this form may be subject to self-employment tax computed on **Schedule SE (Form 1040)**. See **Pub. 533**, Self-Employment Tax, for information on self-employment income. If no income or social security and Medicare taxes were withheld by the payer, you may have to make estimated tax payments if you are still receiving these payments. See **Form 1040-ES**, Estimated Tax for Individuals.

If you are an individual, report the taxable amounts shown on this form on your tax return, as explained below. (Others, such as fiduciaries or partnerships, report the amounts on the corresponding lines of your tax return.)

Boxes 1 and 2. — Report rents from real estate on Schedule E (Form 1040). If you provided significant services to the tenant, sold real estate as a business, or rented personal property as a business, report on Schedule C or C-EZ (Form 1040). For royalties on timber, coal, and iron ore, see **Pub. 544**, Sales and Other Dispositions of Assets.

Box 3. — Report on the "Other income" line on Form 1040 and identify the payment. If it is trade or business income, report this amount on Schedule C, C-EZ, or F (Form 1040). The amount shown may be payments you received as the beneficiary of a deceased employee, prizes, awards, taxable damages, or other taxable income.

Box 4. — Shows backup withholding. For example, persons not furnishing their taxpayer identification number to the payer become subject to backup withholding at a 31% rate on certain payments. See **Form W-9**, Request for Taxpayer Identification Number and Certification, for information on backup withholding. **Include this on your income tax return as tax withheld.**

Box 5. — An amount in this box means the fishing boat operator considers you self-employed. Report this amount on Schedule C or C-EZ (Form 1040). See **Pub. 595**, Tax Guide for Commercial Fishermen.

Box 6. — Report on Schedule C or C-EZ (Form 1040).

Box 7. — Generally, payments for services reported in this box are income from self-employment. Since you received this form, rather than Form W-2, the payer may have considered you self-employed and did not withhold social security or Medicare taxes. Report self-employment income on Schedule C, C-EZ, or F (Form 1040), and **compute the self-employment tax on Schedule SE (Form 1040).** However, if you are not self-employed, report this amount on Form 1040 on the "Wages, salaries, tips, etc." line. Call the IRS for information about how to report any social security and Medicare taxes.

If "EPP" is shown, this is excess golden parachute payments subject to a 20% excise tax. See your Form 1040 instructions for the "Total Tax" line. The unlabled amount is your total compensation.

Box 8. — Report as "Other income" on your tax return. This amount is substitute payments in lieu of dividends or tax-exempt interest received by your broker on your behalf after transfer of your securities for use in a short sale.

Box 9. — An entry in the checkbox means sales to you of consumer products on a buy-sell, deposit-commission, or any other basis for resale have amounted to $5,000 or more. The person filing this return does not have to show a dollar amount in this box. Any income from your sale of these products should generally be reported on Schedule C or C-EZ (Form 1040).

Box 10. — Report on the "Crop insurance proceeds..." line on Schedule F (Form 1040).

Instructions for Recipient

Amounts shown on this form may be subject to self-employment tax computed on **Schedule SE (Form 1040)**. See **Pub. 533**, Self-Employment Tax, for information on self-employment income. If no income or social security and Medicare taxes were withheld by the payer, you may have to make estimated tax payments if you are still receiving these payments. See **Form 1040-ES**, Estimated Tax for Individuals.

If you are an individual, report the taxable amounts shown on this form on your tax return, as explained below. (Others, such as fiduciaries or partnerships, report the amounts on the corresponding lines of your tax return.)

Boxes 1 and 2. — Report rents from real estate on Schedule E (Form 1040). If you provided significant services to the tenant, sold real estate as a business, or rented personal property as a business, report on Schedule C or C-EZ (Form 1040). For royalties on timber, coal, and iron ore, see **Pub. 544**, Sales and Other Dispositions of Assets.

Box 3. — Report on the "Other income" line on Form 1040 and identify the payment. If it is trade or business income, report this amount on Schedule C, C-EZ, or F (Form 1040). The amount shown may be payments you received as the beneficiary of a deceased employee, prizes, awards, taxable damages, or other taxable income.

Box 4. — Shows backup withholding. For example, persons not furnishing their taxpayer identification number to the payer become subject to backup withholding at a 31% rate on certain payments. See **Form W-9**, Request for Taxpayer Identification Number and Certification, for information on backup withholding. **Include this on your income tax return as tax withheld.**

Box 5. — An amount in this box means the fishing boat operator considers you self-employed. Report this amount on Schedule C or C-EZ (Form 1040). See **Pub. 595**, Tax Guide for Commercial Fishermen.

Box 6. — Report on Schedule C or C-EZ (Form 1040).

Box 7. — Generally, payments for services reported in this box are income from self-employment. Since you received this form, rather than Form W-2, the payer may have considered you self-employed and did not withhold social security or Medicare taxes. Report self-employment income on Schedule C, C-EZ, or F (Form 1040), and **compute the self-employment tax on Schedule SE (Form 1040).** However, if you are not self-employed, report this amount on Form 1040 on the "Wages, salaries, tips, etc." line. Call the IRS for information about how to report any social security and Medicare taxes.

If "EPP" is shown, this is excess golden parachute payments subject to a 20% excise tax. See your Form 1040 instructions for the "Total Tax" line. The unlabled amount is your total compensation.

Box 8. — Report as "Other income" on your tax return. This amount is substitute payments in lieu of dividends or tax-exempt interest received by your broker on your behalf after transfer of your securities for use in a short sale.

Box 9. — An entry in the checkbox means sales to you of consumer products on a buy-sell, deposit-commission, or any other basis for resale have amounted to $5,000 or more. The person filing this return does not have to show a dollar amount in this box. Any income from your sale of these products should generally be reported on Schedule C or C-EZ (Form 1040).

Box 10. — Report on the "Crop insurance proceeds..." line on Schedule F (Form 1040).

STF FED3671F.4

Exhibit A-1 *(continued)*

VOID ☐ CORRECTED ☐

PAYER'S name, street address, city, state, and ZIP code		1 Rents $	OMB No. 1545-0115
		2 Royalties $	**199**
		3 Other income $	
PAYER'S Federal identification number	RECIPIENT'S identification number	4 Federal income tax withheld $	5 Fishing boat proceeds $	
RECIPIENT'S name		6 Medical and health care payments $	7 Nonemployee compensation $	
Street address (including apt. no.)		8 Substitute payments in lieu of dividends or interest $	9 Payer made direct sales of $5,000 or more of consumer products to a buyer (recipient) for resale ▶ ☐	**Copy 1** **For State Tax** **Department**
City, state, and ZIP code		10 Crop insurance proceeds $	11 State income tax withheld $	
Account number (optional)		12 State/Payer's state number		

Form **1099-MISC**   Department of the Treasury - Internal Revenue Service

VOID ☐ CORRECTED ☐

PAYER'S name, street address, city, state, and ZIP code		1 Rents $	OMB No. 1545-0115
		2 Royalties $	
		3 Other income $	
PAYER'S Federal identification number	RECIPIENT'S identification number	4 Federal income tax withheld $	5 Fishing boat proceeds $	
RECIPIENT'S name		6 Medical and health care payments $	7 Nonemployee compensation $	
Street address (including apt. no.)		8 Substitute payments in lieu of dividends or interest $	9 Payer made direct sales of $5,000 or more of consumer products to a buyer (recipient) for resale ▶ ☐	**Copy 1** **For State Tax** **Department**
City, state, and ZIP code		10 Crop insurance proceeds $	11 State income tax withheld $	
Account number (optional)		12 State/Payer's state number		

Form **1099-MISC**   Department of the Treasury - Internal Revenue Service

VOID ☐ CORRECTED ☐

PAYER'S name, street address, city, state, and ZIP code		1 Rents $	OMB No. 1545-0115
		2 Royalties $	
		3 Other income $	
PAYER'S Federal identification number	RECIPIENT'S identification number	4 Federal income tax withheld $	5 Fishing boat proceeds $	
RECIPIENT'S name		6 Medical and health care payments $	7 Nonemployee compensation $	
Street address (including apt. no.)		8 Substitute payments in lieu of dividends or interest $	9 Payer made direct sales of $5,000 or more of consumer products to a buyer (recipient) for resale ▶ ☐	**Copy 1** **For State Tax** **Department**
City, state, and ZIP code		10 Crop insurance proceeds $	11 State income tax withheld $	
Account number (optional)		12 State/Payer's state number		

Form **1099-MISC**   Department of the Treasury - Internal Revenue Service

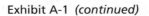

Exhibit A-1 *(continued)*

PAYER'S name, street address, city, state, and ZIP code		1 Rents $	OMB No. 1545-0115	**Miscellaneous Income**
		2 Royalties $	**1995**	
		3 Other income $	Form **1099-MISC**	
PAYER'S Federal identification number	RECIPIENT'S identification number	4 Federal income tax withheld $	5 Fishing boat proceeds $	
RECIPIENT'S name		6 Medical and health care payments $	7 Nonemployee compensation $	**Copy 2** **To be filed**
Street address (including apt. no.)		8 Substitute payments in lieu of dividends or interest $	9 Payer made direct sales of $5,000 or more of consumer products to a buyer (recipient) for resale ▶ ☐	**with recipient's state income**
City, state, and ZIP code		10 Crop insurance proceeds $	11 State income tax withheld $	**tax return, when**
Account number (optional)		12 State/Payer's state number		**required.**

Form **1099-MISC**   Department of the Treasury - Internal Revenue Service

PAYER'S name, street address, city, state, and ZIP code		1 Rents $	OMB No. 1545-0115	**Miscellaneous Income**
		2 Royalties $	**1995**	
		3 Other income $	Form **1099-MISC**	
PAYER'S Federal identification number	RECIPIENT'S identification number	4 Federal income tax withheld $	5 Fishing boat proceeds $	
RECIPIENT'S name		6 Medical and health care payments $	7 Nonemployee compensation $	**Copy 2** **To be filed**
Street address (including apt. no.)		8 Substitute payments in lieu of dividends or interest $	9 Payer made direct sales of $5,000 or more of consumer products to a buyer (recipient) for resale ▶ ☐	**with recipient's state income**
City, state, and ZIP code		10 Crop insurance proceeds $	11 State income tax withheld $	**tax return, when**
Account number (optional)		12 State/Payer's state number		**required.**

Form **1099-MISC**   Department of the Treasury - Internal Revenue Service

PAYER'S name, street address, city, state, and ZIP code		1 Rents $	OMB No. 1545-0115	**Miscellaneous Income**
		2 Royalties $	**1995**	
		3 Other income $	Form **1099-MISC**	
PAYER'S Federal identification number	RECIPIENT'S identification number	4 Federal income tax withheld $	5 Fishing boat proceeds $	
RECIPIENT'S name		6 Medical and health care payments $	7 Nonemployee compensation $	**Copy 2** **To be filed**
Street address (including apt. no.)		8 Substitute payments in lieu of dividends or interest $	9 Payer made direct sales of $5,000 or more of consumer products to a buyer (recipient) for resale ▶ ☐	**with recipient's state income**
City, state, and ZIP code		10 Crop insurance proceeds $	11 State income tax withheld $	**tax return, when**
Account number (optional)		12 State/Payer's state number		**required.**

Form **1099-MISC**   Department of the Treasury - Internal Revenue Service

Exhibit A-1   *(continued)*

☐ VOID   ☐ CORRECTED

PAYER'S name, street address, city, state, and ZIP code		**1** Rents $	OMB No. 1545-0115	**Miscellaneous Income**
		2 Royalties $	**1995**	
		3 Other income $	Form **1099-MISC**	
PAYER'S Federal identification number	RECIPIENT'S identification number	**4** Federal income tax withheld $	**5** Fishing boat proceeds $	**Copy C For Payer**
RECIPIENT'S name		**6** Medical and health care payments $	**7** Nonemployee compensation $	For Paperwork Reduction Act
Street address (including apt. no.)		**8** Substitute payments in lieu of dividends or interest $	**9** Payer made direct sales of $5,000 or more of consumer products to a buyer (recipient) for resale ▶ ☐	Notice and instructions for completing this
City, state, and ZIP code		**10** Crop insurance proceeds $	**11** State income tax withheld $	form, see **Instructions for**
Account number (optional)	2nd TIN Not. ☐	**12** State/Payer's state number		**Forms 1099, 1098, 5498, and W-2G.**

Form **1099-MISC**   Department of the Treasury - Internal Revenue Service

☐ VOID   ☐ CORRECTED

PAYER'S name, street address, city, state, and ZIP code		**1** Rents $	OMB No. 1545-0115	**Miscellaneous Income**
		2 Royalties $	**1995**	
		3 Other income $	Form **1099-MISC**	
PAYER'S Federal identification number	RECIPIENT'S identification number	**4** Federal income tax withheld $	**5** Fishing boat proceeds $	**Copy C For Payer**
RECIPIENT'S name		**6** Medical and health care payments $	**7** Nonemployee compensation $	For Paperwork Reduction Act
Street address (including apt. no.)		**8** Substitute payments in lieu of dividends or interest $	**9** Payer made direct sales of $5,000 or more of consumer products to a buyer (recipient) for resale ▶ ☐	Notice and instructions for completing this
City, state, and ZIP code		**10** Crop insurance proceeds $	**11** State income tax withheld $	form, see **Instructions for**
Account number (optional)	2nd TIN Not. ☐	**12** State/Payer's state number		**Forms 1099, 1098, 5498, and W-2G.**

Form **1099-MISC**   Department of the Treasury - Internal Revenue Service

☐ VOID   ☐ CORRECTED

PAYER'S name, street address, city, state, and ZIP code		**1** Rents $	OMB No. 1545-0115	**Miscellaneous Income**
		2 Royalties $	**1995**	
		3 Other income $	Form **1099-MISC**	
PAYER'S Federal identification number	RECIPIENT'S identification number	**4** Federal income tax withheld $	**5** Fishing boat proceeds $	**Copy C For Payer**
RECIPIENT'S name		**6** Medical and health care payments $	**7** Nonemployee compensation $	For Paperwork Reduction Act
Street address (including apt. no.)		**8** Substitute payments in lieu of dividends or interest $	**9** Payer made direct sales of $5,000 or more of consumer products to a buyer (recipient) for resale ▶ ☐	Notice and instructions for completing this
City, state, and ZIP code		**10** Crop insurance proceeds $	**11** State income tax withheld $	form, see **Instructions for**
Account number (optional)	2nd TIN Not. ☐	**12** State/Payer's state number		**Forms 1099, 1098, 5498, and W-2G.**

Form **1099-MISC**   Department of the Treasury - Internal Revenue Service

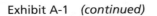

Exhibit A-1   *(continued)*

Payers, Please Note-
Specific information needed to complete this form and other forms in the 1099 series is given in the **1995 Instructions for Forms 1099, 1098, 5498, and W-2G**. A chart in those instructions gives a quick guide to which form must be filed to report a particular payment. You can order those instructions and additional forms by calling 1-800-TAX-FORM (1-800-829-3676).

Furnish Copy B of this form to the recipient by January 31, 1996.
File Copy A of this form with the IRS by February 28, 1996.

Payers, Please Note-
Specific information needed to complete this form and other forms in the 1099 series is given in the **1995 Instructions for Forms 1099, 1098, 5498, and W-2G**. A chart in those instructions gives a quick guide to which form must be filed to report a particular payment. You can order those instructions and additional forms by calling 1-800-TAX-FORM (1-800-829-3676).

Furnish Copy B of this form to the recipient by January 31, 1996.
File Copy A of this form with the IRS by February 28, 1996.

Payers, Please Note-
Specific information needed to complete this form and other forms in the 1099 series is given in the **1995 Instructions for Forms 1099, 1098, 5498, and W-2G**. A chart in those instructions gives a quick guide to which form must be filed to report a particular payment. You can order those instructions and additional forms by calling 1-800-TAX-FORM (1-800-829-3676).

Furnish Copy B of this form to the recipient by January 31, 1996.
File Copy A of this form with the IRS by February 28, 1996.

STF FED3671F.7

Exhibit A-1 *(continued)*

1995

Department of the Treasury
Internal Revenue Service

Instructions for Forms 1099, 1098, 5498, and W-2G

(Including Instructions for Forms 1099-A, 1099-B, 1099-C, 1099-DIV, 1099-G, 1099-INT, 1099-MISC, 1099-OID, 1099-PATR, 1099-R, 1099-S, and 5754)

Section references are to the Internal Revenue Code unless otherwise noted.

Paperwork Reduction Act Notice.—We ask for the information on these forms to carry out the Internal Revenue laws of the United States. You are required to give us the information. We need it to ensure that you are complying with these laws and to allow us to figure and collect the right amount of tax.

The time needed to complete and file the following forms will vary depending on individual circumstances. The estimated average times are:

		Insts. begin on page
1098	7 minutes	8
1099-A	10 minutes	11
1099-B	15 minutes	12
1099-C	11 minutes	13
1099-DIV	14 minutes	14
1099-G	11 minutes	15
1099-INT	12 minutes	15
1099-MISC	14 minutes	17
1099-OID	10 minutes	20
1099-PATR	11 minutes	21
1099-R	20 minutes	22
1099-S	8 minutes	26
5498	7 minutes	29
W-2G	19 minutes	29
1096	10 minutes	(see form)
5754	(see form)	31

If you have comments concerning the accuracy of these time estimates or suggestions for making these forms simpler, we would be happy to hear from you. You can write to the **Internal Revenue Service,** Attention: Tax Forms Committee, PC:FP, Washington, DC 20224. **DO NOT** send these forms to this address. Instead, see **Where To File** on page 5.

Items You Should Note

Changes to Where To File

Some filing sites have changed again. You may have to file with an Internal Revenue Service Center that is different from the one you filed with for 1994. Check the addresses listed on page 5 under **Where To File** for your proper filing location.

Form 1098—Seller-Paid Points

For 1995 and later years, you must report points paid by the seller on the buyer's **Form 1098,** Mortgage Interest Statement. The title of box 2 was changed to "Points paid on purchase of principal residence." See **Points** on page 10.

Filing Forms 1099-A and 1099-C Coordinated; Some Boxes Changed

Rather than filing both **Forms 1099-A,** Acquisition or Abandonment of Secured Property, and **1099-C,** Cancellation of Debt, for the same year, you may be required to file only Form 1099-C. Box 3 on Form 1099-A, previously titled "Gross foreclosure proceeds," was eliminated, and the title of box 4 was changed to "Fair market value of property." On Form 1099-C, the title of box 6 was changed to "Check for bankruptcy," and a new box 7 titled "Fair market value of property" was added. See the instructions for both forms, which begin on pages 11 and 13.

Form 1099-R Changes

New box 9b, Total employee contributions, was added to the 1995 **Form 1099-R,** Distributions From Pensions, Annuities, Retirement or Profit-Sharing Plans, IRAs, Insurance Contracts, etc. See the 1995 Form 1099-R and the instructions for box 9b on page 26.

Distribution codes A, B, and C, used in box 7, were changed to indicate "May be eligible...." See page 26.

Form 945—Withholding Tax Return

Report backup withholding and withholding from gambling winnings, pensions, annuities, IRAs, and military retirement on **Form 945,** Annual Return of Withheld Federal Income Tax. File Form 945 for 1995 by January 31, 1996. Generally, any income tax withheld reported on Forms 1099 or W-2G must be reported on Form 945. Any income tax withheld reported on Form W-2, including withholding on distributions to plan participants from nonqualified plans, must be reported on **Form 941,** Employer's Quarterly Federal Tax Return. For more information, including the deposit requirements for Form 945, see the separate **Instructions for Form 945.**

Use Form 1096 To Send Forms to the IRS

You must send Copies A of all paper Forms 1099, 1098, 5498, and W-2G to the IRS with **Form 1096,** Annual Summary and Transmittal of U.S. Information Returns. Instructions for completing Form 1096 are contained on Form 1096.

REMINDER—Substitute Statements to Recipients

If you are not using the official IRS form (generally Copy B) to furnish statements to recipients, be sure your substitute statements comply with the rules in **Pub. 1179,** Rules and Specifications for Private Printing of Substitute Forms 1096, 1098, 1099 Series, 5498, and W-2G. Pub. 1179, which is revised annually, is a revenue procedure that explains the requirements for format and content of substitute statements to recipients. **If you are using a substitute form to furnish information to recipients, it must comply with the requirements in Pub. 1179.**

Guide to Information Returns

See the chart on pages 32 and 33 for a brief summary of information return reporting rules.

Need Help?

Information Reporting Call Site.—The IRS operates a centralized call site to answer questions about reporting on information returns—Forms 1096, 1098, 1099, 5498, W-2, W-2G, and W-3. If you have questions related to reporting on any of these forms, you may call 304-263-8700 (not a toll-free number) Monday through Friday from 8:30 a.m. to 4:30 p.m. eastern time.

Bulletin Board Service.—The IRS also operates an electronic bulletin board (IRP-BBS). The IRP-BBS offers changes and updates that affect information reporting. By using your personal computer and modem, you can access the IRP-BBS by dialing 304-263-2749. For more information, see **Pub. 1220,** Specifications for Filing Forms 1098, 1099, 5498 and W-2G Magnetically or Electronically.

Internal Revenue Bulletin.—The Internal Revenue Bulletin (IRB), published weekly, contains newly issued regulations, as well as notices, announcements, legislation, court decisions, and other items of general interest. You may find this publication useful to keep you up to date with current developments. The IRB is sold by the Superintendent of Documents, U.S. Government Printing Office, Washington, DC 20402, and is available on a subscription basis. To order the IRB, you can write to the Superintendent of Documents or call 202-512-1800 (not a toll-free number).

Forms and Publications.—You may order forms, instructions, and publications by calling 1-800-TAX-FORM (1-800-829-3676).

Cat. No. 11409F

Exhibit A-1   *(continued)*

Backup Withholding

Interest, dividends, rents, royalties, commissions, nonemployee compensation, and certain other payments (including broker and barter exchange transactions, and certain payments made by fishing boat operators) may be subject to backup withholding at a 31% rate. To be subject to backup withholding, a payment must be a reportable interest or dividend payment under section 6049(a), 6042(a), or 6044 (if the patronage dividend is paid in money or qualified check), or an "other" reportable payment under section 6041, 6041A(a), 6045, 6050A, or 6050N. If the payment is one of these reportable payments, backup withholding will apply if:

1. The payee fails to furnish his or her taxpayer identification number (TIN) to you, OR

2. The IRS notifies you to impose backup withholding because the payee furnished an incorrect TIN, OR

3. You are notified that the payee is subject to backup withholding (under section 3406(a)(1)(C)), OR

4. For interest and dividend accounts opened or instruments acquired after 1983, the payee fails to certify to you, under penalties of perjury, that he or she is not subject to backup withholding under **3** above, OR

5. For interest, dividend, broker, or barter exchange accounts opened or instruments acquired after 1983, or broker accounts considered inactive in 1983, the payee fails to certify, under penalties of perjury, that the TIN provided is correct.

Except as explained in **5** above, reportable "other" payments are subject to backup withholding only if **1** or **2** above applies.

Some payees are exempt from backup withholding. For a list of types of exempt payees and other information, please see **Form W-9,** Request for Taxpayer Identification Number and Certification, and **Instructions for the Requester of Form W-9.**

Real estate transactions reportable under section 6045(e) and canceled debts reportable under section 6050P are not subject to backup withholding.

Generally, the period for which the 31% should be withheld is as follows:

1. Failure to furnish TIN in the manner required.—Withhold on payments made until the TIN is furnished in the manner required. Special backup withholding rules apply if the payee has applied for a TIN. The payee may certify to this on Form W-9 by noting "Applied For" in the TIN block and by signing the form. This form then becomes an "awaiting-TIN certificate," and the payee has 60 days to obtain a TIN and furnish it to you. For information about whether backup withholding applies during the 60-day period, see Temporary Regulations section 35a.9999-3, Q/A-59A. If you do not receive a TIN from the payee within 60 days and you have not already

begun backup withholding, begin backup withholding and continue until the TIN is provided.

2. Notice from the IRS that payee's TIN is incorrect ("B" notice).—You may elect to withhold on any reportable payment made to the account(s) subject to backup withholding after receipt of the "B" notice, but you must withhold on any reportable payment made to the account more than 30 business days after you received the "B" notice. Stop withholding within 30 days after you receive a certified Form W-9 (or acceptable substitute).

Note: The IRS will furnish a notice to you, and you are required to promptly furnish a copy of such notice, or an acceptable substitute, to the payee. For further information, see Regulations section 31.3406(d)-5 and Rev. Proc. 93-37, 1993-2 C.B. 477.

If you receive two incorrect TIN notices within 3 years for the same account, follow the procedures in Regulations section 31.3406(d)-5(g) and Rev. Proc. 93-37.

3. Notice from the IRS that payee is subject to backup withholding due to notified payee underreporting.—Start withholding on payments made on the 31st day after the date you receive notification from the IRS, or you may elect to withhold any time before the 31st day. The IRS will notify you in writing when to stop withholding, or the payee may furnish you a written certification from the IRS stating when withholding is to stop. In most cases, the stop date will be January 1 of the year following the year of the notice.

Note: You must notify the payee when withholding under this procedure starts. For further information, see Temporary Regulations section 35a.3406-2.

4. Payee failure to certify that he or she is not subject to backup withholding.—Withhold on reportable interest and dividends until certification has been received.

For exceptions to these general timing rules, see section 3406(e).

Note: For information about backup withholding on gambling winnings, see the Specific Instructions for Form W-2G for the specific type of gambling winnings later.

Reporting Backup Withholding.—Backup withholding must be reported on **Form 945,** Annual Return of Withheld Federal Income Tax. For more information, see the **Instructions for Form 945.** Also report backup withholding on each Form W-2G, 1099-B, DIV, G, INT, MISC, OID, or PATR used to report the payment.

Additional Information.—For more information about backup withholding, see Temporary Regulations sections 35a.9999-1, 2, and 3, and 35a.3406-1 and 2.

Penalties

The following penalties generally apply to the person required to file information returns. The penalties apply to paper filers as well as magnetic media/electronic filers.

Failure To File Correct Information Returns by the Due Date (Section 6721)

If you fail to file a correct information return by the due date and you cannot show reasonable cause, you may be subject to a penalty. The penalty applies if you fail to file timely, you fail to include all information required to be shown on a return, or you include incorrect information on a return. The penalty also applies if you file on paper when you were required to file on magnetic media, you report an incorrect TIN or fail to report a TIN, or you fail to file paper forms that are machine readable.

The amount of the penalty is based on when you file the correct information return. The penalty is:

● $15 per information return if you correctly file within 30 days (by March 30 if the due date is February 28); maximum penalty $75,000 per year ($25,000 for small businesses, defined later).

● $30 per information return if you correctly file more than 30 days after the due date but by August 1; maximum penalty $150,000 per year ($50,000 for small businesses).

● $50 per information return if you file after August 1 or you do not file required information returns; maximum penalty $250,000 per year ($100,000 for small businesses).

Exceptions to the Penalty.—

1. The penalty will not apply to any failure that you can show was due to reasonable cause and not to willful neglect.

2. An inconsequential error or omission is not considered a failure to include correct information. An inconsequential error or omission does not prevent or hinder the IRS from processing the return, from correlating the information required to be shown on the return with the information shown on the payee's tax return, or from otherwise putting the return to its intended use. Errors and omissions that are never inconsequential are those relating to (a) a TIN, (b) a payee's surname, and (c) any money amounts.

3. *De Minimis Rule for Corrections.*—Even though you cannot show reasonable cause, the penalty for failure to file correct information returns will not apply to a certain number of returns if:

a. You filed those information returns,

b. Either you failed to include all the information required to be shown on a return or you included incorrect information, and

c. You filed corrections of these information returns by August 1.

If you meet all the conditions in **a** through **c,** the penalty for filing incorrect returns (but not for filing late) will not apply to the greater of 10 information returns or ½ of 1% of the total number of information returns you are required to file for the calendar year.

Lower Maximum Penalties for Small Businesses.—For purposes of the lower maximum penalties shown in parentheses

Exhibit A-1 *(continued)*

122 • IRS FORMS AND PUBLICATIONS

above, you are a small business if your average annual gross receipts for the 3 most recent tax years (or for the period you were in existence, if shorter) ending before the calendar year in which the information returns were due are $5 million or less.

Intentional Disregard of Filing Requirements.—If any failure to file a correct information return is due to intentional disregard of the filing and correct information requirements, the penalty is at least $100 per information return with no maximum penalty.

Failure To Furnish Correct Payee Statements (Section 6722)

If you fail to provide correct payee statements and you cannot show reasonable cause, you may be subject to a penalty. The penalty applies if you fail to provide the statement by January 31 (see part H under **General Instructions** later), you fail to include all information required to be shown on the statement, or you include incorrect information on the statement. "Payee statement" has the same meaning as "statement to recipient" as used in part H under **General Instructions.**

The penalty is $50 per statement, regardless of when the correct statement is furnished, with a maximum of $100,000 per year. There is no reduction in the penalty for furnishing a correct statement by August 1.

Exception.—An inconsequential error or omission is not considered a failure to include correct information. An inconsequential error or omission cannot reasonably be expected to prevent or hinder the payee from timely receiving correct information and reporting it on his or her income tax return or from otherwise putting the statement to its intended use. Errors and omissions that are never inconsequential are those relating to (a) a dollar amount, (b) a payee's address, (c) the appropriate form for the information provided (i.e., whether the form is an acceptable substitute for the official IRS form), and (d) whether the statement was furnished in person or by "statement mailing," when required.

Intentional Disregard of Payee Statement Requirements.—If any failure to provide a correct payee statement is due to intentional disregard of the requirements to furnish a correct payee statement, the penalty is at least $100 per payee statement with no maximum penalty.

Forms 1099-R and 5498

The penalties under sections 6721 and 6722 do not apply to Form 1099-R, which is filed under section 6047. The penalty for failure to timely file Form 1099-R is $25 per day with a maximum of $15,000 per year. See section 6652(e).

The penalties under sections 6721 and 6722 do not apply to Form 5498, which is filed under section 408(i). The penalty for failure to timely file Form 5498 is $50 per

return with no maximum. See section 6693.

Caution: *Congress has considered, and may consider again, legislation that would apply the penalties under sections 6721 and 6722 to Forms 1099-R and 5498.*

Magnetic Media/Electronic Reporting

Magnetic media reporting may be required for filing all information returns discussed in this publication. Acceptable forms of magnetic media are magnetic tape, tape cartridge, $3\frac{1}{2}$-, $5\frac{1}{4}$-, and 8-inch diskette. **Pub. 1220,** Specifications for Filing Forms 1098, 1099, 5498 and W-2G Magnetically or Electronically, is the revenue procedure for magnetic media and electronic reporting. Different types of payments, such as interest, dividends, and rents, may be reported on the same tape or other submission.

Electronic submissions are filed using the Information Reporting Bulletin Board System (IRP-BBS). The IRP-BBS operates 24 hours a day, 7 days a week, and is accessed using your personal computer and modem at 304-263-2749. For more information, see Pub. 1220.

Note: *Filing electronically will satisfy the magnetic media filing requirements. Any reference to magnetic media in these instructions includes electronic filing.*

Due Dates.—The due dates for magnetic media reporting are the same as for paper document reporting.

Extension of Time To File.—For information about requesting an extension of time to file, see part B under **General Instructions** later.

Caution: *If you file on magnetic media, do not file the same returns on paper.*

Who Must File on Magnetic Media.—If you are required to file 250 or more information returns, you must file on magnetic media. The 250-or-more requirement applies separately to each type of form. For example, if you must file 500 Forms 1098 and 100 Forms 1099-A, you are not required to file Forms 1099-A on magnetic media, but you must file Forms 1098 on magnetic media.

Note: *Even if you are not required to file on magnetic media, the IRS encourages you to do so. Also, you may file electronically even if you are not required to file on magnetic media.*

The magnetic media filing requirement does not apply if you apply for and receive an undue hardship waiver. See **How To Request a Waiver From Filing on Magnetic Media** later.

Filing Requirement Applies Separately to Originals and Corrections.—The magnetic media filing requirements below apply separately to original returns and corrected returns. Originals and corrections are not aggregated to determine whether you are required to file on magnetic media. For example, if you file 400 Forms 1098 on magnetic media and you are making 75

corrections, your corrections can be filed on paper because the number of corrections for Form 1098 is less than the 250 filing requirement. However, if you were filing 250 or more Form 1098 corrections, they would have to be filed on magnetic media.

How To Get Approval To File on Magnetic Media.—File Form **4419,** Application for Filing Information Returns Magnetically/Electronically, at least 30 days (45 days for some electronic filing) before the due date of the returns. Only one Form 4419 need be filed for all types of returns that will be filed on magnetic media. Once you have received approval, you need not reapply each year. The IRS will provide a written reply to the applicant and further instructions at the time of approval, usually within 30 days. A magnetic media reporting package, which includes all the necessary transmittals, labels, and instructions, will be mailed to all approved filers.

How To Request a Waiver From Filing on Magnetic Media.—To receive a waiver from the required filing of information returns on magnetic media, submit **Form 8508,** Request for Waiver From Filing Information Returns on Magnetic Media, requesting an undue hardship waiver from filing on magnetic media. You cannot apply for a waiver for more than 1 tax year at a time. If you need a waiver for more than 1 tax year, you must reapply at the appropriate time each year.

If a waiver for original returns is approved, any corrections for the same types of returns will be covered under the waiver. However, if you submit original returns on magnetic media but you want to submit your corrections on paper, a waiver must be approved for the corrections if the corrections exceed the 250 filing requirement.

Waiver requests generally must be filed at least 45 days before the due date of the returns. However, new brokers and new barter exchanges may request an undue hardship waiver by filing Form 8508 by the end of the second month following the month in which they became a broker or barter exchange.

If you are seeking, in a single application, approval for filing returns on magnetic media and, if approval is not granted, a waiver from the magnetic media filing requirement, submit both Forms 4419 and 8508.

If you receive an approved waiver, do not send a copy of it to the service center where you file your paper returns. Keep the waiver for your records only.

Penalty.—If you are required to file on magnetic media but fail to do so, and you do not have an approved waiver on record, you may be subject to a penalty of $50 per return for failure to file information returns on magnetic media unless you establish reasonable cause. However, you can file up to 250 returns on paper; those returns will not be subject to a penalty for failure to file on magnetic media.

The penalty applies separately to original returns and corrected returns. See **Filing**
Page 3

Exhibit A-1 *(continued)*

Paper Document Reporting

If you are required to file 250 or more information returns, see **Magnetic Media/Electronic Reporting** earlier.

Common Errors.—Please be sure to check your returns to prevent the following common errors:

1. Duplicate filing. Sending the same information to the IRS more than once.

2. Filer's name, address, and taxpayer identification number are not the same on Form 1096 and Forms 1099, 1098, 5498, or W-2G.

3. Decimal point to show dollars and cents omitted (1000.00).

4. Two or more types of returns submitted with one Form 1096 (e.g., Forms 1099-INT and 1099-MISC with one Form 1096). You must submit a separate Form 1096 with each type of document.

5. Failure to make an entry in box 1a, "Gross dividends and other distributions on stock," on Form 1099-DIV. An amount must be entered in box 1a if any amount is entered in box 1b, 1c, 1d, or 1e.

Required Format.—Because paper forms are read by machines (optical character recognition equipment), all Forms 1096, 1098, 1099, and 5498 must be prepared in accordance with the following instructions. If these instructions are not followed, you may be subject to a penalty of $50 per incorrectly filed document.

1. DO NOT CUT OR SEPARATE the forms that are printed two or three to a sheet (except Form W-2G). Forms 1098, 1099, and 5498 are printed two or three to an 8- by 11-inch sheet. Form 1096 is printed one to an 8- by 11-inch sheet. These forms must be submitted to the IRS on the 8- by 11-inch sheet. If at least one form on the page is correctly completed, you must submit the entire page. Forms W-2G may be separated and submitted as single forms.

Send the forms to the IRS in a flat mailing (not folded). **Note:** *Large envelopes may require extra postage.*

2. NO PHOTOCOPIES of any forms are acceptable. Official forms are available from your IRS district office or by calling 1-800-TAX-FORM (1-800-829-3676).

3. DO NOT STAPLE, tear, or tape any of these forms. It will interfere with the IRS's ability to scan the documents.

4. Pinfeed holes on the form are **NOT** acceptable. Pinfeed strips outside the 8- by 11-inch area must be removed before submission, without tearing or ripping the form. Substitute forms prepared in continuous or strip form must be burst and stripped to conform to the size specified for a single sheet (8 by 11 inches) before they are filed with the IRS.

5. DO NOT change the title of any box on any form. Do not use a form to report information that is not properly reportable on that form. If you are unsure of where to

Page 4

report the data, call 304-263-8700 or your local IRS office.

6. Report information only in the appropriate boxes provided on the forms. Make only one entry in each box unless otherwise indicated in these instructions.

7. DO NOT submit any copy other than Copy A to the IRS.

8. DO NOT use prior year forms unless you are reporting prior year information; do not use subsequent year forms for the current year. Because forms are "read" by machine, you **MUST** use the current year form to report current year information.

9. Use the official forms or substitute forms that meet the specifications in the 1995 **Pub. 1179,** Rules and Specifications for Private Printing of Substitute Forms 1096, 1098, 1099 Series, 5498, and W-2G. If you submit substitute forms that do not meet the current specifications and that are not machine scannable, you may be subject to a penalty of $50 for each return for improper format.

10. DO NOT use dollar signs ($) (they are preprinted on the forms), ampersands (&), asterisks (*), commas (,), or other special characters in money amount boxes.

Suggested Format.—Below are suggestions that will allow the IRS to process the submitted forms in the most economical manner:

1. Type or machine print data entries using 10 pitch (pica) or 12 pitch (elite) black type. Use block print, not script characters. Entries should not be handwritten. Insert data in the middle of the blocks well separated from other printing and guidelines, and take other measures to guarantee a dark black, clear, sharp image.

2. Do not enter 0 (zero) or "None" in money amount boxes when no entry is required. Leave the boxes blank unless the instructions specifically require that you enter a zero. For example, in some cases, you must enter zero to make corrections. See **Corrected Returns** later.

3. You may use the **account number** box for an account number designation. This number must not appear anywhere else on the form, and this box may not be used for any other item. Showing an account number is optional. However, it may be to your benefit to include the recipient's account number on paper documents if your system of records uses the account number rather than the name, social security number or employer identification number for identification purposes. If you furnish the account number, the IRS will include it in future notices to you about backup withholding. If you are using window envelopes to mail statements to recipients, and if you are using reduced rate mail, be sure the account number does not appear in the window because the Postal Service may not accept these for reduced rate mail.

4. Do not enter number signs (#); for example, enter RT 2, not Rt. #2.

General Instructions

A. Who Must File.—See the **Specific Instructions** for each form.

Nominee/Middleman Returns.— Generally, if you receive a Form 1099 for amounts that actually belong to another person, you are considered a nominee recipient. You must file a Form 1099 (the same type of Form 1099 you received) for each of the other owners showing the amounts allocable to each. You must also furnish a Form 1099 to each of the other owners. File Form 1099 with **Form 1096,** Annual Summary and Transmittal of U.S. Information Returns, with the Internal Revenue Service Center for your area. On each Form 1099, list yourself as the "payer" and the other owner as the "recipient." On Form 1096, list yourself as the "filer." A husband or wife is not required to file a nominee return to show amounts owned by the other. The nominee, not the original payer, is responsible for filing the subsequent Forms 1099.

Mergers.—If two corporations merge and the surviving corporation becomes the owner of all the assets and assumes all the liabilities of the absorbed corporation, the reporting requirements explained in this publication will be met if the surviving corporation files Forms 1098, 1099, 5498, and/or W-2G for reportable payments of both corporations. See Rev. Rul. 69-556, 1969-2 C.B. 242.

For information on filing Form 1099-INT for a successor/predecessor corporation, see **Form 1099-INT** later.

Qualified Settlement Funds.—A qualified settlement fund must file information returns as explained in this publication for distributions to claimants if any transferor to the fund would have been required to file if the transferor had made the distributions directly to the claimants.

For distributions to transferors, a fund is subject to the information reporting requirements of sections 6041 and 6041A and may be required to file Form 1099-MISC. For payments made by the fund on behalf of a claimant or transferor, the fund is subject to these same rules and may have to file Form 1099-MISC for the payment to a third party. For information reporting purposes, a payment made by the fund on behalf of a claimant or transferor is considered a distribution to the claimant or transferor and is also subject to information reporting requirements.

The same filing requirements, exceptions, and thresholds apply to qualified settlement funds as apply to any other payer. That is, the fund must determine the character of the payment (e.g., interest, fixed and determinable income, or gross proceeds from broker transactions) and to whom the payment is made (e.g., corporation or individual).

For more information, see Regulations section 1.468B-2(l).

Exhibit A-1 *(continued)*

Payments to Foreign Persons.—See the **Instructions for Forms 1042 and 1042-S,** relating to U.S. source income of foreign persons, and for reporting requirements relating to payments of income items to foreign persons.

B. When To File.—File Form 1096 and Forms 1098, 1099, or W-2G by February 28, 1996. Brokers may file Forms 1096 and 1099-B anytime after the reporting period they elect to adopt (month, quarter, or year), but not later than February 28, 1996. File Form 1096 and Forms 5498 by May 31, 1996. You will meet the requirement to file if the form is properly addressed, mailed, and postmarked on or before the due date. If the regular due date falls on a Saturday, Sunday, or legal holiday, file on the next business day. A business day is any day that is not a Saturday, Sunday, or legal holiday. See part H later about providing Forms 1098, 1099, 5498, and W-2G or statements to recipients.

Reporting period.—Forms 1098, 1099, and W-2G are used to report amounts received, paid, credited, or canceled in the case of Form 1099-C, during the calendar year. Form 5498 is used to report amounts contributed for the calendar year.

Extension.—For paper or magnetic media filing, you may request an extension of time to file by sending **Form 8809,** Request for Extension of Time To File Information Returns, to the address shown on the form. You must request the extension by the due date of the returns for your request to be considered. If your request for an extension is approved, you will have an additional 30 days to file. You may request an additional extension. See Form 8809. For information on extensions for providing statements to recipients, see page 7.

Note: *If you are a magnetic media transmitter requesting extensions of time to file for more than 50 payers, you must submit the extension requests magnetically or electronically. For instructions on submitting extension requests on magnetic media, see Pub. 1220.*

C. Where To File

Caution: *NEW FILING LOCATIONS. Check the addresses below carefully because you may have to file in a service center that is different from the one where you filed last year.*

Send all information returns filed on paper to the following:

If your principal business, office or agency, or legal residence in the case of an individual, is located in	Use the following Internal Revenue Service Center address
Alabama, Arizona, Florida, Georgia, Louisiana, Mississippi, New Mexico, Texas	Austin, TX 73301
Arkansas, Connecticut, Kentucky, Maine, Massachusetts, New Hampshire, New York, Ohio, Rhode Island, Vermont, West Virginia	Cincinnati, OH 45999
Illinois, Indiana, Iowa, Kansas, Michigan, Minnesota, Missouri, Nebraska, North Dakota, Oklahoma, South Dakota, Wisconsin	Kansas City, MO 64999
Delaware, District of Columbia, Maryland, New Jersey, North Carolina, Pennsylvania, South Carolina, Tennessee, Virginia	Memphis, TN 37501
Alaska, California, Colorado, Hawaii, Idaho, Montana, Nevada, Oregon, Utah, Washington, Wyoming	Ogden, UT 84201

If you have no legal residence, principal place of business, or principal office or agency in any Internal Revenue district, file your return with the Internal Revenue Service Center, Cincinnati, OH 45999.

Send all information returns filed magnetically to IRS-Martinsburg Computing Center, P.O. Box 1359, Martinsburg, WV 25401-1359.

D. Filing Returns With the IRS.—The IRS strongly encourages the quality review of data before filing to prevent erroneous notices being mailed to payees (or others for whom information is being reported).

If you must file any Form 1098, 1099, 5498, or W-2G with the IRS, and you are filing paper documents, you must send a **Form 1096,** Annual Summary and Transmittal of U.S. Information Returns, with each type of form as the transmittal document. You must group the forms by form number and submit each group with a separate Form 1096. For example, if you file Forms 1098, 1099-A, and 1099-MISC, complete one Form 1096 to transmit Forms 1098, another Form 1096 to transmit Forms 1099-A, and a third Form 1096 to transmit Forms 1099-MISC. Specific instructions for completing Form 1096 are included on Form 1096. Also see **Transmitters, paying agents, etc.** later. For information about filing corrected returns, see **Corrected Returns** later.

If you are filing on magnetic media, **Form 4804,** Transmittal of Information Returns Reported Magnetically/ Electronically, must accompany your submissions.

For information on the preparation of transmittal documents for magnetic media and paper document reporting (Forms 4804 and 1096), see Rev. Proc. 84-24, 1984-1 C.B. 465, or other current revenue procedure.

If you use paper forms, report payments on the appropriate form, as explained in the **Specific Instructions** later.

See Pub. 1179 on specifications for private printing of information documents. You may not request special consideration. Only forms that conform with the official form and the specifications in Pub. 1179 are acceptable.

Transmitters, paying agents, etc.—A transmitter, service bureau, paying agent, or disbursing agent (hereafter referred to as "agent") may sign Form 1096 or 4804 on behalf of any person required to file

(hereafter referred to as "payer") if the conditions in items **1** and **2** below are met:

1. The agent has the authority to sign the form under an agency agreement (oral, written, or implied) that is valid under state law, and

2. The agent signs the form and adds the caption "For: (Name of payer)."

Signing of the form by an authorized agent on behalf of the payer does not relieve the payer of the liability for penalties for not filing a correct, complete, and timely Form 1096 or 4804 and accompanying returns.

Forms 1098, 1099, 5498, W-2G, or other statements to recipients issued by a service bureau or agent should show the same payer's name as shown on the information returns filed with the IRS.

For information about the election to report and deposit backup withholding under the agent's TIN and how to prepare forms if the election is made, see Rev. Proc. 84-33, 1984-1 C.B. 502 (Pub. 1272).

Keeping copies.—Generally, keep copies of information returns you filed with the IRS or have the ability to reconstruct the data for at least 3 years from the due date of the returns. If backup withholding was imposed and for Form 1099-C, keep copies of information returns for 4 years.

E. Shipping and Mailing.—If you are sending many forms, you may send them in conveniently sized packages. On each package write your name and TIN, number the packages consecutively, and place Form 1096 in package number one. Postal regulations require forms and packages to be sent by First-Class Mail.

F. Recipient Names and Taxpayer Identification Numbers.—Taxpayer identification numbers (TINs) are used to associate and verify amounts reported to the IRS with corresponding amounts on tax returns. Therefore, it is important that you furnish correct names, social security numbers (SSNs) or employer identification numbers (EINs) for recipients on the forms or magnetic media sent to the IRS.

Use Form W-9 to request the recipient's TIN. (You may be subject to a penalty for an incorrect or missing TIN. See **Penalties** on page 2.) You are required to maintain the confidentiality of information obtained on Form W-9 relating to the taxpayer's identity (including SSNs), and you may use such information only to comply with the tax laws.

Note: *If the recipient does not provide a TIN, leave the box for providing the TIN to the IRS blank on the Form 1098, 1099, 5498, or W-2G. See **Backup Withholding** on page 2. Only one recipient TIN can be entered on the form.*

The TIN for individual recipients of information returns is the social security number. But see the information about sole proprietors below. For other recipients, including corporations, partnerships, and estates, it is the EIN.

SSNs have nine digits separated by two hyphens (000-00-0000), and EINs have

---

Exhibit A-1   *(continued)*

nine digits separated by only one hyphen (00-0000000).

Show the full name and address in the section provided on the return. **If payments have been made to more than one recipient or the account is in more than one name, show as the ONLY name on the first name line the name of the recipient whose TIN is shown on the return.** Show the names of any other individual recipients in the area below the first line, if desired. Form W-2G filers see **Form 5754** later.

For **sole proprietors,** show the individual's name on the first name line; on the second name line, you may enter the business name. You may not enter only the business name. For the TIN, enter either the individual's SSN or the EIN of the business (sole proprietorship).

G. Filer's Name, Identification Number, and Address.—The TIN for filers of information returns, including sole proprietors and nominees/middlemen, is the Federal EIN. However, sole proprietors and nominees/middlemen who are not otherwise required to have an EIN should use their social security numbers. A sole proprietor is not required to have an EIN unless he or she must file excise or employment tax returns. See **Pub. 583,** Taxpayers Starting a Business.

The filer's name and TIN should be consistent with the name and number used on the filer's other tax returns. The name of the filer's paying agent or service bureau must not be used in place of the name of the filer.

To obtain an EIN, file **Form SS-4,** Application for Employer Identification Number, with the IRS. If you do not have your EIN by the time you must file information returns, enter "Applied For" in any space where the number must be entered.

Include the room, suite, or other unit number after the street address.

H. Statements to Recipients (Borrowers, Debtors, Participants, Payers/Borrowers, Transferors, or Winners on Certain Forms).—Be sure that the statements you provide to recipients are clear and legible.

If you are not using the official IRS form to furnish statements to recipients, see **Pub. 1179,** Rules and Specifications for Private Printing of Substitute Forms 1096, 1098, 1099 Series, 5498, and W-2G, for specific rules about providing "substitute" statements to recipients. A substitute is any statement other than Copy B (generally) of the official form. You may develop them yourself or buy them from a private printer. However, the substitutes must comply with the format and content requirements specified in Pub. 1179.

Different rules apply to furnishing statements to recipients depending on the type of payment you are reporting and the form you are filing. See the heading below for the type of payment you are reporting. The headings are (1) **Interest, dividend, and royalty payments;** (2) **Real estate transactions;** and (3) **Other payments.**

Interest, dividend, and royalty payments.—For payments of dividends or interest (including original issue discount) under section 6042, 6044, or 6049 (reported on Forms 1099-DIV, 1099-PATR, 1099-INT, or 1099-OID), you are required to furnish an official or substitute Form 1099 to a recipient either in person or in a statement mailing by First-Class Mail. Payers of **royalties** are also required to furnish the statement in person or in a statement mailing by First-Class Mail, but the statement need not be the official form. Statements may be sent by intraoffice mail if you use intraoffice mail to send account information and other correspondence to the recipient.

Statement mailing requirements for Forms 1099-DIV, 1099-INT, 1099-OID, and 1099-PATR, and forms reporting royalties only.—The statement mailing requirements apply only to Forms 1099-DIV (except for section 404(k) dividends), 1099-INT (except for interest reportable under section 6041), 1099-OID, 1099-PATR, and royalties reported under section 6050N (on Form 1099-MISC or 1099-S). In addition to Forms W-2, W-8, W-9, or other 1098, 1099, and 5498 statements, the following enclosures are permitted in a statement mailing: (1) a check, (2) a letter explaining why no check is enclosed, (3) a statement of the person's account shown on Form 1099, and (4) a letter. limited to an explanation of the tax consequences of the information shown on a recipient statement.

A recipient statement may be perforated to a check with respect to the account reported on the recipient statement or to a statement of the recipient's specific account if payments on such account are reflected on the recipient's statement. The check or account statement to which the recipient statement is perforated must contain, in a bold and conspicuous type, the legend "Important Tax Return Document Attached."

No additional enclosures, such as advertising, promotional material, or a quarterly or annual report, are permitted. Even a sentence or two on the yearend statement describing new services offered by the payer is not permitted. However, logos are permitted on the envelope and on any enclosures.

For a statement mailing, the legend "Important Tax Return Document Enclosed" must appear in a bold and conspicuous manner on the outside of the envelope and on each letter, or check or account statement that is not perforated to the recipient statement. This legend is not required on any tax form, tax statement, or permitted letter of tax consequences included in a statement mailing. Further, you need not pluralize the word "document" in the legend simply because more than one recipient statement is enclosed.

Note: *If you provide recipient statements in a "separate mailing" that contains only recipient statements, Forms W-8 and W-9, and a letter limited to the explanation of the tax consequences of the information shown on a recipient statement included in*

the envelope, you are not required to include the legend "Important Tax Return Document Enclosed" on the envelope.

Substitute forms.—You may furnish to the recipient Copy B of the official form, or you may use substitute Forms 1099-DIV, 1099-INT, 1099-OID, and 1099-PATR if they contain the same language as the official forms and they comply with the rules in Pub. 1179, relating to substitute Forms 1099. Applicable box captions and numbers must be clearly identified, using the same wording and numbering as the official form. However, for Form 1099-INT, if your substitute does not contain box 3, "Interest on U.S. Savings Bonds and Treas. obligations," you may omit "not included in box 3" from the box 1 caption. The substitute must show the form number (e.g., Form 1099-INT), form title (e.g., Interest Income), and tax year (e.g., 1995).

If you are using substitutes, the IRS encourages you to use boxes so that the substitute has the appearance of a form. The substitute form must contain the applicable instructions as on the front and back of Copy B of the official form. See Pub. 1179 for additional requirements. For information about substitute Form 1099-MISC for royalties, see **Other payments** below.

Certain "composite" statements are permitted. See Pub. 1179.

Real estate transactions.—You must furnish a statement to the transferor containing the same information reported to the IRS on Form 1099-S. You may use Copy B of Form 1099-S or a substitute form that complies with Pub. 1179 and Regulations section 1.6045-4(m). You may use a Uniform Settlement Statement (under RESPA) as the written statement if it is conformed by including on the statement the legend shown on Form 1099-S and by designating which information is reported to the IRS on Form 1099-S. You may furnish the statement to the transferor in person or by mail. Furnish the statement at or after closing but by January 31 of the following year. The statement mailing requirements explained earlier do not apply to statements to transferors for proceeds from real estate transactions reported on Form 1099-S. However, the statement mailing requirements do apply to statements to transferors for timber royalties reportable under section 6050N on Form 1099-S.

Other payments.—Statements to recipients for Forms 1098, 1099-A, 1099-B, 1099-C, 1099-G, 1099-MISC, 1099-R, 5498, W-2G, 1099-DIV only for section 404(k) dividends reportable under section 6047, or 1099-INT only for interest reportable under section 6041 need not be, but can be, a copy of the paper form filed with the IRS. If you do not use a copy of the paper form, the form number and title of your **substitute** must be the same as the official form. All information required to be reported must be numbered and titled on your substitute in substantially the same manner as on the official form. However, if you are reporting a payment as "Other income" in box 3 of Form 1099-MISC, you may substitute

Exhibit A-1   *(continued)*

appropriate explanatory language for the box title. For example, for payments of accrued wages to a beneficiary of a deceased employee required to be reported on Form 1099-MISC by Rev. Rul. 86-109, you might change the title of box 3 to "Beneficiary payments" or something similar.

Appropriate instructions to the recipient, similar to those on the official form, must be provided to aid in the proper reporting of the items on the recipient's income tax return. For payments reported on Forms 1098, 1099-A, 1099-B, 1099-C, 1099-G, 1099-MISC (except for royalties), 1099-R, 5498, W-2G, 1099-DIV for section 404(k) dividends only, and 1099-INT for interest reportable under section 6041 only. You may combine the statements with other reports or financial or commercial notices, or expand them to include other information of interest to the recipient. Be sure that all copies of the forms are legible.

Certain "composite" statements are permitted. See Pub. 1179.

Time for furnishing forms or statements.—Generally, you must furnish Forms 1098, 1099, and W-2G information by January 31, 1996. However, you may issue them earlier in some situations, as provided by the regulations. For example, you may furnish Form 1099-INT to the recipient on redemption of U.S. Savings Bonds at the time of redemption. Brokers and barter exchanges may furnish Form 1099-B anytime but not later than January 31.

Trustees or issuers of IRAs or SEPs must furnish participants with a statement of the value of the participant's account by January 31, 1996. IRA contribution information must be furnished to the participant by May 31, 1996.

For real estate transactions, you may furnish the statement to the transferor at closing or by mail on or before January 31, 1996.

Filers of Form 1099-G who report state or local income tax refunds, credits, or offsets must furnish the statements to recipients **during** January 1996.

You will meet the requirement to furnish the statement if it is properly addressed, mailed, and postmarked on or before the due date. If the regular due date falls on a Saturday, Sunday, or legal holiday, the due date is the next business day. A business day is any day that is not a Saturday, Sunday, or legal holiday.

Extension.—You may request an extension of time to provide the statements with a letter to IRS-Martinsburg Computing Center, P.O. Box 1359, Martinsburg, WV

25401-1359 or to your district director. The letter must include (a) your name, (b) your TIN, (c) your address, (d) type of return, (e) reason for delay, and (f) the signature of the payer or authorized agent. Your request must be postmarked by the date on which the statements are due to be furnished to recipients. If your request for an extension is approved, you will be granted an extra 15 days to furnish the recipient statements.

I. Corrected Returns.—If you filed a return with the IRS and later discover you made an error on it, you must correct it as soon as possible. For some corrections, you must file two returns (Form 1099, 1098, 5498, or W-2G) with Form 1096 and for some only one return with Form 1096. See the chart that follows for step-by-step instructions for correcting three common errors on paper forms.

To determine whether you are required to submit corrections on magnetic media, see **Magnetic Media/Electronic Reporting** earlier and Pub. 1220.

Follow the step-by-step instructions below for the type of error you need to correct. Be sure you complete all appropriate information on the returns as stated in those instructions. Then file Copy A of the form and Form 1096 with your Internal Revenue Service Center. Please remember not to cut or separate the forms that are two or three to a page. Submit the entire page even if only one of the forms on the page is completed. And do not staple the forms to Form 1096. You must use a separate Form 1096 for each type of return you are correcting, but you may use one Form 1096 for both originals and corrections of the same type of return.

In addition, you must provide statements to recipients showing the corrections as soon as possible.

Note: *If you fail to file correct information returns or furnish a correct payee statement, you may be subject to a penalty. See* **Failure To File Correct Information Returns by the Due Date** *(Section 6721) on page 2 and* **Failure To Furnish Correct Payee Statements** *(Section 6722) on page 3.*

On all Forms 1098, 1099, and 5498, a box is provided for the account number. If the account number was provided on the original return, use this number on the corrected return to help identify the appropriate incorrect return filed when more than one return was filed for a particular individual. The account number may be a checking account number, savings account number, serial number, or any other number assigned to the payee by the filer that is unique and will distinguish the specific account. This number must appear on both the original and corrected returns to properly identify and process the correction.

CORRECTED box.—Enter an "X" in the "CORRECTED" box on Copy A only when you are correcting a form you previously submitted to the IRS. Enter an "X" in the "CORRECTED" box on the copies you give to the recipient (generally, Copy B) only when you are correcting a form previously

furnished to the recipient. When the type of error requires two returns to make the correction, you will mark the "CORRECTED" box only on one of the returns. Refer to the step-by-step instructions chart that follows to determine when you should mark the "CORRECTED" box.

The following chart gives step-by-step instructions for filing corrected returns for three of the most frequently made errors. Correction of errors may require the submission of more than one return. Be sure to read each section thoroughly.

Note: *Regulations section 301.6724-1 (relating to information penalties) does not require you to file corrected returns for missing or incorrect TINs if you meet the reasonable cause criteria. You are merely required to include the correct TIN on the next original return you are required to file. However, if you do not meet the reasonable cause criteria, you should file corrected returns by August 1 to be subject to a reduced penalty.*

In addition, even if you meet the reasonable cause criteria, the IRS encourages you to file corrections for incorrect or missing TINs so that the IRS can update the payees' records.

Step-by-Step Instructions for Filing Corrected Returns on Paper Forms

Error (on Original Return)	How To File the Corrected Return on Paper Forms
1. No payee TIN (SSN or EIN) or incorrect payee TIN, or incorrect name and address. This will require two separate returns to make the correction properly. Read and follow all instructions for both Steps 1 and 2.	**STEP 1:** Identify incorrect return submitted. **Form 1098, 1099, 5498, or W-2G:** 1. Prepare a new information return. 2. Enter an "X" in the "CORRECTED" box at the top of the form. 3. Enter the payer, recipient, and account number information exactly as it appeared on the original incorrect return; HOWEVER, enter "0" (zero) for all money amounts. **STEP 2:** Report correct information. **A. Form 1098, 1099, 5498, or W-2G:** 1. Prepare a new information return. 2. Do NOT enter an "X" in the "CORRECTED" box at the top of the form. Submit the new return as though it was an original. 3. Include all the correct information on the form including the correct TIN and name and address. **B. Form 1096:** 1. Prepare a new transmittal Form 1096. 2. Enter the words "Filed To Correct TIN, Name, and/or Address" in the bottom margin of the form.

Exhibit A-1   *(continued)*

Error (on Original Return)	How To File the Corrected Return on Paper Forms
	3. Provide all requested information on the form as it applies to the returns prepared in Steps 1 and 2.
	4. File Form 1096 and Copies A of the returns with the appropriate service center.
	5. Do NOT include copies of the original return that was filed incorrectly.
2. Incorrect money amount(s) or incorrect address. Follow these instructions if you filed a return when one should not have been filed. This error requires only one return to make the correction. (Follow the instructions under Error 1, instead of these instructions, if you must correct an address AND a name or TIN.)	**A. Form 1098, 1099, 5498, or W-2G:** 1. Prepare a new information return. 2. Enter an "X" in the "CORRECTED" box at the top of the form. 3. Enter the payer, recipient, and account number information exactly as it appeared on the original incorrect return; HOWEVER, enter all correct money amounts in the correct boxes as they should have appeared on the original return, and enter the recipient's correct address. **B. Form 1096:** 1. Follow the instructions under Error 1, Step 2-B, but ignore item B-2. 2. File Form 1096 and Copy A of the return with the appropriate service center. 3. Do NOT include a copy of the original return that was filed incorrectly.
3. Original return was filed using the WRONG type of return. For example, a Form 1099-DIV was filed when a Form 1099-INT should have been filed. This will require two separate returns to make the correction properly. Read and follow all instructions for both Steps 1 and 2.	**STEP 1: Identify incorrect return submitted.** **Form 1098, 1099, 5498, or W-2G:** Follow the instructions under Error 1, Step 1, using the same type of form that was used initially. **STEP 2: Report correct information on the correct type of return.** **A. Form 1098, 1099, 5498, or W-2G:** Follow the instructions under Error 1, Step 2-A, using the proper type of form. **B. Form 1096:** Follow the instructions under Error 1, Step 2-B, except enter the words "Filed To Correct Document Type" in the bottom margin of Form 1096.

J. Void Returns.—An "X" in the "VOID" box will not correct a previously filed return. See part I above for instructions for making corrections.

VOID box.—If a completed or partially completed Form 1098, 1099, or 5498 is incorrect and you want to void it before submission to the IRS, enter an "X" in the "VOID" box at the top of the form. For example, if you make an error while typing or printing a form, you should void it. The return will be disregarded during processing by the IRS. Go to the next form on the page, or to another page, and enter the correct information; but **do not** mark the "CORRECTED" box. Please remember not to cut or separate the forms that are two or three to a page. Submit the entire page even if only one of the forms on the page is a good return.

K. Other Information Returns.—The income information you report on the following returns must not be repeated on the returns discussed in the **Specific Instructions** in this publication:

1. Form W-2 reporting wages and other employee compensation.

2. Forms 1042-S and 1000 reporting income.

3. Form 2439 reporting undistributed long-term capital gains of a regulated investment company.

4. Schedule K-1 of Form 1065 reporting distributive shares to members of a partnership.

5. Schedule K-1 of Form 1041 reporting distributions to beneficiaries of trusts or estates.

6. Schedule K-1 of Form 1120S reporting distributive shares to shareholders of S corporations.

7. Schedule K of Form 1120-IC-DISC reporting actual and constructive distributions to shareholders and deferred DISC income.

8. Schedule Q of Form 1066 reporting income from a REMIC to a residual interest holder.

L. Payments to Corporations and Partnerships.—Reporting generally is not required for payments to corporations except in the case of (1) medical payments (Form 1099-MISC), (2) withheld Federal income tax or foreign tax, (3) barter exchange transactions (Form 1099-B), (4) substitute payments in lieu of dividends and tax-exempt interest (Form 1099-MISC), (5) interest or original issue discount paid or accrued to a regular interest holder of a REMIC (Form 1099-INT or 1099-OID), (6) acquisitions or abandonments of secured property (Form 1099-A), and (7) cancellation of debt (Form 1099-C). For example, reporting is not required for payments of architectural fees to corporations.

However, reporting generally is required for payments to partnerships. For example, payments of $600 or more made in the course of your trade or business to a law firm that is a partnership are reportable on Form 1099-MISC.

M. Earnings on an IRA or SEP.—Generally, any income with respect to an IRA or SEP, such as interest or dividends, is not reported on Forms 1099. But

distributions should be reported on Form 1099-R.

Specific Instructions

If a distribution includes noncash property, show the fair market value of the property at the time of payment.

Although, generally, you are not required to report payments smaller than the minimum described for each form, you may prefer, for economy and your own convenience, to file Copies A for all payments. The IRS encourages this.

Form 1098

Use Form 1098, **Mortgage Interest Statement,** to report mortgage interest (including points, defined later) of $600 or more received by you during the year in the course of your trade or business from an individual, including a sole proprietor. The $600 threshold applies separately to each mortgage; thus, file a separate Form 1098 for each mortgage. You may, at your option, file Form 1098 to report mortgage interest of less than $600, but you are subject to the rules in these instructions.

If an overpayment of interest on an adjustable rate mortgage (ARM) or other mortgage was made in a prior year and you refund (or credit) such overpayment, you may have to file Form 1098 to report the refund (or credit) of the overpayment. See **Reimbursement of Overpaid Interest** later.

Exceptions.—You need not file Form 1098 for interest received from a corporation, partnership, trust, estate, association, or company (other than a sole proprietor) even though an individual is a coborrower and all the trustees, beneficiaries, partners, members, or shareholders of the payer of record are individuals.

Mortgage Defined.—An obligation incurred after 1987 is a mortgage if real property that is located inside or outside the United States secures all or part of the obligation, even though the interest recipient classifies the obligation as other than a mortgage, for example, as a commercial loan.

An obligation incurred after 1984 but before 1988 is a mortgage only if secured primarily by real property.

An obligation in existence on December 31, 1984, is not a mortgage if, at the time the obligation was incurred, the interest recipient reasonably classified the obligation as other than a mortgage, real property loan, real estate loan, or other similar type of obligation. For example, if an obligation incurred in 1983 was secured by real property, but the interest recipient reasonably classified the obligation as a commercial loan because the proceeds were used to finance the borrower's business, the obligation is not considered a mortgage for purposes of this reporting requirement. However, if over half of the obligations in a class established by the interest recipient are primarily secured by

Page 8

Exhibit A-1 *(continued)*

real property, it is not reasonable to classify those obligations as other than mortgages for purposes of this reporting requirement.

Real property includes a manufactured home with a minimum living space of 400 square feet and a minimum width of more than 102 inches of a kind customarily used at a fixed location, including certain mobile homes. See section 25(e)(10).

Lines of credit and credit card obligations.—Interest (other than points) received on any mortgage that is in the form of a line of credit or credit card obligation is reportable regardless of how you classified the obligation. A borrower incurs a line of credit or credit card obligation when the borrower first has the right to borrow against the line of credit or credit card, whether or not the borrower actually borrows an amount at that time.

Who Must File.—File this form if you are engaged in a trade or business and, in the course of such trade or business, you receive from an individual $600 or more of mortgage interest on any one mortgage during the calendar year. You are not required to file this form if the interest is not received in the course of your trade or business. For example, you hold the mortgage on your former personal residence. The buyer makes mortgage payments to you. You are not required to file Form 1098.

If you receive $600 or more of mortgage interest in the course of your trade or business, you are subject to the requirement to file Form 1098, even if you are not in the business of lending money. For example, if you are a real estate developer and you provide financing to an individual to buy a home in your subdivision, and that home is security for the financing, you are subject to this reporting requirement. However, if you are a physician not engaged in any other business and you lend money to an individual to buy your home, you are not subject to this reporting requirement because you did not receive the interest in the course of your trade or business as a physician.

A **governmental unit** (or any subsidiary agency) receiving mortgage interest from an individual of $600 or more must file this form.

For information about who must file to report points, see **Points** later. For information about who must file to report reimbursements of overpaid interest, see **Reimbursement of Overpaid Interest** later.

Cooperative housing corporation.—A cooperative housing corporation is an interest recipient and must file Form 1098 to report an amount received from its tenant-stockholders that represents the tenant-stockholders' proportionate share of interest described in section 216(a)(2). This rule applies only to tenant-stockholders who are individuals and from whom the cooperative has received at least $600 of interest during the year. (See the **Note** under **Box 1**.)

Collection agents.—Generally, if you receive reportable interest payments (other than points) on behalf of someone else and you are the first person to receive the interest, for example, if you are a servicing bank collecting payments for a lender, you must file this form and enter your name, address, and TIN in the recipient entity area. You must file this form even though you do not include the interest received in your income but you merely transfer it to another person. If you wish, you may enter the name of the person for whom you collected the interest in box 4. The person for whom you collected the interest need not file Form 1098.

However, there is an exception to this rule for any period that (1) the first person to receive or collect the interest does not have the information needed to report on Form 1098 and (2) the person for whom the interest is received or collected would receive the interest in its trade or business if the interest were paid directly to such person. If (1) and (2) apply, the person on whose behalf the interest is received or collected is required to report on Form 1098. If interest is received or collected on behalf of another person other than an individual, such person is presumed to receive the interest in a trade or business.

Foreign interest recipient.—If you are not a U.S. person, you must file Form 1098 if the interest is received in the United States. A U.S. person is a citizen or resident of the United States, a domestic partnership or corporation, or a nonforeign estate or trust. If the interest is received outside the United States, you must file Form 1098 if (1) you are a controlled foreign corporation or (2) at least 50% of your gross income from all sources for the 3-year period ending with the close of the tax year preceding the receipt of interest (or for such part of the period as you were in existence) was effectively connected with the conduct of a trade or business in the United States.

Designation agreement.—An interest recipient, including a recipient of points, can designate a qualified person to file Form 1098, to provide a statement to the payer of record, and to provide the Rule of 78s notice. A **qualified person** is either (1) a trade or business in which the interest recipient is under common control as specified in Regulations section 1.414(c)-2 or (2) a designee, named by the lender of record or by a qualified person, who either was involved in the original loan transaction or is a subsequent purchaser of the loan. A **lender of record** is the person who, at the time the loan is made, is named as the lender on the loan documents and whose right to receive payment from the payer of record is secured by the payer of record's principal residence. Even if the lender of record intends to sell or otherwise transfer the loan to a third party after the close of the transaction, such intention does not change who is the lender of record.

The agreement must be in writing, identify the mortgage(s) and calendar years for which the qualified person is to report, and be signed by the designator and the

designee. A designee may report points on Form 1098 (as having been paid directly by the payer of record) only if the designation agreement contains the designator's representation that it did not lend such amount to the payer of record as part of the overall transaction. The agreement need not be filed with the IRS, but the designator must keep a copy of it for 4 years after the close of the year in which the loan is made.

A designated qualified person is subject to any applicable penalties as if it were the interest recipient. Thus, a designator is relieved from liability for any applicable penalties.

Reimbursement of Overpaid Interest.—You are required to report reimbursements of overpaid interest aggregating $600 or more to a payer of record on Form 1098. You are not required to report reimbursements of overpaid interest aggregating less than $600 unless you are otherwise required to file Form 1098. That is, if you did not receive at least $600 of mortgage interest during the year of reimbursement from the person to whom you made the reimbursement, you are not required to file Form 1098 merely to report the reimbursement. However, you may report any reimbursement of overpaid interest that you are not otherwise required to report, but you are subject to the rules in these instructions.

The reimbursement must be reported on Form 1098 for the year in which the reimbursement is made. No change should be made to the prior year Form 1098 because of this reimbursement. Report the total reimbursement even if it is for overpayments made in more than 1 year.

To be reportable, the reimbursement must be a refund or credit of mortgage interest received in a prior year that was required to be reported for that prior year by any interest recipient on Form 1098. Only the person who makes the reimbursement is required to report it on Form 1098. For example, if you bought a mortgage on which interest was overpaid in a prior year, you made a reimbursement of the overpaid interest, and the previous mortgage holder was required to report mortgage interest on Form 1098 in the prior year, you must file Form 1098 to report the reimbursement because you are the one making the reimbursement.

If you reimburse interest in the **same year it is overpaid,** do not report the overpayment on Form 1098 as interest received during the year or as a reimbursement of overpaid interest. For example, if the borrower paid $5,000 and you reimbursed $500 of that amount in 1995, $4,500 should appear in box 1 as interest paid by the borrower. The $500 reimbursement must not appear in box 3.

Example.—In 1993, you received $5,000 of mortgage interest from the payer/borrower and reported that amount on Form 1098 for 1993. In 1995, you determined that interest due on the mortgage for 1993 was $4,500, and the payer/borrower had overpaid $500. You refunded the $500 overpayment to the

Page 9

Exhibit A-1 *(continued)*

payer/borrower in 1995. If you received $600 or more of interest on the mortgage from the payer/borrower in 1995, you must report the $500 refund in box 3 of the 1995 Form 1098. No change to the 1993 Form 1098 is required. If, instead of refunding the $500 overpayment; you credited the payer/borrower's 1995 mortgage interest payments due, $500 is still shown in box 3, and the interest received from the payer/borrower in 1995 shown in box 1 must include the $500 credit.

Interest on reimbursement.—A financial institution (or its middleman) that pays interest of $10 or more on the reimbursement must report that interest (under section 6049) on **Form 1099-INT,** Interest Income. Others that pay interest of $600 or more on the reimbursement must report that interest (under section 6041) on Form 1099-INT. Do not include such interest on Form 1098.

Nonresident Alien Interest Payer.—You must file Form 1098 to report interest paid by a nonresident alien only if all or part of the security for the mortgage is real property located in the United States.

Payer of Record.—The payer of record is the individual carried on your books and records as the principal borrower. If your books and records do not indicate which borrower is the principal borrower, you must designate one.

If you permit a subsequent purchaser of the property to assume the loan without releasing the first purchaser from personal liability, the subsequent purchaser is the payer of record. Such subsequent purchaser's name, address, and TIN must appear on Form 1098.

Multiple Borrowers.—Even though there may be more than one borrower on the mortgage, you are required to prepare Form 1098 only for the **payer of record,** and only if such payer of record is an individual, showing the total interest received on the mortgage. Even if an individual is a coborrower, no Form 1098 is required unless the payer of record is also an individual.

Payments by Third Party.—Report all interest received on the mortgage as received from the borrower, except as explained under **Seller Payments** below. For example, if the borrower's mother makes payments on the mortgage, the interest received from the mother is reportable on Form 1098 as received from the borrower.

However, do not report mortgage interest received from any governmental unit (or any subsidiary agency). For example, do not report any interest received as housing assistance payments from the Department of Housing and Urban Development (HUD) on mortgages insured under section 235 of the National Housing Act.

Seller Payments.—Do not report in box 1 of Form 1098 any interest paid by a seller on a purchaser's-borrower's mortgage, such as on a "buy-down" mortgage. For example, if a real estate developer deposits an amount in escrow and tells

Page 10

you to draw on that escrow account to pay interest on the borrower's mortgage, do not report in box 1 the interest received from that escrow account. As another example, do not report in box 1 any lump sum paid by a real estate developer to pay interest on a purchaser's-borrower's mortgage. However, if you wish, you may use box 4 to report to the payer of record any interest paid by the seller. See **Points** later for information about reporting seller-paid points in box 2.

Rule of 78s Method of Accounting.—If you are permitted by Rev. Proc. 83-40, 1983-1 C.B. 774, or any other revenue procedure, to use the Rule of 78s method to calculate interest earned with respect to a transaction, you may report interest earned under the Rule of 78s method on that transaction as interest received from the borrower in a calendar year. In this case, you must notify borrowers that the Rule of 78s method was used to calculate interest received and that the borrowers may not deduct the amount reported unless the borrowers are also properly using the Rule of 78s method to determine interest deductions. The notification must also state that the Rule of 78s method may be used only in the case of a self-amortizing consumer loan that requires level payments, at regular intervals (at least annually), over a period not in excess of 5 years (with no balloon payment at the end of the loan term), and only when the loan agreement provides for use of the Rule of 78s method to determine interest earned (see Rev. Proc. 83-40 and Rev. Rul. 83-84, 1983-1 C.B. 97). The notice must be furnished to the payer of record on or with the statement of the interest received.

Points.—You must report certain points paid for the purchase of the payer of record's principal residence on Form 1098. You must report points if the points, plus other interest on the mortgage, are $600 or more. For example, if a borrower pays points of $300 and other mortgage interest of $300, the lender has received $600 of mortgage interest and must file Form 1098.

Who must report points.—The lender of record or a qualified person must file Form 1098 to report all points paid by the payer of record in connection with the purchase of the principal residence. If a designation agreement is in effect for a mortgage, only the person designated in the agreement must file Form 1098 to report all points on that mortgage. See **Designation agreement** earlier.

Amounts received directly or indirectly by a mortgage broker are treated as points to the same extent they would be treated as points if paid to and retained by the lender of record. The lender of record must report those points paid to a mortgage broker.

Report the total points on Form 1098 for the year of closing regardless of the accounting method you use to report the points as income for Federal income tax purposes.

Reportable points.—Report on Form 1098 points that meet all the following conditions:

1. They are clearly **designated on the Uniform Settlement Statement** (Form HUD-1) as points; for example, "loan origination fee" (including amounts for VA and FHA loans), "loan discount," "discount points," or "points."

2. They are **computed as a percentage of the stated principal loan amount.**

3. They are **charged under an established business practice** of charging points in the area where the loan was issued and do not exceed the amount generally charged in that area.

4. They are **paid for the acquisition of the payer of record's principal residence,** and the loan is secured by that residence. You may rely on a signed written statement from the payer of record that states whether the proceeds of the loan are for the purchase of the payer of record's principal residence.

5. They are **paid directly by the payer of record.**

Points are paid directly if:

(a) The **payer** of record provides funds that were not borrowed from the lender of record for this purpose as part of the overall transaction. The funds may include down payments, escrow deposits, earnest money applied at closing, and other funds actually paid over by the payer of record at or before closing. OR

(b) The **seller** pays points on behalf of the payer of record. Points paid by the seller to the interest recipient on behalf of the payer of record are treated as paid to the payer of record and then paid directly by the payer of record to the interest recipient.

Report points paid under (a) and (b) above on the payer of record's Form 1098 in box 2.

Do not report on Form 1098 points paid (1) for loans to improve a principal residence, (2) for loans to purchase or improve a residence that is not the payer of record's principal residence, such as a second home, vacation, investment, or trade or business property, (3) for a home equity or line of credit loan, even if secured by the principal residence, (4) for a refinancing (but see **Construction loans** below), including a loan to refinance a debt owed by the borrower under a land contract, a contract for deed, or similar forms of seller financing, (5) in lieu of items ordinarily stated separately on the Form HUD-1, such as appraisal fees, inspection fees, title fees, attorney fees, and property taxes, and (6) to acquire a principal residence to the extent the points are allocable to an amount of principal in excess of $1 million.

Construction loans.—Points paid on a loan to construct a residence (construction loan) or to refinance a loan incurred to construct a residence are reportable on Form 1098 if they:

1. Are clearly designated on the loan documents as points incurred in connection with the loan, such as loan origination fees, loan discount, discount points, or points,

2. Are computed as a percentage of the stated principal loan amount,

3. Conform to an established business practice of charging points in the area where the loan is issued and do not exceed the amount generally charged in the area,

4. Are paid in connection with a loan incurred by the payer of record to construct (or refinance construction of) a residence that is to be used, when completed, as the principal residence of the payer of record,

5. Are paid directly by the payer of record, and

6. Are not allocable to an amount of principal in excess of $1 million.

Amounts paid to refinance a loan to construct a residence are not points to the extent they are allocable to debt that exceeds the debt incurred to construct the residence.

Prepaid Interest.—Report prepaid interest (other than points) only in the year in which it properly accrues. For example, interest received on December 20, 1995, that accrues by December 31 but is not due until February 1, 1996, is reportable on the 1995 Form 1098.

Exception.—Interest received during the current year that will properly accrue in full by January 15 of the following year may be considered received in the current year, at your option, and is reportable on Form 1098 for the current year. However, if any part of an interest payment accrues after January 15, then only the amount that properly accrues by December 31 of the current year is reportable on Form 1098 for the current year. For example, if you receive a payment of interest that accrues for the period December 20 through January 20, you cannot report any of the interest that accrues after December 31 for the current year. You must report the interest that accrues after December 31 on Form 1098 for the following year.

Statements to Payers of Record.—For information about the requirement to furnish a statement to the payer of record, see part H under **General Instructions** earlier.

Recipient's/Lender's Name and Address Box.—Enter the name and address of the filer of Form 1098. Use this same name and address on Form 1096.

Payer's/Borrower's Name and Address Box.—Enter the name and address of the person who paid the interest (payer of record).

Note: *Be careful to enter the recipient's and payer's information in the proper boxes.*

Box 1.—Enter the **interest** (not including points) received on the mortgage from borrowers during the calendar year. Include interest on a mortgage, a home equity loan, or a line of credit or credit card loan secured by real property. Do not include government subsidy payments, seller payments, or prepaid interest that does not meet the exception explained earlier under **Prepaid Interest.** Interest

includes prepayment penalties and late charges unless the late charges are for a specific mortgage service.

Note: *A cooperative housing corporation that receives any cash part of a patronage dividend from the National Consumer Cooperative Bank must reduce the interest to be reported on each tenant-stockholder's Form 1098 by a proportionate amount of the cash payment in the year the cooperative receives the cash payment. See Rev. Proc. 94-40, 1994-1 C.B. 711.*

Box 2.—Enter **points** paid on the purchase of the payer of record's principal residence. For an explanation of reportable points, see **Points** earlier.

Box 3.—Enter the total refund or credit of a prior year(s) overpayment of interest. See **Reimbursement of Overpaid Interest** earlier.

Box 4.—Enter any other item you wish to report to the payer, such as real estate taxes, insurance, or if you are a collection agent, the name of the person for whom you collected the interest. This box is optional and is provided only for your convenience. You do not have to report to the IRS any information provided in this box. You are not required to report the average balance of the mortgage.

Form 1099-A

File Form 1099-A, **Acquisition or Abandonment of Secured Property,** for each borrower if you lend money in connection with your trade or business and, in full or partial satisfaction of the debt, you acquire an interest in property that is security for the debt, or you have reason to know that the property has been abandoned. You need not be in the business of lending money to be subject to this reporting requirement.

Coordination With Form 1099-C.—If, in the same calendar year, a debt is canceled in connection with the acquisition or abandonment of secured property and you would be required to file both Form 1099-A and **Form 1099-C,** Cancellation of Debt, you are required to file Form 1099-C only. You will meet your Form 1099-A filing requirement by making appropriate entries in boxes 5 and 7 on Form 1099-C. You may file both Forms 1099-A and 1099-C, but make no Form 1099-A entries in boxes 5 and 7 on Form 1099-C.

Property.—Property means real property (such as a personal residence), intangible property, or tangible personal property held for investment or used in a trade or business. No reporting is required for a loan made to an individual and secured by an interest in tangible personal property that is neither held for investment nor used in a trade or business. However, you must file Form 1099-A if the personal property is held for both personal use and either for use in a trade or business or for investment.

No reporting is required if the property securing the loan is located outside the United States and the borrower has

furnished the lender a statement, under penalties of perjury, that the borrower is an exempt foreign person (unless the lender knows that the statement is false).

Who Must File.—In addition to the general rule specified above, the following rules apply.

If there are **multiple owners** of undivided interests in a single loan, such as is the case in pools, fixed investment trusts, or other similar arrangements, the trustee, record owner, or person acting in a similar capacity must file Form 1099-A on behalf of all the owners of beneficial interests or participations. In this case, only one form for each borrower must be filed on behalf of all owners with respect to the loan. Similarly, in the case of bond issues, only the trustee or similar person is required to report.

A **governmental unit,** or any of its subsidiary agencies, that lends money secured by property must file Form 1099-A.

A **subsequent holder** of a loan is treated as the lender for purposes of the reporting requirement for events occurring after the loan is transferred to the new holder.

If **more than one person lends** money secured by property and one lender forecloses or otherwise acquires an interest in the property and the sale or other acquisition terminates, reduces, or otherwise impairs the other lenders' security interests in the property, the other lenders must file Form 1099-A for each of their loans. For example, if a first trust holder forecloses on a building, and the second trust holder knows or has reason to know of such foreclosure, the second trust holder must file Form 1099-A for the second trust even though no part of the second trust was satisfied by the proceeds of the foreclosure sale.

Abandonment.—An abandonment occurs when the objective facts and circumstances indicate that the borrower intended to and has permanently discarded the property from use. You have "reason to know" of an abandonment based on all the facts and circumstances concerning the status of the property. You will be deemed to know all the information that would have been discovered through a reasonable inquiry when, in the ordinary course of business, the lender becomes aware or should become aware of circumstances indicating that the property has been abandoned. If you expect to commence a foreclosure, execution, or similar sale within 3 months of the date you had reason to know that the property was abandoned, reporting is required as of the date you acquire an interest in the property or a third party purchases the property at such sale. If you expect to but do not commence such action within 3 months, the reporting requirement arises at the end of the 3-month period.

Statements to Borrowers.—For information about the requirement of furnishing a statement to the borrower, see part H under **General Instructions** earlier.

Page 11

Exhibit A-1 *(continued)*

Box 1.—Enter the date of your acquisition of the secured property or the date you first knew or had reason to know that the property was abandoned. An interest in the property generally is acquired on the earlier of the date title is transferred to the lender or the date possession and the burdens and benefits of ownership are transferred to the lender. If an objection period is provided by law, use the date the objection period expires. If you purchase the property at a sale held to satisfy the debt, such as at a foreclosure or execution sale, use the later of the date of sale or the date the borrower's right of redemption expires. Please use the following format to indicate the date: MMDDYY. For example, for January 7, 1995, enter 010795.

For an abandonment, enter the date you knew or had reason to know that the property was abandoned unless you expect to commence a foreclosure, execution, or similar action within 3 months, as explained earlier. If a third party purchases the property at a foreclosure, execution, or similar sale, the property is treated as abandoned, and you have reason to know of its abandonment on the date of sale.

Box 2.—Enter the balance of the debt outstanding at the time the interest in the property was acquired or on the date you first knew or had reason to know that the property was abandoned. Include only unpaid principal on the original debt. Do not include accrued interest or foreclosure costs.

Box 3.—Make no entry is this box.

Box 4.—For a foreclosure, execution, or similar sale, enter the fair market value of the property. Generally, the gross foreclosure bid price is considered to be the fair market value. If an abandonment or voluntary conveyance to the lender in lieu of foreclosure occurred and you checked "Yes" in box 5, enter the appraised value of the property. Otherwise, make no entry in this box.

Box 5.—Enter an "X" in the applicable box to indicate whether the borrower was personally liable for repayment of the debt at the time the debt was created or, if modified, at the time of the last modification.

Box 6.—Enter a general description of the property. For real property, generally you must enter the address of the property, or, if the address does not sufficiently identify the property, enter the section, lot, and block. For personal property, enter the applicable type, make, and model. For example, describe a car as "Car—1995 Buick Regal." Use a category such as "Office Equipment" to describe more than one piece of personal property, such as six desks and seven typewriters. Enter "CCC" for crops forfeited on Commodity Credit Corporation loans.

Form 1099-B

Any person, including a governmental unit and any subsidiary agency, doing business as a broker or barter exchange must file

Page 12

Form 1099-B, **Proceeds From Broker and Barter Exchange Transactions,** for each person (a) for whom the broker has sold (including short sales) stocks, bonds, commodities, regulated futures contracts, foreign currency contracts, forward contracts, debt instruments, etc., or (b) who exchanged property or services through the barter exchange.

Note: *Report real estate transactions on Form 1099-S discussed later.*

Brokers

The term **broker** means a person who, in the ordinary course of a trade or business, stands ready to effect sales to be made by others. A corporation is a broker if it regularly stands ready to redeem its stock or retire its debt. However, if there are no facts that indicate otherwise, a corporation that purchases odd-lot shares from its stockholders is not a broker. If you manage a farm for someone else, you are not considered a broker.

For a sale of securities through a "cash on delivery" or similar account, only the broker that receives the gross proceeds from the sale against delivery of the securities sold is required to report the sale. However, if such broker's customer is a "second-party broker" that is an exempt recipient, only the second-party broker is required to report the sale.

If the proceeds of a sale are paid in convertible foreign currency, the amount to be reported must be converted into U.S. dollars. You may use the exchange rate on the sales date or the exchange rate on the last business day of the reporting period in which the sale occurs.

Brokers must report each transaction (other than regulated futures or foreign currency contracts) on a separate Form 1099-B. Transactions involving regulated futures or foreign currency contracts are to be reported on an aggregate basis.

To report substitute payments in lieu of dividends and tax-exempt interest, as required by section 6045(d), do not use Form 1099-B. See **Box 8** under **Form 1099-MISC** later.

Form 8308, Report of a Sale or Exchange of Certain Partnership Interests, does not have to be filed if Form 1099-B is required for the transfer of the partnership interest.

No return is required by brokers for:

1. Sales by exempt recipients, including corporations, charitable organizations, individual retirement plans, the United States, a state and political subdivisions.

2. Sales initiated by dealers in securities and financial institutions.

3. Sales by certain custodians and trustees.

4. Sales at issue price of interests in certain regulated investment companies.

5. Obligor payments on:

a. Nontransferable obligations, such as savings bonds or CDs.

b. Obligations for which gross proceeds are reported on other Forms 1099, such as

stripped coupons issued prior to July 1, 1982.

c. Retirement of short-term obligations with original issue discount (reported on Form 1099-INT). However, Form 1099-B is required for the retirement of short-term state obligations having no original issue discount.

d. Callable demand obligations that have no premium or discount.

6. Sales of foreign currency unless under a forward or regulated futures contract that requires delivery of foreign currency.

7. Sales of fractional shares of stock if gross proceeds are less than $20.

8. Retirements of book-entry or registered form obligations if no interim transfers have occurred.

9. Exempt foreign persons.

10. Sales of Commodity Credit Corporation certificates.

11. Spot or forward sales of **agricultural commodities.** Agricultural commodities include grain, feed, livestock, meat, oil seed, timber, or fiber. A spot sale is a sale that results in almost immediate delivery of a commodity. A forward sale is a sale under a forward contract.

However, sales of agricultural commodities under a regulated futures contract, sales of derivative interests in agricultural commodities, and sales of receipts for agricultural commodities issued by a designated warehouse are reportable. A designated warehouse is a warehouse, depository, or other similar entity designated by a commodity exchange in which or out of which a particular type of agricultural commodity is deliverable to satisfy a regulated futures contract. Sales of warehouse receipts issued by any other warehouse are not reportable.

12. Excepted sales designated in a revenue ruling or revenue procedure. The sale of a **precious metal** (gold, silver, platinum, or palladium) in any form that may be used to satisfy a Commodity Futures Trading Commission (CFTC)-approved regulated futures contract (RFC) is an excepted sale if the quantity, by weight or by number of items, is less than the minimum required to satisfy a CFTC-approved RFC. A sale of a precious metal in any form that cannot be used to satisfy a CFTC-approved RFC is an excepted sale.

For example, Form 1099-B is not required to be filed for the sale of a single gold coin in the form and quality deliverable in satisfaction of a CFTC-approved contract since all CFTC contracts for gold coins currently call for delivery of at least 25 coins.

Sales of precious metals for a single customer during a 24-hour period must be aggregated and treated as a single sale to determine if this exception applies. This exception does not apply if the broker knows or has reason to know that a customer, either alone or with a related person, is engaging in sales to avoid information reporting.

Barter Exchanges

A **barter exchange** is any person with members or clients who contract either with each other or with such person to trade or barter property or services either directly or through such person. The term does not include arrangements that provide solely for the informal exchange of similar services on a noncommercial basis. Persons who are not a barter exchange but who trade services do not file Form 1099-B. However, they may be required to file Form 1099-MISC.

Barter exchanges must report each transaction involving noncorporate members or clients of a barter exchange on a separate Form 1099-B. Transactions involving corporate members or clients of a barter exchange may be reported on an aggregate basis.

In the recipient area of the forms, enter information about the member or client that provided the property or services in the exchange.

No return is required by barter exchanges for:

1. Exchanges through a barter exchange having fewer than 100 transactions during the calendar year.

2. Exempt foreign persons.

Brokers and Barter Exchanges

Statements to Recipients.—For information about the requirement to furnish a statement to the proceeds recipient, see part H under **General Instructions** earlier.

2nd TIN Not.—You may enter an "X" in this box if you were notified by the IRS twice within 3 calendar years that the payee provided an incorrect taxpayer identification number (TIN). If you mark this box, you will comply with a safe harbor due diligence requirement of Temporary Regulations section 35a.9999-3, Q/A-89, and the IRS will not send you any further notices about this account. Also see Regulations section 301.6724-1(g).

Box 1a.—For broker transactions, enter the trade date of the sale or exchange. For barter exchanges, enter the date that cash, property, a credit, or scrip is actually or constructively received. Please use the following format to indicate the date: MMDDYY. For example, for January 7, 1995, enter 010795. For aggregate reporting, no entry is required.

Box 1b.—For transactional reporting by brokers, enter the CUSIP (Committee on Uniform Security Identification Procedures) number of the obligation.

Box 2.—Enter the gross proceeds from any disposition of securities (including short sales), commodities, or forward contracts. To determine gross proceeds, you may take into account commissions and option premiums if this treatment is consistent with your books. You may not take into account state and local transfer taxes. Check the applicable box to indicate which amount has been reported to the IRS. Do not include amounts shown in boxes 6 through 9. Any accrued interest on bonds sold between payment dates (or on a payment date) should not be included in this box. Instead, report this accrued interest on Form 1099-INT. A loss from a closing transaction on a forward contract must be shown as a negative amount by enclosing it in parentheses.

Box 3.—Enter the gross amounts received by a member or client of a barter exchange for goods or services. This includes cash received, property or services received, a credit on your books, or scrip issued. **Do not report negative amounts.**

Box 4.—Enter backup withholding. For example, persons who have not furnished their TIN to you in the manner required are subject to withholding at a 31% rate on certain amounts required to be reported on this form.

Box 5.—For broker transactions, enter a brief description of the disposition item, e.g., 100 shares of XYZ Corp. stock. If necessary, abbreviate the description so that it fits within box 5. For regulated futures contracts and forward contracts, enter "RFC" or other appropriate description and **any amount subject to backup withholding,** under Temporary Regulations section 35a.9999-3, Q/A-23. **Note:** *The amount withheld in these situations is to be included in box 4.*

For bartering transactions, show the services or property provided.

Box 6.—Enter the profit or (loss) realized by the customer on closed regulated futures or foreign currency contracts in 1995. For more information on reporting foreign currency contracts, see Temporary Regulations section 35a.9999-3, Q/A-26.

Box 7.—Enter the unrealized profit or (loss) on open regulated futures or foreign currency contracts at the end of 1994.

Box 8.—Enter the unrealized profit or (loss) on open regulated futures or foreign currency contracts as of December 31, 1995.

Box 9.—Enter the aggregate profit or (loss) for the year from regulated futures or foreign currency contracts. Use boxes 6, 7, and 8 to figure the aggregate profit or (loss).

Form 1099-C

Caution: *The following instructions (except those under* **Coordination With Form 1099-A** *and related instructions under* **Box 5** *and* **Box 7** *later) are based on temporary regulations under section 6050P issued in December 1993. Final regulations under section 6050P are expected to be issued in early 1995. For debts discharged before the effective date of those final regulations, no penalties will be imposed if you do not report:*

1. A debt discharged in bankruptcy (under title 11 of the U.S. Code).

2. A debt discharged as the result of the expiration of the statute of limitations for collection of the debt.

3. Any amount other than principal for a debt that arose in connection with a lending transaction. A lending transaction is a transaction in which a lender extends credit, including revolving credit, to a borrower.

4. A debt discharged for a person other than the primary (or first-named) debtor in the case of multiple debtors, for debts incurred before January 1, 1995.

File Form 1099-C, **Cancellation of Debt,** for each debtor for which you canceled (or discharged) a debt (or indebtedness) owed to you of $600 or more and you are a financial institution, a credit union, or a Federal Government agency (including one of the three agencies listed under **Who Must File** below). You must file even though the debtor may not be subject to tax on the canceled debt. That is, you are not required to determine whether the debtor qualifies for exclusion under section 108. For example, debts discharged in bankruptcy are reportable.

You are not required to aggregate multiple discharges of debt of less than $600 during a year unless the separate discharges are under a plan to evade the Form 1099-C reporting requirements.

File Form 1099-C if the debtor is an individual, corporation, partnership, trust, estate, association, or company. Backup withholding does not apply.

Coordination With Form 1099-A.—If, in the same calendar year, a debt is canceled in connection with the acquisition or abandonment of secured property and you would be required to file both Form 1099-C and **Form 1099-A,** Acquisition or Abandonment of Secured Property, you are required to file Form 1099-C only. You will meet your Form 1099-A filing requirement by making appropriate entries in boxes 5 and 7 on Form 1099-C. You may file both Forms 1099-A and 1099-C, but make no Form 1099-A entries in boxes 5 and 7 on Form 1099-C. See the instructions for Form 1099-A earlier and **Box 5** and **Box 7** later.

Who Must File.—File Form 1099-C if you are a financial institution described in section 581 or 591(a) (such as a domestic bank, trust company, building and loan or savings and loan association); a credit union; a Federal executive agency defined in section 6050M, the Federal Deposit Insurance Corporation (FDIC), the Resolution Trust Corporation (RTC), the National Credit Union Administration (NCUA), or any successor or subunit of a Federal executive agency, FDIC, RTC, or NCUA. Also file Form 1099-C if you are a corporation that is a subsidiary of a financial institution or credit union, but only if, because of your affiliation, you are subject to supervision and examination by a Federal or state regulatory agency.

Debt Defined.—A debt is any amount owed to you including principal, interest, penalties, administrative costs, and fines, to the extent they are indebtedness under section 61(a)(12). The amount of debt discharged or canceled may be all or only part of the total amount owed.

When Is a Debt Canceled or Discharged?—A debt is canceled or discharged when an identifiable event

Page 13

Exhibit A-1 *(continued)*

occurs that indicates the debt will never have to be paid by the debtor, taking into account all the facts and circumstances.

An **identifiable event** includes, but is not limited to:

1. A discharge of a debt under title 11 of the U.S. Code (bankruptcy),

2. An agreement between the creditor and the debtor to cancel all or part of a debt (including an agreement that results in an exchange under section 1001), if the last event necessary to cancel the debt has occurred, or

3. A cancellation or extinguishment of the debt by operation of law that makes the debt unenforceable (for example, the statute of limitations for collection of the debt expires).

A bookkeeping entry, such as a deduction for book or regulatory reporting purposes or a partial or full bad debt deduction for tax purposes, is not, alone, an identifiable event. However, such bookkeeping entry is one of the facts and circumstances to take into account to determine if a discharge or cancellation has occurred.

Collection activity by the creditor is another one of the facts and circumstances to take into account to determine if a discharge or cancellation has occurred. In determining that part of a debt is canceled, disregard collection activity on the remaining part of the debt.

Multiple Debtors.—If you cancel a debt with more than one debtor, you must file Form 1099-C for each debtor that had a debt of $600 or more canceled. If the multiple debtors are jointly and severally liable on the debt, report the entire amount of the canceled debt on each debtor's Form 1099-C.

Recordkeeping.—If you are required to file Form 1099-C, you must retain a copy of that form or be able to reconstruct the data for at least 4 years from the due date of the return.

Requesting TINs.—You must make all reasonable efforts to obtain the taxpayer identification number (TIN) of the person whose debt was canceled. You may obtain the TIN when the debt is incurred. If you do not obtain the TIN before the debt is canceled, you must request the debtor's TIN. Your request must clearly notify the debtor that the Internal Revenue Service requires the debtor to furnish its TIN and that failure to furnish such TIN subjects the debtor to a $50 penalty imposed by the IRS. No particular form is required to request the TIN, but if you use Form W-9, you will satisfy the reasonable efforts requirement. A debtor is not required to certify his or her TIN under penalties of perjury.

Statements to Debtors.—Furnish each debtor with Copy B of Form 1099-C or a substitute statement that complies with the requirements of Pub. 1179. See part **H** under **General Instructions** earlier. You have furnished a statement to the debtor if it is mailed to the debtor's last known address.

Box 1.—Enter the date the debt was canceled. See **When Is a Debt Canceled**

Page 14

or **Discharged?** earlier. Use the format MMDDYY to indicate the date. For example, for January 7, 1995, enter 010795.

Box 2.—Enter the amount of the canceled debt. See **Debt Defined** earlier.

Box 3.—Enter any interest included in the canceled debt in box 2.

Box 4.—Enter any penalties, fines, or administrative costs included in the canceled debt in box 2.

Box 5.—Enter a description of the origin of the debt, such as student loan, mortgage, or credit card expenditure. Be as specific as possible. If you are filing a combined Form 1099-C and 1099-A, also enter a description of the property.

Box 6.—Enter an "X" in the checkbox if the debt was discharged in bankruptcy, if known.

Box 7.—Make an entry in this box only if you are filing a combined Form 1099-C and 1099-A. For a foreclosure, execution, or similar sale, enter the fair market value of the property. Generally, the gross foreclosure bid price is considered to be the fair market value. If an abandonment or voluntary conveyance to the lender in lieu of foreclosure occurred, enter the appraised value of the property.

Form 1099-DIV

File Form 1099-DIV, **Dividends and Distributions,** for each person (a) to whom you have paid gross dividends and other distributions on stock (box 1a) of $10 or more, (b) for whom you have withheld and paid any foreign tax on dividends and other distributions on stock, (c) for whom you have withheld any Federal income tax under the backup withholding rules, or (d) to whom you paid $600 or more as part of a liquidation.

Section 404(k) Dividend.—Report on Form 1099-DIV dividends distributed under section 404(k) on stock held by an employee stock ownership plan (ESOP) or a tax credit ESOP. However, if a section 404(k) distribution is made in the same year as a total distribution, the entire amount should be reported as an amount includible in income on Form 1099-R.

Exceptions.—You are not required to file Form 1099-DIV for payments made to certain payees including a corporation, a tax-exempt organization, an individual retirement arrangement (IRA), a U.S. agency, a state, the District of Columbia, a U.S. possession, or a registered securities or commodities dealer.

Dividends.—If you make a payment that may be a dividend, but you are unable to determine whether any part of the payment is a dividend by the time you must file Form 1099-DIV, the entire payment must be reported as a dividend. See regulations under section 6042 for a definition of dividends.

Note: Certain distributions commonly referred to as "dividends" are actually interest and are to be reported on Form 1099-INT. These include so-called

"dividends" on deposit or on share accounts in cooperative banks, credit unions, domestic building and loan associations, domestic and Federal savings and loan associations, and mutual savings banks.

An exempt-interest dividend from a regulated investment company retains its tax-exempt status and is not reported on Form 1099-DIV or 1099-INT.

Substitute Payments in Lieu of Dividends.—For payments received by a broker on behalf of a customer in lieu of dividends as a result of the transfer of a customer's securities for use in a short sale, see **Box 8** under **Form 1099-MISC** later.

RICs.—If a regulated investment company (RIC) declares a dividend in October, November, or December payable to shareholders of record on a specified date in such a month, the dividends are treated as paid by the RIC and received by the shareholders on December 31 of such year as long as the dividends are actually paid by the RIC during January of the following year. Such dividends should be reported on Form 1099-DIV for the year preceding the January they are actually paid. See section 852(b)(7).

If such a dividend paid in January is subject to backup withholding, it must be withheld when the dividend is actually paid. Therefore, backup withhold in January, deposit the withholding when appropriate, and reflect it on Form 945 for the year withheld. However, since the dividend is reportable on Form 1099-DIV in the prior year, the related backup withholding is also reportable on the prior year Form 1099-DIV.

Restricted Stock.—For information about reporting dividends on restricted stock, see Rev. Procs. 80-11, 1980-1 C.B. 616, and 83-38, 1983-1 C.B. 773, and Rev. Rul. 83-22, 1983-1 C.B. 17.

Statements to Recipients.—For an explanation of the requirement to furnish an official form to recipients in person or by statement mailing, see part **H** under **General Instructions** earlier. Also see Pub. 1179.

2nd TIN Not.—You may enter an "X" in this box if you were notified by the IRS twice within 3 calendar years that the payee provided an incorrect taxpayer identification number (TIN). If you mark this box, you will comply with a safe harbor due diligence requirement of Temporary Regulations section 35a.9999-3, Q/A-89, and the IRS will not send you any further notices about this account. Also see Regulations section 301.6724-1(g).

Box 1a.—Enter gross dividends, including those from money market funds, and other distributions on stock. Include reinvested dividends as gross dividends. Include all amounts shown in boxes 1b, 1c, 1d, and 1e. Do not include in box 1a amounts reported in boxes 5 and 6.

Box 1b.—Enter ordinary dividends. Also include this amount in box 1a.

Box 1c.—Enter capital gain distributions. Also include this amount in box 1a.

Exhibit A-1   *(continued)*

Box 1d.—Enter nontaxable distributions, if determinable. Also include this amount in box 1a. (File **Form 5452,** Corporate Report of Nondividend Distributions, if you pay nontaxable distributions to shareholders.)

Box 1e.—Enter the stockholder's pro rata share of certain amounts deductible by a nonpublicly offered regulated investment company in computing its taxable income. This amount is includible in the stockholder's gross income under section 67(c) and must also be included in box 1a.

Box 2.—Enter backup withholding. For example, persons who have not furnished their TIN to you in the manner required are subject to withholding at a 31% rate on certain dividend payments reported on this form.

Box 3.—Enter any foreign tax withheld and paid on dividends and other distributions on stock. A regulated investment company must report only the amount it elects to pass through to the shareholder. Report this amount in U.S. dollars.

Box 4.—Enter the name of the foreign country or U.S. possession to which the withheld tax applies.

Note: *Boxes 5 and 6 apply only to corporations in partial or complete liquidation.*

Box 5.—Enter cash distributed as part of a liquidation. Do not include this amount in box 1a.

Box 6.—Enter noncash distributions made as part of a liquidation. Show the fair market value as of the date of distribution. Do not include this amount in box 1a.

S Corporations

Box 1a.—Report as dividends on Form 1099-DIV only distributions made during 1995 out of accumulated earnings and profits. See section 1368 for more information.

Form 1099-G

File Form 1099-G, **Certain Government Payments,** if you have made certain payments as a unit of a Federal, state, or local government.

Statements to Recipients.—Furnish a copy of Form 1099-G or a substitute statement to each recipient, except as explained below under **Box 2.** Also see part H under **General Instructions** earlier.

Box 1.—Enter payments of $10 or more in **unemployment compensation** including Railroad Retirement Board payments for unemployment.

Box 2.—Enter **refunds, credits, or offsets of state or local income tax** of $10 or more you made to recipients. If recipients deducted the tax paid to a state or local government on their Federal income tax returns, any refunds, credits, or offsets may be taxable to them. If you can determine that the recipient did not claim itemized deductions on the recipient's Federal income tax return for the tax year giving rise to the refund, credit, or offset you are not required to furnish a copy of Form 1099-G or a statement to the recipient. However, you must file Form 1099-G with the IRS in all cases.

A tax on dividends, a tax on net gains from the sale or exchange of a capital asset, and a tax on the net taxable income of an unincorporated business are taxes on gain or profit rather than on gross receipts. Therefore, they are income taxes, and any refund, credit, or offset of $10 or more of these taxes is reportable on Form 1099-G. In the case of the dividends tax and the capital gains tax, if you determine that the recipient did not itemize deductions, as explained above, you are not required to furnish a statement to the recipient. However, in the case of the tax on unincorporated businesses, you must furnish a statement to the recipient in all cases, as this is a tax that applies exclusively to income from a trade or business. See the instructions for box 8 and Rev. Rul. 86-140, 1986-2 C.B. 195.

If you pay interest of $600 or more on the refund, you must file Form 1099-INT and furnish a statement to the recipient. For interest payments of less than $600, if you wish you may enter the amount with an appropriate designation such as "Interest Income" in the blank box on the statement to the recipient.

Box 3.—No entry is required in box 3 if the refund, credit, or offset is for the 1994 tax year. If it is for any other tax year, enter the **year** for which the refund, credit, or offset was made in this box. Also, if the refunds, credits, or offsets are for more than 1 tax year, report the amount for each year on a separate Form 1099-G. Use the format "YYYY" to make the entry in this box. For example, enter 1993, not '93.

Box 4.—Enter **backup withholding.** For example, persons who have not furnished their TIN to you become subject to withholding at a 31% rate on payments required to be reported in box 6 or 7 on this form.

Box 5.—Make no entries in this box.

Box 6.—Enter any amount of a **taxable grant** administered by a Federal, state, or local program to provide subsidized energy financing or grants for projects designed to conserve or produce energy, but only with respect to section 38 property or a dwelling unit located in the United States. Also report amounts of other taxable grants of $600 or more. A Federal grant is ordinarily taxable unless stated otherwise in the legislation authorizing the grant. Do not report scholarship or fellowship grants. See **Scholarships** under **Form 1099-MISC** later.

Box 7.—Enter U.S.D.A. **agricultural subsidy** payments made to recipients during the year. If you are a nominee that received subsidy payments for another person, file Form 1099-G to report the actual owner of the payments, and report the amount of the payments in box 7.

Box 8.—If the amount in box 2 is a refund, credit, or offset attributable to an income tax that applies exclusively to income from a trade or business and is not a tax of general application, enter an "X" in this box.

Form 1099-INT

File Form 1099-INT, **Interest Income,** for each person (1) to whom you paid amounts reportable in boxes 1 and 3 of at least $10 (except for the $600 limit for interest paid in the course of your trade or business described in the instructions below in **Box 1**), (2) for whom you withheld and paid any foreign tax on interest, or (3) from whom you withheld any Federal income tax under the backup withholding rules regardless of the amount of the payment.

Only report interest payments made in the course of your trade or business including Federal, state, and local government agencies and activities deemed nonprofit, or for which you were a nominee/middleman.

Exceptions.—You are not required to file Form 1099-INT for payments made to certain payees including a corporation, a tax-exempt organization, an individual retirement arrangement (IRA), a U.S. agency, a state, the District of Columbia, a U.S. possession, or a registered securities or commodities dealer.

Note: *Do not report tax-exempt or tax-deferred interest, such as interest on municipal bonds or interest that is earned but not distributed from an IRA.*

An exempt-interest dividend from a regulated investment company retains its tax-exempt status and is not reported on Form 1099-INT or 1099-DIV.

When Payment Made.—Generally, interest is paid when it is credited or set apart for a person without any substantial limitation or restriction as to time, manner, or condition of payment. The interest must be made available so that it may be drawn on at any time and its receipt brought within the control and disposition of the person.

For payments made on obligations subject to transactional reporting (e.g., savings bonds, interest coupons, and other demand obligations), interest is paid at the time the obligation is presented for payment. For example, interest on a coupon detached from a bond is paid when it is presented for payment.

Successor/Predecessor Corporation.—A successor corporation and a predecessor corporation may agree that the successor corporation will file one Form 1099-INT for each payee combining the reportable interest paid by both corporations (under section 6049). If the two corporations do not agree, or if other requirements described below are not met, the predecessor must file Forms 1099-INT to report the interest payments it made during the year, and the successor must file Forms 1099-INT to report its own payments.

The combined reporting procedure is available only when all the following conditions are met:

1. The successor corporation acquires substantially all the assets and assumes substantially all the liabilities of the predecessor corporation.

Page 15

Exhibit A-1 *(continued)*

2. During the year of acquisition, but before the acquisition, the predecessor made reportable interest payments to payees.

3. During the year of acquisition, but after the acquisition, the predecessor did not make any reportable interest payments.

Agreement.—The predecessor and successor must agree that the successor assumes the predecessor's entire obligation to file Forms 1099-INT for reportable interest payments made in the year of acquisition. If they so agree and if the successor satisfies the predecessor's obligation, the predecessor is relieved of the obligation to file Forms 1099-INT.

Combined Form 1099-INT.—The Form 1099-INT filed by the successor for each payee must include the reportable interest payments made by the predecessor in the acquisition year and the reportable interest payments made by the successor in that year. Any backup withholding also must be combined on the form. When providing Form 1099-INT, or an acceptable substitute form, to the interest recipient, the successor may include additional information explaining the aggregate reporting of the interest.

Statement required.—By the due date of the Forms 1099-INT, the successor must file a statement containing (1) an indication that Forms 1099-INT are being filed on a combined basis under Rev. Proc. 90-57 and (2) the name, address, and taxpayer identification numbers (TINs) of both the successor and predecessor corporations. This statement must be sent separately from the Form 1099-INT to: IRS-Martinsburg Computing Center, P.O. Box 1359, Attn: Chief, Magnetic Media 2, Martinsburg, WV 25401-1359.

For more information, see Rev. Proc. 90-57, 1990-2 C.B. 641.

Statements to Recipients.—For an explanation of the requirement to furnish an official form to recipients in person or by statement mailing, see part **H** under **General Instructions** earlier. Also see Pub. 1179. If you have furnished Forms 1099-INT to a recipient for amounts received during the year at the time of the transaction, such as you might have done for window transactions, do not include these same amounts in a Form 1099-INT furnished to the same recipient for other payments during the year.

2nd TIN Not.—You may enter an "X" in this box if you were notified by the IRS twice within 3 calendar years that the payee provided an incorrect TIN. If you mark this box, you will comply with a safe harbor due diligence requirement of Temporary Regulations section 35a.9999-3, Q/A-89, and the IRS will not send you any further notices about this account. Also see Regulations section 301.6724-1(g).

Payer's RTN (optional).—If you are a financial institution that wishes to participate in the program for direct deposit of refunds of electronic filers, you may enter your routing and transit number (RTN).

Page 16

Box 1.—Enter interest not included in box 3. Include amounts, whether or not designated as interest, that are paid or credited to any person's account by savings and loan associations, mutual savings banks not having capital stock represented by shares, building and loan associations, cooperative banks, homestead associations, credit unions, or similar organizations. Include interest on bank deposits, accumulated dividends paid by a life insurance company, indebtedness (including bonds, debentures, notes and certificates other than those of the U.S. Treasury) issued in registered form or of a type offered to the public, or from which you withheld Federal income tax or foreign tax. **Also include interest paid in the course of your trade or business** not meeting these criteria, such as interest on delayed death benefits paid by a life insurance company, or interest on a state or Federal income tax refund, if the interest totals $600 or more for any person. In addition, report interest accrued to a REMIC regular interest holder or paid to a CDO holder, as explained below.

Include in box 1 any accrued interest on bonds sold between interest dates (or on a payment date).

Also show original issue discount on short-term obligations of 1 year or less and interest on all bearer certificates of deposit.

Do not include in box 1 interest on tax-free covenant bonds, which is reportable on **Form 1042-S,** Foreign Person's U.S. Source Income Subject to Withholding, or dividends from money market funds, which are reportable on Form 1099-DIV. Also, do not include any description in box 1. If you wish to show a description, use the blank box above box 1.

Box 2.—Enter interest or principal forfeited because of an early withdrawal of time deposits, such as an early withdrawal from a CD, that is deductible from gross income by the recipient. Do not reduce the amount reported in box 1 by the amount of the forfeiture. For detailed instructions for determining the amount of forfeiture deductible by the depositor, see Rev. Ruls. 75-20, 1975-1 C.B. 29, and 75-21, 1975-1 C.B. 367.

Box 3.—Enter interest on U.S. Savings Bonds, Treasury bills, Treasury notes, and Treasury bonds. Do not include this amount in box 1.

If you make payment on a U.S. Savings Bond or other U.S. obligation on which interest is reportable, enter **your** name, address, and Federal identification number on Forms 1099-INT and 1096, not those of the U.S. Treasury Department or the Bureau of Public Debt.

Box 4.—Enter backup withholding. For example, persons who have not furnished their TIN to you in the manner required become subject to withholding at a 31% rate on payments required to be reported in box 1 (which may be reduced by the amount reported in box 2) and box 3 on this form.

Box 5.—Enter any foreign tax withheld and paid on interest. Report this amount in U.S. dollars.

Box 6.—Enter the name of the foreign country or U.S. possession to which the withheld tax applies.

REMICs and Issuers of Collateralized Debt Obligations

Real estate mortgage investment conduits (REMICs), issuers of collateralized debt obligations (CDOs), and any broker or middleman who holds as a nominee a REMIC regular interest or CDO must file Form 1099-INT to report interest of $10 or more, other than original issue discount (OID), accrued to a REMIC regular interest holder during the year or paid to the holder of a CDO. If you are also reporting OID, this interest and the OID can be reported on Form 1099-OID. It is not necessary to file both Forms 1099-INT and 1099-OID. See **Form 1099-OID** later.

You are not required to file or issue Form 1099-INT for exempt recipients including the following holders of a REMIC regular interest or a CDO:

1. A corporation.

2. A broker.

3. A middleman/nominee.

4. A financial institution.

5. An IRA.

6. A tax-exempt organization.

For additional exempt recipients, see Regulations section 1.6049-7(c).

Box 1.—Report in box 1 the amount of interest, other than OID, accrued to each REMIC regular interest holder or paid to a CDO holder for the period during the year for which the return is made. If you are a single-class REMIC (as defined in Temporary Regulations section 1.67-3T(a)(2)(ii)), include in box 1 the regular interest holder's share of investment expenses of the REMIC for the year.

Statements to Holders.—For each Form 1099-INT you are required to file, you must furnish a statement to the REMIC regular interest or CDO holder identified on the form. The statement must contain the information shown on Form 1099-INT, including the legend shown on Copy B of the official Form 1099-INT, and an indication that these items are being furnished to the IRS. The statement must also show the information specified in Regulations section 1.6049-7(f)(2)(i). In addition, the statement furnished by a REMIC must show, for each calendar quarter, the information specified in Regulations section 1.6049-7(f)(3). Also see Regulations section 1.6049-7(f)(3)(ii) for information that may be required to be reported to a real estate investment trust (REIT) that holds a regular interest.

A single-class REMIC (as defined in Temporary Regulations section 1.67-3T(a)(2)(ii)) must include in the statement the investment expenses paid or accrued during each calendar quarter by the REMIC for which the REMIC is allowed

Exhibit A-1 *(continued)*

a deduction under section 212 and the proportionate share of those investment expenses allocated to the regular interest holder.

The statement must be furnished to holders by **March 15.** To meet the statement requirement, you may furnish a copy of Form 1099-INT and a separate statement containing the additional information to the REMIC regular interest or CDO holder.

For information about reporting income to REMIC residual interest holders, see the instructions on **Schedule Q (Form 1066),** Quarterly Notice to Residual Interest Holder of REMIC Taxable Income or Net Loss Allocation.

Form 8811 and Reporting by Brokers or Middlemen.—REMICs and issuers of CDOs must also file **Form 8811,** Information Return for Real Estate Mortgage Investment Conduits (REMICs) and Issuers of Collateralized Debt Obligations, within 30 days after the startup day of the REMIC or issue date of a CDO. The IRS will use the information on Forms 8811 to publish **Pub. 938,** Real Estate Mortgage Investment Conduits (REMICs) Reporting Information, for use by certain brokers, middlemen, corporations, and others specified in Regulations section 1.6049-7(e)(4).

For the requirements that a REMIC or CDO issuer or a broker or middleman who holds a REMIC regular interest or a CDO furnish certain information on request, see Regulations sections 1.6049-7(e) and 1.6049-7(f)(7).

Form 1099-MISC

File Form 1099-MISC, **Miscellaneous Income,** for each person to whom you have paid (1) at least $10 in royalties or broker payments in lieu of dividends or tax-exempt interest (see **Box 8**), (2) at least $600 in rents, services (including parts and materials), prizes and awards, other income payments, and medical and health care payments, or (3) any fishing boat proceeds. In addition, use Form 1099-MISC to report that you made direct sales of at least $5,000 of consumer products to a buyer for resale. You must also file Form 1099-MISC for each person from whom you have withheld any Federal income tax under the backup withholding rules regardless of the amount of the payment. Report only payments made in the course of your trade or business, including those made by Federal, state, or local government agencies and nonprofit organizations.

Caution: *Be sure to report payments in the proper box because the IRS uses this information to determine whether the recipient has properly reported the payment. Generally, amounts reportable in box 7 are subject to self-employment tax. If payments are not subject to this tax and they are not reportable elsewhere on Form 1099-MISC, report the payments in box 3.*

Trade or Business.—Report payments only if you are engaged in a trade or business when payments are made in the course of such trade or business. Thus, personal payments are not reportable. You are engaged in a trade or business if you operate for gain or profit. However, nonprofit organizations are considered to be engaged in a trade or business and are subject to the reporting requirement. Nonprofit organizations subject to the reporting requirements include trusts of qualified pension or profit-sharing plans of employers, certain organizations exempt from tax under section 501(c) or (d), and farmers' cooperatives that are exempt from tax under section 521. Payments by Federal, state, or local government agencies are also reportable.

Exceptions.—Some payments are not required to be reported on Form 1099-MISC, although they may be taxable to the recipient. Payments for which a **Form 1099-MISC is not required** include: (1) payments to a corporation, except those required to be reported in boxes 6 and 8, (2) payments for merchandise, (3) payments of rent to real estate agents, (4) wages paid to employees (report on Form W-2), (5) business travel allowances paid to employees (may be reportable on Form W-2), and (6) PS 58 costs (report on Form 1099-R). See below for additional payments not reportable on Form 1099-MISC.

Fees paid to informants.—A payment to an informant as an award, fee, or reward for information about criminal activity is not required to be reported if the payment is made by a Federal, state, or local government agency, or by a nonprofit organization exempt from tax under section 501(c)(3) that makes the payment to further the charitable purpose of lessening the burdens of government. For more information, see Regulations section 1.6041-3(n).

Scholarships.—*Do not* use Form 1099-MISC to report scholarship or fellowship grants. Scholarship or fellowship grants that are taxable to the recipient because they are paid for teaching, research, or other services as a condition for receiving the grant are considered wages and must be reported on Form W-2. Other taxable scholarship or fellowship payments (to a degree or nondegree candidate) are not required to be reported by you to the IRS on any form. See Notice 87-31, 1987-1 C.B. 475, for more information.

Deceased Employee's Wages Paid to Estate or Beneficiary.—If an employee dies during the year, you must report on Form 1099-MISC the accrued wages, vacation pay, and other compensation paid after the date of death. If you made the payment in the same year the employee died, you must withhold social security and Medicare taxes on the payment and report them only as social security and Medicare wages on the employee's Form W-2 to ensure proper social security and Medicare credit is received. On the Form W-2, show the payment as social security wages (box 3) and Medicare wages and tips (box 5) and the social security and Medicare taxes withheld in boxes 4 and 6; **do not show**

the payment in box 1 of Form W-2. If you made the payment after the year of death, do not report it on Form W-2, and do not withhold social security and Medicare taxes.

Whether the payment is made in the year of death or after the year of death, you also must report it on Form 1099-MISC for the payment to the estate or beneficiary. Report the payment in box 3 (rather than in box 7 as specified in Rev. Rul. 86-109, 1986-2 C.B. 196). Enter the name and TIN of the payment recipient on Form 1099-MISC. For example, if the recipient is an individual beneficiary, enter the name and SSN of the individual; if the recipient is the estate, enter the name and EIN of the estate. The general backup withholding rules apply to this payment.

However, death benefits from qualified and nonqualified deferred compensation plans paid to the estate or beneficiary of a deceased employee are not reportable on Form 1099-MISC but are reportable on Form 1099-R. See the instructions for **Form 1099-R** later in this publication.

Example.—Before Employee A's death on June 15, 1995, A was employed by Employer X and received $10,000 in wages on which Federal income tax of $1,500 was withheld. When A died, X owed A $2,000 in wages and $1,000 in accrued vacation pay. The total of $3,000 was paid to A's estate on July 20, 1995. Because X made the payment during the year of death, X must withhold social security and Medicare taxes on the $3,000 payment and must complete Form W-2 as follows:

● **Box 1**—10000.00 (does not include the $3,000 accrued wages and vacation pay)
● **Box 2**—1500.00
● **Box 3**—13000.00 (includes the $3,000 accrued wages and vacation pay)
● **Box 4**—806.00 (includes 6.2% of the $3,000 accrued wages and vacation pay)
● **Box 5**—13000.00 (includes the $3,000 accrued wages and vacation pay)
● **Box 6**—188.50 (includes 1.45% of the $3,000 accrued wages and vacation pay)

Employer X also must complete Form 1099-MISC as follows:

● **Box 3**—3000.00 (Even though amounts were withheld for social security and Medicare taxes, the gross amount is reported here.)

If Employer X made the payment after the year of death, the $3,000 would not be subject to social security and Medicare taxes and would not be shown on Form W-2. However, the employer would still file Form 1099-MISC.

Employee Business Expense Reimbursements.—Do not use Form 1099-MISC to report employee business expense reimbursements. Payments made to employees under a nonaccountable plan are reportable as wages on Form W-2. Generally, payments made to employees under an accountable plan are not reportable on Form W-2, except in certain cases when you pay per diem or mileage allowance. For more information, see the **Instructions for Form W-2 and Pub. 463,**

Page 17

Exhibit A-1   *(continued)*

Travel, Entertainment, and Gift Expenses. For information on reporting employee moving expense reimbursements on Form W-2, see the Instructions for Form W-2.

Transit Passes and Parking for Independent Contractors.—Although qualified transportation fringes cannot be provided to independent contractors, the de minimis fringe rules for transit passes and parking apply to independent contractors. Tokens or farecards that enable an independent contractor to commute on a public transit system (not including privately-operated van pools) are excludable from the independent contractor's gross income, and therefore not reportable on Form 1099-MISC, if the value of those tokens and farecards in any month is $21 or less. If the value of a pass provided in a month is greater than $21, the full value is includible in gross income and therefore reportable on Form 1099-MISC. The value of parking may be excludable from the gross income of an independent contractor, and therefore not reportable on Form 1099-MISC, if certain requirements are met. See Notice 94-3, 1994-1 C.B. 327, and Regulations sections 1.132-1(b)(2), and 1.132-6(a), (b), and (d)(1).

Independent Contractor or Employee.—Generally, payments to independent contractors are reportable on Form 1099-MISC in box 7. To help you determine whether someone is an independent contractor or an employee, see **Pub. 937**, Employment Taxes.

Note: *To qualify for relief under section 530 of the Revenue Act of 1978 as extended by section 269(c) of P.L. 97-248, about the employment tax status of independent contractors and employees, employers must file Form 1099-MISC. Additional requirements for relief are discussed in Rev. Proc. 85-18, 1985-1 C.B. 518. Also see Notice 87-19, 1987-1 C.B. 455, for special rules that may apply to certain skilled workers, such as engineers, designers, drafters, computer programmers, and systems analysts, and Rev. Rul. 87-41, 1987-1 C.B. 296.*

Directors' Fees.—Directors' fees and other remuneration, including payments made after retirement, are reportable on Form 1099-MISC and must be reported in the year paid. Report them in box 7.

Commissions Paid to Lottery Ticket Sales Agents.—A state that has control over and responsibility for on-line and instant lottery games must file Form 1099-MISC to report commissions, whether paid directly or indirectly, to licensed sales agents. For example, State X retains control over and liability for on-line and instant lottery games. For on-line ticket sales, State X pays commissions by allowing an agent to retain 5% of the ticket proceeds the agent remits to State X. For instant ticket sales, State X pays commissions by providing tickets to the agent for 5% less than the proceeds to be obtained by the agent from the sale of those tickets. If the commissions for the year total $600 or more, they must be reported in box 7 on Form 1099-MISC. The commissions are paid by State X to the agent on the date payment is due from the

Page 18

agent on the statement of account for lottery tickets covered by that statement. See Rev. Rul. 92-96, 1992-2 C.B. 281.

Escrow Agent; Construction Project.—When an escrow agent maintains owner-provided funds in an escrow account for a construction project, performs an oversight function for the construction project, and makes payments for the owner and the general contractor, the escrow agent must file Form 1099-MISC for reportable payments of $600 or more. This requirement applies whether or not the escrow agent is a bank. For more information, see Rev. Rul. 93-70, 1993-2 C.B. 294.

Indian Gaming Profits, Payments to Tribal Members.—If you make payments to members of Indian tribes from the net revenues of class II or class III gaming activities conducted or licensed by the tribes, you must withhold Federal income tax on such payments and file Form 1099-MISC.

File Form 1099-MISC to report the distributions to tribal members. Report the payments in box 3, Other income, and the Federal income tax withheld in box 4. For 1995, when you provide a statement to the tribal member, please also provide an explanation of the income and withholding.

Statements to Recipients.—For information about the requirement of furnishing a statement to each recipient, see part **H** under **General Instructions** earlier.

2nd TIN Not.—You may enter an "X" in this box if you were notified by the IRS twice within 3 calendar years that the payee provided an incorrect taxpayer identification number (TIN). If you mark this box, you will comply with a safe harbor due diligence requirement of Temporary Regulations section 35a.9999-3, Q/A-89, and the IRS will not send you any further notices about this account. Also see Regulations section 301.6724-1(g).

Box 1.—Enter amounts paid to recipients for all types of **rents**, such as real estate rentals paid for office space (unless paid to a real estate agent), machine rentals (for example, hiring a bulldozer to level your parking lot), and pasture rentals (for example, farmers paying for the use of grazing land). If the machine rental is part of a contract that includes both the use of the machine and the operator, the rental should be prorated between the rent of the machine (reported in box 1) and the operator's charge (reported as nonemployee compensation in box 7). Public housing agencies must report in box 1 rental assistance payments made to owners of housing projects. See Rev. Rul. 88-53, 1988-1 C.B. 384.

Coin-operated amusements.—If an arrangement between an owner of coin-operated amusements and an owner of a business establishment where the amusements are placed is a lease of the amusements or the amusement space, the owner of the amusements or the owner of the space, whoever makes the payments, must report the lease payments in box 1 of Form 1099-MISC if the payments total at

least $600. However, if the arrangement is a joint venture, the joint venture must file a Form 1065 and provide each partner with information necessary to report the partner's share of the taxable income. Coin-operated amusements include video games, pinball machines, jukeboxes, pool tables, slot machines, and other machines and gaming devices operated by coins or tokens inserted into the machines by individual users. For more information, see Rev. Rul. 92-49, 1992-1 C.B. 433.

Box 2.—Enter **gross royalty payments** of $10 or more before reduction for severance and other taxes that may have been withheld and paid. Include in this box gross royalties (before reduction for fees, commissions, or expenses) paid by a publisher directly to an author or literary agent or paid by a literary agent to an author. Do not include surface royalties. They should be reported in box 1. Do not report oil or gas payments for a working interest in box 2; report payments for working interests in box 7. Do not report timber royalties made under a pay-as-cut contract; report such timber royalties on Form 1099-S.

Box 3.—Enter **other income** required to be reported on Form 1099-MISC that should not be reported in one of the other boxes on the form.

Enter in box 3 **prizes and awards** that are not for services performed. Include the fair market value of merchandise won on game shows. You must report prizes and awards for employees on Form W-2. (See the Instructions for Form W-2.) Report prizes and awards for services performed by nonemployees, such as an award for the top commission salesperson, in box 7.

Prizes and awards received in recognition of past accomplishments in religious, charitable, scientific, artistic, educational, literary, or civic fields are not reportable if (1) the winners are chosen without action on their part, (2) the winners are not expected to perform future services, **AND** (3) the payer transfers the prize or award to a charitable organization or governmental unit under a designation made by the recipient. See Rev. Proc. 87-54, 1987-2 C.B. 669.

Other items required to be reported in box 3 include the following:

1. Punitive damages paid in cases that do not involve physical injury or sickness and any other taxable damages.

2. Payments to nonemployees specified in, and payments similar to those specified in, Rev. Rul. 65-18, 1965-1 C.B. 32, about payments to patients and members in Department of Veterans Affairs (VA) hospitals and domiciliaries under the VA therapeutic or rehabilitative program.

3. Payments as explained earlier under **Deceased Employee's Wages Paid to Estate or Beneficiary.**

4. Payments as explained earlier under **Indian Gaming Profits, Payments to Tribal Members.**

Box 4.—Enter backup withholding. For example, persons who have not furnished their TIN to you become subject to withholding at a 31% rate on payments required to be reported in boxes 1, 2 (net of severance taxes), 3, 5 (to the extent paid in cash), 6, 7, 8, and 10 on this form.

Also enter any income tax withheld from payments to members of Indian tribes from the net revenues of class II or class III gaming activities conducted or licensed by the tribes.

Box 5.—Enter the share of all proceeds from the sale of a catch or the fair market value of a distribution in kind to each crew member of **fishing boats** with normally fewer than 10 crewmembers.

Box 6.—Enter payments made in the course of your trade or business to each physician or other supplier or provider of **medical or health care services**, including payments made by medical and health care insurers under health, accident, and sickness insurance programs. In the case of a corporation, list the corporation as the recipient rather than the individual providing the services. See Rev. Ruls. 69-595, 1969-2 C.B. 242, and 70-608, 1970-2 C.B. 286.

The exemption from issuing Form 1099-MISC to a corporation does not apply to payments for medical or health care services provided by corporations, including professional corporations.

Box 7.—Enter **nonemployee compensation**. Include fees, commissions, prizes and awards for services performed, or other forms of compensation for services performed for your trade or business by an individual who is not your employee. Include oil and gas payments for a working interest, whether or not services are performed. Also include expenses incurred for the use of an entertainment facility that you treat as compensation to a nonemployee. Do not report in box 7, nor elsewhere on Form 1099-MISC, PS 58 costs (reported on Form 1099-R); an employee's wages, travel or auto allowance, or bonuses (reported on Form W-2); or the cost of group-term life

insurance paid on behalf of a former employee (reported on Form W-2).

Generally, amounts reportable in box 7 are subject to self-employment tax. If payments are not subject to this tax and they are not reportable elsewhere on Form 1099-MISC, report the payments in box 3.

If the following four conditions are met, a payment generally is reportable as nonemployee compensation: (1) you made the payment to someone who is not your employee; (2) you made the payment for services in the course of your trade or business (including government agencies and nonprofit organizations); (3) you made the payment to someone other than a corporation, e.g., an individual or a partnership; and (4) you made payments to the payee of at least $600 during the year.

Examples of payments to be reported in box 7 are:

1. Professional service fees, such as fees to attorneys, accountants, and architects.

2. Fees paid by one professional to another, such as fee-splitting or referral fees.

3. Payments by attorneys to witnesses or experts in legal adjudication.

4. Payment for services, including payment for parts or materials used to perform the services as long as supplying the parts or materials was incidental to providing the service. For example, report the total insurance company payments to an auto repair shop under a repair contract showing an amount for labor and another amount for parts, since furnishing parts was incidental to repairing the auto.

5. Commissions paid to nonemployee salespersons, subject to repayment but not repaid during the calendar year.

6. A fee paid to a nonemployee and travel reimbursement for which the nonemployee did not account to the payer if the fee and reimbursement total at least $600.

7. Payments to nonemployee entertainers for services.

8. Exchanges of services between individuals in the course of their trades or businesses. For example, an attorney represents a painter for nonpayment of business debts in exchange for the painting of the attorney's law offices. The amount reportable by each on Form 1099-MISC is the fair market value of his or her own services performed. However, if the attorney represents the painter in a divorce proceeding, the attorney must report on Form 1099-MISC the value of his or her services, but the painter need not report. The payment by the painter is not made in the course of the painter's trade or business, even though the painting services are of the type normally performed in the course of the painter's trade or business.

9. Taxable fringe benefits for nonemployees. For information on valuation of fringe benefits, see **Pub. 535,** Business Expenses.

10. Gross oil and gas payments for a working interest.

11. Payments to current and former self-employed insurance salespersons and agents for (a) amounts paid after retirement, but calculated as a percentage of commissions received by the individual from the paying company before retirement; (b) renewal commissions; and (c) deferred commissions paid after retirement but for sales made before retirement.

12. Directors' fees as explained earlier under **Directors' Fees.**

13. Commissions paid to licensed lottery ticket sales agents as explained earlier under **Commissions Paid to Lottery Ticket Sales Agents.**

Example.—Ronald Barr is a building contractor. He subcontracts the drywall work to Daniel Joseph, a sole proprietor who does business as ABC Drywall. During the year, Mr. Barr pays Mr. Joseph

9595	☐ VOID	☐ CORRECTED			
PAYER'S name, street address, city, state, and ZIP code		1 Rents $	OMB No. 1545-0115		
Ronald Barr XYZ Builders 123 Maple Ave. Oaktown, VA 22000		2 Royalties $	19**95**	**Miscellaneous Income**	
		3 Other income $	Form 1099-MISC		
PAYER'S Federal identification number 10-9999999	RECIPIENT'S identification number 123-45-6789	4 Federal income tax withheld $	5 Fishing boat proceeds $	**Copy A**	
RECIPIENT'S name Daniel Joseph ABC Drywall		6 Medical and health care payments $	7 Nonemployee compensation $ 5500.00	**For Internal Revenue Service Center**	
		8 Substitute payments in lieu of dividends or interest $	9 Payer made direct sales of $5,000 or more of consumer products to a buyer (recipient) for resale ▶ ☐	File with Form 1096.	
Street address (including apt. no.) 456 Flower Ln.				For Paperwork Reduction Act	
City, state, and ZIP code Oaktown, VA 22000		10 Crop insurance proceeds $	11 State income tax withheld $	Notice and instructions for completing this form,	
Account number (optional)	2nd TIN Not. ☐	12 State/Payer's state number		see **Instructions for Forms 1099, 1098, 5498, and W-2G.**	

Form **1099-MISC**   Cat. No. 14425J   Department of the Treasury - Internal Revenue Service

Do NOT Cut or Separate Forms on This Page

Page 19

Exhibit A-1 *(continued)*

$5,500.00. Mr. Barr must file Form 1099-MISC because he paid Mr. Joseph $600 or more in the course of his trade or business, and Mr. Joseph is not a corporation. Form 1099-MISC is completed as shown above.

Golden Parachute Payments.—A typical golden parachute payment is one made by a corporation to a certain officer, shareholder, or highly paid individual when a change in the ownership or control of the corporation occurs or when a change in the ownership of a substantial part of the corporate assets occurs. See section 280G for more information.

In box 7, report any excess golden parachute payments to a nonemployee. Enter the letters "EPP" next to this amount. Also enter the total compensation, including any golden parachute payments. Your entry should be in the following format:

300000EPP
400000

Box 8.—Enter aggregate payments of at least $10 received by a broker for a customer in lieu of **dividends or tax-exempt interest** as a result of the transfer of a customer's securities for use in a short sale. File Form 1099-MISC with the IRS and furnish a copy to the customer for whom you received the payment. However, for substitute payments in lieu of dividends, do not file Form 1099-MISC nor furnish it to your customer if your customer is an **individual,** unless you have reason to know on the record date of the dividend payment that such substitute dividend payment is in lieu of (1) an exempt-interest dividend, (2) a capital gain dividend, (3) a return of capital, or (4) a dividend subject to a foreign tax credit. File Form 1099-MISC for and furnish a copy to an individual for whom you received a payment in lieu of tax-exempt interest. If you are not required to make a report on Form 1099-MISC for substitute dividends of at least $10, you must report the substitute dividends on Form 1099-DIV.

Substitute payment means a payment in lieu of (1) tax-exempt interest to the extent that interest (including OID) has accrued while the short sale was open and (2) a dividend if the ex-dividend date is after the transfer of stock for use in a short sale and before the closing of the short sale.

For more information about reporting substitute payments, see Regulations section 1.6045-2.

Box 9.—Sales by you of $5,000 or more of **consumer products** to a person on a buy-sell, deposit-commission, or other commission basis for resale (by the buyer or any other person) anywhere other than in a permanent retail establishment. Enter an "X" in the checkbox in box 9. Do not enter a dollar amount here.

If you are reporting an amount in box 7, you may also check box 9 on the same Form 1099-MISC.

The report you must give to the recipient for these direct sales need not be made on the official form. It may be in the form of a

Page 20

letter showing this information along with commissions, prizes, awards, etc.

Box 10.—Enter **crop insurance proceeds** paid to farmers by insurance companies, unless the farmer has informed the insurance company that expenses have been capitalized under section 278, 263A, or 447.

Boxes 11 and 12.—These boxes, and Copies 1 and 2, are provided for your convenience only and need not be completed for the IRS. If you withhold state income tax, you may enter it in box 11. In box 12, enter the abbreviated name of the state and the payer's state identification number, assigned by the state. Use Copy 1 to provide information to the state, and Copy 2 as the recipient's copy for use in filing the state income tax return.

Form 1099-OID

File Form 1099-OID, **Original Issue Discount,** if the original issue discount (OID) includible in gross income is at least $10 and you are any of the following: (1) an issuer with any bond outstanding or other evidence of indebtedness in registered or bearer form issued with OID; (2) an issuer of certificates of deposit (CDs) made, purchased, or renewed after 1970 if the term of the obligation or deposit is more than 1 year; (3) a financial institution having other deposit arrangements, such as time deposits or bonus-savings plans having a term in excess of 1 year provided the payment of interest is deferred until maturity; (4) a broker or other middleman holding an OID obligation, including CDs, as nominee for the actual owner; or (5) a real estate mortgage investment conduit (REMIC) or issuer of a collateralized debt obligation (CDO). Also, file Form 1099-OID in any case in which you are required to deduct and withhold taxes even if the amount of the OID is less than $10.

Original Issue Discount.—Original issue discount means the difference between the stated redemption price at maturity and the issue price of a debt instrument. In the case of a stripped bond or coupon, OID is the difference between the stated redemption price at maturity and the acquisition price. A discount of less than 1/4 of 1% of the stated redemption price at maturity, multiplied by the number of full years from the date of issue to maturity, is considered to be zero.

Reporting OID.—You must prepare a Form 1099-OID for each person who is a holder of record of the obligation if the OID includible in the holder's gross income is at least $10.

For REMICs and CDOs, see the discussion about REMICs and CDOs later.

Ordinarily, you will file only one Form 1099-OID for the depositor or holder of a particular obligation for the calendar year. If a person holds more than one discount obligation, issue separate Forms 1099-OID for each obligation. However, if a person holds more than one certificate of the same issue for the same period of time

during the calendar year, and if Form 1099-OID amounts are proportional, you may treat all such certificates as one discount obligation and file a single Form 1099-OID.

For time deposits and face-amount certificates, use the actual date of deposit and compute OID on a straight-line, monthly prorated basis for obligations issued before July 2, 1982, and on a daily economic accrual basis for obligations issued after July 1, 1982.

If you are a broker or middleman who holds a bank CD as nominee, whether or not you sold the CD to the owner, you must determine the amount of OID includible in the income of the owner, if any, and report it on Form 1099-OID.

Pub. 1212, List of Original Issue Discount Instruments, contains information on certain outstanding publicly offered discount obligations.

Issuers of certain publicly offered debt instruments having OID must file **Form 8281,** Information Return for Publicly Offered Original Issue Discount Instruments, within 30 days after the date of issuance. The information provided on that form will enable the IRS to update Pub. 1212. See Form 8281 for details.

Exceptions.—You are not required to file Form 1099-OID for payments made to certain payees including a corporation, a tax-exempt organization, an individual retirement arrangement (IRA), a U.S. agency, a state, the District of Columbia, a U.S. possession, or a registered securities or commodities dealer.

Do not report interest on U.S. Savings Bonds on this form. Report it on Form 1099-INT. Also report OID on obligations with a term of 1 year or less on Form 1099-INT.

Statements to Recipients.—For an explanation of the requirement to furnish an official form to recipients in person or by statement mailing, see part **H** under **General Instructions** earlier. Also see Pub. 1179.

2nd TIN Not.—You may enter an "X" in this box if you were notified by the IRS twice within 3 calendar years that the payee provided an incorrect taxpayer identification number (TIN). If you mark this box, you will comply with a safe harbor due diligence requirement of Temporary Regulations section 35a.9999-3, Q/A-89, and the IRS will not send you any further notices about this account. Also see Regulations section 301.6724-1(g).

Box 1.—Report the OID on the obligation for the part of the year it was owned by the record holder. For REMICs and CDOs, see the discussion about REMICs and CDOs later.

Box 2.—Enter any interest other than OID paid or credited on this obligation during the year. Some OID instruments pay regular interest, in addition to the OID, at certain intervals during the life of the instrument. However, if OID is the only interest on this obligation, leave this box blank. Interest reported here must not be reported on Form 1099-INT. For REMICs

Exhibit A-1   *(continued)*

and CDOs, see the discussion about REMICs and CDOs later.

Box 3.—Enter amounts of interest or principal forfeited because of an early withdrawal, such as an early withdrawal from a CD, that are deductible from gross income by the recipient. Do not reduce the amounts in boxes 1 and 2 by the amount of the forfeiture. For detailed instructions for determining the amount of forfeiture deductible by the holder, see Rev. Ruls. 75-20, 1975-1 C.B. 29, and 75-21, 1975-1 C.B. 367.

Box 4.—Enter backup withholding. For example, persons who have not furnished their TIN to you in the manner required become subject to withholding at a 31% rate on amounts required to be reported in boxes 1 and 2 (which may be reduced by the amount reported in box 3) limited to the cash paid on these obligations.

Box 5.—Enter the CUSIP number, if any; if there is no CUSIP number, the abbreviation for the stock exchange, the abbreviation for the issuer used by the stock exchange, the coupon rate, and the year of maturity (e.g., NYSE XYZ 12½ 98). If the issuer of the obligation is other than the payer, show the name of the issuer.

REMICs and Issuers of Collateralized Debt Obligations

Real estate mortgage investment conduits (REMICs), issuers of collateralized debt obligations (CDOs), and any broker or middleman who holds as a nominee a REMIC regular interest or CDO must file Form 1099-OID to report OID of $10 or more accrued to a REMIC regular interest holder or a holder of a CDO. Also use Form 1099-OID to report other interest accrued to a REMIC regular interest holder during the year or paid to a holder of a CDO. Use Form 1099-INT to report interest if no OID is includible in the regular interest holder's or CDO holder's income for the year.

You are not required to file or issue Form 1099-OID for exempt recipients including the following holders of a REMIC regular interest or a CDO:

1. A corporation.
2. A broker.
3. A middleman/nominee.
4. A financial institution.
5. An IRA.
6. A tax-exempt organization.

For additional exempt recipients, see Regulations section 1.6049-7(c).

Box 1.—Report in box 1 the aggregate amount of OID includible in the gross income of each REMIC regular interest or CDO holder for the period during the year for which the return is made.

Box 2.—Report in box 2 any amount of interest, other than OID, accrued to each REMIC regular interest holder or paid to each CDO holder. If you are a single-class REMIC (as defined in Temporary Regulations section 1.67-3T(a)(2)(ii)), include in box 2 the regular interest holder's share of investment expenses of the REMIC for the year.

Statements to Holders.—For each Form 1099-OID you are required to file, you must furnish a statement to the REMIC regular interest or CDO holder identified on the form. The statement must contain the information shown on Form 1099-OID, including the legend shown on Copy B of the official Form 1099-OID, and an indication that these items are being furnished to the IRS. The statement must also show the information specified in Regulations section 1.6049-7(f)(2)(ii). In addition, the statement furnished by a REMIC must show, for each calendar quarter, the information specified in Regulations section 1.6049-7(f)(3). Also see Regulations section 1.6049-7(f)(3)(ii) for information that may be required to be reported to a real estate investment trust (REIT) that holds a regular interest.

A single-class REMIC (as defined in Temporary Regulations section 1.67-3T(a)(2)(ii)) must include in the statement the investment expenses paid or accrued during each calendar quarter by the REMIC for which the REMIC is allowed a deduction under section 212 and the proportionate share of those investment expenses allocated to the regular interest holder.

The statement must be furnished to holders by **March 15.** To meet the statement requirement, you may furnish a copy of Form 1099-OID and a separate statement containing the additional information to the REMIC regular interest or CDO holder.

For information about reporting income to REMIC residual interest holders, see the instructions on **Schedule Q (Form 1066),** Quarterly Notice to Residual Interest Holder of REMIC Taxable Income or Net Loss Allocation.

Form 8811 and Reporting by Brokers or Middlemen.—REMICs and issuers of CDOs must also file **Form 8811,** Information Return for Real Estate Mortgage Investment Conduits (REMICs) and Issuers of Collateralized Debt Obligations, within 30 days after the startup day of the REMIC or issue date of a CDO. The IRS will use the information on Forms 8811 to publish **Pub. 938,** Real Estate Mortgage Investment Conduits (REMICs) Reporting Information, for use by certain brokers, middlemen, corporations, and others specified in Regulations section 1.6049-7(e)(4).

For the requirements that a REMIC or CDO issuer or a broker or middleman who holds a REMIC regular interest or a CDO furnish certain information on request, see Regulations sections 1.6049-7(e) and 1.6049-7(f)(7).

Form 1099-PATR

File Form 1099-PATR, **Taxable Distributions Received From Cooperatives,** for each person to whom the cooperative has paid at least $10 in patronage dividends and other distributions described in section 6044(b) or from whom you withheld any Federal income tax under

the backup withholding rules regardless of the amount of the payment. A cooperative determined to be primarily engaged in the retail sale of goods or services that are generally for personal, living, or family use of the members may ask for and receive exemption from filing Form 1099-PATR. See **Form 3491,** Consumer Cooperative Exemption Application, for information about how to apply for this exemption.

Report dividends paid on cooperatives' capital stock on Form 1099-DIV.

Statements to Recipients.—For an explanation of the requirement to furnish an official form to recipients in person or by statement mailing, see part **H** under **General Instructions** earlier. Also see Pub. 1179.

2nd TIN Not.—You may enter an "X" in this box if you were notified by the IRS twice within 3 calendar years that the payee provided an incorrect taxpayer identification number (TIN). If you mark this box, you will comply with a safe harbor due diligence requirement of Temporary Regulations section 35a.9999-3, Q/A-89, and the IRS will not send you any further notices about this account. Also see Regulations section 301.6724-1(g).

Box 1.—Enter the total patronage dividends paid in cash (qualified or "consent" checks), qualified written notices of allocation (face amount), and other property (except nonqualified written notices of allocation).

Box 2.—Enter the total nonpatronage distributions paid in cash (qualified or "consent" checks), qualified written notices of allocation (face amount), and other property (not including nonqualified written notices of allocation). This box applies only to farmers' cooperatives exempt from tax under section 521.

Box 3.—Enter the total per-unit retain allocations paid in cash, qualified per-unit retain certificates (face amount), and other property.

Box 4.—Enter backup withholding. For example, persons who have not furnished their TIN to you in the manner required become subject to withholding at a 31% rate on payments required to be reported in boxes 1, 2, 3, and 5 to the extent such payments are in cash or qualified check. See Temporary Regulations section 35a.9999-3, Q/A-10 for more information on backup withholding by cooperatives.

Box 5.—Enter all redemptions of nonqualified written notices of allocation issued as patronage dividends, nonqualified written notices of allocation issued as nonpatronage allocations (applicable only to farmers' cooperatives qualifying under section 521), and nonqualified per-unit retain certificates, issued with respect to marketing.

Pass-Through Credits.—Report in the appropriate boxes the patron's share of unused credits that the cooperative is passing through to this patron:

Box 6.—See the **Note** below.

Box 7.—Energy investment credit.

Box 8.—Jobs credit.

Page 21

Exhibit A-1 *(continued)*

Box 9.—Patron's Alternative Minimum Tax Adjustments.—Enter the total alternative minimum tax (AMT) patronage dividend adjustment for the patron and/or the total AMT per-unit retain allocation adjustment for the patron.

Note: *If you are passing through other credits, such as the Indian employment credit, use box 6 or the blank box under boxes 8 and 9. Label the credit.*

Form 1099-R

File Form 1099-R, **Distributions From Pensions, Annuities, Retirement or Profit-Sharing Plans, IRAs, Insurance Contracts, etc.,** for each person to whom you have made any designated distribution from profit-sharing or retirement plans, IRAs, annuities, pensions, insurance contracts, survivor income benefit plans, permanent and total disability payments under life insurance contracts, charitable gift annuities, etc., whether or not you withheld Federal income tax.

If part of the distribution is taxable and part is nontaxable, file a Form 1099-R reporting the entire distribution. However, if the total amount of the gross distribution paid to someone for the year is less than $1, a Form 1099-R need not be filed for that person.

Also report death benefit payments made by employers that are **not** made as part of a pension, profit-sharing, or retirement plan. (See the instructions for box 1 later.)

For loans from qualified plans, section 403(a) annuity plans, section 403(b) contracts, or modified endowment contracts treated as distributions, see sections 72(p) and 72(e)(4)(A). A deemed distribution under section 72(p) or 72(e)(4) could be an early distribution under section 72(t) or 72(v), respectively.

Generally, do not report payments subject to withholding of social security and Medicare taxes on this form. Report such payments on Form W-2.

Reportable disability payments made from a retirement plan should be reported on Form 1099-R.

Do not report amounts totally exempt from tax such as workmen's compensation and Department of Veterans Affairs (VA) payments.

Military Retirement Pay.—Payments to military retirees are reportable on Form 1099-R. Military retirement pay awarded as a property settlement to a former spouse is reportable on Form 1099-R under the name and taxpayer identification number of the recipient, not those of the military retiree.

Payments of survivor benefit annuities are also reportable on Form 1099-R.

Nonqualified Plans.—Report any reportable distributions from commercial annuities on Form 1099-R. Report distributions to plan participants from nonqualified deferred compensation plans, including section 457 plans, on Form W-2, not on Form 1099-R. However, report

Page 22

distributions to beneficiaries of deceased employees on Form 1099-R. Report distributions to beneficiaries in boxes 1 and 2a and use Code 4 in box 7.

Charitable Gift Annuities.—If cash or capital gain property is donated in exchange for a charitable gift annuity, distributions from the annuity are reportable on Form 1099-R. Report in box 1 the total amount distributed during the year. Report in box 2a the taxable amount. If any amount is taxable as a capital gain, report it in box 3. Report in box 5 any nontaxable amount. Enter Code F in box 7. See Regulations section 1.1011-2(c) Example 8.

Life Insurance, Annuity, and Endowment Contracts.—Report on Form 1099-R payments of matured or redeemed annuity, endowment, and life insurance contracts. However, you need not file Form 1099-R to report the surrender of a life insurance contract if it is reasonable to believe that none of the payment is includible in the income of the recipient. If you are reporting the surrender of a life insurance contract on Form 1099-R, enter Code 7 in box 7.

Also report premiums paid by a trustee or custodian for current life or other insurance protection (PS 58 costs). PS 58 costs are not subject to the 10% early distribution tax under section 72(t).

*Section 1035 exchange.—*A tax-free section 1035 exchange is the exchange of (1) a life insurance contract for another life insurance, endowment, or annuity contract, (2) an endowment contract for an annuity contract or for another endowment contract that provides for regular payments to begin no later than they would have begun under the old contract, and (3) an annuity contract for another annuity contract. However, the distribution of other property or the cancellation of a contract loan at the time of the exchange may be taxable and reportable on a separate Form 1099-R.

These exchanges of contracts are generally reportable on Form 1099-R. However, if (1) the exchange occurs within the same company, (2) the exchange is solely a contract for contract exchange, as defined above, that does not result in a designated distribution, and (3) the company maintains adequate records of the policyholder's basis in the contracts, reporting on Form 1099-R is not required. For example, a life insurance contract issued by Company X received in exchange solely for another life insurance contract previously issued by Company X is not reportable on Form 1099-R as long as the company maintains the required records. (See Rev. Proc. 92-26, 1992-1 C.B. 744.)

For those section 1035 exchanges that are reportable on Form 1099-R, enter the total value of the contract in box 1, 0 (zero) in box 2a, the total premiums paid in box 5, and Code 6 in box 7.

IRA and SEP Distributions.—Distributions from an individual retirement arrangement (IRA) or simplified employee pension (SEP) must be reported in boxes 1 and 2a regardless of the amount. You may mark

the "Taxable amount not determined" box in box 2b. But see the instructions for box 2a for how to report the withdrawal of contributions under section 408(d)(4). Also see **Direct Rollovers and Transfers** below for information on trustee-to-trustee transfers. The direct rollover provisions do not apply to distributions from IRAs and SEPs.

IRA Revocation.—If an IRA is revoked during its first 7 days (under Regulations section 1.408-6(d)(4)(ii)), the distribution from the IRA must be reported. In addition, Form 5498 must be filed to report any regular or rollover contribution to an IRA that is revoked. Trustee-to-trustee transfers from one IRA to another are not reportable on either Form 5498 or Form 1099-R.

If a regular contribution is made to an IRA that later is revoked, and distribution is made to the taxpayer, enter the gross distribution in box 1 of Form 1099-R. If no earnings are distributed, enter 0 (zero) in box 2a and Code 8 in box 7. If earnings are distributed, enter the amount of earnings in box 2a. Such earnings could be subject to the early distribution tax under section 72(t). If they are subject to that tax, enter Code 1 in box 7; if the earnings are not subject to that tax, enter Code 8.

Note: *If you know that the taxpayer deducted the contribution, report the total amount distributed in box 2a and use the appropriate code in box 7.*

If a rollover contribution is made to an IRA that later is revoked, and distribution is made to the taxpayer, enter in boxes 1 and 2a of Form 1099-R the gross distribution and the appropriate code in box 7. Follow this same procedure for a transfer from one IRA to another IRA that later is revoked. The distribution could be subject to the early distribution tax under section 72(t).

If an employer SEP contribution is made and the SEP is revoked by the employee, report the distribution as fully taxable.

For more information, see Rev. Proc. 91-70, 1991-2 C.B. 899.

DECs.—If you are reporting a total distribution from a plan that includes a distribution of deductible voluntary employee contributions (DECs), file two Forms 1099-R—one to report the distribution of DECs, the other to report the distribution from the other part of the plan. Report the distribution of DECs in boxes 1 and 2a on the separate Form 1099-R. However, for the direct rollover (explained below) of funds that include DECs, file only one Form 1099-R to report the direct rollover of the entire amount. In this case, it is not necessary to report the direct rollover of DECs on a separate Form 1099-R.

Direct Rollovers and Transfers.—You must report a direct rollover of an eligible rollover distribution. A direct rollover is the direct payment of the distribution to an eligible retirement plan, including an IRA. An **eligible rollover distribution** is the taxable part of any distribution (including net unrealized appreciation) from a qualified plan (or tax-sheltered annuity but

Exhibit A-1 *(continued)*

not an IRA) except (1) one of a series of substantially equal periodic payments (at least annually) made for the life (or life expectancy) of the employee or for the joint lives (or life expectancies) of the employee and the employee's beneficiary or for a specified period of 10 years or more, and (2) any part of a distribution that is a minimum distribution required by section 401(a)(9). Other exceptions may apply. See Codes G and H under **Box 7** later.

Amounts paid under an annuity contract purchased for and distributed to a participant under a qualified plan can qualify as eligible rollover distributions. (See Notice 93-26, 1993-1 C.B. 308.) An offset amount to repay a plan loan can be an eligible rollover distribution. An amount equal to the offset can be rolled over, but the plan is not required to permit a participant a direct rollover of an offset amount. A deemed distribution of a plan loan under section 72(p) cannot be an eligible rollover distribution. (See Notice 93-3, 1993-1 C.B. 293.)

For information on withholding on eligible rollover distributions that are not direct rollovers, see **Box 4** later. For more information on direct rollovers, see Temporary Regulations sections 1.401(a)(31)-1T, 1.402(c)-2T, 1.402(f)-2T, 1.403(b)-2T, and 31.3405(c)-1T.

Report a direct rollover in box 1 and 0 (zero) in box 2a. You do not have to report capital gain in box 3 or net unrealized appreciation in box 6. Prepare the form using the name and social security number of the person for whose benefit the funds were rolled over (generally the participant), not those of the trustee of the IRA or other plan to which the funds were rolled.

If part of the distribution is a direct rollover and part is distributed to the recipient, prepare two Forms 1099-R.

Do not report **transfers** between trustees or issuers (unless they are direct rollovers from qualified plans) that involve no payment or distribution of funds to the participant including a trustee-to-trustee transfer from one IRA to another or one tax-sheltered (section 403(b)) arrangement to another. However, a trustee-to-trustee transfer from a conduit IRA to a qualified plan is considered a distribution and subsequent rollover and must be reported.

You may have to report exchanges of insurance contracts, including an exchange under section 1035, under which any designated distribution may be made. For a section 1035 exchange that is in part taxable, file a separate Form 1099-R to report the taxable amount. See **Section 1035 exchange** earlier.

Explanation to Recipients Before Eligible Rollover Distributions (Section 402(f) Notice).—No more than 90 days and no fewer than 30 days before making an eligible rollover distribution, the plan administrator must provide a written explanation to the recipient. The plan administrator must explain the rollover rules, the special tax treatment for lump-sum distributions, the direct rollover option, and the mandatory 20%

withholding rules. Notice 92-48, 1992-2 C.B. 377, contains a model notice the plan administrator can use to satisfy this requirement. Notice 93-26 explains an exception to the 30-day rule and special rules for tax-sheltered (section 403(b)) annuities.

Beneficiaries.—Prepare Form 1099-R using the name and taxpayer identification number (TIN) of the beneficiary or estate, not those of the decedent. If there are multiple beneficiaries, report on each Form 1099-R only the amount paid to the beneficiary whose name appears on the Form 1099-R, and enter the percentage in box 9a, if applicable.

Nonresident Aliens.—If income tax is withheld under section 3405 on a distribution to a nonresident alien, report the distribution and withholding on Form 1099-R. Also file **Form 945,** Annual Return of Withheld Federal Income Tax, to report the withholding. If income tax is withheld under section 1441, report the distribution and withholding on Forms 1042 and 1042-S.

Corrective Distributions.—For reporting the distribution of excess deferrals, excess contributions, and excess aggregate contributions, see **Code 8** under **Box 7** later.

Excess Annual Additions Under Section 415.—You must report on Form 1099-R distributions made under Regulations section 1.415-6(b)(6)(iv) of elective deferrals or a return of employee contributions (and gains attributable to such employee contributions) to reduce excess annual additions arising from the allocation of forfeitures, a reasonable error in estimating a participant's compensation, or a reasonable error in determining the amount of elective deferrals that may be made for an individual under the limits of section 415.

Such distributions are not eligible rollover distributions although they are subject to income tax withholding under section 3405. They are not subject to social security, Medicare, or Federal Unemployment Tax Act (FUTA) taxes. In addition, such distributions are not subject to the early distributions tax under section 72(t) nor the excess distributions tax under section 4980A.

You may report the distribution of elective deferrals and employee contributions (and gains attributable to such employee contributions) on the same Form 1099-R. However, if other distributions are made during the year, they must be reported on a separate Form 1099-R. Because the distribution of elective deferrals is fully taxable (no part of the distribution is a return of the investment in the contract), report the total amount of the distribution in boxes 1 and 2a. Leave box 5 blank, and enter Code E in box 7. For a return of employee contributions plus gains, enter the gross distribution in box 1, the gains attributable to the employee contributions being returned in box 2a, and the employee contributions being returned in box 5. Enter Code E in box 7.

For more information, see Rev. Proc. 92-93, 1992-2 C.B. 505.

Failing the ADP or ACP Test After a Total Distribution.—If you make a total distribution in 1995 and file a Form 1099-R with the IRS and then discover in 1996 that the plan failed either the section 401(k)(3) ADP (actual deferral percentage) test for 1995 and you compute excess contributions or the section 401(m)(2) ACP (actual contribution percentage) test and you compute excess aggregate contributions, you must recharacterize part of the total distribution as excess contributions or excess aggregate contributions. First, file a CORRECTED Form 1099-R for 1995 for the correct amount of the total distribution (not including the amount recharacterized as excess contributions or excess aggregate contributions). Second, file a NEW Form 1099-R for 1995 for the excess contributions or excess aggregate contributions.

To avoid a late filing penalty if the new Form 1099-R is filed after the due date, enter in the bottom margin of Form 1096 the words "Filed To Correct Excess Contributions."

You should also issue copies of the Forms 1099-R to the plan participant with an explanation of why these new forms are being issued.

Missing Participants.—The IRS administers a letter-forwarding program that could help plan administrators contact missing retirement plan participants (or possibly their beneficiaries). To inform individuals of their rights to benefits under a retirement plan, the IRS will forward letters from plan administrators to the missing individuals if the administrators provide the names and social security numbers of the missing individuals. However, the IRS cannot disclose individuals' addresses or give confirmation of letter delivery. All undelivered letters will be destroyed.

For further information, see Rev. Proc. 94-22, 1994-1 C.B. 608, or contact the Disclosure Officer at your IRS district office.

Filer.—The payer or plan administrator must file Form 1099-R using the same name and employer identification number used to deposit any tax withheld and to file the annual withholding tax return (Form 945).

Statements to Recipients.—For information about the requirement to furnish a statement to each recipient, see part H under **General Instructions** earlier.

Box 1.—Enter the **total amount of the distribution** before income tax or other deductions were withheld. Include direct rollovers, premiums paid by a trustee or custodian for current life or other insurance protection (PS 58 costs), and the gross amount of IRA or SEP distributions in this box. However, in the case of a distribution by a trust representing CDs redeemed early, report the net amount distributed. Also, see **Box 6.**

Page 23

Exhibit A-1 *(continued)*

Example for Computing Amount Eligible for Capital Gain Election (See Box 3.)

Step I: Total Taxable Amount

Total distribution		XXXXX
Less: 1. Current actuarial value of any annuity	XXXXX	
2. Employee contributions (minus any amounts previously distributed that were not includible in the employee's gross income)	XXXXX	
3. Net unrealized appreciation in the value of any employer securities that were a part of the lump-sum distribution . .	XXXXX	XXXXX
Total taxable amount		XXXXX

Step II: Capital Gain

$$\text{Total taxable amount (from Step I)} \times \frac{\text{Months of active participation before 1974}}{\text{Total months of active participation}} = \text{Capital gain}$$

Include in this box the value of U.S. Savings Bonds distributed from the plan. Enter the appropriate taxable amount in box 2a. Please furnish a statement to the plan participant showing the value of each bond at the time of distribution. This will provide him or her with the information necessary to figure the interest income on each bond when it is redeemed.

In addition to reporting death benefit payments made from a plan, report here any **death benefit payments** made by employers that are not made as part of a pension, profit-sharing, or retirement plan. Also enter this amount in box 2a. Enter Code 4 in box 7. For example, the board of directors of XYZ Corporation votes to pay the widow of one of its employees a lump-sum "death benefit." This amount must be reported in boxes 1 and 2a, and Code 4 must be shown in box 7.

For a section 1035 exchange, see **Section 1035 exchange** under **Life Insurance, Annuity, and Endowment Contracts** earlier.

Box 2a.—Generally, you must enter the amount includible as income. However, if you are unable to reasonably compute the data needed to compute the **taxable amount,** leave this box blank. Do not include excludable or tax-deferred amounts reportable in boxes 5, 6, and 8.

For a direct rollover from a qualified plan or tax-sheltered annuity or for a nontaxable section 1035 exchange of life insurance, annuity, or endowment contracts, enter 0 (zero) in box 2a.

Include PS 58 costs that were reported in box 1. However, do not report PS 58 costs and a distribution on the same Form 1099-R. Use a separate Form 1099-R for each. Enter Code 9 in box 7 for PS 58 costs. See Regulations section 1.72-16(b) and Rev. Ruls. 55-747, 1955-2 C.B. 228, and 66-110, 1966-1 C.B. 12, for information on the cost of premiums paid by an employees' trust under a qualified plan for current life insurance protection taxable to plan participants or their beneficiaries.

If you made periodic life annuity distributions from a qualified employee plan under section 401(a), from an employee annuity under section 403(a), or from an annuity contract under section

Page 24

403(b), and the annuity starting date is after July 1, 1986, you may elect to use a simplified safe harbor method to compute the taxable amount. However, for purposes of computing the taxable amount to enter in box 2a, assume the distribution is **not** eligible for the death benefit exclusion. See Notice 88-118, 1988-2 C.B. 450.

Generally, you are not required to compute the taxable amount of an **IRA or SEP** nor designate whether any part of a distribution is a return of basis attributable to nondeductible contributions. Therefore, report the total amount distributed from an IRA or SEP in box 2a. This will be the same amount reported in box 1. You may mark the "Taxable amount not determined" box in box 2b. However, in the case of a distribution by a trust representing CDs redeemed early, report the net amount distributed. Do not include any amount paid for IRA insurance protection in this box. For a distribution of contributions plus earnings from an IRA under section 408(d)(4) (previously excess contributions), report the gross distribution in box 1 and only the earnings in box 2a, and enter Code 8 or P, whichever is applicable, in box 7. For a distribution of contributions without earnings after the due date of the individual's return, under section 408(d)(5), enter 0 (zero). Include DEC distributions in this box.

Losses.—If a distribution is a loss, do not enter a negative amount in this box. For example, if stock is distributed but the value is less than the employee's aftertax contributions, enter the value of the stock in box 1; leave box 2a blank, and enter the employee's contributions in box 5.

Box 2b—Taxable amount not determined.—Enter an "X" in this box only if you are unable to reasonably obtain the data needed to compute the taxable amount. If you mark this box, leave box 2a blank unless you are reporting an IRA distribution. Please make every effort to compute the taxable amount. See Notice 88-118 for the simplified safe harbor method of computing certain taxable amounts for certain life annuity distributions from qualified plans and tax-sheltered (section 403(b)) annuities.

Box 2b—Total distribution.—Enter an "X" in this box only if the payment shown in

box 1 is a total distribution. A total distribution is one or more distributions within 1 tax year in which the entire balance of the account is distributed. Any distribution that does not meet this definition is not a total distribution. If periodic or installment payments are made, mark this box in the year the final payment is made.

Box 3.—For lump-sum distributions from qualified plans only, enter the amount in box 2a eligible for the **capital gain** election under section 1122(h)(3) of the Tax Reform Act of 1986 for participants born before 1936 (or their beneficiaries). Enter the full amount eligible for the capital gain election. You should not complete this box for a direct rollover.

To compute the months of an employee's active participation before 1974, count as 12 months any part of a calendar year in which an employee actively participated under the plan; for active participation after 1973, count as 1 month any part of a month in which the employee actively participated under the plan. See the example at the top of this page.

Active participation begins with the first month in which an employee became a participant under the plan and ends with the earliest of:

1. The month in which the employee received a lump-sum distribution under the plan;

2. In the case of an employee, other than a self-employed person or owner-employee, the month in which the employee separates from service;

3. The month in which the employee dies; or

4. For a self-employed person or owner-employee, the first month in which the employee becomes disabled (within the meaning of section 72(m)(7)).

For a charitable gift annuity, see **Charitable Gift Annuities** earlier.

Box 4.—Enter any **Federal income tax withheld.** This withholding is subject to deposit rules, and the withholding tax return is **Form 945,** Annual Return of Withheld Federal Income Tax.

Note: *The amount withheld cannot be more than the sum of the cash and the fair market value of property (excluding employer securities) received in the distribution.*

For **periodic payments** that are not eligible rollover distributions, withhold on the taxable part as though the periodic payments were wages, based on the recipient's **Form W-4P,** Withholding Certificate for Pension or Annuity Payments. The recipient may request additional withholding on Form W-4P or claim exemption from withholding. If a recipient does not submit a Form W-4P, withhold by treating the recipient as married with three withholding allowances. See **Circular E,** Employer's Tax Guide, for wage withholding tables.

Note: *Rather than Form W-4P, military retirees should give you **Form W-4,***

Exhibit A-1 *(continued)*

Employee's Withholding Allowance Certificate.

Withhold 10% of the taxable part of a **nonperiodic distribution** that is not an eligible rollover distribution. The recipient may request additional withholding on Form W-4P or claim exemption from withholding.

If a payee fails to furnish his or her correct TIN to you in the manner required, or if the IRS notifies you before any distribution that the TIN furnished is incorrect, a payee cannot claim exemption from withholding. Backup withholding does not apply.

Withhold 20% of an **eligible rollover distribution** from a qualified plan that is not a direct rollover. A recipient cannot claim exemption from withholding for such a distribution; however, no withholding is required for a direct rollover. Although the same rules generally apply to an eligible rollover distribution from a tax-sheltered annuity, a special effective date may apply. Any net unrealized appreciation excludable from gross income under section 402(e)(4) is not included in the amount of any eligible rollover distribution that is subject to 20% withholding. (See Notice 93-3.) You are not required to withhold 20% of an eligible rollover distribution that, when aggregated with other eligible rollover distributions made to one person during the year, is less than $200. Form W-4P is not required for an eligible rollover distribution since 20% withholding is mandatory.

The 20% withholding does not apply to distributions from IRAs. For purposes of withholding, assume that the entire amount of an IRA distribution is taxable (except for the distribution of contributions under sections 408(d)(4), in which only the earnings are taxable, and 408(d)(5)).

Even though you may be using Code 1 in box 7 to designate an early distribution subject to the 10% tax specified in sections 72(q), (t), or (v), you are not required to withhold that tax.

See Cir. E and the **Instructions for Form 945** for more withholding information.

Box 5.—Enter the **employee's contributions** to a profit-sharing or retirement plan, or **insurance premiums.** The entry in box 5 can include the tax-free part of any of the following: (a) contributions actually made by the employee over the years under the retirement or profit-sharing plan that were required to be included in the income of the employee when contributed ("aftertax contributions"), (b) contributions made by the employer but considered to have been contributed by the employee under section 72(f), (c) the accumulated cost of premiums paid for life insurance protection, taxable to the employee in previous years and in the current year under Regulations section 1.72-16 (PS 58 costs) (only if the life insurance contract itself is distributed), and (d) premiums paid on commercial annuities. Do not include contributions to IRAs, SEPs, DECs, 401(k) plans, or any

contribution to a retirement plan that was not an aftertax contribution.

Generally, for qualified plans, tax-sheltered annuities, and nonqualified commercial annuities, enter in box 5 the employee contributions or insurance premiums recovered tax free during the year based on the method you used to determine the taxable amount to be entered in box 2a. If periodic payments began before 1993, you are not required to, but you are encouraged to, report in box 5. Also, you may have to report the total employee contributions in box 9b. See **Box 9b** later.

If a total distribution is made, the total employee contributions or insurance premiums available to be recovered tax free must be shown only in box 5. If any previous distributions were made, any amount recovered tax free in prior years must not appear in box 5. See **Box 9b** later for more information about reporting total employee contributions.

If you are unable to reasonably obtain the data necessary to compute the taxable amount, leave boxes 2a and 5 blank, and mark the box in box 2b.

For more information, see Rev. Proc. 92-86, 1992-2 C.B. 495.

For charitable gift annuities, see **Charitable Gift Annuities** earlier.

Box 6.—Use this box if a distribution includes securities of the employer corporation (or a subsidiary or parent corporation) and you can compute the **net unrealized appreciation (NUA)** in the employer's securities. Enter all the NUA in employer securities if this is a lump-sum distribution. If this is not a lump-sum distribution, enter only the NUA in employer securities attributable to employee contributions. See Regulations section 1.402(a)-1(b) for the determination of the NUA. Also see Notice 89-25 (Q/A-1), 1989-1 C.B. 662. Include the NUA in box 1 but not in box 2a. You do not have to complete this box for a direct rollover.

Box 7.—Enter the appropriate **code(s)** from the list below that shows the type of distribution being made. Also, enter an "X" in the IRA/SEP checkbox if the distribution is from an IRA or SEP.

Read the codes carefully and enter the appropriate codes accurately because the IRS uses the codes to help determine whether the recipient has properly reported the distribution. If the codes you enter are incorrect, the IRS may improperly propose changes to the recipient's taxes.

Use the codes below for distributions from IRAs, SEPs, Keoghs, qualified plans, commercial annuities, insurance contracts, etc.

A numeric code must be entered, except when Code P, D, E, F, G, or H is used. When applicable, you may enter a numeric and an alpha code. For example, when using a Code P for an IRA distribution under section 408(d)(4), you may also enter Code 1, if it applies. Or for a normal distribution from a qualified plan that qualifies for 5- or 10-year averaging, enter Codes 7 and A. For a direct rollover

to an IRA for the surviving spouse of a deceased participant, enter Codes 4 and G. Do not use Code 4 with Code H.

Only two numeric combinations are permitted: Codes 8 and 1, or 8 and 2. If two other numeric codes are applicable, you must file more than one Form 1099-R. For example, if part of a distribution is premature (Code 1) and part is not, one Form 1099-R must be filed for the part to which Code 1 applies and another Form 1099-R for the part that is a normal distribution, Code 7. In addition, for the distribution of excess deferrals, excess contributions, or excess aggregate contributions, parts of the distribution may be taxable in two or three different years. Thus, separate Forms 1099-R must be filed using Code 8, P, or D to indicate the year the amount is taxable.

If part of an eligible rollover distribution is paid in a direct rollover and part is not, you must file a separate 1099-R for each part showing the appropriate code on each form. If part of a distribution is an eligible rollover distribution and part is not (e.g., a minimum distribution required by section 401(a)(9)) and the part that is an eligible rollover distribution is directly rolled over, you must file a separate Form 1099-R to report each part.

Codes.—

1—Early (premature) distribution, no known exception. Use Code 1 only if the employee/taxpayer has not reached age 59½, and only if none of the exceptions under section 72(q), (t), or (v) are known to apply. For example, if a hardship distribution is made for medical expenses, you probably will not know if the medical expense exception under section 72(t) applies. Therefore, use Code 1.

2—Early (premature) distribution, exception applies (as defined in section 72(q), (t), or (v)). Use Code 2 only if the employee/taxpayer has not reached age 59½ to indicate that an exception under 72(q), (t), or (v) applies. However, instead of Code 2, use Code 3 or 4, whichever applies, for an early distribution due to disability or death.

3—Disability.

4—Death. Use Code 4 regardless of the age of the employee/taxpayer to indicate payment to a decedent's beneficiary, including an estate or trust. Also use it for death benefit payments made by an employer but not made as part of a pension, profit-sharing, or retirement plan.

5—Prohibited transaction.

6—Section 1035 exchange. Use Code 6 to indicate the tax-free exchange of life insurance, annuity, or endowment contracts under section 1035.

7—Normal distribution. Use Code 7 for a normal distribution from any plan, including an IRA or SEP, if the employee/taxpayer is at least 59½. Also use Code 7 to report a distribution from a life insurance, annuity, or endowment contract and for reporting income from a failed life insurance contract under section 7702(g) and (h). (See Rev. Rul. 91-17, 1991-1 C.B. 190.) Generally, use Code 7 if no other code applies.

Page 25

Exhibit A-1 *(continued)*

8—Excess contributions plus earnings/excess deferrals (and/or earnings) taxable in 1995. Use Code 8 for an IRA distribution under section 408(d)(4), unless Code P applies. Also use this code for corrective distributions of excess deferrals, excess contributions, and excess aggregate contributions, unless Code P or D applies. For information about reporting corrective distributions, see Notice 89-32, 1989-1 C.B. 671; Notice 88-33, 1988-1 C.B. 513; and Notice 87-77, 1987-2 C.B. 385. (Notice 88-33 was modified by Rev. Proc. 91-44, 1991-2 C.B. 733, to provide that the income allocable to an excess contribution to a SARSEP (salary reduction simplified employee pension) is includible in gross income in the year withdrawn from the IRA.) Also see **IRA Revocation** earlier.

9—PS 58 costs. Use Code 9 to report premiums paid by a trustee or custodian for current life or other insurance protection (PS 58 costs). See **Box 2a** for more information.

P—Excess contributions plus earnings/ excess deferrals taxable in 1994. See the explanation for Code 8. The IRS suggests that anyone using Code P for the refund of an IRA contribution under section 408(d)(4) advise payees, at the time the distribution is made, that the earnings are taxable in the year in which the contribution was made.

A—May be eligible for 5- or 10-year averaging. Use Code A to indicate that the distribution is eligible for the averaging method of computing the tax on lump-sum distributions under section 402(d). To determine whether the distribution may be eligible for averaging, you need not consider whether the recipient used averaging (or capital gain treatment) in the past.

B—May be eligible for death benefit exclusion. Use Code B to indicate that the distribution is eligible for the death benefit exclusion under section 101(b).

C—May be eligible for both A and B.

D—Excess contributions plus earnings/excess deferrals taxable in 1993. See the explanation for Code 8.

E—Excess annual additions under section 415. Use Code E alone. Do not use Code 1 or 2 with Code E.

F—Charitable gift annuity.

G—Direct rollover to IRA. Do not use this code for a distribution from an IRA. Do not use this code with any other code except Code 4, when applicable.

H—Direct rollover to qualified plan or tax-sheltered annuity. Do not use this code with any other code.

Box 8.—Enter the current **actuarial value** of an annuity contract that is a part of a lump-sum distribution. Do not include this item in boxes 1 and 2a.

To determine the value of an annuity contract, show the value as an amount equal to the current actuarial value of the annuity contract, reduced by an amount equal to the excess of the employee's contributions over the cash and other

Page 26

property (not including the annuity contract) distributed.

If an annuity contract is part of a multiple recipient lump-sum distribution, enter in box 8, along with the current actuarial value, the percentage of the total annuity contract each Form 1099-R represents.

Box 9a.—If this is a total distribution and it is made to **more than one person,** enter the **percentage** received by the person whose name appears on Form 1099-R. You need not complete this box for IRA or SEP distributions or for a direct rollover.

Box 9b.—If a distribution is payable in the form of a life annuity eligible for the simplified safe harbor method under Notice 88-118 (qualified plans and tax-sheltered (section 403(b)) annuities), you must also report the **total employee contributions** remaining to be recovered tax free. Report the total employee contributions only in the year periodic payments begin.

If any previous distributions were made, any amount recovered tax free in prior years must not appear in this box. In addition, you need not report the total employee contributions if the distribution is not eligible for the simplified safe harbor method under Notice 88-118.

For a total distribution, the total employee contributions must be shown only in box 5. See **Box 5** earlier.

Boxes 10–15.—These boxes and Copies 1 and 2 are provided for your convenience only and need not be completed for the IRS. Use the **state and local information** boxes to report distributions and taxes for two states or localities. Keep the information for each state or locality separated by the broken line. If state or local income tax has been withheld on this distribution, you may enter it in boxes 10 and 13, as appropriate. In box 11, enter the abbreviated name of the state and the payer's state identification number. The state number is the payer's identification number assigned by the individual state. In box 14, enter the name of the locality. In boxes 12 and 15 you may enter the amount of the state or local distribution. Copy 1 may be used to provide information to the state or local tax department, and Copy 2 may be used as the recipient's copy for use in filing a state or local income tax return.

Form 1099-S

File Form 1099-S, **Proceeds From Real Estate Transactions,** to report the sale or exchange of real estate.

Note: *You are not required to indicate on Form 1099-S that the transferor's (seller's) financing was Federally subsidized. Also, you are not required to enter (1) both total gross proceeds **and** the allocated gross proceeds for a multiple transferor transaction (enter either one or the other); (2) an indication that the transferor may receive property or services for an obligation having a stated principal amount; or (3) an indication that, in connection with a contingent payment transaction, the*

transferor may receive gross proceeds that cannot be determined with certainty under the regulations and is not included in gross proceeds.

Reportable Real Estate.—Generally, reporting is required if the transaction consists in whole or in part of the sale or exchange for money, indebtedness, property, or services, of any present or future ownership interest in any of the following:

1. Improved or unimproved land, including air space.

2. Inherently permanent structures, including any residential, commercial, or industrial building.

3. A condominium unit and its appurtenant fixtures and common elements, including land.

4. Stock in a cooperative housing corporation (as defined in section 216).

*Sale or exchange.—*A sale or exchange includes any transaction properly treated as a sale or exchange for Federal income tax purposes, even if the transaction is not currently taxable. For example, a sale of a principal residence is a reportable sale even though the transferor may be entitled to defer recognition of the gain on the sale because of the purchase of a new residence under section 1034 or because the transferor is entitled to exclude the gain under section 121 because of being age 55. Likewise, a transfer to a corporation that qualifies for nonrecognition of gain under section 351 is a reportable exchange. In addition, a transfer under a land contract is reportable in the year in which the parties enter into the contract.

*Ownership interest.—*An ownership interest includes fee simple interests, life estates, reversions, remainders, and perpetual easements. It also includes any previously created rights to possession or use for all or part of any particular year, e.g., a leasehold, easement, or timeshare, if such rights have a remaining term of at least 30 years, including any period for which the holder may renew such rights, determined on the date of closing. For example, a preexisting leasehold on a building with an original term of 99 years and a remaining term of 35 years on the closing date is an ownership interest; however, if the remaining term is 10 years, it is not an ownership interest. An ownership interest does not include any option to acquire real estate.

*Involuntary conversion.—*A sale of real estate under threat or imminence of seizure, requisition, or condemnation is generally a reportable transaction.

Exceptions.—The following is a list of transactions that are **not reportable.** However, you may choose to report them; but if you do, the return filed and the statement furnished to the transferor must comply with the reporting rules.

1. Any transaction in which the transferor is a corporation (or is considered to be a corporation under Regulations section 1.6045-4(d)(2)), a governmental unit, including a foreign government or an international organization, or an exempt volume transferor. Under this rule, if there are exempt and nonexempt transferors, you must file Form 1099-S only for the nonexempt transferors.

Exempt volume transferor.—An exempt volume transferor is someone who sold or exchanged during the year, who expects to sell or exchange during the year, or who did sell or exchange in either of the 2 previous years, at least 25 separate items of reportable real estate to at least 25 separate transferees. In addition, each item of reportable real estate must have been held, at the date of closing, or will be held, primarily for sale or resale to customers in the ordinary course of a trade or business. You are not required to report an exempt volume transferor's transactions if you receive the penalties of perjury certification required by Regulations section 1.6045-4(d)(3).

2. Any transaction that is not a sale or exchange, including a bequest, a gift (including a transaction treated as a gift under section 1041), and a financing or refinancing that is not related to the acquisition of real estate.

3. A transfer in full or partial satisfaction of a debt secured by the property. This includes a foreclosure, a transfer in lieu of foreclosure, or an abandonment.

4. A de minimis transfer for less than $600. A transaction is de minimis if it can be determined with certainty that the total money, services, and property received or to be received is less than $600, as measured on the closing date. For example, if a contract for sale provides for total consideration of "$1.00 plus other valuable consideration," the transfer is not a de minimis transfer unless you can determine that the "other valuable consideration" is less than $599, as measured on the closing date. The $600 rule applies to the transaction as a whole, not separately to each transferor.

The following are also not reportable if the transaction is not related to the sale or exchange of reportable real estate:

1. An interest in crops or surface or subsurface natural resources, i.e., timber, water, ores, and other natural deposits, whether or not such crops or natural resources are severed from the land.

2. A burial plot or vault.

3. A manufactured structure used as a dwelling that is manufactured and assembled at a location different from that where it is used, but only if such structure is not affixed, on the closing date, to a foundation. This exception applies to an unaffixed mobile home.

Timber Royalties.—Report on Form 1099-S payments of timber royalties made under a pay-as-cut contract, reportable under section 6050N. For more information, see Announcement 90-129, 1990-48 I.R.B. 10.

Gross Proceeds.—See Box 2 later.

Who Must File.—Generally, the person responsible for closing, as explained in **1** below, is required to file Form 1099-S. If no one is responsible for closing, the

person required to file Form 1099-S is explained in **2** below. However, you may designate the person required to file Form 1099-S in a written agreement, as explained under **3** below.

Note: *For each transaction, please be sure that only one person is responsible for filing and that only one Form 1099-S is filed for each transferor.*

1. If you are the **person responsible for closing the transaction,** you must file Form 1099-S. If a Uniform Settlement Statement, prescribed under the Real Estate Settlement Procedures Act of 1974 (RESPA), is used, the person responsible for closing is the person listed as the settlement agent on that statement. A Uniform Settlement Statement includes any amendments, variations, or substitutions that may be prescribed under RESPA if any such form requires disclosure of the transferor and transferee, the application of the proceeds, and the name of the settlement agent or other person responsible for preparing the settlement statement.

If a Uniform Settlement Statement is not used, or no settlement agent is listed, the person responsible for closing is the person who prepares the closing statement, including a settlement statement or other written document that identifies the transferor, transferee, and real estate transferred, and that describes how the proceeds are to be disbursed.

If no closing statement is used, or if two or more statements are used, the person responsible for closing is, in the following order: **(a)** the transferee's attorney if the attorney is present at the delivery of either the transferee's note or a significant part of the cash proceeds to the transferor or if the attorney prepares or reviews the preparation of the documents transferring legal or equitable ownership; **(b)** the transferor's attorney if the attorney is present at the delivery of either the transferee's note or a significant part of the cash proceeds to the transferor or if the attorney prepares or reviews the preparation of the documents transferring legal or equitable ownership; or **(c)** the disbursing title or escrow company that is most significant in disbursing gross proceeds. If there is more than one attorney described in (a) or (b), the one whose involvement is most significant is the person responsible for filing.

2. If no one is responsible for closing the transaction as explained in **1** above, the person responsible for filing is, in the following order: **(a)** the mortgage lender, **(b)** the transferor's broker, **(c)** the transferee's broker, or **(d)** the transferee.

For purposes of **2** above, apply the following definitions:

a. Mortgage lender means a person who lends new funds in connection with the transaction, but only if the loan is at least partially secured by the real estate. If there is more than one lender, the one who lends the most new funds is the mortgage lender. If several lenders advance equal amounts of new funds, and no other person advances a greater amount of new

funds, the mortgage lender is the one who has the security interest that is most senior in priority. Amounts advanced by the transferor are not treated as new funds.

b. Transferor's broker means the broker who contracts with the transferor and who is compensated for the transaction.

c. Transferee's broker means the broker who significantly participates in the preparation of the offer to acquire the property or who presents such offer to the transferor. If there is more than one such person, the transferee's broker is the one who most significantly participates in the preparation of the acquisition offer. If there is no such person, the one who most significantly participates in the presentation of the offer is the transferee's broker.

d. Transferee means the person who acquires the greatest interest in the property. If no one acquires the greatest interest, the transferee is the person listed first on the ownership transfer documents.

3. Designation agreement.—You can enter into a designation agreement at or before closing to designate who must file Form 1099-S for the transaction. The agreement will identify the person responsible for filing if such designated person signs the agreement. It is not necessary that all parties to the transaction (or that more than one party) enter into the agreement.

You may be designated in the agreement as the person who must file if you are the person responsible for closing (as explained in **1** above), the transferee's or transferor's attorney (as explained in **1** above), a title or escrow company that is most significant in terms of the gross proceeds disbursed, or the mortgage lender (as explained in **2a** above).

The designation agreement may be in any form and may be included on the closing statement. It must identify by name and address the person designated as the person responsible for filing; it must include the names and addresses of each person entering into the agreement; it must be signed and dated by all persons entering into the agreement; it must include the names and addresses of the transferor and transferee; and it must include the address and any other information necessary to identify the property. Each person who signs the agreement must retain it for 4 years.

Employees, Agents, and Partners.—If an employee, agent, or partner, acting within the scope of such person's employment, agency, or partnership, participates in a real estate transaction, only the employer, principal, or partnership (not the employee, agent, or partner) may be the reporting person. However, the participation of a person listed on the Uniform Settlement Statement as the settlement agent acting as an agent of another is not attributed to the principal.

Foreign Transferors.—Sales or exchanges involving foreign transferors are reportable on Form 1099-S. For information on the transferee's responsibility to withhold income tax when a U.S. real property

Page 27

Exhibit A-1 *(continued)*

interest is acquired from a foreign person, see **Pub. 515**, Withholding of Tax on Nonresident Aliens and Foreign Corporations, and **Form 8288**, U.S. Withholding Tax Return for Dispositions by Foreign Persons of U.S. Real Property Interests.

Multiple Transferors.—For multiple transferors of the same real estate, you must file a separate Form 1099-S for each transferor. At or before closing, you must request from the transferors an allocation of the gross proceeds among the transferors. The request and the response are not required to be in writing. You must make a reasonable effort to contact all transferors of whom you have knowledge. However, you may rely on the unchallenged response of any transferor, and you need not make additional contacts with other transferors after at least one complete allocation is received (100% of gross proceeds, whether or not received in a single response). If you receive the allocation, report gross proceeds on each Form 1099-S accordingly.

You are not required to, but you may, report gross proceeds in accordance with an allocation received after the closing date but before the due date of Form 1099-S (without extensions). However, you cannot report gross proceeds in accordance with an allocation received on or after the due date of Form 1099-S (without extensions).

If no gross proceeds are allocated to a transferor because no allocation or an incomplete allocation is received, you must report the total unallocated gross proceeds on the Form 1099-S made for that transferor. If you do not receive any allocation or you receive conflicting allocations, report on each transferor's Form 1099-S the total unallocated gross proceeds.

Husband and wife.—If the transferors were husband and wife, at the time of closing, who held the property as joint tenants, tenants by the entirety, tenants in common, or as community property, treat them as a single transferor. Only one Form 1099-S showing either of them as the transferor is required. You need not request an allocation of gross proceeds if husband and wife are the only transferors. But if you receive an uncontested allocation of gross proceeds from them, file Form 1099-S for each spouse according to the allocation. If there are other transferors, you must make a reasonable effort to contact either the husband or wife to request an allocation.

Partnerships.—If the property is transferred by a partnership, file only one Form 1099-S for the partnership, not separate Forms 1099-S for each partner.

Multiple Assets Sold.—If real estate is sold or exchanged and other assets are sold or exchanged in the same transaction, report the total gross proceeds from the entire transaction on Form 1099-S.

Taxpayer Identification Numbers (TINs).—You must request the transferor's TIN no later than the time of closing. The TIN request need not be made in a

Page 28

separate mailing. Rather, it may be made in person or in a mailing that includes other items. The transferor is required to furnish his or her TIN and to certify that the TIN is correct.

You may request a TIN on **Form W-9,** Request for Taxpayer Identification Number and Certification. Alternatively, you may provide a written statement to the transferor similar to the following: "You are required by law to provide [insert name of person responsible for filing] with your correct taxpayer identification number. If you do not provide [insert name of person responsible for filing] with your correct taxpayer identification number, you may be subject to civil or criminal penalties imposed by law." The solicitation must contain space for the name, address, and TIN of the transferor, and a place to certify under penalties of perjury that the TIN furnished is the correct TIN of the transferor. The certification must read similar to: "Under penalties of perjury, I certify that the number shown on this statement is my correct taxpayer identification number." If you use a Uniform Settlement Statement (under RESPA), you may provide a copy of such statement, appropriately modified to solicit the TIN, to the transferor. Keep the Form W-9 or substitute form in your records for 4 years.

Separate Charge Prohibited.—The law prohibits any person required to file Form 1099-S from separately charging any customer a fee for complying with the requirements to file Form 1099-S.

Statements to Transferors.—For information about the requirement to furnish a statement to the transferor, see part H under **General Instructions** earlier.

Filer's Name and Address Box.—Enter the name and address of the person who is filing Form 1099-S. This information must be the same as the filer information reported on Form 1096.

Transferor's Name and Address Box.— Enter the name and address of the seller or other transferor of the real estate. If a husband and wife are joint sellers, it is only necessary to enter one name and the TIN for that person on the form.

Box 1.—Enter the closing date. If a Uniform Settlement Statement (under RESPA) is used, the closing date is the date shown as the settlement date on such statement. If a Uniform Settlement Statement is not used, the closing date is the earlier of the date title transfers or the date the economic burdens and benefits of ownership shift to the transferee. Please use the following format to indicate the date: MMDDYY. For example, for January 7, 1995, enter 010795.

Box 2.—Enter the gross proceeds from the sale or exchange of real estate. Gross proceeds means any cash received or to be received for the real property by or on behalf of the transferor, including the stated principal amount of a note payable to or for the benefit of the transferor and including a note or mortgage paid off at settlement. If the transferee assumes a liability of the transferor or takes the

property subject to a liability, such liability is treated as cash and is includible as part of gross proceeds. For a contingent payment transaction, include the maximum determinable proceeds. Also see **Multiple Assets Sold** earlier.

If you are reporting a like-kind exchange of property for which no gross proceeds are reportable, enter 0 (zero) in box 2 and mark the checkbox in box 4.

Gross proceeds do not include the value of property or services received or to be received by, or on behalf of, the transferor or separately stated cash received for personal property, such as draperies, carpeting, or a washer and dryer.

Do not reduce gross proceeds by any expenses paid by the transferor, such as sales commissions, deed preparation, advertising, and legal expenses. If a Uniform Settlement Statement (under RESPA) is used for a transfer of real estate for cash and notes only, gross proceeds generally will be the contract sales price shown on that statement. If other property or services are exchanged, see **Box 4** below.

Contingent payment transaction.—A contingent payment transaction is one in which the receipt, by or on behalf of the transferor, is subject to a contingency. The maximum determinable proceeds means the greatest amount of gross proceeds possible if all the contingencies are satisfied. If the maximum amount of gross proceeds cannot be determined with certainty, the maximum determinable proceeds are the greatest amount that can be determined with certainty.

Box 3.—Enter the address of the property, including the city, state, and ZIP code, and if the address does not sufficiently identify the property, also enter a legal description, such as section, lot, and block. For timber royalties, enter "Timber."

Box 4.—If the transferor received or will receive property (other than cash and consideration treated as cash in computing gross proceeds) or services as part of the consideration for the property, enter an "X" in the checkbox in box 4.

Box 5.—For a real estate transaction involving a residence, enter real estate tax paid in advance that is allocable to the purchaser. You do not have to report an amount as allocable to the purchaser for real estate taxes paid in arrears. You may use the appropriate information included on the HUD-1, or comparable form, provided at closing. For example, a residence is sold in a county where the real estate tax is paid annually in advance. The seller paid real estate taxes of $1,200 for the year in which the sale took place. The sale occurred at the end of the ninth month of the real estate tax year. Therefore, $300 of the tax paid in advance is allocated to the buyer, by reference to the amount of real estate tax shown on the HUD-1 as paid by the seller in advance, and is reported in box 5.

Caution: *The information about reporting real estate taxes in box 5 is based on Notice 93-4, 1993-1 C.B. 295. If the reporting requirement is expanded, the IRS*

Exhibit A-1 *(continued)*

Form 5498

File Form 5498, **Individual Retirement Arrangement Information,** with the IRS on or before May 31, 1996, for each person for whom you maintained an individual retirement arrangement (IRA) or simplified employee pension (SEP) during 1995. For all SEPs, complete only box 4 for the value of the account; do not report employer SEP contributions in box 1, including those made under section 408(k)(6), relating to a salary reduction SEP (SARSEP), on Form 5498. For an IRA, complete all applicable boxes. If no IRA contributions were made for 1995, complete only box 4.

For contributions made between January 1 and April 15, 1996, trustees and issuers should obtain the participant's designation of the year for which the contributions are made.

Direct Rollovers and Transfers.—You must report the receipt of a direct rollover from a qualified plan or tax-sheltered annuity. Report a direct rollover in box 2. For information on direct rollovers of eligible rollover distributions, see **Form 1099-R** earlier.

However, do not report a direct trustee-to-trustee transfer from one IRA to another. For reporting purposes, contributions and rollovers do not include these transfers.

Statements to Participants.—Trustees or issuers of IRAs or SEPs must provide participants with a statement of the December 31, 1995, value of the participant's account by January 31, 1996, in any written format. Trustees or issuers of IRAs must provide participants with contribution information by May 31. You are not required to provide information to the IRS or to participants as to whether a contribution is deductible or nondeductible. In addition, the participant is not required to tell you whether a contribution is deductible or nondeductible.

If the trustee or issuer furnished a statement of the fair market value of the IRA to the participant by January 31, 1996, and no contributions were made to the IRA by the participant for 1995, the trustee or issuer need not furnish another statement (or Form 5498) to the participant to report zero contributions. However, Form 5498 must be filed with the IRS by May 31, 1996, to report the December 31, 1995, fair market value of the IRA. This rule also applies to beneficiary accounts under the inherited IRA rules below.

Note: *If the trustee or issuer does not furnish another statement to the participant because no contributions were made for the year, the statement of the fair market value of the account must contain a legend designating which information is being furnished to the Internal Revenue Service.*

Total Distribution, No Contributions.— Generally, if a total distribution was made from an IRA during the year and no contributions were made for that year, you need not file Form 5498 nor furnish the annual statement to reflect that the fair market value on December 31 was zero.

Distributions.—Report distributions from IRAs and SEPs on Form 1099-R. For a distribution of contributions plus earnings, report the distribution on Form 1099-R using the applicable code.

Inherited IRAs.—In the year an IRA owner dies, you, as an IRA trustee or issuer, generally must file a Form 5498 and furnish an annual statement for the decedent and a Form 5498 and an annual statement for each nonspouse beneficiary. An IRA holder must be able to identify the source of each IRA he or she holds for purposes of figuring the taxation of a distribution from an IRA. Thus, the decedent's name must be shown on the beneficiary's Form 5498 and annual statement. For example, you may enter "Brian Young as beneficiary of Joan Smith" or something similar that signifies that the IRA was once owned by Joan Smith. You may abbreviate the word "beneficiary" as, for example, "benef."

For a spouse beneficiary, unless the spouse makes the IRA his or her own by making contributions to the account, including a rollover contribution, or by not taking distributions required by section 401(a)(9)(B), treat the spouse as a nonspouse beneficiary for reporting purposes. If the spouse makes the IRA his or her own, report on Form 5498 and the annual statement without the beneficiary designation.

Fair market value.—On the decedent's Form 5498 and annual statement, you must enter the fair market value of the IRA on the date of death in box 4. Or you may choose the alternate reporting method and report the fair market value as of the end of the year in which the decedent died. This alternate value will usually be zero because you will be reporting the end-of-year valuation on the beneficiary's Form 5498 and annual statement, and the same figure should not be shown on both the beneficiary's and decedent's Form 5498. If you choose to report using the alternate method, you must inform the executor or administrator of the decedent's estate of his or her right to request a date-of-death valuation. If you use the language for box 4 on the back of Copy B of the official 1995 Form 5498, or you use the official Copy B, you will have met this notice requirement.

On the beneficiary's Form 5498 and annual statement, the fair market value of that beneficiary's share of the IRA as of the end of the year must be shown in box 4. Every year thereafter that the IRA exists, you must file Form 5498 and furnish an annual statement for each beneficiary who has not received a total distribution of his or her share of the IRA showing the fair market value at the end of the year and identifying the IRA as described above.

However, if a beneficiary takes a total distribution of his or her share of the IRA in the year of death, you need not file a Form 5498 nor furnish an annual statement for that beneficiary.

If you have no knowledge of the death of an IRA owner until after you are required to file Form 5498 (May 31), you are not required to file a corrected Form 5498 nor furnish a corrected annual statement. However, you must still provide the date-of-death valuation in a timely manner to the executor or administrator upon request.

For more information about the reporting requirements for inherited IRAs, see Rev. Proc. 89-52, 1989-2 C.B. 632.

Desert Storm Contributions.—For information about reporting contributions for a prior year made by a qualifying Desert Storm/Shield individual, see Notice 91-17, 1991-1 C.B. 319, and the 1994 Form 5498 instructions.

Box 1.—Enter **regular contributions** to an IRA made in 1995 and through April 15, 1996, designated for 1995. Also include employee contributions to an IRA under a SEP plan but only those that would be subject to the deduction limit under section 219. Report gross contributions, including the amount allocable to the cost of life insurance (see **Box 3**) and including any excess contributions, even if the excess contributions were withdrawn. If an excess contribution is treated as a contribution in a subsequent year, do not report it on Form 5498 for the subsequent year. It has already been reported as a contribution on Form 5498 for the year it was actually contributed.

Box 2.—Enter **rollover contributions,** including direct rollovers from a qualified plan or tax-sheltered annuity, made to an IRA received by you during 1995.

Box 3.—For endowment contracts only, enter the amount included in box 1 allocable to the **cost of life insurance.**

Box 4.—Enter the **fair market value** of the IRA or SEP account on December 31. For inherited IRAs, see **Inherited IRAs** earlier.

Form W-2G

The requirements for filing Form W-2G, **Certain Gambling Winnings,** and for withholding on certain gambling winnings depend on the type of gambling, the amount of the gambling winnings, and generally the ratio of the winnings to the wager.

The types of gambling are grouped as follows:

1—Horse Racing, Dog Racing, Jai Alai, and Other Wagering Transactions Not Discussed Later

2—Sweepstakes, Wagering Pools, and Lotteries (Including State-Conducted Lotteries)

3—Keno, Bingo, and Slot Machines

Reportable Gambling Winnings.—If you pay "reportable gambling winnings," you must file Form W-2G with the IRS and provide a statement to the winner. Generally, gambling winnings are reportable if the amount paid reduced, at the option of the payer, by the wager is (1) $600 or more and (2) at least 300 times the amount of the wager. However, these

Exhibit A-1 *(continued)*

two requirements do not apply to winnings from keno, bingo, and slot machines. If the winnings from a keno game (reduced by the wager) are $1,500 or more, they are reportable gambling winnings. If the winnings (not reduced by the wager) from a bingo game or slot machine play are $1,200 or more, they are reportable gambling winnings.

Regular Gambling Withholding.—A payer of certain gambling winnings (not including winnings from keno, bingo, and slot machines) is required to withhold 28% from such winnings and report this amount as Federal income tax withheld in box 2 on Form W-2G. This is referred to as regular gambling withholding. It applies if gambling winnings are more than $5,000 and are from (1) a sweepstakes, wagering pool, or nonstate-conducted lottery, or (2) other wagering transactions when the winnings are at least 300 times the amount wagered. Regular gambling withholding applies to the total amount of gross proceeds (the amount of winnings less the amount wagered) not merely to the amount in excess of $5,000. Report regular gambling withholding on **Form 945,** Annual Return of Withheld Federal Income Tax.

Noncash payments.—Noncash payments, such as automobiles, must be taken into account at their fair market values for purposes of reporting and withholding. If the fair market value exceeds $5,000, after deducting the price of the wager, it is subject to regular gambling withholding. In such a case, the tax that must be withheld is computed under either of two methods as follows: (1) if payment of the withholding tax is made by the winner to the payer of winnings, 28% of the noncash payment less the amount of the wager is the withholding; (2) if the payer of winnings also pays the withholding tax on behalf of the winner, 38.88% of the noncash payment (less the wager) is the withholding. If the method under (2) is used, the sum of the noncash payment and withholding tax is entered in box 1 of Form W-2G. See Notice 93-7, 1993-1 C.B. 297.

Backup Withholding.—If a winner fails to furnish a payer of reportable gambling winnings with a correct taxpayer identification number (TIN), the payer is required to withhold 31% of the proceeds and to report this amount as Federal income tax withheld in box 2 on Form W-2G unless the winnings are already subject to regular gambling withholding as explained above. This is referred to as backup withholding. Backup withholding applies to the amount of the winnings reduced, at the option of the payer, by the amount wagered and not merely to the amounts of such reportable payments in excess of $600, $1,200, or $1,500 (the thresholds for information reporting). See the instructions for each type of gambling for detailed rules for backup withholding. Report backup withholding on **Form 945,** Annual Return of Withheld Federal Income Tax.

A payer may use **Form W-9,** Request for Taxpayer Identification Number and

Certification, to request the TIN of the recipient.

Foreign Persons.—Payments of certain gambling winnings to a nonresident alien individual or a foreign corporation are not subject to reporting or withholding on Form W-2G or **Form 5754,** Statement by Person(s) Receiving Gambling Winnings, since such payments are subject to withholding under sections 1441(a) and 1442(a) and are reportable on Forms 1042 and 1042-S.

State Tax Information.—If state income tax withholding is required on gambling winnings in your state, you may want to complete boxes 13 and 14 on Form W-2G. Copy 1 of the form may be used to provide information to the state, and Copy 2 may be used as the winner's copy for use in filing a state income tax return. The state identification number is assigned by the individual state.

Form 5754.—If the person receiving the winnings is not the actual winner, or is a member of a group of winners, see **Form 5754** later.

Statements to Winners.—For information about the requirement to furnish a statement to the winner, see part H under **General Instructions** earlier.

1—Horse Racing, Dog Racing, Jai Alai, and Other Wagering Transactions Not Discussed Later

File Form W-2G for every person to whom you pay $600 or more in gambling winnings if such winnings are at least 300 times the amount of the wager. You must withhold Federal income tax, at the rate of 28%, from the amount of winnings less the amount wagered if such winnings less the wager exceed $5,000 and if the winnings are at least 300 times the amount of the wager. If the winner of reportable gambling winnings does not provide a TIN, you must backup withhold at the rate of 31% on such winnings that are not subject to regular gambling withholding under the preceding sentence. That is, if the winnings are at least $600 but not more than $5,000 and are at least 300 times the wager, backup withholding applies to the amount of the winnings reduced, at the option of the payer, by the amount wagered.

In the case of multiple wagers sold on one ticket, such as the $12 box bet on a Big Triple or Trifecta, the wager will be considered to be six $2 bets and not one $12 bet for purposes of computing the amount to be reported or withheld. Winnings on a $12 box bet must be reported if they are $600 or more, and Federal income tax must be withheld if the proceeds amount to more than $5,000 or, in the event the proceeds do not exceed $5,000, if the recipient fails to provide a TIN.

Identical wagers (for example, two $2 bets on a particular horse to win the same race) are aggregated for purposes of the reporting and withholding requirements. Also, winnings from identical wagers that are not part of the payment for which the

Form W-2G is being prepared are aggregated for purposes of withholding to determine if the total amount of proceeds from identical wagers is more than $5,000. If the person presenting the ticket for payment is the sole owner of the ticket, Form W-2G should be completed showing the name, address, and identification number of the winner. If regular gambling withholding is required, the winner must sign the Form W-2G, under penalties of perjury, stating that he or she is the sole owner and that the information listed on the form is correct. In this case, Form 5754 is not used.

Box 1.—Enter payments of $600 or more if the payment is at least 300 times the amount of the wager.

Box 2.—Enter the amount of Federal income tax withheld, whether regular withholding or backup withholding.

Box 3.—Enter the type of wager if other than a regular race bet, for example, Daily Double or Big Triple.

Box 4.—Enter the date of the winning event. This is not the date the money was paid if paid after the date of the race (or game).

Box 5.—Not applicable.

Box 6.—Enter the race (or game) applicable to the winning ticket.

Box 7.—Enter the amount of additional winnings from identical wagers.

Box 8 or 10.—Enter the cashier and/or window number making the winning payment.

Boxes 11 and 12.—Enter the identification numbers of the person receiving the winnings.

Box 13.—(optional) Enter the abbreviated name of the state and your state identification number.

Box 14.—(optional) Enter the amount of state income tax withheld.

2—Sweepstakes, Wagering Pools, and Lotteries (Including State-Conducted Lotteries)

File Form W-2G for each person to whom you pay $600 or more in gambling winnings from a sweepstakes, wagering pool, or lottery (including a state-conducted lottery) if such winnings are at least 300 times the amount of the wager. You must withhold Federal income tax, at the rate of 28%, from the amount of winnings less the amount wagered if such winnings less the wager exceed $5,000. If the recipient of such reportable gambling winnings does not provide a TIN, you must impose backup withholding at the rate of 31% on any such winnings that are not subject to regular gambling withholding under the terms of the preceding sentence. That is, if the winnings are at least $600 but not more than $5,000 and are at least 300 times the wager, backup withholding applies to the amount of the winnings reduced, at the option of the payer, by the amount wagered. These requirements apply to church raffles, charity drawings, etc.

Page 30

Installment payments of $5,000 or less are subject to regular 28% gambling withholding if the aggregate proceeds from such wager will exceed $5,000.

If payments are to be made for the life of a person (or for the lives of more than one person), and it is actuarially determined that the aggregate proceeds from such wager are expected to exceed $5,000, such payments are subject to regular 28% gambling withholding.

The price of the wager must be deducted from the total winnings to determine whether withholding is required and at the option of the payer to determine whether reporting is required. The deduction for the cost of the wager should be made at the time of the first payment.

A payment of winnings is considered made when it is paid, either actually or constructively, to the winner. Winnings are constructively paid when they are credited to, or set apart for, that person without any substantial limitation or restriction on the time, manner, or condition of payment.

When a third party makes the payments, as in the case of an insurance company handling the winnings as an annuity, that third party must deduct and withhold.

Box 1.—Enter payments of $600 or more.

Box 2.—Enter the amount of Federal income tax withheld, whether regular gambling withholding or backup withholding.

Box 3.—Enter the type of wager (such as raffle or 50-50 drawing) or the name of the lottery (such as Instant, Big 50, or Baker's Dozen) and the price of the wager (50¢, $1, etc.).

Box 4.—Enter the date of the winning transaction, such as the date of the drawing of the winning number. This might not be the date the winnings are paid.

Box 5.—For a state lottery, enter the ticket number or other identifying number.

Boxes 6 through 8 and 10.— Not applicable.

Boxes 11 and 12.—For other than state lotteries, enter the identification numbers of the person receiving the winnings.

Box 13.—(optional) Enter the abbreviated name of the state and your state identification number.

Box 14.—(optional) Enter the amount of state income tax withheld.

3—Keno, Bingo, and Slot Machines

File Form W-2G for every person to whom you pay $1,200 or more in gambling winnings from bingo or slot machines, or $1,500 or more from keno after the price of the wager for the winning keno game is deducted. If the winnings are of a noncash nature, the fair market value of the item won is to be considered the amount of the winnings. Total all winnings from each bingo or keno game. Winnings and losses from other wagering transactions are not to be taken into account in arriving at the $1,200 or $1,500 figure. If the recipient of reportable gambling winnings from bingo, keno, or slot machines does not provide a TIN, you must backup withhold at the rate of 31% on any such winnings. Backup withholding applies to the amount of the winnings reduced, at the option of the payer, by the amount wagered. Regular gambling withholding does not apply to winnings from keno, bingo, or slot machines.

Box 1.—Enter payments of $1,200 or more from bingo or slot machines or payments of $1,500 or more from keno.

Box 2.—Enter the amount of any backup withholding.

Box 3.—Enter the type of wager, such as keno, bingo, and slot machines, and the amount of the wager.

Box 4.—Enter the date of the winning transaction.

Box 5.—Enter the ticket number, card number (and color, if applicable), machine serial number, or any other information that will help identify the winning transaction.

Boxes 6 and 7.—Not applicable.

Box 8.—Enter the initials of the person paying the winnings.

Box 10.—Enter the location of the person paying the winnings, if applicable.

Boxes 11 and 12.—Enter the identification numbers of the person receiving the winnings.

Box 13.—(optional) Enter the abbreviated name of the state and your state identification number.

Box 14.—(optional) Enter the amount of state income tax withheld.

Form 5754

Form 5754, **Statement by Person(s) Receiving Gambling Winnings,** is used only in preparing Form W-2G when the person receiving gambling winnings subject to reporting or withholding is not the actual winner or is a member of a group of two or more winners on the same winning ticket. The payer is required to file Forms W-2G based on Form 5754.

The person receiving the winnings must furnish all the information required by Form 5754. However, a recipient of winnings from a state-conducted lottery need not provide identification other than his or her taxpayer identification number. Part I lists the identification of the person to whom the winnings are paid, and Part II lists the actual winners, their respective shares of the winnings, and any additional winnings from identical wagers.

In Part II, the person receiving the winnings must provide the name, address, identification number, respective share of the winnings, and additional winnings from identical wagers for each of the winners. In addition, if regular gambling withholding is required, the form must be signed, under penalties of perjury, and dated by the person receiving the winnings. The form must be returned to the payer for preparation of Form W-2G for each of the persons listed as winners. Forms W-2G may be issued immediately or by January 31 following the year of the payment. Do **not send Form 5754 to the IRS.** Keep it for your records.

Withholding and Forms W-2G for Multiple Winners.—If more than one person shares in the winnings from a single wager, the total amount of the winnings (less the amount wagered) will determine the amount of the proceeds for purposes of reporting and withholding. Do not allocate winnings to each winner before determining whether the withholding or reporting thresholds were reached.

For example, E purchases a sweepstakes ticket for $1 on behalf of himself and S, who contributes an equal amount of the ticket price and who will share equally in any winnings. The ticket wins $5,002. Since the winnings ($5,002 - $1 = $5,001) are more than $5,000, you must withhold 28% of $5,001. You must prepare Form W-2G for E and for S, using the information furnished to you on Form 5754.

Exhibit A-1   *(continued)*

Guide to Information Returns *(If any date shown falls on a Saturday, Sunday, or legal holiday, the due date is the next business day.)*

Form	Title	What To Report	Amounts To Report	Due Date To IRS	Due Date To Recipient (unless indicated otherwise)
1042-S	Foreign Person's U.S. Source Income Subject to Withholding	Payments subject to withholding under Chapter 3 of the Code, including interest, dividends, royalties, pensions and annuities, gambling winnings, and compensation for personal services.	All amounts	March 15	March 15
1098	Mortgage Interest Statement	Mortgage interest (including points) you received in the course of your trade or business from individuals and reimbursements of overpaid interest.	$600 or more	February 28	(To Payer/Borrower) January 31
1099-A	Acquisition or Abandonment of Secured Property	Information about the acquisition or abandonment of property that is security for a debt for which you are the lender.	All amounts	February 28	(To Borrower) January 31
1099-B	Proceeds From Broker and Barter Exchange Transactions	Sales or redemptions of securities, futures transactions, commodities, and barter exchange transactions.	All amounts	February 28	January 31
1099-C	Cancellation of Debt	Cancellation of a debt owed to a financial institution, credit union, RTC, FDIC, NCUA, or Federal Government agency.	$600 or more	February 28	January 31
1099-DIV	Dividends and Distributions	Distributions, such as dividends, capital gain distributions, or nontaxable distributions, that were paid on stock, and distributions in liquidation.	$10 or more, except $600 or more for liquidations	February 28	January 31
1099-G	Certain Government Payments	Unemployment compensation, state and local income tax refunds, agricultural payments, and taxable grants.	$10 or more for unemployment and tax refunds; $600 or more for all others	February 28	January 31
1099-INT	Interest Income	Interest income not including interest on an IRA.	$10 or more ($600 or more in some cases)	February 28	January 31
1099-MISC	Miscellaneous Income (Also, use this form to report the occurrence of direct sales of $5,000 or more of consumer goods for resale.)	Rent or royalty payments; prizes and awards that are not for services, such as winnings on TV or radio shows.	$600 or more, except $10 or more for royalties	February 28	January 31
		Payments to crew members by owners or operators of fishing boats. Report payments of proceeds from sale of catch.	All payments		
		Payments to a physician, physicians' corporation, or other supplier of health and medical services. Issued mainly by medical assistance programs or health and accident insurance plans.	$600 or more		
		Payments for services performed for a trade or business by people not treated as its employees. Examples: fees to subcontractors or directors, expenses incurred for use of an entertainment facility treated as compensation to a nonemployee, and golden parachute payments.	$600 or more		
		Substitute dividend and tax-exempt interest payments reportable by brokers.	$10 or more		
		Crop insurance proceeds.	$600 or more		
1099-OID	Original Issue Discount	Original issue discount.	$10 or more	February 28	January 31
1099-PATR	Taxable Distributions Received From Cooperatives	Distributions from cooperatives to their patrons.	$10 or more	February 28	January 31
1099-R	Distributions From Pensions, Annuities, Retirement or Profit-Sharing Plans, IRAs, Insurance Contracts, etc.	Distributions from retirement or profit-sharing plans, IRAs, SEPs, or insurance contracts.	All amounts	February 28	January 31
1099-S	Proceeds From Real Estate Transactions	Gross proceeds from the sale or exchange of real estate.	Generally, $600 or more	February 28	January 31
4789	Currency Transaction Report	Each deposit, withdrawal, exchange of currency, or other payment or transfer by, through, or to financial institutions (other than casinos) that involves a transaction in currency of more than $10,000.	Over $10,000	Within 15 days after the date of the transaction	Not required

Exhibit A-1 *(continued)*

Guide to Information Returns *(Continued)*

Form	Title	What To Report	Amounts To Report	Due Date To IRS	Due Date To Recipient (unless indicated otherwise)
5471	Information Return of U.S. Persons With Respect To Certain Foreign Corporations	U.S. persons who are officers, directors, or shareholders in certain foreign corporations report information required by sections 6035, 6038, and 6046, and to compute income under sections 951–964.	See form instructions	Due date of income tax return	None
5472	Information Return of a 25% Foreign-Owned U.S. Corporation or a Foreign Corporation Engaged in a U.S. Trade or Business	Transactions between a 25% foreign-owned domestic corporation or a foreign corporation engaged in a trade or business in the United States and a related party as required by sections 6038A and 6038C.	See form instructions	Due date of income tax return	None
5498	Individual Retirement Arrangement Information	Contributions (including rollover contributions) to an individual retirement arrangement (IRA), and the value of an IRA or simplified employee pension (SEP) account.	All amounts	May 31	(To Participant) (for value of account) January 31 (for contributions) May 31
8027	Employer's Annual Information Return of Tip Income and Allocated Tips	Receipts from food or beverage operations, tips reported by employees, and allocated tips.	See separate instructions	Last day of February	Allocated tips are shown on Form W-2, due January 31
8300	Report of Cash Payments Over $10,000 Received in a Trade or Business	Payments in cash (including certain monetary instruments) or foreign currency received in one transaction, or two or more related transactions, in the course of a trade or business. Does not apply to banks and financial institutions filing **Form 4789**, Currency Transaction Report, and casinos that are required to report such transactions on **Form 8362**, Currency Transaction Report by Casinos, or, generally, to transactions outside the United States.	Over $10,000	Within 15 days after the date of the transaction	(To Payer) January 31
8308	Report of a Sale or Exchange of Certain Partnership Interests	Sales or exchanges of a partnership interest involving unrealized receivables or substantially appreciated inventory items.	(Transaction only)	Generally, attach to Form 1065	(To Transferor and Transferees) January 31
W-2G	Certain Gambling Winnings	Gambling winnings from horse racing, dog racing, jai alai, lotteries, keno, bingo, slot machines, sweepstakes, and wagering pools.	Generally, $600 or more; $1,200 or more from bingo or slot machines; $1,500 or more from keno	February 28	January 31
926	Return by a U.S. Transferor of Property to a Foreign Corporation, Foreign Estate or Trust, or Foreign Partnership	Transfers of property to a foreign corporation, estate, trust, or partnership; also used to pay excise tax under section 1491 and to report information under section 6038B.	See form instructions	Day of transfer; for section 6038B, attach to tax return	None
W-2	Wage and Tax Statement	Wages, tips, other compensation, withheld income, social security, and Medicare taxes, and advance earned income credit (EIC) payments. Include bonuses, vacation allowances, severance pay, moving expense payments, some kinds of travel allowances, and third-party payments of sick pay.	See separate instructions	**To SSA** Last day of February	**To Recipient** January 31
TD F 90-22.1	Report of Foreign Bank and Financial Accounts	Financial interest in or signature or other authority over a foreign bank account, securities account, or other financial account.	Over $10,000	**To Treasury Dept.** June 30	**To Recipient** None

Exhibit A-1 *(continued)*

Types of Payments

Below is an alphabetical list of some payments and the forms to file to report them. The list was developed to help you determine which form to file. However, it is not a complete list of all payments, and the absence of a payment from the list does not indicate that the payment is not reportable.

Type of Payment	Report on Form	Type of Payment	Report on Form	Type of Payment	Report on Form
Abandonment	1099-A	Discharge of indebtedness	1099-C	Mortgage interest	1098
Advance earned income credit	W-2	Dividends	1099-DIV	Moving expense	W-2
Agriculture payments	1099-G	Education expense reimbursement:		Nonemployee compensation	1099-MISC
Allocated tips	W-2	Employee	W-2	Nonqualified plan distribution	W-2
Annuities	1099-R	Nonemployee	1099-MISC	Beneficiaries	1099-R
Auto reimbursements:		Employee business expense		Original issue discount (OID)	1099-OID
Employee	W-2	reimbursement	W-2	Patronage dividends	1099-PATR
Nonemployee	1099-MISC	Employee compensation	W-2	Pension	1099-R
Awards:		Excess deferrals, excess		Points	1098
Employee	W-2	contributions, distributions of	1099-R	Prizes:	
Nonemployee	1099-MISC	Fees:		Employee	W-2
Barter exchange income	1099-B	Employee	W-2	Nonemployee	1099-MISC
Bonuses:		Nonemployee	1099-MISC	Profit-sharing plan	1099-R
Employee	W-2	Fishing boat crew members		PS 58 costs	1099-R
Nonemployee	1099-MISC	proceeds	1099-MISC	Qualified plan distributions	1099-R
Broker transactions	1099-B	Foreclosures	1099-A	Real estate transactions	1099-S
Cancellation of debt	1099-C	Foreign persons' income	1042-S	Refunds, state and local tax	1099-G
Car expense:		401(k) contributions	W-2	Rents	1099-MISC
Employee	W-2	404(k) dividend	1099-DIV	Retirement	1099-R
Nonemployee	1099-MISC	Gambling winnings	W-2G	Royalties	1099-MISC
Charitable gift annuities	1099-R	Golden parachute:		Timber, pay-as-cut contract	1099-S
Christmas bonuses:		Employee	W-2	Sales:	
Employee	W-2	Nonemployee	1099-MISC	Real estate	1099-S
Nonemployee	1099-MISC	Grants, taxable	1099-G	Securities	1099-B
Commissions:		Health care services	1099-MISC	Section 1035 exchange	1099-R
Employee	W-2	Income tax refunds, state		SEP contributions	W-2
Nonemployee	1099-MISC	and local	1099-G	SEP distributions	1099-R
Commodities transactions	1099-B	Indian gaming profits		Severance pay	W-2
Compensation:		paid to tribal members	1099-MISC	Sick pay	W-2
Employee	W-2	Interest income	1099-INT	Substitute payments in lieu of	
Nonemployee	1099-MISC	Interest, mortgage	1098	dividends or tax-exempt	
Crop insurance proceeds	1099-MISC	IRA contributions	5498	interest	1099-MISC
Damages	1099-MISC	IRA/SEP distributions	1099-R	Supplemental unemployment	W-2
Debt cancellation	1099-C	Life insurance contract		Tips	W-2
Dependent care payments	W-2	distributions	1099-R	Unemployment benefits	1099-G
Direct rollovers	1099-R, 5498	Liquidation, distributions in	1099-DIV	Vacation allowance:	
Direct sales of consumer		Medical services	1099-MISC	Employee	W-2
products for resale	1099-MISC	Mileage:		Nonemployee	1099-MISC
Directors' fees	1099-MISC	Employee	W-2	Wages	W-2
		Nonemployee	1099-MISC		
		Military retirement	1099-R		

Exhibit A-1   *(continued)*

Printed on recycled paper

Exhibit A-1 *(continued)*

U.S. Department of Justice

Immigration and Naturalization Service

OMB No. 1115-0136

Employment Eligibility Verification

Please read instructions carefully before completing this form. The instructions must be available during completion of this form. **ANTI-DISCRIMINATION NOTICE. It is illegal to discriminate against work eligible individuals. Employers CANNOT specify which document(s) they will accept from an employee. The refusal to hire an individual because of a future expiration date may also constitute illegal discrimination.**

Section 1. Employee Information and Verification. To be completed and signed by employee at the time employment begins

Print Name: Last	First	Middle Initial	Maiden Name

Address (Street Name and Number)	Apt. #	Date of Birth (month/day/year)

City	State	Zip Code	Social Security #

I am aware that federal law provides for imprisonment and/or fines for false statements or use of false documents in connection with the completion of this form.	I attest, under penalty of perjury, that I am (check one of the following): ☐ A citizen or national of the United States ☐ A Lawful Permanent Resident (Alien # A _____ ☐ An alien authorized to work until _____ (Alien # or Admission # _____

Employee's Signature	Date (month/day/year)

Preparer and/or Translator Certification. *(To be completed and signed if Section 1 is prepared by a person other than the employee.) I attest, under penalty of perjury, that I have assisted in the completion of this form and that to the best of my knowledge the information is true and correct.*

Preparer's/Translator's Signature	Print Name

Address (Street Name and Number, City, State, Zip Code)	Date (month/day/year)

Section 2. Employer Review and Verification. To be completed and signed by employer. Examine one document from List A OR examine one document from List B and one from List C as listed on the reverse of this form and record the title, number and expiration date, if any, of the document(s)

List A	OR	List B	AND	List C
Document title: _____		_____		_____
Issuing authority: _____		_____		_____
Document #: _____		_____		_____
Expiration Date (if any): _____		_____		_____
Document #: _____				
Expiration Date (if any): _____				

CERTIFICATION - I attest, under penalty of perjury, that I have examined the document(s) presented by the above-named employee, that the above-listed document(s) appear to be genuine and to relate to the employee named, that the employee began employment on *(month/day/year)* _____ **and that to the best of my knowledge the employee is eligible to work in the United States. (State employment agencies may omit the date the employee began employment).**

Signature of Employer or Authorized Representative	Print Name	Title

Business or Organizaton Name	Address (Street Name and Number, City, State, Zip Code)	Date (month/day/year)

Section 3. Updating and Reverification. To be completed and signed by employer

A. New Name (if applicable)	B. Date of rehire (month/day/year) (if applicable)

C. If employee's previous grant of work authorization has expired, provide the information below for the document that establishes current employment eligibility.

Document Title: _____ Document #: _____ Expiration Date (if any): _____

I attest, under penalty of perjury, that to the best of my knowledge, this employee is eligible to work in the United States, and if the employee presented document(s), the document(s) I have examined appear to be genuine and to relate to the individual.

Signature of Employer or Authorized Representative	Date (month/day/year)

Form I-9 (Rev. 11-21-91) N

ISA

STF FED7459F

Exhibit A-2   Form I-9 Employment Eligibility Verification, and Instructions

INSTRUCTIONS
PLEASE READ ALL INSTRUCTIONS CAREFULLY BEFORE COMPLETING THIS FORM.

Anti-Discrimination Notice. It is illegal to discriminate against any individual (other than an alien not authorized to work in the U.S.) in hiring, discharging, or recruiting or referring for a fee because of that individual's national origin or citizenship status. It is illegal to discriminate against work eligible individuals. Employers Cannot specify which document(s) they will accept from an employee. The refusal to hire an individual because of a future expiration date may also constitute illegal discrimination.

Section 1 - Employee All employees, citizens and noncitizens, hired after November 6, 1986, must complete Section 1 of this form at the time of hire, which is the actual beginning of employment. The employer is responsible for ensuring that Section 1 is timely and properly completed.

Preparer/Translator Certification. The Preparer/Translator Certification must be completed if Section 1 is prepared by a person other than the employee. A preparer/translator may be used only when the employee is unable to complete Section 1 on his/her own. However, the employee must still sign Section 1 personally.

Section 2 - Employer For the purpose of completing this form, the term "employer" includes those recruiters and referrers for a fee who are agricultural associations, agricultural employers, or farm labor contractors.

Employers must complete Section 2 by examining evidence of identity and employment eligibility within three (3) business days of the date employment begins. If employees are authorized to work, but are unable to present the required document(s) within three business days, they must present a receipt for the application of the document(s) within three business days and the actual document(s) within ninety (90) days. However, if employers hire individuals for a duration of less than three business days, Section 2 must be completed at the time employment begins. Employers must record: 1) document title; 2) issuing authority; 3) document number, 4) expiration date, if any; and 5) the date employment begins. Employees must sign and date the certification. Employees must present original documents. Employers may, but are not required to, photocopy the document(s) presented. These photocopies may only be used for the verification process and must be retained with the I-9. However, employers are still responsible for completing the I-9.

Section 3 - Updating and Reverification Employers must complete Section 3 when updating and/or reverifying the I-9. Employers must reverify employment eligibility of their employees on or before the expiration date recorded in Section 1. Employers CANNOT specify which document(s) they will accept from an employee.

- If an employee's name has changed at the time this form is being updated/ reverified, complete Block A.

- If an employee is rehired within three (3) years of the date this form was originally completed and the employee is still eligible to be employed on the same basis as previously indicated on this form (updating), complete Block B and the signature block.

- If an employee is rehired within three (3) years of the date this form was originally completed and the employee's work authorization has

expired or if a current employee's work authorization is about to expire (reverification), complete Block B and:
- examine any document that reflects that the employee is authorized to work in the U.S. (see List A or C),
- record the document title, document number and expiration date (if any) in Block C, and
- complete the signature block.

Photocopying and Retaining Form I-9.A blank I-9 may be reproduced provided both sides are copied. The Instructions must be available to all employees completing this form. Employers must retain completed I-9s for three (3) years after the date of hire or one (1) year after the date employment ends, whichever is later.

For more detailed information, you may refer to the INS Handbook for Employers, (Form M-274). You may obtain the handbook at your local INS office.

Privacy Act Notice. The authority for collecting this information is the Immigration Reform and Control Act of 1986, Pub. L. 99-603 (8 U.S.C. 1324a).

This information is for employers to verify the eligibility of individuals for employment to preclude the unlawful hiring, or recruiting or referring for a fee, of aliens who are not authorized to work in the United States.

This information will be used by employers as a record of their basis for determining eligibility of an employee to work in the United States. The form will be kept by the employer and made available for inspection by officials of the U.S. Immigration and Naturalization Service, the Department of Labor, and the Office of Special Counsel for Immigration Related Unfair Employment Practices.

Submission of the information required in this form is voluntary. However, an individual may not begin employment unless this form is completed since employers are subject to civil or criminal penalties if they do not comply with the Immigration Reform and Control Act of 1986.

Reporting Burden. We try to create forms and instructions that are accurate, can be easily understood, and which impose the least possible burden on you to provide us with information. Often this is difficult because some immigration laws are very complex. Accordingly, the reporting burden for this collection of information is computed as follows: 1) learning about this form, 5 minutes; 2) completing the form, 5 minutes; and 3) assembling and filing (recordkeeping) the form, 5 minutes, for an average of 15 minutes per response. If you have comments regarding the accuracy of this burden estimate, or suggestions for making this form simpler, you can write to both the Immigration and Naturalization Service, 425 I Street, N.W., Room 5304, Washington, D. C. 20536; and the Office of Management and Budget, Paperwork Reduction Project, OMB No. 1115-0136, Washington, D.C. 20503.

EMPLOYERS MUST RETAIN COMPLETED I-9
PLEASE DO NOT MAIL COMPLETED I-9 TO INS

STF FED7459I.1

Exhibit A-2   *(continued)*

Lists of Acceptable Documents

LIST A		List B		List C
Documents that Establish Both Identity and Employment Eligibility	**OR**	**Documents that Establish Identity**	**AND**	**Documents that Establish Employment Eligibility**

LIST A — Documents that Establish Both Identity and Employment Eligibility

1. U.S. Passport (unexpired or expired)

2. Certificate of U.S. Citizenship (INS Form N-560 or N-561)

3. Certificate of Naturalization (INS Form N-550 or N-570)

4. Unexpired foreign passport, with I-551 stamp or attached INS Form I-94 indicating unexpired employment authorization

5. Alien Registration Receipt Card with photograph (INS Form I-151 or I-551)

6. Unexpired Temporary Resident Card (INS Form I-688)

7. Unexpired Employment Authorization Card (INS Form I-688A)

8. Unexpired Reentry Permit (INS Form I-327)

9. Unexpired Refugee Travel Document (INS Form I-571)

10. Unexpired Employment Authorization Document issued by the INS which contains a photograph (INS Form I-688B)

List B — Documents that Establish Identity

1. Driver's license or ID card issued by a state or outlying possession of the United States provided it contains a photograph or information such as name, date of birth, sex, height, eye color, and address

2. ID card issued by federal, state, or local government agencies or entities provided it contains a photograph or information such as name, date of birth, sex, height, eye color, and address

3. School ID card with a photograph

4. Voter's registration card

5. U.S. Military card or draft record

6. Military dependent's ID card

7. U.S. Coast Guard Merchant Mariner Card

8. Native American tribal document

9. Driver's license issued by a Canadian government authority

For persons under age 18 who are unable to present a document listed above:

10. School record or report card

11. Clinic, doctor, or hospital record

12. Day-care or nursery school record

List C — Documents that Establish Employment Eligibility

1. U.S. social security card issued by the Social Security Administration (other than a card stating it is not valid for employment)

2. Certification of Birth Abroad issued by the Department of State (Form FS-545 or Form DS-1350)

3. Original or certified copy of a birth certificate issued by a state, county, municipal authority or outlying possession of the United States bearing an official seal

4. Native American tribal document

5. U.S. Citizen ID Card (INS Form I-197)

6. ID Card for use of Resident Citizen in the United States (INS Form I-179)

7. Unexpired employment authorization document issued by the INS (other than those listed under List A)

Illustrations of many of these documents appear in Part 8 of the Handbook for Employers (M-274)

Form I-9 Rev. (11-21-91) N

STF FED7459I.2

Exhibit A-2   *(continued)*

Handbook for Employers

Instructions to Federal Form I-9:

(Employment Eligibility Verification Form)

If you have questions after reviewing this Handbook, please contact your local INS office at the address found in the back of this Handbook. Direct your letter to the attention of the Employer Relations Officer.
DO NOT CONTACT THE INTERNAL REVENUE SERVICE (IRS)

M-274 (Rev. 11/21/91) N

Exhibit A-2   *(continued)*

To United States Employers:

Thank you for your cooperation and assistance. For the past five years, you have worked with us to implement the employment eligibility verification and employer sanctions provisions of the Immigration Reform and Control Act of 1986. Your teamwork has made the law a success, ensuring fairness in applying the law and preserving jobs for those who are legally eligible to work - citizens and nationals and aliens authorized to work in the United States.

Based on comments and suggestions received from the public and our experience in these first years, we have revised the Employment Eligibility Verification Form (I-9) and expanded this Handbook for Employers. We have sought to simplify and clarify.

This Handbook provides a step-by-step explanation of what you as an employer must do to meet your responsibilities under the law. It also explains the responsibilities and rights of employees in the hiring and verification process. We have included additional illustrations of documents that may be used to establish identity and employment eligibility. The Handbook also provides expanded information about how to avoid employment discrimination based on citizenship or national origin.

The Immigration and Naturalization Service thanks you for your compliance with these requirements, now an established part of our nation's laws. We are counting on your continued cooperation.

Gene McNary
Commissioner
Immigration and Naturalization Service

STF FED74591.4

Exhibit A-2   *(continued)*

Contents

This Handbook is divided into eight (8) parts:

This handbook includes two copies of Form I-9. At the back, you will find a list of INS offices for you to contact if you need more information.

United States Department of Justice

Immigration and Naturalization Service

November 1991

Part One

Why Employers Must Verify Employment Eligibility of New Employees

In recent years, Congress has worked to reform our nation's immigration laws. These reforms, the result of a bipartisan effort, preserve our tradition of legal immigration while closing the door to illegal entry. The employer sanctions provisions, found at Section 274A of the Immigration and Nationality Act, were added by the Immigration Reform and Control Act of 1986 (IRCA). These provisions further changed with the passage of the Immigration Act of 1990. References to "the Act" in this Handbook refer to the Immigration and Nationality Act, as amended.

Employment is often the magnet that attracts persons to come to or stay in the United States illegally. The purpose of the employer sanctions law is to remove this magnet by requiring employers to hire only persons who may legally work here: citizens and nationals of the United States and aliens authorized to work. To comply with the law, you must verify the identity and employment eligibility of anyone you hire, and complete and retain a Form I-9 like the one contained in this Handbook.

In addition, the law obliges you not to discriminate against individuals on the basis of national origin or citizenship, or to require more or different documents from a particular individual. (See Part 4.)

This law has been strongly supported by the public. Employers have joined, and continue to join, the effort to protect our heritage of legal immigration. This cooperation has made jobs available to American citizens and to aliens who are authorized to work in our country. In addition to being the law, it is good business practice for you to verify the identity and employment eligibility of your workers. The law deserves your support.

The Form I-9 was developed for verifying that persons are eligible to work in the United States. You should have completed a Form I-9 for everyone you have hired after November 6, 1986. The law requires you as an employer to:

- Ensure that your employees fill out Section 1 of the Form I-9 when they start to work;

Exhibit A-2 *(continued)*

- Review document(s) establishing each employee's identity and eligibility to work;

- Properly complete Section 2 of the Form I-9;

- Retain the Form I-9 for 3 years after the date the person begins work or 1 year after the person's employment is terminated, whichever is later; and

- Make the Form I-9 available for inspection to an officer of the Immigration and Naturalization Service (INS), the Department of Labor (DOL), or the Office of Special Counsel for Immigration Related Unfair Employment Practices (OSC) upon request. You will be given at least 3 days advance notice.

    Note: *This does not preclude the INS, the DOL, or the OSC from obtaining warrants based on probable cause for entry onto the premises of suspected violators without advance notice.*

If you are an agricultural association, agricultural employer, or farm labor contractor who employs people, or recruits or refers people for a fee, these requirements apply to you. (See Part 6.)

If you employ anyone for domestic work in your private home on a regular basis (such as every week), these requirements apply to you.

If you are self-employed, you do not need to complete a Form I-9 on yourself unless you are also an employee of a business entity, such as a corporation or partnership, in which case the business entity is required to complete a Form I-9 on you.

The instructions in this Handbook will help you assess your responsibilities for completing the form and complying with the law.

New Developments in the Law

The Immigration Act of 1990

On November 29, 1990, the President signed into law the Immigration Act of 1990 which amended the Immigration and Nationality Act. You should be aware of several provisions in this new law which affect your responsibilities as an employer.

New Anti-Discrimination Provisions

For the purpose of satisfying the employment eligibility verification requirements, an employer cannot request that an employee present more or different documents than are required. Also, an employer cannot refuse to honor documents which on their face reasonably appear to be genuine and to relate to the person presenting them. The new law makes these actions unfair immigration-related employment practices. (See Part 4.)

New Document Fraud Provisions

Under the new law, it is unlawful for anyone knowingly to engage in any of the following activities for the purpose of satisfying a requirement of the Act:

- To forge, counterfeit, alter, or falsely make any document;

- To use, attempt to use, possess, obtain, accept, or receive any forged, counterfeit, altered, or falsely made document;

- To use or attempt to use any document lawfully issued to a person other than the possessor (including a deceased individual); or

- To accept or receive any document lawfully issued to a person other than the possessor (including a deceased individual) for the purpose of complying with the employment eligibility verification requirements. (See Part 5.)

Where to Get the Form I-9

Two copies of the Form I-9 are included in this Handbook. If you need more forms, you can photocopy or print the forms, provided both sides are reproduced. The Instructions page must also be made available to both you and the employee during the completion of the form. You may obtain a limited number of copies from the INS or you may order them in bulk from the Superintendent of Documents at the following address:

> Superintendent of Documents
> U.S. Government Printing Office
> Washington, D.C. 20402

STF FED7459I.6

Exhibit A-2   *(continued)*

Part Two

When You Must Complete the Form I-9

Every time you hire any person to perform labor or services in return for wages or other remuneration, you must complete the Form I-9. This requirement applies to everyone hired after November 6, 1986.

Ensure that the employee fully completes Section 1 of the form at the time of the hire - when the employee begins work.

Review the employee's document(s) and fully complete Section 2 of the form within 3 business days of the hire.

If you hire a person for less than 3 business days, Sections 1 and 2 of the Form I-9 must be fully completed at the time of the hire - when the employee begins work.

You **DO NOT** need to complete a Form I-9 for:

- Persons hired before November 7, 1986, who are continuing in their employment and have a reasonable expectation of employment at all times;

- Persons you employ for casual domestic work in a private home on a sporadic, irregular, or intermittent basis;

- Persons who are independent contractors; or

- Persons who provide labor to you who are employed by a contractor providing contract services (e.g., employee leasing).

    Note: You cannot contract for the labor of an alien if you know the alien is not authorized to work in the United States.

Part Three

How to Complete the Form I-9

Section 1

- Have your employees complete Section 1 at the time of the hire - when they begin to work - by filling in the correct information and signing and dating the form.

- If your employees cannot complete Section 1 by themselves or if they need the form translated, someone may assist them. The preparer or translator must read the form to the employee, assist him or her in completing Section 1, and have the employee sign or mark the form in the appropriate place. The preparer or translator must then complete the Preparer/Translator Certification block on the Form I-9.

- You are responsible for reviewing and ensuring that your employees fully and properly complete Section 1.

Section 2

- Employees must present to you an original document or documents that establish identity and employment eligibility within 3 business days of the date employment begins. Some documents establish both identity and employment eligibility (List A). Other documents establish identity only (List B) or employment eligibility only (List C). Employees can choose which document(s) they want to present from the lists of acceptable documents. These lists appear in Part 8 of this Handbook and on the back of the Form I-9. You must examine the original document or documents presented by the employee and then fully complete Section 2 of the Form I-9.

- You must examine one document from List A or one from List B and one from List C. Record the title, issuing authority, number, and expiration date (if any) of the document(s); fill in the date of hire and correct information in the certification block; and sign and date the Form I-9. You must accept any document(s) (from List A) or combination of documents (one from List B and one from List C) presented by the individual which reasonably appear on their face to be genuine and to relate to the person presenting them. You may not specify which document(s) an employee must present.

Exhibit A-2 *(continued)*

- If employees are unable to present the required document(s) within 3 business days of the date employment begins, they must present a receipt for the application for the document(s) within 3 business days. The employees must have indicated, by having checked an appropriate box in Section 1, that they are already eligible to be employed in the United States.When they provide you with a receipt showing that they have applied for a document evidencing that eligibility, you should record the document title in Section 2 of the Form I-9 and write the word"receipt" and any document number in the "Document #" space.The employee must present the actual document within 90 days of the date employ ment begins. At that time, you should cross out the word "receipt" and any accompanying document number, insert the numberfrom the actual document presented, and initial and date the change.

- You must retain the Form I-9 for 3 years after the date employment begins or 1 year after the person's employment is terminated, whichever is later.

Future Expiration Dates

Future expiration dates may appear on the Form I-9 or on the employment authorization documents of aliens, including, among others, permanent residents, temporary residents, and refugees. INS includes expiration dates even on documents issued to aliens with permanent work authorization. The existence of a future expiration date:

- Does not preclude continuous employment authorization;

- Does not mean that subsequent employment authorization will not be granted; and

- Should not be considered in determining whether the alien is qualified for a particular position.

Consideration of a future employment authorization expiration date in determining whether an alien is qualified for a particularjobmayconstituteemploymentdiscrimination.(See Part 4.) You will, however, need to reverify the employee's eligibility to work when any expiration date on the Form I-9 is reached.

Reverifying Employment Authorization for Current Employees

When an employee's work authorization expires, you must reverify his or her employment eligibility. You may use Section 3 of the Form I-9 or, if Section 3 has already been used for a previous reverification or update, use a new Form I-9. If you use a new form, you should write the employee's name in Section 1, complete Section 3, and retain the new form with the original. The employee must present a document that shows either an extension of the employee's initial employment authorization or new work authorization. If the employee cannot provide you with proof of current work authorization, you cannot continue to employ that person.

To maintain continuous employment eligibility, an employee with temporary work authorization should apply for new work authorization at least 90 days before the current expiration date. If the Service fails to adjudicate the application for employment authorization within 90 days, then the employee will be authorized for employment on Form I-688B for a period not to exceed 240 days.

You must reverify on the Form I-9 not later than the date the employee's work authorization expires.

Reverifying or Updating Employment Authorization for Rehired Employees

When you rehire an employee, you must ensure that he or she is still authorized to work. You may do this by completing a new Form I-9 or you may reverify or update the original form by completing Section 3.

If you rehire an employee who has previously completed a Form I-9, you may reverify on the employee's original Form I-9 (or on a new Form I-9 if Section 3 of the original has already been used) if:

- You rehire the employee within 3 years of the initial date of hire; and

- The employee's previous grant of work authorization has expired but he or she is currently eligible to work on a different basis or under a new grant of work authorization than when the original Form I-9 was completed.

STF FED7459I.8

Exhibit A-2 *(continued)*

To reverify, you must:

- Record the date of rehire;

- Record the document title, number, and expiration date (if any) of any document(s) presented;

- Sign and date Section 3; and

- If you are reverifying on a new form, write the employee's name in Section 1.

If you rehire an employee who has previously completed a Form I-9, you may update on the employee's original Form I-9 or on a new Form I-9 if:

- You rehire the employee within 3 years of the initial date of hire; and

- The employee is still eligible to work on the same basis as when the original Form I-9 was completed.

To update, you must:

- Record the date of rehire;

- Sign and date Section 3; and

- If you are updating on a new form, write the employee's name in Section 1.

In all of the situations described above with respect to re-hired employees, you always have the option of completing Sections 1 and 2 of a new Form I-9 instead of completing Section 3.

Minors (Individuals Under Age 18)

If a minor - a person under the age of 18 - cannot present a List A document or an identity document from List B, the Form I-9 should be completed in the following way:

- A parent or legal guardian must complete Section 1 and write "Individual under age 18" in the space for the employee's signature;

- The parent or legal guardian must complete the "Preparer/Translator Certification" block;

- You should write "Individual under age 18" in Section 2, List B, in the space after the words "Document #"; and

- The minor must present a List C document showing his or her employment eligibility. You should record the required information in the appropriate space in Section 2.

Handicapped Employees (Special Placement)

If a person with a handicap, who is placed in a job by a non-profit organization or as part of a rehabilitation program, cannot present a List A document or an identity document from List B, the Form I-9 should be completed in the following way:

- A representative of the nonprofit organization, or a parent or a legal guardian, must complete Section 1 and write "Special Placement" in the space for the employee's signature;

- The representative, parent, or legal guardian must complete the "Preparer/Translator Certification" block;

- You should write "Special Placement" in Section 2, List B, in the space after the words "Document #"; and

- The handicapped employee must present a List C document showing his or her employment eligibility. You should record the required information in the appropriate space in Section 2.

Exhibit A-2 *(continued)*

6

Section 1: To be completed by the **EMPLOYEE**

STEP 1
Fill in the personal information.

STEP 2
Check the box for work eligibility.
Fill in other information if appli-
cable.

STEP 3
Read, sign, and date.

STEP 4
(Preparer/Translator only)
Read, fill in information, sign, and
date.

Section 2: To be completed by the **EMPLOYER**

STEP 5
Examine the document(s) and fill in
the document title, issuing authority,
number, and expiration date (if any)
in the space provided.

STEP 6
Read, fill in information (including
the date employment begins in the
certification), sign, and date.

Section 3: To be completed by the **EMPLOYER**

STEP 7
Fill in the new name and/or date
of rehire (if applicable).

STEP 8
Examine the document(s) and
fill in the document title, number,
and expiration date (if any) in the
space provided.

STEP 9
Read, sign, and date.

STF FED7459L10

Exhibit A-2 *(continued)*

Part Three of this Handbook gives instructions for completing the Form I-9 for minors and handicapped individuals who are unable to present a List A document or a List B (identity) document. This example shows a completed Form I-9 in which a parent has attested to a minor employee's identity.

Section 1: To be completed by the **PARENT, LEGAL GUARDIAN, OR REPRESENTATIVE OF THE NONPROFIT ORGANIZATION**

Step 1
Fill in the personal information.

Step 2
Check the box for work eligibility. Fill in other information as required.

Step 3
Read, then write "Individual under age18" in the space for the employee's signature.

Step 4
(Preparer/Translator)
Read, fill in information, sign, and date.

Section 2: To be completed by the **EMPLOYER**

Step 5
Examine a List C document establishing employment eligibility. Fill in thedocu-ment title, issuing authority, number,and expiration date (if any) in the space provided. Under List B, write "Individual under age 18" in the space provided for "Document #."

STEP 6
Read, fill in information, sign, and date.

STF FED7459t.11

Exhibit A-2 *(continued)*

Part Four

Unlawful Discrimination

General Provisions

The Immigration and Nationality Act, as amended, and Title VII of the Civil Rights Act of 1964, as amended, prohibit employment discrimination. Employers with 4 or more employees are prohibited from discriminating against any person (other than an unauthorized alien) in hiring, discharging, or recruiting or referring for a fee because of a person's national origin, or in the case of a citizen or protected individual, because of a person's citizenship status. Employers with 15 or more employees may not discriminate against any person on the basis of national origin in hiring, discharge, recruitment, assignment, compensation, or other terms and conditions of employment.

Note: For the definition of a "protected individual," see Question #41 on Page 18 of this Handbook.

In practice, this means that employers must treat all employees the same when completing the Form I-9. Employers cannot set different employment eligibility verification standards or require that different documents be presented by different groups of employees. Employees can choose which documents they want to present from the lists of acceptable documents. An employer cannot request that an employee present more or different documents than are required or refuse to honor documents which on their face reasonably appear to be genuine and to relate to the person presenting them. An employer cannot refuse to accept a document, or refuse to hire an individual, because a document has a future expiration date. For example, temporary resident aliens have registration cards and persons granted asylum have INS work authorization documents that will expire, but they are ordinarily granted extensions of their employment authorization and they are protected by law from discrimination.

Generally, employers who have 4 or more employees cannot limit jobs to United States citizens to the exclusion of authorized aliens. Such a limitation may only be applied to a specific position when required by law, regulation, or executive order; when required by a Federal, state, or local government contract; or when the Attorney General determines that United States citizenship is essential for doing business with an agency or department of the Federal, state, or local government.

On an individual basis, an employer may legally prefer a United States citizen or national over an equally qualified alien to fill a specific position. **However, an employer may not adopt a blanket policy of always preferring a qualified citizen over a qualified alien.**

Verification of identity and employment eligibility is not required until an individual actually starts work. The Form I-9 should be completed at the same point in the employment process for all employees. Different procedures should not be established based on an individual's appearance, name, accent, or other factors.

Procedures for Filing Complaints

Discrimination charges may be filed by an individual who believes he or she is the victim of employment discrimination, a person acting on behalf of such an individual, or an INS officer who has reason to believe that discrimination has occurred.

Charges of national origin discrimination against employers with 4 to 14 employees, and all charges of citizenship status discrimination against employers with 4 or more employees, should be filed with the Office of Special Counsel for Immigration Related Unfair Employment Practices (OSC) within the Department of Justice.

Discrimination charges must be filed with the OSC within 180 days of the discriminatory act. Upon receipt of a discrimination charge, the OSC will notify the employer within 10 days that the charges have been filed and that an investigation will be conducted. If the OSC has not filed a complaint with an administrative law judge within 120 days of receiving a charge of discrimination, it will notify the person making the charge of its determination not to file a complaint. The person making the charge (other than an INS officer) may file a complaint with an administrative law judge within 90 days after receiving the notice from the OSC. In addition, the OSC may still file a complaint within this 90-day period. The administrative law judge will conduct a hearing and issue a decision.

An employer is prohibited from taking retaliatory action against a person who has filed a charge of discrimination or who was a witness or otherwise participated in the investigation of another person's complaint. Such retaliatory action is a violation of the Act's anti-discrimination provision and of Title VII.

Exhibit A-2 *(continued)*

Additional Information

For more information about immigration-related discrimination, contact the Office of Special Counsel for Immigration Related Unfair Employment Practices, P.O. Box 65490, Washington, D.C., 20035-5490, or call 1-800-255-7688 or for the hearing impaired TDD 1-800-237-2515. In Washington, D.C., call (202) 653-8121 or TDD (202) 296-0168.

For more information on Title VII and policies and procedures of the Equal Employment Opportunity Commission, call 1-800-USA-EEOC.

Part Five

Penalties for Prohibited Practices

A.   UNLAWFUL EMPLOYMENT

1.   Civil Penalties

If an investigation reveals that an employer has knowingly hired or knowingly continued to employ an unauthorized alien, or has failed to comply with the employment eligibility verification requirements, with respect to employees hired after November 6, 1986, the INS may take action. When the INS intends to impose penalties, a Notice of Intent to Fine (NIF) is issued. Employers who receive a NIF may request a hearing before an administrative law judge. If a request for a hearing is not received within 30 days, the penalty will be imposed and a Final Order will be issued. When a Final Order is issued, the penalty is final and unappealable.

- Hiring or continuing to employ unauthorized aliens

Employers determined to have knowingly hired unauthorized aliens (or to be continuing to employ aliens knowing that they are or have become unauthorized to work in the United States) may be ordered to cease and desist from such activity, and pay a civil money penalty as follows:

  ° First Offense. Not less than $250 and not more than $2,000 for each unauthorized alien;

  ° Second Offense. Not less than $2,000 and not more than $5,000 for each unauthorized alien; or

  ° Subsequent Offenses. Not less than $3,000 and not more than $10,000 for each unauthorized alien.

After November 6, 1986, if an employer uses a contract, subcontract, or exchange entered into, renegotiated, or extended, to obtain the labor of an alien and knows the alien is not authorized to work in the United States, the employer will be considered to have knowingly hired an unauthorized alien. The employer will be subject to the penalties set forth above.

Exhibit A-2   *(continued)*

- Failing to comply with the Form I-9 requirements

  Employers who fail to properly complete, retain, and/or make available for inspection Forms I-9 as required by law may face civil money penalties of not less than $100 and not more than $1,000 for each employee for whom the Form I-9 was not properly completed, retained, and/or made available.

- Requiring indemnification

  Employers found to have required a bond or indemnity from an employee against liability under the employer sanctions laws may be ordered to pay a civil money penalty of $1,000 for each violation and to make restitution, either to the person who was required to pay the indemnity, or, if that person cannot be located, to the United States Treasury.

- Good faith defense

  If an employer can show that he or she has complied with the Form I-9 requirements, then the employer has established a "good faith" defense with respect to a charge of knowingly hiring an unauthorized alien, unless the government can show that the employer had actual knowledge of the unauthorized status of the employee.

2. **Criminal Penalties**

- Engaging in a pattern or practice of knowingly hiring or continuing to employ unauthorized aliens

  Persons or entities who are convicted of having engaged in a pattern or practice of knowingly hiring unauthorized aliens (or continuing to employ aliens knowing that they are or have become unauthorized to work in the United States) after November 6, 1986, may face fines of up to $3,000 per employee and/or 6 months imprisonment.

- Engaging in fraud or false statements, or otherwise misusing visas, immigration permits, and identity documents

  People who use fraudulent identification or employment eligibility documents, or documents that were lawfully issued to another person, or who make a false statement or attestation for purposes of satisfying the employment eligibility verification requirements, may be fined, or imprisoned for up to 5 years, or both.

B. UNLAWFUL DISCRIMINATION

If an investigation reveals that an employer has engaged in unfair immigration-related employment practices under the Act, the OSC or the EEOC may take action. An employer will be ordered to stop the prohibited practice and may be ordered to take one or more of the following steps:

- Hire or reinstate, with or without back pay, individuals directly injured by the discrimination;

- Lift any restrictions on an employee's assignments, work shifts, or movements;

- Post notices to employees about their rights and about employers' obligations;

- Educate all personnel involved in hiring and in complying with the employer sanctions and anti-discrimination laws about the requirements of these laws; and/or

- Remove a false performance review or false warning from an employee's personnel file.

Employers may also be ordered to pay a civil money penalty as follows:

- First Offense. Not less than $250 and not more than $2,000 for each individual discriminated against;

- Second Offense. Not less than $2,000 and not more than $5,000 for each individual discriminated against;

- Subsequent Offenses. Not less than $3,000 and not more than $10,000 for each individual discriminated against; or

- Unlawful Request for More or Different Documents. Not less than $100 and not more than $1,000 for each individual discriminated against.

Employers may also be ordered to keep certain records regarding the hiring of applicants and employees. If a court decides that the losing party's claim has no reasonable basis in fact or law, the court may award attorneys' fees to prevailing parties other than the United States.

Exhibit A-2 *(continued)*

C. CIVIL DOCUMENT FRAUD

If an investigation reveals that an individual has knowingly committed or participated in acts relating to document fraud (see Part 1), the INS may take action. When the INS intends to impose penalties, a Notice of Intent to Fine (NIF) is issued. Persons who receive a NIF may request a hearing before an administrative law judge. If a request for a hearing is not received within 30 days, the penalty will be imposed and a Final Order will be issued. When a Final Order is issued, this penalty is final and unappealable.

Individuals may be ordered to pay a civil money penalty as follows:

- First Offense. Not less than $250 and not more than $2,000 for each fraudulent document used, accepted, or created and each instance of use, acceptance, or creation;or

- Subsequent Offenses. Not less than $2,000 and not more than $5,000 for each fraudulent document used, accepted, or created and each instance of use, acceptance, or creation.

Part Six

Instructions for Recruiters and Referrers for a Fee

Under the Immigration and Nationality Act, as amended by the Immigration Act of 1990, it is unlawful for an agricultural association, agricultural employer, or farm labor contractor to hire, or to recruit or refer for a fee, an individual for employment in the United States without complying with the employment eligibility verification requirements. This provision applies to those agricultural associations, agricultural employers, and farm labor contractors who recruit persons for a fee and those who refer persons or provide documents or information about persons to employers in return for a fee.

This limited class of recruiters and referrers for a fee must complete the Form I-9 when a person they refer is hired. The Form I-9 must be fully completed within 3 business days of the date employment begins, or, in the case of an individual hired for less than 3 business days, at the time employment begins.

Recruiters and referrers for a fee may designate agents, such as national associations or employers, to complete the verification procedures on their behalf. If the employer is designated as the agent, the employer should provide the recruiter or referrer with a photocopy of the Form I-9. However, recruiters and referrers are still responsible for compliance with the law and may be found liable for violations of the law.

Recruiters and referrers for a fee must retain the Form I-9 for 3 years after the date the referred individual was hired by the employer. They must also make available Forms I-9 for inspection to an INS, DOL, or OSC officer after 3 days (72 hours) advance notice.

NOTE: This does not preclude the INS, the DOL, or the OSC from obtaining warrants based on probable cause for entry onto the premises of suspected violaters without advance notice.

The penalties for failing to comply with the Form I-9 requirements and for requiring indemnification, as described in Part 5, apply to this limited class of recruiters and referers for a fee.

Note: All recruiters and referers for a fee are still liable for knowingly recruiting or referring for a fee aliens not authorized to work in the United States.

STF FED7459I.15

Exhibit A-2   *(continued)*

Part Seven

Some Questions You May Have About the Form I-9

Questions About the Verification Process

1. **Q. Do citizens and nationals of the United States need to prove they are eligible to work?**

   A. Yes. While citizens and nationals of the United States are automatically eligible for employment, they too must present the required documents and complete an I-9. Citizens of the United States include persons born in Puerto Rico, Guam, the Virgin Islands, and the Northern Mariana Islands. Nationals of the United States include persons born in American Samoa, including Swains Island.

2. **Q. Do I need to complete an I-9 for everyone who applies for a job with my company?**

   A. No. You need to complete I-9s only for people you actually hire. For purposes of this law, a person is "hired" when he or she begins to work for you.

3. **Q. If someone accepts a job with my company but will not start work for a month, can I complete the I-9 when the employee accepts the job?**

   A. Yes. The law requires that you complete the I-9 only when the person actually begins working. However, you may complete the form earlier, as long as you complete the form at the same point in the employment process for all employees.

4. **Q. I understand that I must complete an I-9 for anyone I hire to perform labor or services in return for wages or other remuneration. What is "remuneration"?**

   A. Remuneration is anything of value given in exchange for labor or services rendered by an employee, including food and lodging.

5. **Q. Do I need to fill out an I-9 for independent contractors or their employees?**

   A. No. For example, if you contract with a construction company to perform renovations on your building, you do not have to complete I-9s for that company's employees. The construction company is responsible for completing the I-9s for its own employees. However, you must not knowingly use contract labor to circumvent the law against hiring unauthorized aliens.

6. **Q. What should I do if the person I hire is unable to provide the required documents within 3 business days of the date employment begins?**

   A. If an employee is unable to present the required document or documents within 3 business days of the date employment begins, the employee must produce a receipt showing that he or she has applied for the document. In addition, the employee must present the actual document to you within 90 days of the hire. The employee must have indicated on or before the time employment began, by having checked an appropriate box in Section 1, that he or she is already eligible to be employed in the United States.

   NOTE: Employees hired for less than 3 business days must produce the actual document(s) and the I-9 must be fully completed at the time employment begins.

7. **Q. Can I fire an employee who fails to produce the required documents within 3 business days?**

   A. Yes. You can terminate an employee who fails to produce the required document or documents, or a receipt for a document, within 3 business days of the date employment begins. However, you must apply these practices uniformly to all employees If an employee has presented a receipt for a document, he or she must produce the actual document within 90 days of the date employment begins.

STF FED7459I.16

Exhibit A-2 *(continued)*

8. **Q.** **What happens if I properly complete a Form I-9 and INS discovers that my employee is not actually authorized to work?**

A. You cannot be charged with a verification violation. You will also have a good faith defense against the imposition of employer sanctions penalties for knowingly hiring an unauthorized alien, unless the government can show you had actual knowledge of the unauthorized status of the employee, if you have done the following:

   ° Ensured that employees fully and properly completed Section 1 of the I-9 at the time employment began;

   ° Reviewed the required documents which should have reasonably appeared to have been genuine and to have related to the person presenting them;

   ° Fully and properly completed Section 2 of the I-9, and signed and dated the employer certification;

   ° Retained the I-9 for the required period of time; and

   ° Made the I-9 available upon request to an INS, DOL, or OSC officer.

Questions About Documents

9. **Q.** **May I specify which documents I will accept for verification?**

A. No. The employee can choose which document(s) he or she wants to present from the lists of acceptable documents. You must accept any document (from List A) or combination of documents (one from List B and one from List C) listed on the I-9 and found in Part 8 of this Handbook which reasonably appear on their face to be genuine and to relate to the person presenting them. To do otherwise could be an unfair immigration-related employment practice. Individuals who look and/or sound foreign must not be treated differently in the hiring or verification process.

10. **Q.** **If an employee writes down an Alien Number or Admission Number when completing Section 1 of the I-9, can I ask to see a document with that number?**

A. No. Although it is your responsibility as an employer to ensure that your employees fully complete Section 1 at the time employment begins, there is no requirement that employees present any document to complete this section.

When you complete Section 2, you may not ask to see a document with the employee's Alien Number or Admission Number or otherwise specify which document(s) an employee may present.

11. **Q.** **What is my responsibility concerning the authenticity of document(s) presented to me?**

A. You must examine the document(s) and, if they reasonably appear on their face to be genuine and to relate to the person presenting them, you must accept them. To do otherwise could be an unfair immigration-related employment practice. If the document(s) do not reasonably appear on their face to be genuine or to relate to the person presenting them, you must not accept them.

12. **Q.** **Why are certain documents listed in both List B and List C? If these documents are evidence of both identity and employment eligibility, why aren't they found in List A?**

A. Three documents can be found in both List B and List C: the U.S. Citizen ID Card and the ID Card for use of Resident Citizen in the U.S. - acceptable as ID Cards in List B - and a Native American tribal document. Although these documents are evidence of both identity and employment eligibility, they are not found in List A because List A documents are limited to those designated by Congress in the law. An employee can establish both identity and employment eligibility by presenting one of these documents. You should record the document title, issuing authority, number, and expiration date (if any) for that document in the appropriate space for both List B and List C.

STF FED7459I.17

Exhibit A-2 *(continued)*

13. **Q. Why is a Canadian driver's license acceptable as a List B document and not a Mexican driver's license?**

A. The United States-Canada Free-Trade Agreement and other reciprocal agreements between these 2 countries form the basis for accepting a Canadian driver's license as a List B identity document. No such reciprocal agreements currently exist between the United States and Mexico that would allow or permit the use of a Mexican driver's license as a List B identity document.

14. **Q. May I accept an expired document?**

A. You may accept an expired United States Passport. You may also accept an expired document from List B to establish identity. However, the document must reasonably appear on its face to be genuine and to relate to the person presenting it. You cannot accept any other expired documents.

15. **Q. How can I tell if an INS-issued document has expired?**

A. Some INS-issued documents, such as previous versions of the Alien Registration Receipt Card (I-151 and I-551), do not have expiration dates and are valid indefinitely. However, the 1989 revised version of the Alien Registration Receipt Card (I-551), which is rose-colored with computer readable data on the back, features a 2-year or 10-year expiration date. Other INS issued documents, such as the Temporary Resident Card (I-688) and the Employment Authorization Card (I-688A or I-688B) also have expiration dates. These dates can be found either on the face of the document or on a sticker attached to the back of the document.

16. **Q. Some people are presenting me with Social Security Cards that have been laminated. May I accept such cards as evidence of employment eligibility?**

A. You may not accept a laminated Social Security Card as evidence of employment eligibility if the card states on the back "not valid if laminated." Lamination of such cards renders them invalid. Metal or plastic reproductions of Social Security Cards are not acceptable.

17. **Q. Some people are presenting me with printouts from the Social Security Administration with their name, Social Security Number, date of birth, and their parents' names. May I accept such printouts in place of a Social Security Card as evidence of employment eligibility?**

A. No. Only a person's official Social Security Card is acceptable.

18. **Q. What should I do if persons present Social Security Cards marked "NOT VALID FOR EMPLOYMENT," but state they are now authorized to work?**

A. You should ask them to provide another document to establish their employment eligibility, since such Social Security Cards do not establish this.

19. **Q. What should I do if one of my employees tells me that his or her Social Security Number is invalid?**

A. You should tell the employee to get a proper Social Security Number by completing a Form SS-5 This form is available from the Social Security Administration. You do not need to amend your employment tax returns. However, when the employee gives you the new number, you should file a Form W-2C with the Social Security Administration for the years in which you reported income and withholding under the incorrect number. You will not be penalized or fined for the years during which you reported employees under incorrect numbers.

You should also be aware that any Social Security Number starting with a "9" is not a valid Social Security Number. Employees who are using such numbers should be instructed to get a proper Social Security Number using a Form SS-5.

20. **Q. May I accept a photocopy of a document presented by an employee?**

A. No. Employees must present original documents. The only exception is that an employee may present a certified copy of a birth certificate.

STF FED7459I.18

Exhibit A-2 *(continued)*

21. **Q.** I noticed on the Form I-9 that under List A there are 2 spaces for document numbers and expiration dates. Does this mean I have to see 2 List A documents?

    A. No. One of the documents found in List A is an unexpired foreign passport with an attached INS Form I-94. The Form I-9 provides space for you to record the document number and expiration date for both the passport and the INS Form I-94.

22. **Q.** When I review an employee's identity and employment eligibility documents, should I make copies of them?

    A. The law does not require you to photocopy documents. However, if you wish to make photocopies, you should do so for all employees, and you should retain each photocopy with the I-9. Photocopies must not be used for any other purpose. Photocopying documents does not relieve you of your obligation to fully complete Section 2 of the I-9 nor is it an acceptable substitute for proper completion of the I-9 in general.

    NOTE 1: Although a Certificate of Naturalization (INS Forms N-550 and N-570) provides across the face of the document that it may not be copied, such certificates may be copied in this limited situation.

    NOTE 2: *Copies of documents retained by Federal government employers must be kept separately from an employee's official personnel folder.*

Questions About Completing and Retaining the Form I-9

23. **Q.** When do I fill out the I-9 if I hire someone for less than 3 business days?

    A. You must complete both Sections 1 and 2 of the I-9 at the time of the hire. This means the I-9 must be fully completed when the person starts to work.

24. **Q.** What should I do if I rehire a person who previously filled out an I-9?

    A. You do not need to complete a new I-9 if you rehire the person within 3 years of the date that the I-9 was originally completed, and the employee is still eligible to work. You should review the previously completed I-9, and if the employee's work authorization has not expired, note the date of rehire in the Updating and Reverification Section on the I-9 (Section 3), and sign in the appropriate space. If the employee's work authorization has expired, you also need to examine a document that reflects that the employee is authorized to work in the U.S., and record the document title, number, and expiration date (if any) in Section 3.

25. **Q.** What should I do if I need to update or reverify an I-9 for an employee who filled out an earlier version of the form?

    A. You may line through any outdated information and initial and date any updated information. You may also choose, instead, to complete a new I-9.

26. **Q.** Do I need to complete a new I-9 when one of my employees is promoted within my company or transfers to another company office at a different location?

    A. No. You do not need to complete a new I-9 for such promoted or transferred employees.

STF FED7459I.19

Exhibit A-2 *(continued)*

27. **Q. What do I do when an employee's work authorization expires?**

A. You will need to reverify on the I-9 in order to continue to employ the person. Reverification must occur not later than the date that work authorization expires. The employee must present a document that shows either an extension of the employee's initial employment authorization or new work authorization. You must review this document and, if it reasonably appears on its face to be genuine and to relate to the person presenting it, record the document title, number, and expiration date (if any), in the Updating and Reverification Section on the I-9 (Section 3), and sign in the appropriate space. You may want to establish a calendar call-up system for employees whose employment authorization will expire in the future.

NOTE: You cannot refuse to accept a document because it has a future expiration date. You must accept any document (from List A or List C) listed on the I-9 and in Part 8 of this Handbook which on its face reasonably appears to be genuine and to relate to the person presenting it. To do otherwise could be an unfair immigration-related employment practice.

28. **Q. Can I avoid reverifying the I-9s by not hiring persons whose employment authorization has an expiration date?**

A. You cannot refuse to hire persons solely because their employment authorization is temporary. The existence of a future expiration date does not preclude continuous employment authorization for an employee and does not mean that subsequent employment authorization will not be granted. In addition, consideration of a future employment authorization expiration date in determining whether an alien is qualified for a particular job could be an unfair immigration-related employment practice.

29. **Q. As an employer, do I have to fill out all the I-9s myself?**

A. No. You may designate someone to fill out the I-9s for you, such as a personnel officer, foreman, agent, or anyone else acting in your interest. However, you are still liable for any violations of the employer sanctions laws.

30. **Q. Can I contract with someone to complete the I-9s for my business?**

A. Yes. You can contract with another person or business to verify employees' identity and work eligibility and to complete the I-9s for you. However, you are still responsible for the contractor's actions and are liable for any violations of the employer sanctions laws.

31. **Q. As an employer, can I negotiate my responsibility to complete the I-9s in a collective bargaining agreement with a union?**

A. Yes. However, you are still liable for any violations of the employer sanctions laws. If the agreement is for a multi-employer bargaining unit, certain rules apply. The association must track the employee's hire and termination dates each time the employee is hired or terminated by an employer in the multi-employer association.

32. **Q. What are the requirements for retaining the I-9?**

A. If you are an employer, you must retain the I-9 for 3 years after the date employment begins or 1 year after the date the person's employment is terminated, whichever is later. If you are an agricultural association, agricultural employer, or farm labor contractor, you must retain the I-9 for 3 years after the date employment begins for persons you recruit or refer for a fee.

STF FED7459I.20

Exhibit A-2   *(continued)*

33. **Q. Will I get any advance notice if an INS, DOL, or OSC officer wishes to inspect my I-9s?**

A. Yes. The officer will give you at least 3 days (72 hours) advance notice before the inspection. If it is more convenient for you, you may waive the 3-day notice. You may also request an extension of time in which to produce the I-9s. The INS, DOL, or OSC officer will not need to show you a subpoena or a warrant at the time of the inspection.

NOTE: This does not preclude the INS, the DOL, or the OSC from obtaining warrants based on probable cause for entry onto the premises of suspected violators without advance notice.

Failure to provide the I-9s for inspection is a violation of the employer sanctions laws and could result in the imposition of civil money penalties.

34. **Q. Do I have to complete an I-9 for Canadians who entered the United States under the Free Trade Agreement?**

A. Yes. You must complete an I-9 for all employees. Canadians must show identity and employment eligibility documents just like all other employees.

35. **Q. If I acquire a business, can I rely on the I-9s completed by the previous owner/employer?**

A. Yes. However, you also accept full responsibility and liability for all I-9s completed by the previous employer relating to individuals who are continuing in their employment.

36. **Q. If I am a recruiter or referrer for a fee, do I have to fill out I-9s on persons whom I recruit or refer?**

A. No, with three exceptions. Agricultural associations, agricultural employers, and farm labor contractors are still required to complete I-9s on all individuals who are recruited or referred for a fee. However, all recruiters and referrers for a fee must still complete I-9s for their own employees hired after November 6, 1986. Also, all recruiters and referrers for a fee are still liable for knowingly recruiting or referring for a fee aliens not authorized to work in the United States.

37. **Q. Can I complete Section 1 of the I-9 for an employee?**

A. Yes. You may help an employee who needs assistance in completing Section 1 of the I-9. However, you must also complete the "Preparer/Translator Certification" block. The employee must still sign the certification block in Section 1.

38. **Q. If I am a business entity (corporation, partnership, etc.), do I have to fill out I-9s on my employees?**

A. Yes, you must complete I-9s for all of your employees, including yourself.

Exhibit A-2 *(continued)*

39. **Q.** I have heard that some state employment agencies can certify that people they refer are eligible to work. Is that true?

A. Yes. State employment agencies may elect to provide persons they refer with a certification of employment eligibility. If one of these agencies refers potential employees to you with a job order or other appropriate referral form, and the agency sends you a certification within 21 business days of the referral, you do not have to check documents or complete an I-9 if you hire that person. However, you must review the certification to ensure that it relates to the person hired and observe the person sign the certification. You must also retain the certification as you would an I-9 and make it available for inspection, if requested. You should check with your state employment agency to see if it provides this service and become familiar with its certification document.

Questions About Avoiding Discrimination

40. **Q.** How can I avoid discriminating against certain employees while still complying with this law?

A. You can avoid discriminating against certain employees and still comply with the law by applying the employment eligibility verification procedures of this law to all newly hired employees and by hiring without respect to the national origin or citizenship status of those persons authorized to work in the United States. To request to see identity and employment eligibility documents only from persons of a particular origin, or from persons who appear or sound foreign, is a violation of the employer sanctions laws and may also be a violation of Title VII of the Civil Rights Act of 1964. You should not discharge present employees, refuse to hire new employees, or otherwise discriminate on the basis of foreign appearance, accent, language, or name.

41. **Q.** I know that the Act prohibits discrimination on the basis of citizenship status against "protected individuals." Who are protected individuals?

A. Protected individuals include citizens or nationals of the United States, lawful permanent residents, temporary residents, and persons granted refugee or asylee status. The term does not include aliens in one of those classes who fail to make a timely application for naturalization after they become eligible.

42. **Q.** Can I be charged with discrimination if I contact the INS about a document presented to me that does not reasonably appear to be genuine and relate to the person presenting it?

A. No. The anti-discrimination provisions of the Act only apply to the hiring and discharging of individuals. While you are not legally required to inform the INS of such situations, you may do so if you choose to.

STF FED7459l.22

Exhibit A-2 *(continued)*

Questions About Employees Hired Before November 6, 1986

43. **Q. Does this law apply to my employees if I hired them before November 7, 1986?**

   A. No. You are not required to complete I-9s for employees hired before November 7, 1986. However, if you choose to complete I-9s for these employees, you should do so for all your current employees hired before November 7, 1986.

   NOTE: This "grandfather" status does not apply to seasonal employees, or to employees who change employers within a multi-employer association.

44. **Q. What if an employee was hired before November 7, 1986, but has taken an approved leave of absence?**

   A. You do not need to complete an I-9 for that employee if the employee is continuing in his or her employment and has a reasonable expectation of employment at all times. However, if that employee has quit or been terminated, or is an alien who has been removed from the United States, you will need to complete an I-9 for that employee.

45. **Q. Will I be subject to employer sanctions penalties if an employee I hired before November 7, 1986, is an illegal alien?**

   A. No. You will not be subject to employer sanctions penalties for retaining an illegal alien in your workforce if the alien was hired before November 7, 1986. However, the fact that an illegal alien was on your payroll before November 7, 1986, does not give him or her any right to remain in the United States. Unless the alien obtains permission from the INS to remain in the United States, he or she is subject to apprehension and removal.

Questions About Federal Income Tax Obligations

46. **Q. What advice should I give to my employees applying to legalize their status concerning their Federal income tax obligations?**

   A. You can advise employees that when they apply to INS for permanent resident status, they will be given an IRS publication explaining requirements for filing Form -4 or W-4A to insure correct withholding of tax records (if an invalid social security number was used) and other guidelines relating to tax benefits.

47. **Q. What advice should I give to newly-hired employees who ask about their Federal income tax obligations?**

   A. First, you can tell them it is important to have a valid social security number and to properly complete a W-4 or W-4A so that the employer can withhold the proper amount for income tax. Second, you can encourage employees to apply for social security numbers for their dependent children who will be five years old or older by the end of the year. Since 1987, such numbers have been required to be provided for dependents claimed on tax returns.

STF FED74591.23

Exhibit A-2 *(continued)*

Part Eight

Acceptable Documents for Verifying Employment Eligibility

The following documents have been designated for determining employment eligibility by the Act. A person must present a document or documents that establish identity and employment eligibility. A comprehensive list of acceptable documents can be found on the next page of this Handbook and on the back of the Form I-9. Samples of many of the acceptable documents appear on the following pages.

To establish both identity and employment eligibility, a person can present a passport, an Alien Registration Receipt Card, or one of the other documents from List A.

If a person does not present a document from List A, he or she must present one document from List B which establishes identity and one document from List C which establishes employment eligibility.

To establish identity only, a person must present a document from List B, such as a state-issued driver's license, a state-issued identification card, or one of the other documents listed.

To establish employment eligibility only, a person must present a document from List C, such as a Social Security Card, a United States birth certificate, or one of the other documents listed.

If a person is unable to present the required document(s) within 3 business days of the date employment begins, he or she must present (within 3 business days) a receipt showing that he or she has applied for the document. The person then must present the actual document within 90 days of the date employment begins. The person must have indicated on or before the time employment began, by having checked an appropriate box in Section 1, that he or she is already eligible to be employed in the United States.

LIST A

Documents That Establish Both Identity and Employment Eligibility

- United States Passport (unexpired or expired)

- Certificate of United States Citizenship (INS Form N-560 or N-561)

- Certificate of Naturalization (INS Form N-550 or N-570)

- Unexpired foreign passport which:

  ° contains an unexpired stamp which reads "Processed for I-551. Temporary Evidence of Lawful Admission for permanent residence. Valid until _____. Employment authorized;" or

  ° has attached to it a Form I-94 bearing the same name as the passport and containing an employment authorization stamp, so long as the period of endorsement has not yet expired, and the proposed employment is not in conflict with any restrictions or limitations identified on the Form I-94.

  NOTE: For more detailed information concerning the Form I-94, see page 23 of this Handbook.

- Alien Registration Receipt Card (INS Form I-151 or I-551) provided that it contains a photograph of the bearer

- Unexpired Temporary Resident Card (INS Form I-688)

- Unexpired Employment Authorization Card (INS Form I-688A)

- Unexpired reentry permit (INS Form I-327)

- Unexpired Refugee Travel document (INS Form I-571)

- Unexpired Employment Authorization Document issued by the INS which contains a photograph (INS Form I-688B)

STF FED7459I.24

Exhibit A-2 *(continued)*

LIST B

Documents That Establish Identity

For individuals 18 years of age or older:

- Driver's license or ID card issued by a state or outlying possession of the United States provided it contains a photograph or information such as name, date of birth, sex, height, eye color, and address

- ID card issued by federal, state, or local government agencies or entities provided it contains a photograph or information such as name, date of birth, sex, height, eye color, and address (including U.S. Citizen ID Card [INSForm I-197] and ID Card for use of Resident Citizen inthe U.S. [INS Form I-179])

- School identification card with a photograph

- Voter's registration card

- United States military card or draft record

- Military dependent's identification card

- United States Coast Guard Merchant Mariner Card

- Native American tribal document

- Driver's license issued by a Canadian government authority

For individuals under the age of 18 who are unable to present one of the documents listed above:

- School record or report card

- Clinic, doctor, or hospital record

- Day-care or nursery school record

LIST C

Documents That Establish Employment Eligibility

- U.S. Social Security Number Card other than one which has printed on its face "NOT VALID FOR EMPLOYMENT"

  NOTE: *This must be a card issued by the Social Security Administration; a facsimile (such as a metal or plastic reproduction) is not an acceptable document.*

- Certification of Birth Abroad issued by the Department of State (Form FS-545 or Form DS-1350)

- Original or certified copy of a birth certificate issued by a state, county, municipal authority, or outlying possession of the United States bearing an official seal

- Native American tribal document

- U.S. Citizen ID Card (INS Form I-197) ID Card for Use of Resident Citizen in the U.S. (INS Form I-179)

- Unexpired employment authorization document issued by the INS

STF FED7459I.25

Exhibit A-2   *(continued)*

Document List A
Documents That Establish Both Identity and Employment Eligibility
The following illustrations in this handbook do not necessarily reflect the actual size of the documents.

United States Passport
Issued by the Department of State to United States citizens and nationals.

Certificate of United States Citizenship
N-560 or N-561
Issued by INS to individuals who: 1) derived citizenship through parental naturalization; 2) acquired citizenship at birth abroad through a United States parent or parents; or 3) acquired citizenship through application by United States citizen adoptive parent(s); and who, pursuant to section 341 of the Act, have applied for a certificate of citizenship.

Certificate of Naturalization
N-550 or N-570
Issued by INS to naturalized United States citizens.

Certificate of Naturalization
N-550
Issued by INS to naturalized United States citizens who file for naturalization after October 1, 1991.

STF FED7459I.26

Exhibit A-2   *(continued)*

Unexpired Foreign Passport with I-551 Stamp

I-94 Arrival/Departure Record

Arrival-departure record issued by INS to nonimmigrant aliens. An individual in possession of the departure portion of this document may only be employed if the document bears an "employment authorization" stamp or employment incident to the nonimmigrant classification is authorized with a specific employer (i.e. A-1, A-2, A-3, C-2, C-3, E-1, E-2, G-1, G-2, G-3, G-4, G-5, H-1A, H-1B, H-2A, H-2B, H-3, I, L-1, O-1, O-2, P-1, P-2, P-3, Q, NATO 1-7 and TC). The expiration date is noted on the Form I-94.

STF FED7459I.27

Exhibit A-2 *(continued)*

Alien Registration Receipt Card I-151

Issued by INS prior to June 1978, to lawful permanent resident aliens. There are numerous versions of this card because it was periodically revised. Although this card is no longer issued, it is valid indefinitely. This card is also commonly referred to as a "green card" although most versions were blue.

Alien Registration Receipt Card (Resident Alien Card) I-551

Issued by INS after March 1977, to lawful permanent resident aliens. Although this card is no longer issued, it is valid indefinitely. This card is commonly referred to as a "green card" and is the replacement for the Form I-151. This version is white with a blue logo.

Alien Registration Receipt Card (Conditional Resident Alien Card) I-551

Issued by INS after January 1987, to conditional permanent resident aliens such as alien spouses of United States citizens or lawful permanent resident aliens. It is similar to the I-551 issued to permanent resident aliens. Although this card is no longer issued, it is valid for 2 years from the date of admission or adjustment. The expiration date is stated on the back of the card. This version is white with a blue logo.

Alien Registration Receipt Card (Resident Alien Card) I-551

Currently issued by INS since 1989 to both conditional and lawful permanent resident aliens. Although it is similar to the previously issued I-551s, this card is valid only for a limited period of time - 2 years from the date of admission or adjustment for conditional permanent resident aliens and 10 years from issuance for lawful permanent resident aliens. The expiration date is stated on the front of the card. This version is rose-colored with a blue logo.

STF FED74591.28

Exhibit A-2 *(continued)*

Temporary Resident Card I-688

Issued by INS to aliens granted temporary resident status under the Legalization or Special Agricultural Worker program. It is valid until the expiration date stated on the face of the card or on the sticker(s) placed on the back of the card.

Employment Authorization Card I-688A

Issued by INS to applicants for temporary resident status after their interview for Legalization or Special Agricultural Worker status. It is valid until the expiration date stated on the face of the card or on the sticker(s) placed on the back of the card.

STF FED7459I.29

Exhibit A-2 *(continued)*

26

Employment Authorization Card I -688B

Issued by INS to aliens granted temporary employment authorization in the U.S. The expiration date is noted on the face of the card

Unexpired Re-Entry Permit I-327

Issued by INS to lawful permanent resident aliens before they leave the United States for a 1-2 year period.

STF FED7459I30

Exhibit A-2   *(continued)*

Unexpired Refugee Travel Document I-571
Issued by INS to aliens who have been granted refugee status. The expiration date is stated on page four (4).

Exhibit A-2   *(continued)*

Document List B

Documents That Establish Identity Only

The following illustrations in this handbook do not necessarily reflect the actual size of the documents.

Sample Driver's License

A driver's license issued by any state or outlying possession of the United States (including the District of Columbia, Puerto Rico, the Virgin Islands, Guam, the Northern Mariana Islands, and American Samoa) or by a Canadian government authority is acceptable if it contains a photograph or other identifying information such as name, date of birth, sex, height, color of eyes, and address.

Sample State Identification Card

An identification card issued by any state (including the District of Columbia, Puerto Rico, the Virgin Islands, Guam, and the Northern Mariana Islands) or by a local government is acceptable if it contains a photograph or other identifying information such as name, date of birth, sex, height, color of eyes, and address.

See List C for ID cards issued by INS.

STF FED74591.32

Exhibit A-2   *(continued)*

Document List C

Documents That Establish Employment Eligibility Only

The following illustrations in this handbook do not necessarily reflect the actual size of the documents.

Social Security Card (other than one stating "Not Valid For Employment," metal or plastic reproductions, or certain laminated cards.) There are many versions of this card.

Certifications of Birth Issued by the Department of State

FS-545	DS-1350
Issued by U.S. embassies and consulates overseas to United States citizens born abroad.	Issued by the U.S. Department of State to United States citizens born abroad.

Exhibit A-2 *(continued)*

United States Citizen Identification Card I-197

Issued by INS to United States citizens. Although INS no longer issues this card, it is valid indefinitely.

Identification Card for Use of Resident Citizen in the United States I-179

Issued by INS to United States citizens who are residents of the United States. Although INS no longer issues this card, it is valid indefinitely.

STF FED74591.34

Exhibit A-2   *(continued)*

I-20 ID Card Accompanied by a Form I-94

The Form I-94 for F-1 nonimmigrant students must be accompanied by an I-20 Student ID endorsed with employment authorization by the Designated School Official for off-campus employment or curriculum practical training. INS will issue Form I-688B (Employment Authorization Document) to all students (F-1 and M-1) authorized for a post-completion practical training period.

Form I-20 Student ID (Reverse)

Endorsement by Designated School Official for Employment Authorization.

STF FED7459I.35

Exhibit A-2   *(continued)*

REMEMBER:

- Hiring employees without complying with the employment eligibility verification requirements is a violation of the employer sanctions laws.

- This law requires employees hired after NOVEMBER 6, 1986 to present documentation that establishes identity and employment eligibility, and employers to record this information on Forms I-9.

- Employers may not discriminate against employees on the basis of national origin or citizenship status.

If you have questions after reviewing this Handbook, please contact your local INS office at the address found in the back of this Handbook. Direct your letter to the attention of the Employer Relations Officer.
DO NOT CONTACT THE INTERNAL REVENUE SERVICE (IRS)

STF FED7459L37

Exhibit A-2 *(continued)*

Form SS-4
(Rev. December 1995)
Department of the Treasury
Internal Revenue Service

Application for Employer Identification Number

(For use by employers, corporations, partnerships, trusts, estates, churches, government agencies, certain individuals, and others. See instructions.)
► Keep a copy for your records.

EIN

OMB No. 1545-0003

Please type or print clearly.

1 Name of applicant (Legal name) (See instructions.)	

2 Trade name of business (if different from name on line 1)	**3** Executor, trustee, "care of" name	

4a Mailing address (street address) (room, apt., or suite no.)	**5a** Business address (if different from address in lines 4a and 4b)
4b City, state, and ZIP code	**5b** City, state, and ZIP code

6 County and state where principal business is located

7 Name of principal officer, general partner, grantor, owner, or trustor — SSN required (See instructions.) ►

8a Type of entity (Check only one box.) (See instructions.)

☐ Sole proprietor (SSN) _____
☐ Partnership   ☐ Personal service corp.
☐ REMIC   ☐ Limited liability co.
☐ State/local government   ☐ National Guard
☐ Other nonprofit organization (specify) ►
☐ Other (specify) ►

☐ Estate (SSN of decedent) _____
☐ Plan administrator - SSN _____
☐ Other corporation (specify) ►
☐ Trust   ☐ Farmers' cooperative
☐ Federal Government/military   ☐ Church or church-controlled organization
(enter GEN if applicable)

8b If a corporation, name the state or foreign country (if applicable) where incorporated

State	Foreign country

9 Reason for applying (Check only one box.)

☐ Started new business (specify) ►
☐ Hired employees
☐ Created a pension plan (specify type) ►

☐ Banking purpose (specify) ►
☐ Changed type of organization (specify) ►
☐ Purchased going business
☐ Created a trust (specify) ►
☐ Other (specify) ►

10 Date business started or acquired (Mo., day, year) (See instructions.)

11 Closing month of accounting year (See instructions.)

12 First date wages or annuities were paid or will be paid (Mo., day, year). **Note:** *If applicant is a withholding agent, enter date income will first be paid to nonresident alien. (Mo., day, year)* .... ►

13 Highest number of employees expected in the next 12 months. **Note:** *If the applicant does not expect to have any employees during the period, enter -0-. (See instructions.)* .... ►	Nonagricultural	Agricultural	Household

14 Principal activity (See instructions.) ►

15 Is the principal business activity manufacturing? .... ☐ Yes ☐ No
If "Yes," principal product and raw material used ►

16 To whom are most of the products or services sold? Please check the appropriate box.   ☐ Business (wholesale)
☐ Public (retail)   ☐ Other (specify) ►   ☐ N/A

17a Has the applicant ever applied for an identification number for this or any other business? .... ☐ Yes ☐ No
Note: *If "Yes," please complete lines 17b and 17c.*

17b If you checked "Yes" on line 17a, give applicant's legal name and trade name shown on prior application, if different than name shown on line 1 or 2 above.
Legal name ►   Trade name ►

17c Approximate date when and city and state where the application was filed. Enter previous employer identification number if known.

Approximate date when filed (Mo., day, year)	City and state where filed	Previous EIN

Under penalties of perjury, I declare that I have examined this application, and to the best of my knowledge and belief, it is true, correct, and complete.

Business telephone number (include area code)

Fax telephone number (include area code)

Name and title (Please type or print clearly.) ►

Signature ►   Date ►

Note: *Do not write below this line. For official use only.*

Please leave blank ►	Geo.	Ind.	Class	Size	Reason for applying

For Paperwork Reduction Act Notice, see page 4.
ISA

Form **SS-4** (Rev. 12-95)

STF FED7769F

Exhibit A-3   Form SS-4 Application for Employer Identification Number, and Instructions

General Instructions

Section references are to the Internal Revenue Code unless otherwise noted.

Purpose of Form

Use Form SS-4 to apply for an employer identification number (EIN). An EIN is a nine-digit number (for example, 12-3456789) assigned to sole proprietors, corporations, partnerships, estates, trusts, and other entities for filing and reporting purposes. The information you provide on this form will establish your filing and reporting requirements.

Who Must File

You must file this form if you have not obtained an EIN before and:

• You pay wages to one or more employees including household employees.

• You are required to have an EIN to use on any return, statement, or other document, even if you are not an employer.

• You are a withholding agent required to withhold taxes on income, other than wages, paid to a nonresident alien (individual, corporation, partnership, etc.). A withholding agent may be an agent, broker, fiduciary, manager, tenant, or spouse, and is required to file Form 1042, Annual Withholding Tax Return for U.S. Source Income of Foreign Persons.

• You file Schedule C, Profit or Loss From Business, or Schedule F, Profit or Loss From Farming, of Form 1040, U.S. Individual Income Tax Return, and have a Keogh plan or are required to file excise, employment, information, or alcohol, tobacco or firearms returns.

The following must use EINs even if they do not have any employees:

• State and local agencies who serve as tax reporting agents for public assistance recipients, under Rev. Proc. 80-4, 1980-1 C.B. 581, should obtain a separate EIN for this reporting. See Household employer on page 3.

• Trusts, except the following:

1. Certain grantor-owned revocable trusts. (See the Instructions for Form 1041.)

2. Individual Retirement Arrangement (IRA) trusts, unless the trust has to file Form 990-T, Exempt Organization Business Income Tax Return. (See the Instructions for Form 990-T.)

3. Certain trusts that are considered household employers can use the trust EIN to report and pay the social security and Medicare taxes, Federal unemployment tax (FUTA) and withheld Federal income tax. A separate EIN in not necessary.

• Estates

• Partnerships

• REMICs (real estate mortgage investment conduits) (See the Instructions for Form 1066, U.S. Real Estate Mortgage Investment Conduit Income Tax Return.)

• Corporations

• Nonprofit organizations (churches, clubs, etc.)

• Farmers' cooperatives

• Plan administrators (A plan administrator is the person or group of persons specified as the administrator by the instrument under which the plan is operated.)

When To Apply for a New EIN

New Business. — If you become the new owner of an existing business, do not use the EIN of the former owner. IF YOU ALREADY HAVE AN EIN, USE THAT NUMBER. If you do not have an EIN, apply for one on this form. If you become the "owner" of a corporation by acquiring its stock, use the corporation's EIN.

Changes in Organization or Ownership. —If you already have an EIN, you may need to get a new one if either the organization or ownership of your business changes. If you incorporate a sole proprietorship or form a partnership, you must get a new EIN. However, do not apply for a new EIN if you change only the name of your business.

Note: *If you are electing to be an "S corporation," be sure you file Form 2553, Election by a Small Business Corporation.*

File Only one Form SS-4. —File only one Form SS-4, regardless of the number of business operated or trade names under which a business operates. However, each corporation in an affiliated group must file a separate application.

EIN Applied for, But Not Received. —If you do not have an EIN by the time a return is due, write "Applied for" and the date you applied in the space shown for the number. Do not show your social security number as an EIN on returns.

If you do not have an EIN by the time a tax deposit is due, send your payment to the Internal Revenue Service Center for your filing area. (See Where To Apply below.) Make your check or money order payable to Internal Revenue Service and show your name (as shown on Form SS-4) address, type of tax, period covered, and date you applied for an EIN. Send an explanation with the deposit.

For more information about EINs, see Pub. 583, Starting a Business and Keeping Records, and Pub. 1635, Understanding Your EIN.

How To Apply

You can apply for an EIN either by mail or by telephone. You can get an EIN immediately by calling the Tele-Tin phone number for the service center for your state, or you can send the completed Form SS-4 directly to the service center to receive your EIN in the mail.

Application by Tele-TIN. —Under the Tele-TIN program, you can receive your EIN over the telephone and use it immediately to file a return or make a payment. To receive an EIN by phone, complete Form SS-4, then call the Tele-TIN phone number listed for your state under Where To Apply. The person making the call must be authorized to sign the form. (See Signature block on page 4.)

An IRS representative will use the information from the Form SS-4 to establish your account and assign you an EIN. Write the number you are given on the upper right-hand corner of the form, sign and date it.

Mail or FAX the signed SS-4 within 24 hours to the Tele-Tin Unit at the service center address for your state. The IRS representative will give you the FAX number. The FAX numbers are also listed in Pub. 1635.

Taxpayer representatives can receive their client's EIN by phone if they first send a facsimile (FAX) of a completed Form 2848, Power of Attorney and Declaration of Representative, or Form 8821, Tax Information Authorization, to the Tele-TIN unit. The Form 2848 or Form 8821 will be used solely to release the EIN to the representative authorized on the form.

Application by Mail. —Complete Form SS-4 at least 4 to 5 weeks before you will need an EIN. Sign and date the application and mail it to the service center address for your state. You will receive your EIN in the mail in approximately 4 weeks.

Where To Apply

The Tele-TIN phone numbers listed below will involve a long-distance charge to callers outside of the local calling area and can be used only to apply for an EIN. THE NUMBERS MAY CHANGE WITHOUT NOTICE. Use 1-800-829-1040 to verify a number or to ask about an application by mail or other Federal tax matters.

If your principal business, office or agency, or legal residence in the case of an individual, is located in: ▼	Call the Tele-TIN Phone number shown or file with the Internal Revenue Service Center at: ▼
Florida, Georgia, South Carolina	Attn: Entity Control Atlanta, GA 39901 (404) 455-2360
New Jersey, New York City and counties of Nassau, Rockland, Suffolk, and Westchester	Attn: Entity Control Holtsville, NY 00501 (516) 447-4955
New York (all other counties), Connecticut, Maine, Massachusetts, New Hampshire, Rhode Island, Vermont	Attn: Entity Control Andover, MA 05501 (508) 474-9717
Illinois, Iowa, Minnesota, Missouri, Wisconsin	Attn: Entity Control Stop 57A 2306 E. Bannister Rd. Kansas City, MO 64131 (816) 926-5999
Delaware, District of Columbia, Maryland, Pennsylvania, Virginia	Attn: Entity Control Philadelphia, PA 19255 (215) 574-2400
Indiana, Kentucky, Michigan, Ohio, West Virginia	Attn: Entity Control Cincinnati, OH 45999 (606) 292-5467
Kansas, New Mexico, Oklahoma, Texas	Attn: Entity Control Austin, TX 73301 (512) 460-7843

STF FED7769L1

Exhibit A-3 *(continued)*

Alaska, Arizona, California
(counties of Alpine, Amador,
Butte, Calaveras, Colusa, Contra
Costa, Del Norte, El Dorado,
Glenn, Humboldt, Lake, Lassen,
Marin, Mendocino, Modoc, — Attn: Entity Control
Napa, Nevada, Placer, Plumas, — Mail Stop 6271-T
Sacramento, San Joaquin, — P.O. Box 9950
Shasta, Sierra, Siskiyou, Solano, — Ogden, UT 84409
Sonoma, Sutter, Tehama, Trinity, — (801) 620-7645
Yolo, and Yuba), Colorado,
Idaho, Montana, Nebraska,
Nevada, North Dakota, Oregon,
South Dakota, Utah,
Washington, Wyoming

California (all other — Attn: Entity Control
counties), Hawaii — Fresno, CA 93888
— (209) 452-4010

Alabama, Arkansas, — Attn: Entity Control
Louisiana, Mississippi, — Memphis, TN 37501
North Carolina, Tennessee — (901) 546-3920

If you have no legal residence, principal place of business, or principal office or agency in any state, file your form with the Internal Revenue Service Center, Philadelphia, PA 19255 or call 215-574-2400.

Specific Instructions

The instructions that follow are for those items that are not self-explanatory. Enter N/A (nonapplicable) on the lines that do not apply.

Line 1. — Enter the legal name of the entity applying for the EIN exactly as it appears on the social security card, charter, or other applicable legal document.

Individuals. — Enter the first name, middle initial, and last name, If you are a sole proprietor, enter your individual name, not your business name. Do not use abbreviations or nicknames.

Trusts. — Enter the name of the trust.

Estate of a decedent. — Enter the name of the estate.

Partnership. — Enter the legal name of the partnership agreement. Do not list the names of the partners on line 1. See the specific instructions for line 7.

Corporations. — Enter the corporate name as it appears in the corporation charter or other legal document creating it.

Plan administrators. — Enter the name of the plan administrator. A plan administrator who already has an EIN should use that number.

Line 2. — Enter the trade name of the business if different from the legal name. The trade name is the "doing business as" name.

Note: *Use the full legal name on line 1 on all tax returns filed for the entity. However, if you enter a trade name on line 2 and choose to use the trade name instead of the legal name, enter the trade name on all returns you file. To prevent processing delays and errors, always use either the legal name only or the trade name only on all tax returns.*

Line 3. — Trusts enter the name of the trustee. Estates enter the name of the executor, administrator, or other fiduciary. If the entity applying has a designated person to receive tax information, enter that person's name as the "care of" person. Print or type the first name, middle initial, and last name.

Line 7. — Enter the first name, middle initial, last name, and social security number (SSN) of a principal officer if the business is a corporation; of a general partner if a partnership; or of a grantor, owner, or trustor if a trust.

Line 8a. — Check the box that best describes the type of entity applying for the EIN. If not specifically mentioned, check the "Other" box and enter the type of entity. Do not enter N/A.

Sole proprietor. — Check this box if you file Schedule C or F (Form 1040) and have a Keogh plan, or are required to file exise, employment, information, or alcohol, tobacco, or firearms returns. Enter you SSN in the space provided.

REMIC. — Check this box if the entity has elected to be treated as a real estate mortgage investment conduit (REMIC). See the Instructions for Form 1066 for more information.

Other nonprofit organization. — Check this box if the nonprofit organization is other than a church or church-controlled organization and specify the type of nonprofit organization (for example, an educational organization).

If the organization also seeks tax-exempt status, you must file either Package 1023 or Package 1024, Application for Recognition of Exemption. Get Pub. 557, Tax-Exempt Status for your Organization, for more information.

Group exemption number (GEN). — If the organization is covered by a group exemption letter, enter the four-digit GEN. (Do not confuse the GEN with the nine-digit EIN.) If you do not know the GEN, contact the parent organization. Get Pub. 557 for more information about group exemption numbers.

Withholding agent. — If you are a withholding agent required to file Form 1042, check the "Other" box and enter "Withholding agent.

Personal service corporation. — Check this box if the entity is a personal service corporation. An entity is a personal service corporation for a tax year only if:

● The principal activity of the entity during the testing period (prior tax year) for the tax year is the performance of personal services substantially by employee-owners, and

● The employee-owners own 10% of the fair market value of the outstanding stock in the entity on the last day of the testing period.

Personal Services include performance of services in such fields as health, law, accounting, or consulting. For more information about personal service corporations, see the Instructions for Form 1120, U.S. Corporation Income Tax Return, and Pub. 542, Tax information on Corporations.

Limited liability co. — See the definition of limited liability company in the Instructions for Form 1065. If you are classified as a partnership for Federal income tax purposes mark the "Limited liability co." checkbox. If you are classified as a corporation for Federal income tax purposes, mark the "Other corporation" checkbox and write "Limited liability co." in the space provided.

Plan administrator. — If the plan administrator is an individual, enter the plan administrator's SSN in the space provided.

Other Corporation. — This box is for any corporation other than a personal service corporation. If you check this box, enter the type of corporation (such as insurance company) in the space provided.

Household employer. — If you are an individual, check the "Other" box and enter "Household employer" and your SSN. If you are a state or local agency serving as a tax reporting agent for public assistance recipients who become household employers, check the "Other" box and enter "Household employer agent." If you are a trust that qualifies as a household employer, you do not need a separate EIN for reporting tax information relating to household employees; use the EIN of the trust.

Line 9. — Check only one box. Do not enter N/A.

Started new business. — Check this box if you are starting a new business that requires an EIN. If you check this box, enter the type of business being started. Do not apply if you already have an EIN and are only adding another place of business.

Hired employees. — Check this box if the existing business is requesting an EIN because it has hired or is hiring employees and is therefore required to file employment tax returns. Do not apply if you already have an EIN and are only hiring employees. For information on the applicable employment taxes for family members, see Circular E, Employer's Tax Guide (Publication 15).

Created a pension plan. — Check this box if you have created a pension plan and need this number for reporting purposes. Also, enter the type of plan created.

Banking purpose. — Check this box if you are requesting an EIN for banking purpose only, and enter the banking purpose (for example, a bowling league for depositing dues or an investment club for dividend and interest reporting).

Changed type of organization. — Check this box if the business is changing its type of organization, for example, if the business was a sole proprietorship and has been incorporated or has become a partnership. If you check this box, specify in the space provided the type of change made, for example, "from sole proprietorship to partnership."

Purchased going business. — Check this box if you purchased an existing business. Do not use the former owner's EIN. Do not apply for a new EIN if you already have one. Use your own EIN.

Created a trust. — Check this box if you created a trust, and enter the type of trust created.

STF FED7769l.2

Exhibit A-3 *(continued)*

Note: *Do not file this form if you are the grantor/owner of certain revocable trusts. You must use your SSN for the trust. See the instructions for Form 1041.*

Other (specify). — Check this box if you are requesting an EIN for any reason other than those for which there are checkboxes, and enter the reason.

Line 10. — If you started a new business, enter the starting date of the business. If the business you acquired is already operating, enter the date you acquired the business. Trusts should enter the date the trust was legally created. Estates should enter the date of death of decedent whose name appears on line 1 or the date when the estate was legally funded.

Line 11. — Enter the last month of your accounting year or tax year. An accounting or tax year is usually 12 consecutive months, either a calendar year or a fiscal year (including a period of 52 or 53 weeks). A calendar year is 12 consecutive months ending on December 31. A fiscal year is either 12 consecutive months ending on the last day of any month other than December or a 52-53 week year. For more information on accounting periods, see Pub. 538, Accounting Periods and methods.

Individuals. — Your tax year generally will be a calendar year.

Partnerships. — Partnerships generally must adopt the tax year of either (a) the majority partners; (b) the principal partners; (c) the tax year that results in the least aggregate (total) deferral of income; or (d) some other tax year. (See the Instructions for Form 1065, U.S. Partnership Return of income, for more information.)

REMIC. — REMICs must have a calendar year as their tax year.

Personal service corporations. — A personal service corporation generally must adopt a calendar year unless:

● It can establish a business purpose for having a different tax year, or

● It elects under section 444 to have a tax year other than a calendar year.

Trusts. — Generally, a trust must adopt a calendar year except for the following:

● Tax exempt trusts,

● Charitable trusts, and

● Grantor-owned trusts.

Line 12. — If the business has or will have employees, enter the date on which the business began or will begin to pay wages. If the business does not plan to have employees, enter N/A.

Withholding agent. — Enter the date you began or will begin to pay income to a nonresident alien. This also applies to individuals who are required to file Form 1042 to report alimony paid to a nonresident alien.

Line 13. — For a definition of agricultural labor (farmworker), see Circular A, Agricultural Employer's Tax Guide (Publication 51).

Line 14. — Generally, enter the exact type of business being operated (for example, advertising agency, farm, food or beverage establishment, labor union, real estate agency, steam laundry, rental of coin-operated vending machine, or investment club). Also state if the business will involve the sale or distribution of alcoholic beverages.

Governmental. — Enter the type of organization (state, county, school district, municipality, etc.).

Nonprofit organization (other than governmental). — Enter whether organized for religious, educational, or humane purposes, and the principal activity (for example, religious organization-hospital, charitable).

Mining and quarrying. — Specify the process and the principal product (for example, mining bituminous coal, contract drilling for oil, or quarrying dimension stone).

Contract construction. — Specify whether general contracting or special trade contracting. Also, show the type of work normally performed (for example, general contractor for residential buildings or electrical subcontractor).

Food or beverage establishments. — Specify the type of establishment and state whether you employ workers who receive tips (for example, lounge — yes).

Trade. — Specify the type of sales and the principal line of goods sold (for example, wholesale dairy products, manufacturer's representative for mining machinery, or retail hardware).

Manufacturing. — Specify the type of establishment operated (for example, sawmill or vegetable cannery).

Signature block. — The application must be signed by (a) the individual, if the applicant is an individual, (b) the president, vice president, or other principal officer, if the applicant is a corporation, (c) a responsible and duly authorized member or officer having knowledge of its affairs, if the applicant is a partnership or other unincorporated organization, or (d) the fiduciary, if the applicant is a trust or estate.

Some Useful Publication

You may get the following publications for additional information on the subjects covered on this form. To get these and other free forms and publications, call 1-800-TAX-FORM (1-800-829-3676). You should receive your order or notification of its status within 7 to 15 workdays of your call.

Use your computer. — If you subscribe to an on-line service, ask if IRS information is available and, if so, how to access it. You can also get information through IRIS, the Internal Revenue Information Services, on FedWorld, a government bulletin board. Tax forms, instructions, publications, and other IRS information, are available through IRIS.

IRIS is accessible directly by calling 703-321-8020. On the Internet, you can telnet to

fedworld.gov. or, for file transfer protocol services, connect to ftp.fedworld.gov. If you are using the WorldWide Web, connect to http://www.ustreas.gov

FedWorld's help desk offers technical assistance on accessing IRIS (not tax help) during regular business hour at 703-487-4608. The IRIS menus offer information on available file formats and software needed to read and print files. You must print the forms to use them; the forms are not designed to be filled out on-screen.

Tax forms, instructions, and publication are also available on CD-ROM, including prior-year forms starting with the 1991 tax year. For ordering information and software requirements, contact the Government Printing Office's Superintendent of Documents (202-512-1800) or Federal Bulletin Board (202-512-1387).

Pub. 1635, Understanding Your EIN

Pub. 15, Employer's Tax Guide

Pub. 15-A, Employer's Supplemental Tax Guide

Pub. 538, Accounting Periods and Methods

Pub. 541, Tax Information on Partnerships

Pub. 542, Tax Information on Corporations

Pub. 557, Tax-Exempt Status for Your Organization

Pub. 583, Starting a Business and Keeping Records

Package 1023, Application for Recognition of Exemption

Package 1024, Application for Recognition of Exemption Under Section 501(a) or for Determination Under Section 120

Paperwork Reduction Act Notice

We ask for the information on this form to carry out the Internal Revenue laws of the United States. You are required to give us the information. We need it to ensure that you are complying with these laws and to allow us to figure and collect the right amount of tax.

The time needed to complete and file this form will vary depending on individual circumstances. The estimated average time is:

Recordkeeping	7 min.
Learning about the law or the form	18 min.
Preparing the form	45 min.
Copying, assembling, and sending the form to the IRS	20 min.

If you have comments concerning the accuracy of these time estimates or suggestions for making this form simpler, we would be happy to hear from you. You can write to the Tax Forms Committee, Western Area Distribution Center, Rancho Cordova, CA 95743-0001. Do not send this form to this address. Instead, see Where To Apply on page 2.

STF FED7769I.3

Exhibit A-3   *(continued)*

Form W-4 (1995)

Want More Money In Your Paycheck?
If you expect to be able to claim the earned income credit for 1995 and a child lives with you, you may be able to have part of the credit added to your take-home pay. For details, get Form W-5 from your employer.

Purpose. Complete Form W-4 so that your employer can withhold the correct amount of Federal income tax from your pay.

Exemption From Withholding. Read line 7 of the certificate below to see if you can claim exempt status. If exempt, complete line 7; but do not complete lines 5 and 6. No Federal income tax will be withheld from your pay. Your exemption is good for 1 year only. It expires February 15, 1996.

Note: You cannot claim exemption from withholding if (1) your income exceeds $650 and includes unearned income (e.g., interest and dividends) and (2) another

person can claim you as a dependent on their tax return.

Basic Instructions. Employees who are not exempt should complete the Personal Allowances Worksheet. Additional worksheets are provided on page 2 for employees to adjust their withholding allowances based on itemized deductions, adjustments to income, or two-earner/two-job situations. Complete all worksheets that apply to your situation. The worksheets will help you figure the number of withholding allowances you are entitled to claim. However, you may claim fewer allowances than this.

Head of Household. Generally, you may claim head of household filing status on your tax return only if you are unmarried and pay more than 50% of the costs of keeping up a home for yourself and your dependent(s) or other qualifying individuals.

Nonwage Income. If you have a large amount of nonwage income, such as interest or dividends, you should consider making estimated tax payments

using Form 1040-ES. Otherwise, you may find that you owe additional tax at the end of the year.

Two Earners/Two Jobs. If you have a working spouse or more than one job, figure the total number of allowances you are entitled to claim on all jobs using worksheets from only one Form W-4. This total should be divided among all jobs. Your withholding will usually be most accurate when all allowances are claimed on the W-4 filed for the highest paying job and zero allowances are claimed for the others.

Check Your Withholding. After your W-4 takes effect, you can use Pub. 919, Is My Withholding Correct for 1995?, to see how the dollar amount you are having withheld compares to your estimated total annual tax. We recommend you get Pub. 919 especially if you used the Two Earner/Two Job Worksheet and your earnings exceed $150,000 (Single) or $200,000 (Married). Call 1-800-829-3676 to order Pub. 919. Check your telephone directory for the IRS assistance number for further help.

Personal Allowances Worksheet

A Enter "1" for **yourself** if no one else can claim you as a dependent . . . . **A** _____

B Enter "1" if:
- You are single and have only one job; or
- You are married, have only one job, and your spouse does not work; or
- Your wages from a second job or your spouse's wages (or the total of both) are $1,000 or less.   . . . . **B** _____

C Enter "1" for your **spouse**. But, you may choose to enter -0- if you are married and have either a working spouse or more than one job (this may help you avoid having too little tax withheld) . . . . **C** _____

D Enter number of **dependents** (other than your spouse or yourself) you will claim on your tax return . . . . **D** _____

E Enter "1" if you will file as **head of household** on your tax return (see conditions under Head of Household above) . . . . **E** _____

F Enter "1" if you have at least $1,500 of **child or dependent care expenses** for which you plan to claim a credit . **F** _____

G Add lines A through F and enter total here. Note: This amount may be different from the number of exemptions you claim on your return . . . ▶ **G** _____

For accuracy
do all
worksheets
that apply.
- If you plan to **itemize or claim adjustments to income** and want to reduce your withholding, see the Deductions and Adjustments Worksheet on page 2.
- If you are **single** and have **more than one job** and your combined earnings from all jobs exceed $30,000 OR if you are **married** and have a **working spouse or more than one job** and the combined earnings from all jobs exceed $50,000, see the Two-Earner Two-Job Worksheet on page 2 if you want to avoid having too little tax withheld.
- If **neither** of the above situations applies, stop here and enter the number from line G on line 5 of Form W-4 below.

- - - - - - - - - - - - - Cut here and give the certificate to your employer. Keep the top portion for your records. - - - - - - - - - - - - -

Form **W-4**

Department of the Treasury
Internal Revenue Service

Employee's Withholding Allowance Certificate

▶ For Privacy Act and Paperwork Reduction Act Notice, see reverse.

OMB No. 1545-0010

1995

1 Type or print your first name and middle initial	Last name		2 Your social security number

Home address (number and street or rural route)	3 ☐ Single ☐ Married ☐ Married, but withhold at higher Single rate.
	Note: If married, but legally separated, or spouse is a nonresident alien, check the Single box.
City or town, state, and ZIP code	4 If your last name differs from that on your social security card, check here and call 1-800-772-1213 for a new card . . . . ▶ ☐

5 Total number of allowances you are claiming (from line G above or from the worksheets on page 2 if they apply) . . . . **5** _____

6 Additional amount, if any, you want withheld from each paycheck . . . . **6** $ _____

7 I claim exemption from withholding for 1995 and I certify that I meet **BOTH** of the following conditions for exemption:
- Last year I had a right to a refund of **ALL** Federal income tax withheld because I had **NO** tax liability; **AND**
- This year I expect a refund of **ALL** Federal income tax withheld because I expect to have **NO** tax liability.

If you meet both conditions, enter "EXEMPT" here . . . . ▶ **7**

Under penalties of perjury, I certify that I am entitled to the number of withholding allowances claimed on this certificate or entitled to claim exempt status.

Employee's signature ▶ _____ Date ▶ _____ , 19 _____

8 Employer's name and address (Employer: Complete 8 and 10 only if sending to the IRS)	9 Office code (optional)	10 Employer identification number

Cat. No. 10220Q

STF FED8105F 1

Exhibit A-4   Form W-4 Employee's Withholding Allowance Certificate, and Instructions (Revised March 1994)

Deductions and Adjustments Worksheet

Note: *Use this worksheet only if you plan to itemize deductions or claim adjustments to income on your 1995 tax return.*

1 Enter an estimate of your 1995 itemized deductions. These include qualifying home mortgage interest, charitable contributions, state and local taxes (but not sales taxes), medical expenses in excess of 7.5% of your income, and miscellaneous deductions. (For 1995, you may have to reduce your itemized deductions if your income is over $114,700 ($57,350 if married filing separately). Get Pub. 919 for details.) ...... **1** $ _____

2 Enter: { $6,550 if married filing jointly or qualifying widow(er) }
         { $5,750 if head of household   } .... **2** $ _____
         { $3,900 if single   }
         { $3,275 if married filing separately   }

3 **Subtract** line 2 from line 1. If line 2 is greater than line 1, enter -0- .... **3** $ _____
4 Enter an estimate of your 1995 adjustments to income. These include alimony paid and deductible IRA contributions ... **4** $ _____
5 **Add** lines 3 and 4 and enter the total .... **5** $ _____
6 Enter an estimate of your 1995 nonwage income (such as dividends or interest) .... **6** $ _____
7 **Subtract** line 6 from line 5. Enter the result, but not less than -0- .... **7** $ _____
8 **Divide** the amount on line 7 by $2,500 and enter the result here. Drop any fraction .... **8** _____
9 Enter the number from Personal Allowances Worksheet, line G, on page 1 .... **9** _____
10 **Add** lines 8 and 9 and enter the total here. If you plan to use the Two-Earner/Two-Job Worksheet, also enter this total on line 1 below. Otherwise, **stop here** and enter this total on Form W-4, line 5, on page 1 .... **10** _____

Two-Earner/Two-Job Worksheet

Note: *Use this worksheet only if the instructions for line G on page 1 direct you here.*

1 Enter the number from line G on page 1 (or from line 10 above if you used the Deductions and Adjustments Worksheet) . **1** _____
2 Find the number in **Table 1** below that applies to the **LOWEST** paying job and enter it here .... **2** _____
3 If line 1 is **GREATER THAN OR EQUAL TO** line 2, subtract line 2 from line 1. Enter the result here (if zero, enter -0-) and on Form W-4, line 5, on page 1. **DO NOT** use the rest of this worksheet .... **3** _____

Note: *If line 1 is **LESS THAN** line 2, enter -0- on Form W-4, line 5, on page 1. Complete lines 4-9 to calculate the additional withholding amount necessary to avoid a year end tax bill.*

4 Enter the number from line 2 of this worksheet .... **4** _____
5 Enter the number from line 1 of this worksheet .... **5** _____
6 **Subtract** line 5 from line 4 .... **6** _____
7 Find the amount in **Table 2** below that applies to the **HIGHEST** paying job and enter it here ...... **7** $ _____
8 **Multiply** line 7 by line 6 and enter the result here. This is the additional annual withholding amount needed .... **8** $ _____
9 Divide line 8 by the number of pay periods remaining in 1995. (For example, divide by 26 if you are paid every other week and you complete this form in December 1994.) Enter the result here and on Form W-4, line 6, page 1. This is the additional amount to be withheld from each paycheck ...... **9** $ _____

Table 1: Two-Earner/Two-Job Worksheet

Married Filing Jointly				All Others	
If wages from **LOWEST** paying job are—	Enter on line 2 above	If wages from **LOWEST** paying job are—	Enter on line 2 above	If wages from **LOWEST** paying job are—	Enter on line 2 above
0 - $3,000	0	39,001 - 50,000	9	0 - $4,000	0
3,001 - 6,000	1	50,001 - 55,000	10	4,001 - 10,000	1
6,001 - 11,000	2	55,001 - 60,000	11	10,001 - 14,000	2
11,001 - 16,000	3	60,001 - 70,000	12	14,001 - 19,000	3
16,001 - 21,000	4	70,001 - 80,000	13	19,001 - 23,000	4
21,001 - 27,000	5	80,001 - 90,000	14	23,001 - 45,000	5
27,001 - 31,000	6	90,001 and over	15	45,001 - 60,000	6
31,001 - 34,000	7			60,001 - 70,000	7
34,001 - 39,000	8			70,001 and over	8

Table 2: Two-Earner/Two-Job Worksheet

Married Filing Jointly		All Others	
If wages from **HIGHEST** paying job are—	Enter on line 7 above	If wages from **HIGHEST** paying job are—	Enter on line 7 above
0 - $50,000	$380	0 - $30,000	$380
50,001 - 100,000	700	30,001 - 60,000	700
100,001 - 130,000	780	60,001 - 110,000	780
130,001 - 230,000	900	110,001 - 230,000	900
230,001 and over	990	230,001 and over	990

STF FED8105F.2

Exhibit A-4   *(continued)*

Form W-9
(Rev. March 1994)
Department of the Treasury
Internal Revenue Service

Request for Taxpayer
Identification Number and Certification

Give form to the requester. Do NOT send to the IRS.

Please print or type

Name (If joint names, list first and circle the name of the person or entity whose number you enter in Part I below. **See instructions on page 2 if your name has changed**)

Business name (Sole proprietors see instructions on page 2.)

Please check appropriate box: ☐ Individual/Sole proprietor ☐ Corporation ☐ Partnership ☐ Other ▶ _____

Address (number, street, and apt. or suite no.)

Requester's name and address (optional)

City, state, and ZIP code

Part I	**Taxpayer Identification Number (TIN)**

List account number(s) here (optional)

Enter your TIN in the appropriate box. For individuals, this is your social security number (SSN). For sole proprietors, see the instructions on page 2. For other entities, it is your employer identification number (EIN). If you do not have a number, see **How To Get a TIN** below.

Note: *If the account is in more than one name, see the chart on page 2 for guidelines on whose number to enter.*

Social security number

OR

Employer identification number

Part II	For Payees Exempt From Backup Withholding (See Part II instructions on page 2)

▶

Part III	**Certification**

Under penalties of perjury, I certify that:

1. The number shown on this form is my correct taxpayer identification number (or I am waiting for a number to be issued to me), **and**

2. I am not subject to backup withholding because: **(a)** I am exempt from backup withholding, or **(b)** I have not been notified by the Internal Revenue Service that I am subject to backup withholding as a result of a failure to report all interest or dividends, or **(c)** the IRS has notified me that I am no longer subject to backup withholding.

Certification Instructions.—You must cross out item 2 above if you have been notified by the IRS that you are currently subject to backup withholding because of underreporting interest or dividends on your tax return. For real estate transactions, item 2 does not apply. For mortgage interest paid, the acquisition or abandonment of secured property, cancellation of debt, contributions to an individual retirement arrangement (IRA), and generally payments other than interest and dividends, you are not required to sign the Certification, but you must provide your correct TIN. (Also see **Part III instructions** on page 2.)

Sign Here Signature ▶ _____ Date ▶ _____

Section references are to the Internal Revenue Code.

Purpose of Form.—A person who is required to file an information return with the IRS must get your correct TIN to report income paid to you, real estate transactions, mortgage interest you paid, the acquisition or abandonment of secured property, cancellation of debt, or contributions you made to an IRA. Use Form W-9 to give your correct TIN to the requester (the person requesting your TIN) and, when applicable, (1) to certify the TIN you are giving is correct (or you are waiting for a number to be issued), (2) to certify you are not subject to backup withholding, or (3) to claim exemption from backup withholding if you are an exempt payee. Giving your correct TIN and making the appropriate certifications will prevent certain payments from being subject to backup withholding.

Note: *If a requester gives you a form other than a W-9 to request your TIN, you must use the requester's form if it is substantially similar to this Form W-9.*

What Is Backup Withholding?—Persons making certain payments to you must withhold and pay to the IRS 31% of such payments under certain conditions. This is called "backup withholding." Payments that could be subject to backup withholding include interest, dividends, broker and barter exchange transactions, rents, royalties, nonemployee pay, and certain payments from fishing boat operators. Real estate transactions are not subject to backup withholding.

If you give the requester your correct TIN, make the proper certifications, and report all your taxable interest and dividends on your tax return, your payments will not be subject to backup withholding. Payments you receive will be subject to backup withholding if:

1. You do not furnish your TIN to the requester, or

2. The IRS tells the requester that you furnished an incorrect TIN, or

3. The IRS tells you that you are subject to backup withholding because you did not report all your interest and dividends on your tax return (for reportable interest and dividends only), or

4. You do not certify to the requester that you are not subject to backup withholding under 3

above (for reportable interest and dividend accounts opened after 1983 only), or

5. You do not certify your TIN. See the Part III instructions for exceptions.

Certain payees and payments are exempt from backup withholding and information reporting. See the Part II instructions and the separate **Instructions for the Requester of Form W-9.**

How To Get a TIN.—If you do not have a TIN, apply for one immediately. To apply, get **Form SS-5,** Application for a Social Security Number Card (for individuals), from your local office of the Social Security Administration, or **Form SS-4,** Application for Employer Identification Number (for businesses and all other entities), from your local IRS office.

If you do not have a TIN, write "Applied For" in the space for the TIN in Part I, sign and date the form, and give it to the requester. Generally, you will then have 60 days to get a TIN and give it to the requester. If the requester does not receive your TIN within 60 days, backup withholding, if applicable, will begin and continue until you furnish your TIN.

Form **W-9** (Rev. 3-94)

ISA

STF FED8132F.1

Exhibit A-5   Form W-9 Request for Taxpayer Identification Number and Certification, and Instructions

Department of the Treasury
Internal Revenue Service

Instructions for the Requester of Form W-9

(March 1994)

Request for Taxpayer Identification Number and Certification

Section references are to the Internal Revenue Code, unless otherwise noted.

These instructions supplement the instructions on the Form W-9, for the requester. The payee may also need these instructions.

Substitute Form W-9

You may use a substitute Form W-9 (your own version) as long as it is substantially similar to the official Form W-9 and conforms to Temporary Regulations section 35a.9999-1, Q/A-36. You may not use a substitute form to require the payee, by signing, to agree to provisions unrelated to TIN certification.

TIN Applied For

If the payee returns the Form W-9 with "Applied For" written in Part I, the payee must provide you with a TIN within 60 days. During this 60-day period, you have two options for withholding on reportable interest or dividend payments. For other reportable payments, if you do not receive the payee's TIN within the 60 days you must backup withhold, until the payee furnishes you with his or her TIN.

Option 1.—You must backup withhold on any withdrawals the payee makes from the account after 7 business days after you receive the Form W-9.

Option 2.—You must backup withhold on any reportable interest or dividend payments made to the payee's account, regardless of whether the payee makes any withdrawals. Backup withholding under this option must begin no later than 7 business days after you receive the Form W-9. Under this option, you must refund the amounts withheld if you receive the payee's certified TIN within the 60-day period and the payee was not otherwise subject to backup withholding during the period.

Payees and Payments Exempt From Backup Withholding

The following is a list of payees exempt from backup withholding and for which no information reporting is required. For interest and dividends, all listed payees are exempt except item **(9)**. For broker transactions, payees listed in items **(1)** through **(13)** and a person registered under the Investment Advisers Act of 1940 who regularly acts as a broker are exempt. Payments subject to reporting under sections 6041 and 6041A are generally exempt from backup withholding only if made to payees described in items **(1)** through **(7)**, except a corporation that provides medical and health care services or bills and collects payments for such services is not exempt from backup withholding or information reporting. Only payees described in items **(2)** through **(6)** are exempt from backup withholding for barter exchange transactions, patronage dividends, and payments by certain fishing boat operators.

(1) A corporation.

(2) An organization exempt from tax under section 501(a), or an IRA, or a custodial account under section 403(b)(7).

(3) The United States or any of its agencies or instrumentalities.

(4) A state, the District of Columbia, a possession of the United States, or any of their political subdivisions or instrumentalities.

(5) A foreign government or any of its political subdivisions, agencies, or instrumentalities.

(6) An international organization or any of its agencies or instrumentalities.

(7) A foreign central bank of issue.

(8) A dealer in securities or commodities required to register in the United States or a possession of the United States.

(9) A futures commission merchant registered with the Commodity Futures Trading Commission.

(10) A real estate investment trust.

(11) An entity registered at all times during the tax year under the Investment Company Act of 1940.

(12) A common trust fund operated by a bank under section 584(a).

(13) A financial institution.

(14) A middleman known in the investment community as a nominee or listed in the most recent publication of the American Society of Corporate Secretaries, Inc., Nominee List.

(15) A trust exempt from tax under section 664 or described in section 4947.

Payments of **dividends and patronage dividends** generally not subject to backup withholding include the following:

● Payments to nonresident aliens subject to withholding under section 1441.

● Payments to partnerships not engaged in a trade or business in the United States and that have at least one nonresident partner.

● Payments of patronage dividends not paid in money.

Cat. No. 20479P

Exhibit A-5 *(continued)*

Note: *Writing "Applied For" on the form means that you have already applied for a TIN OR that you intend to apply for one soon.*

As soon as you receive your TIN, complete another Form W-9, include your TIN, sign and date the form, and give it to the requester.

Penalties

Failure To Furnish TIN.—If you fail to furnish your correct TIN to a requester, you are subject to a penalty of $50 for each such failure unless your failure is due to reasonable cause and not to willful neglect.

Civil Penalty for False Information With Respect to Withholding.—If you make a false statement with no reasonable basis that results in no backup withholding, you are subject to a $500 penalty.

Criminal Penalty for Falsifying Information.—Willfully falsifying certifications or affirmations may subject you to criminal penalties including fines and/or imprisonment.

Misuse of TINs.—If the requester discloses or uses TINs in violation of Federal law, the requester may be subject to civil and criminal penalties.

Specific Instructions

Name.—If you are an individual, you must generally enter the name shown on your social security card. However, if you have changed your last name, for instance, due to marriage, without informing the Social Security Administration of the name change, please enter your first name, the last name shown on your social security card, and your new last name.

Sole Proprietor.—You must enter your **individual** name. (Enter either your SSN or EIN in Part I.) You may also enter your business name or "doing business as" name on the business name line. Enter your name as shown on your social security card and business name as it was used to apply for your EIN on Form SS-4.

Part I—Taxpayer Identification Number (TIN) You must enter your TIN in the appropriate box. If you are a sole proprietor, you may enter your SSN or EIN. Also see the chart on this page for further clarification of name and TIN combinations. If you do not have a TIN, follow the instructions under **How To Get a TIN** on page 1.

Part II—For Payees Exempt From Backup Withholding

Individuals (including sole proprietors) are **not** exempt from backup withholding. Corporations are exempt from backup withholding for certain payments, such as interest and dividends. For a complete list of exempt payees, see the separate Instructions for the Requester of Form W-9.

If you are exempt from backup withholding, you should still complete this form to avoid possible erroneous backup withholding. Enter your correct TIN in Part I, write "Exempt" in Part II, and sign and date the form. If you are a nonresident alien or a foreign entity not subject to backup withholding, give the requester a completed **Form W-8**, Certificate of Foreign Status.

Part III—Certification

For a joint account, only the person whose TIN is shown in Part I should sign.

1. Interest, Dividend, and Barter Exchange Accounts Opened Before 1984 and Broker Accounts Considered Active During 1983. You must give your correct TIN, but you do not have to sign the certification.

2. Interest, Dividend, Broker, and Barter Exchange Accounts Opened After 1983 and Broker Accounts Considered Inactive During 1983. You must sign the certification or backup withholding will apply. If you are subject to backup withholding and you are merely providing your correct TIN to the requester, you must cross out item **2** in the certification before signing the form.

3. Real Estate Transactions. You must sign the certification. You may cross out item 2 of the certification.

4. Other Payments. You must give your correct TIN, but you do not have to sign the certification unless you have been notified of an incorrect TIN. Other payments include payments made in the course of the requester's trade or business for rents, royalties, goods (other than bills for merchandise), medical and health care services, payments to a nonemployee for services (including attorney and accounting fees), and payments to certain fishing boat crew members.

5. Mortgage Interest Paid by You, Acquisition or Abandonment of Secured Property, Cancellation of Debt, or IRA Contributions. You must give your correct TIN, but you do not have to sign the certification.

Privacy Act Notice

Section 6109 requires you to give your correct TIN to persons who must file information returns with the IRS to report interest, dividends, and certain other income paid to you, mortgage interest you paid, the acquisition or abandonment of secured property, cancellation of debt, or contributions you made to an IRA. The IRS uses the numbers for identification purposes and to help verify the accuracy of your tax return. You must provide your TIN whether or not you are

required to file a tax return. Payers must generally withhold 31% of taxable interest, dividend, and certain other payments to a payee who does not give a TIN to a payer. Certain penalties may also apply.

What Name and Number To Give the Requester

For this type of account:	Give name and SSN of:
1. Individual	The individual
2. Two or more individuals (joint account)	The actual owner of the account or; if combined funds, the first individual on the account[1]
3. Custodian account of a minor (Uniform Gift to Minors Act)	The minor[2]
4. a. The usual revocable savings trust (grantor is also trustee)	The grantor-trustee[1]
b. So-called trust account that is not a legal or valid trust under state law	The actual owner[1]
5. Sole proprietorship.	The owner[3]

For this type of account:	Give name and EIN of:
6. Sole proprietorship	The owner[3]
7. A valid trust, estate, or pension trust	Legal entity[4]
8. Corporate	The corporation
9. Association, club, religious, charitable, educational, or other tax-exempt organization	The organization
10. Partnership	The partnership
11. A broker or registered nominee	The broker or nominee
12. Account with the Department of Agriculture in the name of a public entity (such as a state or local government, school district, or prison) that receives agricultural program payments	The public entity

[1] List first and circle the name of the person whose number you furnish.

[2] Circle the minor's name and furnish the minor's SSN.

[3] You must show your individual name, but you may also enter your business or "doing business as" name. You may use either your SSN or EIN.

[4] List first and circle the name of the legal trust, estate, or pension trust. (Do not furnish the TIN of the personal representative or trustee unless the legal entity itself is not designated in the account title.)

Note: *If no name is circled when more than one name is listed, the number will be considered to be that of the first name listed.*

STF FED8132F.2

Exhibit A-5   *(continued)*

- Payments made by certain foreign organizations.

Payments of **interest** generally not subject to backup withholding include the following:

- Payments of interest on obligations issued by individuals.

Note: *The payee may be subject to backup withholding if this interest is $600 or more and is paid in the course of your trade or business and the payee has not provided his or her correct TIN to you.*

- Payments of tax-exempt interest (including exempt-interest dividends under section 852).

- Payments described in section 6049(b)(5) to nonresident aliens.

- Payments on tax-free covenant bonds under section 1451.

- Payments made by certain foreign organizations.

- Mortgage interest paid to you.

Payments that are not subject to information reporting are also not subject to backup withholding. For details, see sections 6041, 6041A(a), 6042, 6044, 6045, 6049, 6050A, and 6050N, and their regulations.

For more information on backup withholding and your requirements, get **Pub. 1679,** A Guide to Backup Withholding, and **Pub. 1281,** Backup Withholding on Missing and Incorrect TINs.

Names and TINs To Use for Information Reporting

Show the full name and address as provided on the Form W-9 on the appropriate information return. If payments have been made to more than one recipient or the account is in more than one name, enter ONLY on the first name line the name of the recipient whose TIN is shown on the information return. Show the names of any other individual recipients in the area below the first name line, if desired.

For sole proprietors, show the individual's name on the first name line. On the second name line, you may enter the business name if provided. You may not enter only the business name. For the TIN, enter either the individual's SSN or the EIN of the business (sole proprietorship).

Notices From the IRS About Your Payees

We will send you a notice if the payee's name and TIN on the information return you filed do not match our records. You may need to send a "B" Notice to the payee to solicit his or her TIN. See Pub. 1679 and Pub. 1281 for copies of the two different "B" Notices.

Page 2

Printed on recycled paper

Exhibit A-5   *(continued)*

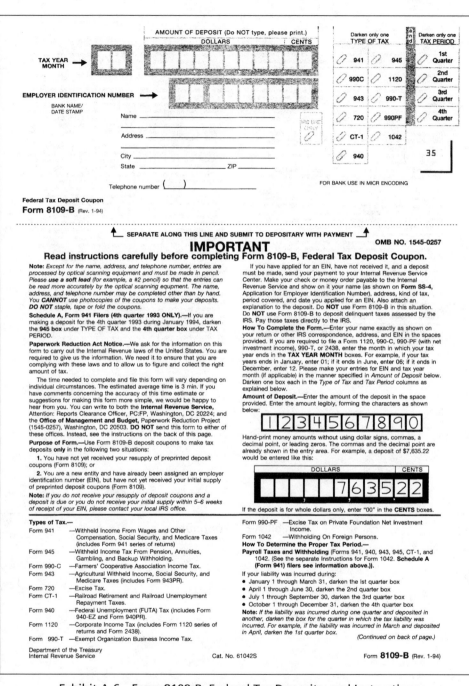

AMOUNT OF DEPOSIT (Do NOT type, please print.)

DOLLARS | CENTS

TAX YEAR MONTH →

EMPLOYER IDENTIFICATION NUMBER →

BANK NAME/
DATE STAMP

Name _____

Address _____

City _____

State _____ ZIP _____

Telephone number ( )

Darken only one
TYPE OF TAX

941   945
990C   1120
943   990-T
720   990PF
CT-1   1042
940

Darken only one
TAX PERIOD

1st Quarter
2nd Quarter
3rd Quarter
4th Quarter

35

FOR BANK USE IN MICR ENCODING

Federal Tax Deposit Coupon
Form 8109-B (Rev. 1-94)

- -

↑ SEPARATE ALONG THIS LINE AND SUBMIT TO DEPOSITARY WITH PAYMENT ↑

IMPORTANT

OMB NO. 1545-0257

Read instructions carefully before completing Form 8109-B, Federal Tax Deposit Coupon.

Note: *Except for the name, address, and telephone number, entries are processed by optical scanning equipment and must be made in pencil. Please **use a soft lead** (for example, a #2 pencil) so that the entries can be read more accurately by the optical scanning equipment. The name, address, and telephone number may be completed other than by hand. You **CANNOT** use photocopies of the coupons to make your deposits. **DO NOT** staple, tape or fold the coupons.*

Schedule A, Form 941 Filers (4th quarter 1993 ONLY).—If you are making a deposit for the 4th quarter 1993 during January 1994, darken the **945 box** under TYPE OF TAX and the **4th quarter box** under TAX PERIOD.

Paperwork Reduction Act Notice.—We ask for the information on this form to carry out the Internal Revenue laws of the United States. You are required to give us the information. We need it to ensure that you are complying with these laws and to allow us to figure and collect the right amount of tax.

The time needed to complete and file this form will vary depending on individual circumstances. The estimated average time is 3 min. If you have comments concerning the accuracy of this time estimate or suggestions for making this form more simple, we would be happy to hear from you. You can write to both the **Internal Revenue Service,** Attention: Reports Clearance Officer, PC:FP, Washington, DC 20224; and the **Office of Management and Budget,** Paperwork Reduction Project (1545-0257), Washington, DC 20503. **DO NOT** send this form to either of these offices. Instead, see the instructions on the back of this page.

Purpose of Form.—Use Form 8109-B deposit coupons to make tax deposits **only** in the following two situations:

1. You have not yet received your resupply of preprinted deposit coupons (Form 8109); or

2. You are a new entity and have already been assigned an employer identification number (EIN), but have not yet received your initial supply of preprinted deposit coupons (Form 8109).

Note: *If you do not receive your resupply of deposit coupons and a deposit is due or you do not receive your initial supply within 5–6 weeks of receipt of your EIN, please contact your local IRS office.*

If you have applied for an EIN, have not received it, and a deposit must be made, send your payment to your Internal Revenue Service Center. Make your check or money order payable to the Internal Revenue Service and show on it your name (as shown on **Form SS-4,** Application for Employer Identification Number), address, kind of tax, period covered, and date you applied for an EIN. Also attach an explanation to the deposit. Do **NOT** use Form 8109-B in this situation. Do **NOT** use Form 8109-B to deposit delinquent taxes assessed by the IRS. Pay those taxes directly to the IRS.

How To Complete the Form.—Enter your name exactly as shown on your return or other IRS correspondence, address, and EIN in the spaces provided. If you are required to file a Form 1120, 990-C, 990-PF (with net investment income), 990-T, or 2438, enter the month in which your tax year ends in the **TAX YEAR MONTH** boxes. For example, if your tax years ends in January, enter 01; if it ends in June, enter 06; if it ends in December, enter 12. Please make your entries for EIN and tax year month (if applicable) in the manner specified in *Amount of Deposit* below. Darken one box each in the *Type of Tax* and *Tax Period* columns as explained below.

Amount of Deposit.—Enter the amount of the deposit in the space provided. Enter the amount legibly, forming the characters as shown below:

1234567890

Hand-print money amounts without using dollar signs, commas, a decimal point, or leading zeros. The commas and the decimal point are already shown in the entry area. For example, a deposit of $7,635.22 would be entered like this:

DOLLARS		CENTS
	7 6 3 5	2 2

If the deposit is for whole dollars only, enter "00" in the **CENTS** boxes.

Types of Tax.—

Form 941	—Withheld Income From Wages and Other Compensation, Social Security, and Medicare Taxes (includes Form 941 series of returns)
Form 945	—Withheld Income Tax From Pension, Annuities, Gambling, and Backup Withholding.
Form 990-C	—Farmers' Cooperative Association Income Tax.
Form 943	—Agricultural Withheld Income, Social Security, and Medicare Taxes (includes Form 943PR).
Form 720	—Excise Tax.
Form CT-1	—Railroad Retirement and Railroad Unemployment Repayment Taxes.
Form 940	—Federal Unemployment (FUTA) Tax (includes Form 940-EZ and Form 940PR).
Form 1120	—Corporate Income Tax (includes Form 1120 series of returns and Form 2438).
Form 990-T	—Exempt Organization Business Income Tax.

Form 990-PF —Excise Tax on Private Foundation Net Investment Income.

Form 1042 —Withholding On Foreign Persons.

How To Determine the Proper Tax Period.—

Payroll Taxes and Withholding (Forms 941, 940, 943, 945, CT-1, and 1042. (See the separate Instructions for Form 1042. **Schedule A (Form 941) filers see information above.)).**

If your liability was incurred during:
- January 1 through March 31, darken the lst quarter box
- April 1 through June 30, darken the 2nd quarter box
- July 1 through September 30, darken the 3rd quarter box
- October 1 through December 31, darken the 4th quarter box

Note: *If the liability was incurred during one quarter and deposited in another, darken the box for the quarter in which the tax liability was incurred. For example, if the liability was incurred in March and deposited in April, darken the 1st quarter box.*

(Continued on back of page.)

Department of the Treasury
Internal Revenue Service

Cat. No. 61042S

Form **8109-B** (Rev. 1-94)

Exhibit A-6   Form 8109-B, Federal Tax Deposits, and Instructions

Excise Taxes For Form 720, follow the instructions on the front page for Forms 941, 940, etc., **but** for exceptions see separate instructions for Form 720. For Form 990-PF, with net investment income, follow the instructions below for Form 1120, 990-C, etc.

Income Taxes (Form 1120, 990-C, 990-T, and 2438).—

To make a deposit for the current tax year for any quarter, darken **only** the 1st quarter box. Such deposits apply to estimated income tax payments.

Example 1: If your tax year ends on December 31, 1994, and a deposit for 1994 is being made between January 1 and December 31, 1994, darken the 1st quarter box.

Example 2: If your tax year ends on June 30, 1994, and a deposit for that fiscal year is being made between July 1, 1993 and June 30, 1994, darken the 1st quarter box.

To make a deposit for the prior tax year, darken **only** the 4th quarter box. Such deposits include the following:

• Deposits of balance due shown on the return (Forms 1120, 990-C, and 990-T (corporate filers), and Forms 990-PF and 990-T (trust filers)).

• Deposits of balance due shown on **Form 7004,** Application for Automatic Extension of Time To File Corporation Income Tax Return (be sure to darken the 1120, 990-C, or 990-T box as appropriate).

• Deposits of balance due (from Forms 990-T (trust filers) and 990-PF filers) shown on **Form 2758,** Application for Extension of Time To File Certain Excise, Income, Information, and Other Returns (be sure to darken the 990-PF or 990-T box as appropriate).

• Deposits of tax due shown on Form 2438 (darken the 1120 box).

Example 1: If your tax year ends on December 31, 1994, and a deposit for 1994 is being made after that date, darken the 4th quarter box.

Example 2: If your tax year ends on June 30, 1994, and a deposit for that fiscal year is being made after that date, darken the 4th quarter box.

How To Ensure Your Deposit is Credited to the Correct Account.—

1. Make sure your name and EIN are correct;

2. Prepare only one coupon for each type of tax deposit;

3. Darken only one box for the type of tax you are depositing; and

4. Darken only one box for the tax period for which you are making a deposit.

Telephone number.—A space is provided on the deposit coupon for you to enter your daytime telephone number. Our purpose for requesting it is to allow us to contact you if we have difficulty processing your deposit coupon.

Miscellaneous.—The IRS USE ONLY box is used during our processing to ensure proper crediting to your account. Do **not** darken this box when making a deposit.

Note: *DO NOT deposit delinquent taxes assessed by IRS. Pay those taxes directly to the IRS.*

How To Make Deposits.—Mail or deliver the completed coupon with the appropriate payment for the amount of the deposit to a qualified depositary for Federal taxes or to the Federal Reserve bank (FRB) servicing your geographic area. Make checks or money orders payable to that depositary or FRB. Federal agencies deposit at FRBs only. To help ensure proper crediting of your account, include your EIN, the type of tax (e.g., Form 940), and the tax period to which the payment applies on your check or money order.

Deposits at Depositaries.—Authorized depositaries are required to accept cash, postal money orders drawn to the order of the depositary, or checks or drafts drawn on and to the order of the depositary. If you want to make a tax deposit with a depositary by a check drawn on another financial institution, you may do so only if the depositary is willing to accept that payment as a deposit of Federal taxes.

Deposits at FRBs.—If you want to make a deposit at an FRB, you must make that deposit with the FRB servicing your area with a check or payment for which immediate credit is given according to the funds availability schedule of the receiving FRB. A personal check is not an immediate credit item. The FRB servicing your area can provide information regarding what are considered immediate credit items.

Timeliness of Deposits.—The IRS determines whether deposits are on time by the date they are received by an authorized depositary or collected by an FRB. However, a deposit received by the authorized depositary or FRB after the deposit due date will be considered timely if the taxpayer establishes that it was mailed in the United States on or before the second day before the due date.

Note: *If you are required to deposit any taxes more than once a month, any deposit of $20,000 or more must be made by its due date to be timely.*

When To Make Deposits.—Instructions are provided in IRS publications and tax returns. Copies of these documents and other information concerning tax procedures can be obtained from most IRS offices.

Penalties.—You may be charged a penalty for not making deposits when due or in sufficient amounts, unless you have reasonable cause. This penalty may also apply if you mail or deliver Federal tax deposits to IRS offices, rather than to authorized depositaries or FRBs. Additionally, **a trust fund recovery penalty may apply to any responsible person who willfully fails to collect, account for, and pay over trust fund taxes.** For more information on penalties, see Circular E, Employer's Tax Guide.

Exhibit A-6   *(continued)*

AS A TAXPAYER

A s a taxpayer, you have the right to be treated fairly, professionally, promptly, and courteously by Internal Revenue Service employees. Our goal at the IRS is to protect your rights so that you will have the highest confidence in the integrity, efficiency, and fairness of our tax system. To ensure that you always receive such treatment, you should know about the many rights you have at each step of the tax process.

Free Information and Help in Preparing Returns

You have the right to information and help in complying with the tax laws. In addition to the basic instructions we provide with the tax forms, we make available a great deal of other information.

Taxpayer publications. We publish over 100 free taxpayer information publications on various subjects. One of these, Publication 910, *Guide to Free Tax Services*, is a catalog of the free services and publications we offer. You can order all publications and any tax forms or instructions you need by calling us toll-free at 1-800-TAX-FORM (829-3676).

Other assistance. We provide walk-in tax help at many IRS offices and recorded telephone information on many topics through our *Tele-Tax* system. The telephone numbers for *Tele-Tax*, and the topics covered, are in certain tax forms' instructions and publications. Many of our materials are available in Braille (at regional libraries for the handicapped) and in Spanish. We provide help for the hearing-impaired via special telephone equipment.

We have informational videotapes that you can borrow. In addition, you may want to attend our education programs for specific groups of taxpayers, such as farmers and those with small businesses.

In cooperation with local volunteers, we offer free help in preparing tax returns for low-income and elderly taxpayers through the Volunteer Income Tax Assistance (VITA) and Tax Counseling for the Elderly (TCE) Programs. You can get information on these programs by calling the toll-free telephone number for your area.

Copies of tax returns. If you need a copy of your tax return for an earlier year, you can get one by filling out Form 4506, *Request for Copy of Tax Form*, and paying a small fee. However, you often only need certain information, such as the amount of your reported income, the number of your exemptions, and the tax shown on the return. You can get this information free if you write or visit an IRS office or call the toll-free number for your area.

Privacy and Confidentiality

You have the right to have your personal and financial information kept confidential. People who prepare your return or represent you *must* keep your information confidential.

You also have the right to know why we are asking you for information, exactly how we will use any information you give, and what might happen if you do not give the information.

Information sharing. Under the law, we can share your tax information with State tax agencies and, under strict legal guidelines, the Department of Justice and other federal agencies. We can also share it with certain foreign governments under tax treaty provisions.

Courtesy and Consideration

You are always entitled to courteous and considerate treatment from IRS employees. If you ever feel that you are not being treated with fairness, courtesy, and consideration by an IRS employee, you should tell the employee's supervisor.

Protection of Your Rights

The employees of the Internal Revenue Service will explain and protect your rights as a taxpayer at all times. If you feel that this is not the case, you should discuss the problem with the employee's supervisor.

Complaints

If for any reason you have a complaint about the IRS, you may write to the District Director or Service Center Director for your area. We will give you the name and address if you call our toll-free phone number listed later.

Representation and Recordings

Throughout your dealings with us, you can represent yourself, or, generally with proper written authorization, have someone represent you in your absence. During an interview, you can have someone accompany you.

Department of the Treasury
Internal Revenue Service
Publication 1 (Rev. 10-90)

Cat. No. 64731W

Exhibit A-7   Your Rights as a Taxpayer

If you want to consult an attorney, a certified public accountant, an enrolled agent, or any other person permitted to represent a taxpayer during an interview for examining a tax return or collecting tax, we will stop and reschedule the interview. We cannot suspend the interview if you are there because of an administrative summons.

You can generally make an audio recording of an interview with an IRS Collection or Examination officer. Your request to record the interview should be made in writing, and must be received 10 days before the interview. You must bring your own recording equipment. We also can record an interview. If we do so, we will notify you 10 days before the meeting and you can get a copy of the recording at your expense.

Payment of Only the Required Tax

You have the right to plan your business and personal finances so that you will pay the least tax that is due under the law. You are liable only for the correct amount of tax. Our purpose is to apply the law consistently and fairly to all taxpayers.

If Your Return is Questioned

We accept most taxpayers' returns as filed. If we inquire about your return or select it for examination, it does not suggest that you are dishonest. The inquiry or examination may or may not result in more tax. We may close your case without change. Or, you may receive a refund.

Examination and inquiries by mail. We handle many examinations and inquiries entirely by mail. We will send you a letter with either a request for more information

or a reason why we believe a change needs to be made to your return. If you give us the requested information or provide an explanation, we may or may not agree with you and we will explain the reasons for any changes. You should not hesitate to write to us about anything you do not understand. If you cannot resolve any questions through the mail, you can request a personal interview. You can appeal through the IRS and the courts. You will find instructions with each inquiry or in Publication 1383, *Correspondence Process*.

Examination by interview. If we notify you that we will conduct your examination through a personal interview, or you request such an interview, you have the right to ask that the examination take place at a reasonable time and place that is convenient for both you and the IRS. If the time or place we suggest is not convenient, the examiner will try to work out something more suitable. However, the IRS makes the final determination of how, when, and where the examination will take place. You will receive an explanation of your rights and of the examination process either before or at the interview.

If you do not agree with the examiner's report, you may meet with the examiner's supervisor to discuss your case further.

Repeat examinations. We try to avoid repeat examinations of the same items, but this sometimes happens. If we examined your tax return for the same items in either of the 2 previous years and proposed no change to your tax liability, please contact us as soon as possible so we can see if we should discontinue the repeat examination.

Explanation of changes. If we propose any changes to your return, we will explain the reasons for the changes. It is

important that you understand these reasons. You should not hesitate to ask about anything that is unclear to you.

Interest. You must pay interest on additional tax that you owe. The interest is generally figured from the due date of the return. But if our error caused a delay in your case, and this was grossly unfair, we may reduce the interest. Only delays caused by procedural or mechanical acts not involving the exercise of judgment or discretion qualify. If you think we caused such a delay, please discuss it with the examiner and file a claim for refund.

Business taxpayers. If you are in an individual business, the rights covered in this publication generally apply to you. If you are a member of a partnership or a shareholder in a small business corporation, special rules may apply to the examination of your partnership or corporation items. The examination of partnership items is discussed in Publication 556, *Examination of Returns, Appeal Rights, and Claims for Refund.* The rights covered in this publication generally apply to exempt organizations and sponsors of employee plans.

An Appeal of the Examination Findings

If you don't agree with the examiner's findings, you have the right to appeal them. During the examination process, you will be given information about your appeal rights. Publication 5, *Appeal Rights and Preparation of Protests for Unagreed Cases*, explains your appeal rights in detail and tells you exactly what to do if you want to appeal.

Appeals Office. You can appeal the findings of an examination within the IRS through our Appeals Office. Most

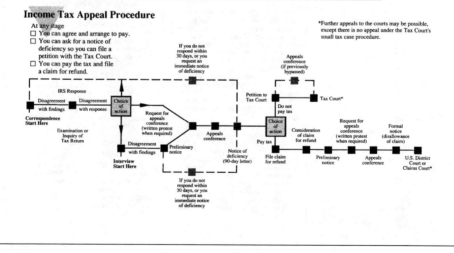

Income Tax Appeal Procedure

At any stage
☐ You can agree and arrange to pay.
☐ You can ask for a notice of deficiency so you can file a petition with the Tax Court.
☐ You can pay the tax and file a claim for refund.

*Further appeals to the courts may be possible, except there is no appeal under the Tax Court's small tax case procedure.

Exhibit A-7 *(continued)*

differences can be settled through this appeals system without expensive and time-consuming court trials. If the matter cannot be settled to your satisfaction in Appeals, you can take your case to court.

Appeals to the courts. Depending on whether you first pay the disputed tax, you can take your case to the U.S. Tax Court, the U.S. Claims Court, or your U.S. District Court. These courts are entirely independent of the IRS. As always, you can represent yourself or have someone admitted to practice before the court represent you.

If you disagree about whether you owe additional tax, you generally have the right to take your case to the U.S. Tax Court if you have not yet paid the tax. Ordinarily, you have 90 days from the time we mail you a formal notice (called a "notice of deficiency") telling you that you owe additional tax, to file a petition with the U.S. Tax Court. You can request simplified small tax case procedures if your case is $10,000 or less for any period or year. A case settled under these procedures cannot be appealed.

If you have already paid the disputed tax in full, you may file a claim for refund. If we disallow the claim, you can appeal the findings through our Appeals Office. If you do not accept their decision or we have not acted on your claim within 6 months, then you may take your case to the U.S. Claims Court or your U.S. District Court.

Recovering litigation expenses. If the court agrees with you on most issues in your case, and finds that our position was largely unjustified, you may be able to recover some of your administrative and litigation costs. To do this, you must have used all the administrative remedies available to you within the IRS. This includes going through our Appeals system and giving us all the information necessary to resolve the case.

Publication 556, *Examination of Returns, Appeal Rights, and Claims for Refund*, will help you more fully understand your appeal rights.

Fair Collection of Tax

Whenever you owe tax, we will send you a bill describing the tax and stating the amounts you owe in tax, interest, and penalties. Be sure to check any bill you receive to make sure it is correct. You have the right to have your bill adjusted if it is incorrect, so you should let us know about an incorrect bill right away.

If we tell you that you owe tax because of a math or clerical error on your return, you have the right to ask us to send you a formal notice (a "notice of deficiency") so that you can dispute the tax, as discussed earlier. You do not have to pay the additional tax at the same time that you ask us for the formal notice, if you ask for it within 60 days of the time we tell you of the error.

If the tax is correct, we will give you a specific period of time to pay the bill in full. If you pay the bill within the time allowed, we will not have to take any further action.

We may request that you attend an interview for the collection of tax. You will receive an explanation of your rights and of the collection process either before or at the interview.

Your rights are further protected because we are not allowed to use tax enforcement results to evaluate our employees.

Payment arrangements. You should make every effort to pay your bill in full. If you can't, you should pay as much as you can and contact us right away. We may ask you for a complete financial statement to determine how you can pay the amount due. Based on your financial condition, you may qualify for an installment agreement. We can arrange for these payments to be made through payroll deduction. We will give you copies of all agreements you make with us.

If we approve a payment agreement, the agreement will stay in effect only if:

You give correct and complete financial information,

You pay each installment on time,

You satisfy other tax liabilities on time,

You provide current financial information when asked, and

We determine that collecting the tax is not at risk.

Following a review of your current finances, we may change your payment agreement. We will notify you 30 days before any change to your payment agreement and tell you why we are making the change.

We will not take any enforcement action (such as recording a tax lien or levying on or seizing property), until after we have tried to contact you and given you the chance to voluntarily pay any tax due. Therefore, it is very important for you to respond right away to our attempts to contact you (by mail, telephone, or personal visit). If you do not respond, we may have no choice but to begin enforcement action.

Release of liens. If we have to place a lien on your property (to secure the amount of tax due), we must release the lien no later than 30 days after finding that you have paid the entire tax and certain charges, the assessment has become legally unenforceable, or we have accepted a bond to cover the tax and certain charges.

Recovery of damages. If we knowingly or negligently fail to release a lien under the circumstances described above, and you suffer economic damages because of our failure, you can recover your actual economic damages and certain costs.

If we recklessly or intentionally fail to follow the laws and regulations

for the collection of tax, you can recover actual economic damages and certain costs.

In each of the two situations above, damages and costs will be allowed within the following limits. You must exhaust all administrative remedies available to you. The damages will be reduced by the amount which you could have reasonably prevented. You must bring suit within 2 years of the action.

Incorrect lien. You have the right to appeal our filing of a Notice of Federal Tax Lien if you believe we filed the lien in error. If we agree, we will issue a certificate of release, including a statement that we filed the lien in error.

A lien is incorrect if:

You paid the entire amount due before we filed the lien,

The time to collect the tax expired before we filed the lien,

We made a procedural error in a deficiency assessment, or

We assessed a tax in violation of the automatic stay provisions in a bankruptcy case.

Levy. We will generally give you 30 days notice before we levy on any property. The notice may be given to you in person, mailed to you, or left at your home or workplace. On the day you attend a collection interview because of a summons, we cannot levy your property unless the collection of tax is in jeopardy.

Property that is exempt from levy. If we must seize your property, you have the legal right to keep:

Necessary clothing and schoolbooks,

A limited amount of personal belongings, furniture, and business or professional books and tools,

Unemployment and job training benefits, workers' compensation, welfare, certain disability payments, and certain pension benefits,

The income you need to pay court-ordered child support,

Mail,

An amount of weekly income equal to your standard deduction and allowable personal exemptions, divided by 52, and

Your main home, unless collection of tax is in jeopardy or the district director (or assistant) approves the levy in writing.

If your bank account is levied after June 30, 1989, the bank will hold your account up to the amount of the levy for 21 days. This gives you time to settle any disputes concerning ownership of the funds in the account.

We generally must release a levy issued after June 30, 1989, if:

You pay the tax, penalty, and interest for which the levy was made,

The IRS determines the release will help collect the tax,

Exhibit A-7 *(continued)*

You have an approved installment agreement for the tax on the levy,

The IRS determines the levy is creating an economic hardship, or

The fair market value of the property exceeds the amount of the levy and release would not hinder the collection of tax.

If at any time during the collection process you do not agree with the collection officer, you can discuss your case with his or her supervisor.

If we seize your property, you have the right to request that it be sold within 60 days after your request. You can request a time period greater than 60 days. We will comply with your request unless it is not in the best interest of the government.

Access to your private premises. A court order is not generally needed for a collection officer to seize your property. However, you don't have to allow the employee access to your private premises, such as your home or the non-public areas of your business, if the employee does not have court authorization to be there.

Withheld taxes. If we believe that you were responsible for seeing that a corporation paid us income and social security taxes withheld from its employees, and the taxes were not paid, we may look to you to pay an amount based on the unpaid taxes. If you feel that you don't owe this, you have the right to discuss the case with the collection officer's supervisor. You may also request an appeals hearing within 30 days of our proposed assessment of employment taxes. You generally have the same IRS appeal rights as other taxpayers. Because the U.S. Tax Court has no jurisdiction in this situation, you must pay at least part of the withheld taxes and file a claim for refund in order to take the matter to the U.S. District Court or U.S. Claims Court.

The amount of tax withheld from your wages is determined by the W-4, *Employees Withholding Allowance Certificate*, you give your employer. If your certificate is incorrect, the IRS may instruct your employer to increase the amount. We may also assess a penalty. You have the right to appeal the decision. Or, you can file a claim for refund and go to the U.S. Claims Court or U.S. District Court.

Publications 586A, *The Collection Process (Income Tax Accounts)*, and 594, *The Collection Process (Employment Tax Accounts)*, will help you understand your rights during the collection process.

The Collection Process

To stop the process at any stage, you should pay the tax in full. If you cannot pay the tax in full, contact us right away to discuss possible ways to pay the tax.

Start here

First notice and demand for unpaid tax

10 days later

Enforcement authority arises (a notice of a lien may be filed)

Up to 3 more notices sent over a period of time asking for payment

Notice of intent to levy is sent by certified mail (final notice)

30 days later

Enforcement action to collect the tax begins (levy, seizure, etc.)

Refund of Overpaid Tax

Once you have paid all your tax, you have the right to file a claim for a refund if you think the tax is incorrect. Generally, you have 3 years from the date you filed the return or 2 years from the date you paid the tax (whichever is later) to file a claim. If we examine your claim for any reason, you have the same rights that you would have during an examination of your return.

Interest on refunds. You will receive interest on any income tax refund delayed more than 45 days after the **later** of either the date you filed your return or the date your return was due.

Checking on your refund. Normally, you will receive your refund about 6 weeks after you file your return. If you have not received your refund within 8 weeks after mailing your return, you may check on it by calling the toll-free Tele-Tax number in the tax forms' instructions.

If we reduce your refund because you owe a debt to another Federal agency or because you owe child support, we must notify you of this action. However, if you have a question about the debt that caused the reduction, you should contact the other agency.

Cancellation of Penalties

You have the right to ask that certain penalties (but not interest) be cancelled (abated) if you can show reasonable cause for the failure that led to the penalty (or can show that you exercised due diligence, if that is the applicable standard for that penalty).

If you relied on wrong advice you received from IRS employees on the toll-free telephone system, we will cancel certain penalties that may result. But you have to show that your reliance on the advice was reasonable.

If you relied on incorrect written advice from the IRS in response to a written request you made after January 1,

1989, we will cancel any penalties that may result. You must show that you gave sufficient and correct information and filed your return after you received the advice.

Special Help to Resolve Your Problems

We have a Problem Resolution Program for taxpayers who have been unable to resolve their problems with the IRS. If you have a tax problem that you cannot clear up through normal channels, write to the Problem Resolution Office in the district or Service Center with which you have the problem. You may also reach the Problem Resolution Office by calling the IRS taxpayer assistance number for your area. If you are hearing-impaired with TV/Telephone (TTY) access, you may call 1-800-829-4059.

If your tax problem causes (or will cause) you to suffer a significant hardship, additional assistance is available. A significant hardship may occur if you cannot maintain necessities such as food, clothing, shelter, transportation, and medical treatment.

There are two ways you can apply for relief. You can submit Form 911, *Application for Taxpayer Assistance Order to Relieve Hardship*, which you can order by calling 1-800-TAX-FORM (829-3676). You can choose instead to call 1-800-829-1040, to request relief from your hardship. The Taxpayer Ombudsman, Problem Resolution Officer, or other official will then review your case and may issue a Taxpayer Assistance Order (TAO), to suspend IRS action.

Taxpayer Assistance Numbers

You should use the telephone number shown in the white pages of your local telephone directory under U.S. Government, Internal Revenue Service, Federal Tax Assistance. If there is not a specific number listed, call toll-free 1-800-829-1040.

You can also find these phone numbers in the instructions for Form 1040. You may also use these numbers to reach the Problem Resolution Office. Ask for the Problem Resolution Office when you call.

U.S. taxpayers abroad may write for information to:

Internal Revenue Service
Attn: IN:C:TPS
950 L'Enfant Plaza South, S.W.
Washington, D.C. 20024

You can also contact your nearest U.S. Embassy for information about what services and forms are available in your location.

*U.S. Government Printing Office: 1995 — 384-754

Exhibit A-7   *(continued)*

Profit or Loss From Business

(Sole Proprietorship)

Department of the Treasury
Internal Revenue Service   (99)

☐ **Partnerships, joint ventures, etc., must file Form 1065.**

☐ **Attach to Form 1040 or Form 1041.**   ☐ **See Instructions for Schedule C (Form 1040).**

Attachment
Sequence No. **09**

Name of proprietor	Social security number (SSN)

A Principal business or profession, including product or service (see page C-1)

B Enter principal business code
(see page C-6) ☐

C Business name. If no separate business name, leave blank.

D Employer ID number (EIN), if any

E Business address (including suite or room no.) ☐_____
City, town or post office, state, and ZIP code

F Accounting method: **(1)** ☐ Cash **(2)** ☐ Accrual   **(3)** ☐ Other (specify) ☐_____

G Method(s) used to
value closing inventory: **(1)** ☐ Cost **(2)** ☐ Lower of cost
or market **(3)** ☐ Other (attach
explanation) **(4)** ☐ Does not apply (if
checked, skip line H)

	Yes	No

H Was there any change in determining quantities, costs, or valuations between opening and closing inventory? If "Yes," attach
explanation ....

I Did you "materially participate" in the operation of this business during 1995? If "No," see page C-2 for limit on losses.............

J If you started or acquired this business during 1995, check here .... ☐ ☐

Part I   Income

1	Gross receipts or sales. **Caution:** If this income was reported to you on Form W-2 and the "Statutory employee" box on that form was checked, see page C-2 and check here .... ☐ ☐	**1**	
2	Returns and allowances	**2**	
3	Subtract line 2 from line 1	**3**	
4	Cost of goods sold (from line 40 on page 2)	**4**	
5	**Gross profit.** Subtract line 4 from line 3	**5**	
6	Other income, including Federal and state gasoline or fuel tax credit or refund (see page C-2)	**6**	
7	**Gross income.** Add lines 5 and 6 .... ☐	**7**	

Part II   Expenses. Enter expenses for business use of your home **only** on line 30.

8	Advertising	**8**		**19**	Pension and profit-sharing plans	**19**	
9	Bad debts from sales or services (see page C-3)	**9**		**20**	Rent or lease (see page C-4):		
				a	Vehicles, machinery, and equipment	**20a**	
10	Car and truck expenses (see page C-3)	**10**		**b**	Other business property	**20b**	
11	Commissions and fees	**11**		**21**	Repairs and maintenance	**21**	
12	Depletion	**12**		**22**	Supplies (not included in Part III)	**22**	
13	Depreciation and section 179 expense deduction (not included in Part III) (see page C-3)	**13**		**23**	Taxes and licenses	**23**	
				24	Travel, meals, and entertainment:		
14	Employee benefit programs (other than on line 19)	**14**		**a**	Travel	**24a**	
15	Insurance (other than health) ..	**15**		**b**	Meals and entertainment		
16	Interest:			**c**	Enter 50% of line 24b subject to limitations (see page C-4)		
a	Mortgage (paid to banks, etc.) .	**16a**					
b	Other	**16b**		**d**	Subtract line 24c from line 24b .	**24d**	
17	Legal and professional services	**17**		**25**	Utilities	**25**	
				26	Wages (less employment credits)	**26**	
18	Office expense	**18**		**27**	Other expenses (from line 46 on page 2)	**27**	

28	**Total expenses** before expenses for business use of home. Add lines 8 through 27 in columns .... ☐	**28**	
29	Tentative profit (loss). Subtract line 28 from line 7	**29**	
30	Expenses for business use of your home. Attach **Form 8829**	**30**	
31	**Net profit or (loss).** Subtract line 30 from line 29.		
	☐ If a profit, enter on **Form 1040, line 12,** and ALSO on **Schedule SE, line 2** (statutory employees, see page C-5). Estates and trusts, enter on Form 1041, line 3.		
	☐ If a loss, you MUST go on to line 32.	**31**	
32	If you have a loss, check the box that describes your investment in this activity (see page C-5).		
	☐ If you checked 32a, enter the loss on **Form 1040, line 12,** and ALSO on **Schedule SE, line 2** (statutory employees, see page C-5). Estates and trusts, enter on Form 1041, line 3.	**32a** ☐ All investment is at risk. **32b** ☐ Some investment is not at risk.	
	☐ If you checked 32b, you MUST attach **Form 6198.**		

For Paperwork Reduction Act Notice, see Form 1040 instructions.

Schedule C (Form 1040) 1995

STF FED2615F.1

Exhibit A-8   Form 1040, Schedule C, Profit or Loss From Business,
and Instructions

Part III   **Cost of Goods Sold** (see page C-5)

33	Inventory at beginning of year. If different from last year's closing inventory, attach explanation	33	
34	Purchases less cost of items withdrawn for personal use	34	
35	Cost of labor. Do not include salary paid to yourself	35	
36	Materials and supplies	36	
37	Other costs	37	
38	Add lines 33 through 37	38	
39	Inventory at end of year	39	
40	**Cost of goods sold.** Subtract line 39 from line 38. Enter the result here and on page 1, line 4	40	

Part IV   **Information on Your Vehicle. Complete this part ONLY if you are claiming car or truck expenses on line 10 and are not required to file Form 4562 for this business. See the instructions for line 13 on page C-3 to find out if you must file.**

41   When did you place your vehicle in service for business purposes? (month, day, year) ☐ _____ .

42   Of the total number of miles you drove your vehicle during 1995, enter the number of miles you used your vehicle for:

a   Business _____ b Commuting _____ c Other_____

43   Do you (or your spouse) have another vehicle available for personal use? . . . . ☐ Yes   ☐ No

44   Was your vehicle available for use during off-duty hours? . . . . ☐ Yes   ☐ No

45a   Do you have evidence to support your deduction? . . . . ☐ Yes   ☐ No
  b   If "Yes," is the evidence written? . . . . ☐ Yes   ☐ No

Part V   **Other Expenses.** List below business expenses not included on lines 8-26 or line 30.

46	**Total other expenses.** Enter here and on page 1, line 27	46

STF FED2615F.2

Exhibit A-8   *(continued)*

Instructions for Schedule C, Profit or Loss From Business

Use Schedule C to report income or loss from a business you operated or a profession you practiced as a sole proprietor. Also, use Schedule C to report wages and expenses you had as a statutory employee. An activity qualifies as a business if your primary purpose for engaging in the activity is for income or profit and you are involved in the activity with continuity and regularity. For example, a sporadic activity or a hobby does not qualify as a business. To report income from a nonbusiness activity, see the Instructions for Form 1040, line 21.

Small businesses and statutory employees with gross receipts of $25,000 or less and expenses of $2,000 or less may be able to file Schedule C-EZ, Net Profit From Business, instead of Schedule C. See Schedule C-EZ to find out if you qualify to file it.

This activity may subject you to state and local taxes and other requirements such as business licenses and fees. Check with your state and local governments for more information.

General Instructions

A Change To Note

The standard mileage rate has been increased to 30 cents for each mile of business use in 1995. See the instructions for line 10.

Other Schedules and Forms You May Have To File

Schedule A to deduct interest, taxes, and casualty losses not related to your business.

Schedule E to report rental real estate and royalty income or (loss) that is not subject to self-employment tax.

Schedule F to report profit or (loss) from farming.

Schedule SE to pay self-employment tax on income from any trade or business.

Form 4562 to claim depreciation on assets placed in service in 1995, to claim amortization that began in 1995, or to report information on listed property.

Form 4684 to report a casualty or theft gain or loss involving property used in your trade or business or income-producing property.

Form 4797 to report sales, exchanges, and involuntary conversions (other than from a casualty or theft) of trade or business property.

Form 8271 if you are claiming or you are reporting on Schedule C or C-EZ any income, deduction, loss, credit, or other tax benefit from a tax shelter.

Form 8594 to report certain purchases or sales of groups of assets that constitute a trade or business.

Form 8824 to report like-kind exchanges.

Form 8829 to claim expenses for business use of your home.

Heavy Vehicle Use Tax

If you use certain highway trucks, truck-trailers, tractor-trailers, or buses in your trade or business, you may have to pay a Federal highway motor vehicle use tax. Get Form 2290, Heavy Vehicle Use Tax Return, to see if you owe this tax.

Information Returns

You may have to file information returns for wages paid to employees, certain payments of fees and other nonemployee compensation, interest, rents, royalties, real estate transactions, annuities, and pensions. You may also have to file an information return if you sold $5,000 or more of consumer products to a person on a buy-sell, deposit-commission, or other similar basis for resale. For more information, get the Instructions for Forms 1099, 1098, 5498, and W-2G.

If you received cash of more than $10,000 in one or more related transactions in the course of your trade or business, you may have to file Form 8300. For details, get Pub. 1544, Reporting Cash Payments of Over $10,000.

Additional Information

Get Pub. 334, Tax Guide for Small Business, for more details on business income and expenses.

Specific Instructions

Filers of Form 1041

Do not complete the block labeled "Social security number." Instead, enter your employer identification number (EIN) on line D.

Line A

Describe the business or professional activity that provided your principal source of income reported on line 1. If you owned more than one business, you must complete a separate Schedule C for each business. Give the general field or activity and the type of product or service. If your general field or activity is wholesale or retail trade, or services connected with production services (mining, construction, or manufacturing), also give the type of customer or client. For example, "wholesale sale of hardware to retailers" or "appraisal of real estate for lending institutions."

Line D

You need an employer identification number (EIN) only if you had a Keogh plan or were required to file an employment, excise, estate, trust, or alcohol, tobacco, and firearms tax return. If you need an EIN, file Form SS-4, Application for Employer Identification Number. If you do not have an EIN, leave line D blank. Do not enter your SSN.

Line E

Enter your business address. Show a street address instead of a box number. Include the suite or room number, if any. If you conducted the business from your home located at the address shown on Form 1040, page 1, you do not have to complete this line.

Line F

You must use the cash method on your return unless you kept account books. If you kept such books, you can use the cash method or the accrual method. However, if inventories are required, you must use the accrual method for sales and purchases. Special rules apply to long-term contracts. See Internal Revenue Code section 460 for details. The method used must clearly reflect your income.

If you use the cash method, show all items of taxable income actually or constructively received during the year (in cash, property, or services). Income is constructively received when it is credited to your account or set aside for you to use. Also, show amounts actually paid during the year for deductible expenses.

If you use the accrual method, report income when you earn it and deduct expenses when you incur them even if you do not pay them during the tax year.

Accrual-basis taxpayers are put on a cash basis for deducting business expenses owed to a related cash-basis taxpayer. Other rules determine the timing of deductions based on economic performance. Get Pub. 538, Accounting Periods and Methods.

To change your accounting method (including treatment of inventories), you must usually get permission from the IRS. In general, file Form 3115, Application for Change in Accounting Method, within the first 180 days of the tax year in which you want to make the change.

Line G

Your inventories can be valued at cost; cost or market value, whichever is lower; or any other method approved by the IRS.

Line I

Participation, for purposes of the following seven material participation tests, generally

C-1

STF FED2615I.1

Exhibit A-8 *(continued)*

includes any work you did in connection with an activity if you owned an interest in the activity at the time you did the work. The capacity in which you did the work does not matter. However, work is not treated as participation if it is work that an owner would not customarily do in the same type of activity and one of your main reasons for doing the work was to avoid the disallowance of losses or credits from the activity under the passive activity rules.

Work you did as an investor in an activity is not treated as participation in the activity unless you were directly involved in the day-to-day management or operations of the activity. Work done as an investor includes:

1. Studying and reviewing financial statements or reports on operations of the activity.

2. Preparing or compiling summaries or analyses of the finances or operations of the activity for your own use.

3. Monitoring the finances or operations of the activity in a nonmanagerial capacity.

Participation by your spouse during the tax year in an activity you own can be counted as your participation in the activity. This applies even if your spouse did not own an interest in the activity and whether or not you and your spouse file a joint return for the tax year.

Material Participation. For purposes of the passive activity rules, you materially participated in the operation of this trade or business activity during 1995 if you meet any of the following seven tests:

1. You participated in the activity for more than 500 hours during the tax year.

2. Your participation in the activity for the tax year was substantially all of the participation in the activity of all individuals (including individuals who did not own any interest in the activity) for the tax year.

3. You participated in the activity for more than 100 hours during the tax year, and you participated at least as much as any other person for the tax year. This includes individuals who did not own any interest in the activity.

4. The activity is a significant participation activity for the tax year, and you participated in all significant participation activities for more than 500 hours during the year. An activity is a "significant participation activity" if it involves the conduct of a trade or business, you participated in the activity for more than 100 hours during the tax year, and you did not materially participate under any of the material participation tests (other than this test 4).

5. You materially participated in the activity for any 5 of the prior 10 tax years.

6. The activity is a personal service activity in which you materially participated for any 3 prior tax years. A personal service activity is an activity that involves performing personal services in the fields of health, law, engineering, architecture, accounting, actuarial science, performing arts, consulting, or any other trade or business in which capital is not a material income-producing factor.

7. Based on all the facts and circumstances, you participated in the activity on a regular, continuous, and substantial basis during the tax year. But you do not meet this test if you participated in the activity for

100 hours or less during the tax year. Your participation in managing the activity does not count in determining if you meet this test if any person (except you) —

a. Received compensation for performing management services in connection with the activity, or

b. Spent more hours during the tax year than you spent performing management services in connection with the activity (regardless of whether the person was compensated for the services).

If you meet any of the above tests, check the "Yes" box.

If you do not meet any of the above tests, check the "No" box. This business is a passive activity. If you have a loss from this business, see Limit on Losses below. If you have a profit from this business activity but have current-year losses from other passive activities or you have prior-year unallowed passive activity losses, see the Instructions for Form 8582, Passive Activity Loss Limitations.

Exception for Oil and Gas. If you are filing Schedule C to report income and deductions from an oil or gas well in which you own a working interest directly or through an entity that does not limit your liability, check the "Yes" box. The activity of owning the working interest is not a passive activity regardless of your participation in the activity.

Limit on Losses. If you checked the "No" box and you have a loss from this business, you may have to use Form 8582 to figure your allowable loss, if any, to enter on Schedule C, line 31. Generally, you can deduct losses from passive activities only to the extent of income from passive activities.

For more details, get Pub. 925, Passive Activity and At-Risk Rules.

Line J

If you started or acquired this business in 1995, check the box on line J. Also, check the box if you are reopening or restarting this business after temporarily closing it, and you did not file a 1994 Schedule C or C-EZ for this business.

Part I. Income

Line 1

Enter gross receipts or sales from your business. Be sure to include on this line amounts you received in your trade or business as shown on Form 1099-MISC, Miscellaneous Income.

Statutory Employees. If you received a Form W-2 and the "Statutory employee" box in box 15 of that form was checked, report your income and expenses related to that income on Schedule C or C-EZ. Enter your statutory employee income from box 1 of Form W-2 on line 1 of Schedule C or C-EZ, and check the box on that line. Social security and Medicare tax should have been withheld from your earnings; therefore, you do not owe self-employment tax on these earnings.

Statutory employees include full-time life insurance agents, certain agent or commission drivers and traveling salespersons, and certain homeworkers.

If you had both self-employment income and statutory employee income, do not combine these amounts on a single Schedule C or C-EZ. In this case, you must file two Schedules C. You cannot use Schedule C-EZ.

Installment Sales. Generally, the installment method may not be used to report income from the sale of (a) personal property regularly sold under the installment method or (b) real property held for resale to customers. But the installment method may be used to report income from sales of certain residential lots and timeshares if you elect to pay interest on the tax due on that income after the year of sale. See Internal Revenue Code section 453(l)(2)(B) for details. If you make this election, include the interest on Form 1040, line 54, and write "453(l)(3)" and the amount of the interest on the dotted line to the left of line 54.

If you use the installment method, attach a schedule to your return. Show separately for 1995 and the 3 preceding years: gross sales, cost of goods sold, gross profit, percentage of gross profit to gross sales, amounts collected, and gross profit on amounts collected.

Line 2

Enter such items as returned sales, rebates, and allowances from the sales price.

Line 6

Report on line 6 amounts from finance reserve income, scrap sales, bad debts you recovered, interest (such as on notes and accounts receivable), state gasoline or fuel tax refunds you got in 1995, credit for Federal tax paid on gasoline or other fuels claimed on your 1994 Form 1040, prizes and awards related to your trade or business, and other kinds of miscellaneous business income. Include amounts you received in your trade or business as shown on Form 1099-PATR, Taxable Distributions Received From Cooperatives. Also, include any recapture of the deduction for clean-fuel vehicles used in your business and clean-fuel vehicle refueling property. For more details, get Pub. 535, Business Expenses.

If the business use percentage of any listed property (defined in the instructions for line 13) decreased to 50% or less in 1995, report on this line any recapture of excess depreciation, including any section 179 expense deduction. Use Form 4797, Sales of Business Property, to figure the recapture. Also, if the business use percentage drops to 50% or less on leased listed property (other than a vehicle), include on this line any inclusion amount. Get Pub. 946, How To Depreciate Property, to figure the amount.

Part II. Expenses

Capitalizing Costs of Property. If you produced real or tangible personal property or acquired property for resale, certain expenses attributable to the property must be included in inventory costs or capitalized. In addition to direct costs, producers of inventory property must also include part of certain indirect costs in their inventory. Purchasers of personal property acquired for resale must include part of certain indirect

C-2

Exhibit A-8   *(continued)*

costs in inventory only if the average annual gross receipts for the 3 prior tax years exceed $10 million. Also, you must capitalize part of the indirect costs that benefit real or tangible personal property constructed for use in a trade or business, or non-inventory property produced for sale to customers. Reduce the amounts on lines 8-26 and Part V by amounts capitalized. For more details, see Pub. 538.

Exception for Creative Property. If you are an artist, author, or photographer, you may be exempt from the capitalization rules. However, your personal efforts must have created (or reasonably be expected to create) the property. This exception does not apply to any expense related to printing, photographic plates, motion picture films, video tapes, or similar items. These expenses are subject to the capitalization rules. For more details, see Pub. 538.

Line 9

Caution: *Cash method taxpayers cannot take a bad debt deduction unless the amount was previously included in income.*

Include debts and partial debts from sales or services that were included in income and are definitely known to be worthless. If you later collect a debt that you deducted as a bad debt, include it as income in the year collected. For more details, see Pub. 535.

Line 10

You can deduct the actual cost of running your car or truck, or take the standard mileage rate. You must use actual costs if you did not own the vehicle or if you used more than one vehicle simultaneously in your business (such as in fleet operations).

If you deduct actual costs, include on line 10 the business portion of expenses for gasoline, oil, repairs, insurance, tires, license plates, etc. Show depreciation on line 13 and rent or lease payments on line 20a.

If you want to take the standard mileage rate, multiply the number of business miles by 30 cents a mile. Add to this amount your parking fees and tolls, and enter the total on line 10.

For more details, get Pub. 917, Business Use of a Car.

Information on Your Vehicle. If you claim any car and truck expenses, you must provide certain information on the use of your vehicle by completing:

☐ Part IV of Schedule C or Part III of Schedule C-EZ if (a) you are claiming the standard mileage rate, you lease your vehicle, or your vehicle is fully depreciated and (b) you are not required to file Form 4562, Depreciation and Amortization, for any other reason. If you used more than one vehicle during the year, attach your own schedule with the information requested in Part IV of Schedule C, or Part III of Schedule C-EZ, for each additional vehicle.

☐ Part V of Form 4562 if you are claiming depreciation on your vehicle or you are required to file Form 4562 for any other reason (see the instructions for line 13 below).

Line 12

Enter your deduction for depletion on this line. If you have timber depletion, attach Form T, Forest Activities Schedules. See Pub. 535 for details.

Line 13

Depreciation and Section 179 Expense Deduction. Depreciation is the annual deduction allowed to recover the cost or other basis of business or investment property with a useful life of more than 1 year. You can also depreciate improvements made to leased business property. However, stock in trade, inventories, and land are not depreciable.

Depreciation starts when you first use the property in your business or for the production of income. It ends when you take the property out of service, deduct all your depreciable cost or other basis, or no longer use the property in your business or for the production of income.

For property placed in service after 1980, see the Instructions for Form 4562 to figure the amount of depreciation to enter on line 13. For property placed in service before 1981, figure depreciation from your own books and records.

You may also choose under Internal Revenue Code section 179 to expense part of the cost of certain property you bought in 1995 for use in your business. See the Instructions for Form 4562 for more details.

When To Attach Form 4562. You must complete and attach Form 4562 only if:

☐ You are claiming depreciation on property placed in service during 1995, or

☐ You are claiming depreciation on listed property (defined below), regardless of the date it was placed in service, or

☐ You are claiming a section 179 expense deduction.

If you acquired depreciable property for the first time in 1995, see Pub. 946.

Listed property generally includes, but is not limited to:

☐ Passenger automobiles weighing 6,000 pounds or less.

☐ Any other property used for transportation if the nature of the property lends itself to personal use, such as motorcycles, pickup trucks, etc.

☐ Any property used for entertainment or recreational purposes (such as photographic, phonographic, communication, and video recording equipment).

☐ Cellular telephones or other similar telecommunications equipment placed in service after 1989.

☐ Computers or peripheral equipment.

Exceptions. Listed property does not include photographic, phonographic, communication, or video equipment used exclusively in your trade or business or at your regular business establishment. It also does not include any computer or peripheral equipment used exclusively at a regular business establishment owned or leased by the person operating the establishment. For purposes of these exceptions, a portion of your home is treated as a regular business establishment only if that portion meets the requirements under Internal Revenue Code section 280A(c)(1) for deducting expenses for the business use of your home.

If the business use percentage of any listed property decreased to 50% or less in 1995, see the instructions for line 6 on page C-2.

Line 14

Deduct contributions to employee benefit programs that are not an incidental part of a pension or profit-sharing plan included on line 19. Examples are accident and health plans, group-term life insurance, and dependent care assistance programs.

Do not include on line 14 any contributions you made on your behalf as a self-employed person to an accident and health plan or for group-term life insurance. You may be able to deduct on Form 1040, line 26, part of the amount you paid for health insurance on behalf of yourself, your spouse, and dependents, even if you do not itemize your deductions. See the Form 1040 instructions on page 21 for more details.

Line 15

Deduct premiums paid for business insurance on line 15. Deduct on line 14 amounts paid for employee accident and health insurance. Do not deduct amounts credited to a reserve for self-insurance or premiums paid for a policy that pays for your lost earnings due to sickness or disability. For more details, see Pub. 535.

Lines 16a and 16b

Interest Allocation Rules. The tax treatment of interest expense differs depending on its type. For example, home mortgage interest and investment interest are treated differently. "Interest allocation" rules require you to allocate (classify) your interest expense so it is deducted (or capitalized) on the correct line of your return and gets the right tax treatment. These rules could affect how much interest you are allowed to deduct on Schedule C or C-EZ.

Generally, you allocate interest expense by tracing how the proceeds of the loan were used. See Pub. 535 for details.

If you paid interest in 1995 that applies to future years, deduct only the part that applies to 1995. If you paid interest on a debt secured by your main home and any of the proceeds from that debt were used in connection with your trade or business, see Pub. 535 to figure the amount that is deductible on Schedule C or C-EZ.

If you have a mortgage on real property used in your business (other than your main home), enter on line 16a the interest you paid for 1995 to banks or other financial institutions for which you received a Form 1098, Mortgage Interest Statement. If you didn't receive a Form 1098, enter the interest on line 16b.

If you paid $600 or more of mortgage interest, the recipient should send you a Form 1098 or similar statement showing the total interest received from you during 1995. This statement must be sent to you by January 31, 1996. If you paid more mortgage interest to financial institutions than is shown on Form 1098 or similar statement, see Pub.

C-3

STF FED2615I.3

Exhibit A-8 *(continued)*

535 to find out if you can deduct the additional interest. If you can, enter the amount on line 16a. Attach a statement to your return explaining the difference. Write "See attached" in the left margin next to line 16a.

If you and at least one other person (other than your spouse if you file a joint return) were liable for and paid interest on the mortgage and the other person received the Form 1098, report your share of the interest on line 16b. Attach a statement to your return showing the name and address of the person who received the Form 1098. In the left margin next to line 16b, write "See attached."

Do not deduct interest you paid or accrued on debts allocable to investment property. This interest is generally deducted on Schedule A (Form 1040). For details, get Pub. 550, Investment Income and Expenses.

Line 17

Include on this line fees for tax advice related to your business and for preparation of the tax forms related to your business.

Line 19

Enter your deduction for contributions to a pension, profit-sharing, or annuity plan, or plans for the benefit of your employees. If the plan includes you as a self-employed person, enter contributions made as an employer on your behalf on Form 1040, line 27, not on Schedule C.

Generally, you must file one of the following forms if you maintain a pension, profit-sharing, or other funded-deferred compensation plan. The filing requirement is not affected by whether or not the plan qualified under the Internal Revenue Code, or whether or not you claim a deduction for the current tax year.

Form 5500. Complete this form for each plan with 100 or more participants.

Form 5500-C/R or 5500-EZ. Complete the applicable form for each plan with fewer than 100 participants.

There is a penalty for failure to timely file these forms.

For more information, get Pub. 560, Retirement Plans for the Self-Employed.

Lines 20a and 20b

If you rented or leased vehicles, machinery, or equipment, enter on line 20a the business portion of your rental cost. But if you leased a vehicle for a term of 30 days or more, you may have to reduce your deduction by an amount called the inclusion amount.

You may have to do this if—

The lease term began:	And the vehicle's fair market value on the first day of the lease exceeded:
During 1995	$15,500
During 1994	14,600
During 1993	14,300
During 1992	13,700
During 1991	13,400
After 1986 but before 1991	12,800

If the lease term began after June 18, 1984, but before January 1, 1987, see Pub. 917 to find out if you have an inclusion amount.

See Pub. 917 to figure your inclusion amount.

Enter on line 20b amounts paid to rent or lease other property, such as office space in a building.

Line 21

Deduct the cost of repairs and maintenance. Include labor, supplies, and other items that do not add to the value or increase the life of the property. Do not deduct the value of your own labor. Do not deduct amounts spent to restore or replace property; they must be capitalized.

Line 23

You can deduct the following taxes on this line:

☐ State and local sales taxes imposed on you as the seller of goods or services. If you collected this tax from the buyer, you must also include the amount collected in gross receipts or sales on line 1.

☐ Real estate and personal property taxes on business assets.

☐ Social security and Medicare taxes paid to match required withholding from your employees' wages. Also, Federal unemployment tax paid. Reduce your deduction by the amount of the current year credit shown on line 4 of Form 8846, Credit for Employer Social Security and Medicare Taxes Paid on Certain Employee Tips.

☐ Federal highway use tax.

Do not deduct on this line:

☐ Federal income taxes, including your self-employment tax. However, you may deduct one-half of your self-employment tax on Form 1040, line 25.

☐ Estate and gift taxes.

☐ Taxes assessed to pay for improvements, such as paving and sewers.

☐ Taxes on your home or personal use property.

☐ State and local sales taxes on property purchased for use in your business. Instead, treat these taxes as part of the cost of the property.

☐ State and local sales taxes imposed on the buyer that you were required to collect and pay over to the state or local governments. These taxes are not included in gross receipts or sales nor are they a deductible expense. However, if the state or local government allowed you to retain any part of the sales tax you collected, you must include that amount as income on line 6.

☐ Other taxes not related to your business.

Line 24a

Enter your expenses for lodging and transportation connected with overnight travel for business while away from your tax home. Generally, your tax home is your main place of business regardless of where you maintain your family home. You cannot deduct expenses paid or incurred in connection with employment away from home if that period of

employment exceeds 1 year. Also, you cannot deduct travel expenses for your spouse, your dependent, or any other individual unless that person is your employee, the travel is for a bona fide business purpose, and the expenses would otherwise be deductible by that person.

Do not include expenses for meals and entertainment on this line. Instead, see the instructions for lines 24b and 24c below.

You cannot deduct expenses for attending a foreign convention unless it is directly related to your trade or business and it is as reasonable for the meeting to be held outside the North American area as within it. These rules apply to both employers and employees. Other rules apply to luxury water travel.

For more details, get Pub. 463, Travel, Entertainment, and Gift Expenses.

Lines 24b and 24c

On line 24b, enter your total business meal and entertainment expenses. Include meals while traveling away from home for business. Instead of the actual cost of your meals while traveling away from home, you may use the standard meal allowance. For more details, see Pub. 463.

Business meal expenses are deductible only if they are (a) directly related to or associated with the active conduct of your trade or business, (b) not lavish or extravagant, and (c) incurred while you or your employee is present at the meal.

You cannot deduct any expense paid or incurred for a facility (such as a yacht or hunting lodge) used for any activity usually considered entertainment, amusement, or recreation.

Also, you cannot deduct amounts paid or incurred for membership dues in any club organized for business, pleasure, recreation, or other social purpose. This includes country clubs, golf and athletic clubs, airline and hotel clubs, and clubs operated to provide meals under conditions favorable to business discussion. But it does not include civic or public service organizations, professional organizations (such as bar and medical associations), business leagues, trade associations, chambers of commerce, boards of trade, and real estate boards, unless a principal purpose of the organization is to entertain, or provide entertainment facilities for, members or their guests.

There are exceptions to these rules as well as other rules that apply to sky-box rentals and tickets to entertainment events. See Pub. 463.

Generally, you may deduct only 50% of your business meal and entertainment expenses, including meals incurred while traveling away from home on business. However, you may fully deduct meals and entertainment furnished or reimbursed to an employee if you properly treat the expense as wages subject to withholding. You may also fully deduct meals and entertainment provided to a nonemployee to the extent the expenses are includible in the gross income of that person and reported on Form 1099-MISC.

Figure how much of the amount on line 24b is subject to the 50% limit. Then, enter one-half of that amount on line 24c.

C-4

Exhibit A-8 *(continued)*

Line 25

Deduct only utility expenses paid or incurred for your trade or business.

Local Telephone Service. If you used your home phone for business, do not deduct the base rate (including taxes) of the first phone line into your residence. But you can deduct expenses for any additional costs you incurred for business that are more than the cost of the base rate for the first phone line. For example, if you had a second line, you can deduct the business percentage of the charges for that line, including the base rate charges.

Line 26

Enter the total salaries and wages paid or incurred for the tax year. Do not include salaries and wages deducted elsewhere on your return or amounts paid to yourself. Reduce your deduction by the current year credits claimed on:

☐ **Form 5884,** Jobs Credit.

☐ **Form 8844,** Empowerment Zone Employment Credit.

☐ **Form 8845,** Indian Employment Credit.

Caution: *If you provided taxable fringe benefits to your employees, such as personal use of a car, do not deduct as wages the amount applicable to depreciation and other expenses claimed elsewhere.*

Line 30

Business Use of Your Home. You may be able to deduct certain expenses for business use of your home, subject to limitations. Generally, any amount not allowed as a deduction for 1995 because of the limitations can be carried over to 1996. You must attach Form 8829, Expenses for Business Use of Your Home, if you claim this deduction.

For details, see the Instructions for Form 8829, and get Pub. 587, Business Use of Your Home.

Line 31

If you have a loss, the amount of loss you can deduct this year may be limited. Go on to line 32 before entering your loss on line 31. If you answered "No" to Question I on Schedule C, also see the Instructions for Form 8582. Enter the net profit or deductible loss here. Combine this amount with any profit or loss from other businesses, and enter the total on Form 1040, line 12, and Schedule SE, line 2. Estates and trusts should enter the total on Form 1041, line 3.

If you have a net profit on line 31, this amount is earned income and may qualify you for the earned income credit if you meet certain conditions. See the Instructions for Form 1040, line 57, on page 27 for more details.

Statutory Employees. If you are filing Schedule C to report income and expenses as a statutory employee, include your net profit or deductible loss from line 31 with other Schedule C amounts on Form 1040, line 12. However, do not report this amount on Schedule SE, line 2. If you are required to file Schedule SE because of other self-employment income, see the Instructions for Schedule SE.

Line 32

At-Risk Rules. Generally, if you have (a) a business loss and (b) amounts in the business for which you are not at risk, you will have to complete Form 6198, At-Risk Limitations, to figure your allowable loss.

The at-risk rules generally limit the amount of loss (including loss on the disposition of assets) you can claim to the amount you could actually lose in the business.

Check box 32b if you have amounts for which you are not at risk in this business, such as the following.

☐ Nonrecourse loans used to finance the business, to acquire property used in the business, or to acquire the business that are not secured by your own property (other than property used in the business). However, there is an exception for certain nonrecourse financing borrowed by you in connection with holding real property.

☐ Cash, property, or borrowed amounts used in the business (or contributed to the business, or used to acquire the business) that are protected against loss by a guarantee, stop-loss agreement, or other similar arrangement (excluding casualty insurance and insurance against tort liability).

☐ Amounts borrowed for use in the business from a person who has an interest in the business, other than as a creditor, or who is related under Internal Revenue Code section 465(b)(3) to a person (other than you) having such an interest.

If all amounts are at risk in this business, check box 32a and enter your loss on line 31. But if you answered "No" to Question I, you may need to complete Form 8582 to figure your allowable loss to enter on line 31. See the Instructions for Form 8582 for more details.

If you checked box 32b, get Form 6198 to determine the amount of your deductible loss and enter that amount on line 31. But if you answered "No" to Question I, your loss may be further limited. See the Instructions for Form 8582. If your at-risk amount is zero or less, enter zero on line 31. Be sure to attach Form 6198 to your return. If you checked box 32b and you do not attach Form 6198, the processing of your tax return may be delayed.

Statutory Employees. Include your deductible loss with other Schedule C amounts on Form 1040, line 12. Do not include this amount on Schedule SE, line 2.

Any loss from this business not allowed for 1995 because of the at-risk rules is treated as a deduction allocable to the business in 1996. For more details, see the Instructions for Form 6198 and Pub. 925.

Part III. Cost of Goods Sold

If you engaged in a trade or business in which the production, purchase, or sale of merchandise was an income-producing factor, merchandise inventories must be taken into account at the beginning and end of your tax year.

Note: *Certain direct and indirect expenses must be capitalized or included in inventory. See the instructions for Part II.*

Part V. Other Expenses

Include all ordinary and necessary business expenses not deducted elsewhere on Schedule C. List the type and amount of each expense separately in the space provided. Enter the total on lines 46 and 27. Do not include the cost of business equipment or furniture, replacements or permanent improvements to property, or personal, living, and family expenses. Do not include charitable contributions. Also, you may not deduct fines or penalties paid to a government for violating any law. For more details on business expenses, see Pub. 535.

Amortization. Include amortization in this part. For amortization that begins in 1995, you must complete and attach Form 4562.

You may amortize:

☐ The cost of pollution-control facilities.

☐ Amounts paid for research and experimentation.

☐ Certain business startup costs.

☐ Qualified forestation and reforestation costs.

☐ Amounts paid to acquire, protect, expand, register, or defend trademarks or trade names.

☐ Goodwill and certain other intangibles.

In general, you may not amortize real property construction period interest and taxes. Special rules apply for allocating interest to real or personal property produced in your trade or business.

At-Risk Loss Deduction. Any loss from this activity that was not allowed as a deduction last year because of the at-risk rules is treated as a deduction allocable to this activity in 1995.

Capital Construction Fund. Do not claim on Schedule C or C-EZ the deduction for amounts contributed to a capital construction fund set up under the Merchant Marine Act of 1936. To take the deduction, reduce the amount that would otherwise be entered as taxable income on Form 1040, line 37, by the amount of the deduction. In the margin to the left of line 37, write "CCF" and the amount of the deduction. For more information, get Pub. 595, Tax Guide for Commercial Fishermen.

Deduction for Clean-Fuel Vehicles and Clean-Fuel Vehicle Refueling Property. You may deduct part of the cost of qualified clean-fuel vehicle property used in your business and qualified clean-fuel vehicle refueling property. See Pub. 535 for more details.

Disabled Access Credit and the Deduction for Removing Barriers to Individuals With Disabilities and the Elderly. You may be able to claim a tax credit of up to $5,000 for eligible expenditures paid or incurred in 1995 to provide access to your business for individuals with disabilities. See Form 8826, Disabled Access Credit, for more details. You can also deduct up to $15,000 of costs paid or incurred in 1995 to remove architectural or transportation barriers to individuals with disabilities and the elderly. However, you cannot take both the credit and the deduction on the same expenditures.

C-5

STF FED2615I.5

Exhibit A-8   *(continued)*

Principal Business or Professional Activity Codes

Locate the major category that best describes your activity. Within the major category, select the activity code that most closely identifies the business or profession that is the principal source of your sales or receipts. Enter this 4-digit code on line B of Schedule C or C-EZ. For example, real estate agent is under the major category of "Real Estate," and the code is "5520."

Note: *If your principal source of income is from farming activities, you should file Schedule F (Form 1040), Profit or Loss From Farming.*

Agricultural Services, Forestry, Fishing

Code

- 1990 Animal services, other than breeding
- 1933 Crop services
- 2113 Farm labor & management services
- 2246 Fishing, commercial
- 2238 Forestry, except logging
- 2212 Horticulture, gardening, & landscaping
- 2469 Hunting & trapping
- 1974 Livestock breeding
- 0836 Logging
- 1958 Veterinary services, including pets

Construction

- 0018 Operative builders (for own account)

Building Trades, Including Repairs

- 0414 Carpentering & flooring
- 0455 Concrete work
- 0273 Electrical work
- 0299 Masonry, dry wall, stone, & tile
- 0257 Painting & paper hanging
- 0232 Plumbing, heating, & air conditioning
- 0430 Roofing, siding, & sheet metal
- 0885 Other building trade contractors (excavation, glazing, etc.)

General Contractors

- 0075 Highway & street construction
- 0059 Nonresidential building
- 0034 Residential building
- 3889 Other heavy construction (pipe laying, bridge construction, etc.)

Finance, Insurance, & Related Services

- 6064 Brokers & dealers of securities
- 6080 Commodity contracts brokers & dealers; security & commodity exchanges
- 6148 Credit institutions & mortgage bankers
- 5702 Insurance agents or brokers
- 5744 Insurance services (appraisal, consulting, inspection, etc.)
- 6130 Investment advisors & services
- 5777 Other financial services

Manufacturing, Including Printing & Publishing

- 0679 Apparel & other textile products
- 1115 Electric & electronic equipment
- 1073 Fabricated metal products
- 0638 Food products & beverages
- 0810 Furniture & fixtures
- 0695 Leather footwear, handbags, etc.
- 0836 Lumber & other wood products
- 1099 Machinery & machine shops
- 0877 Paper & allied products
- 1057 Primary metal industries
- 0851 Printing & publishing
- 1032 Stone, clay, & glass products
- 0653 Textile mill products
- 1883 Other manufacturing industries

Mining & Mineral Extraction

- 1537 Coal mining
- 1511 Metal mining
- 1552 Oil & gas
- 1719 Quarrying & nonmetallic mining

Real Estate

- 5538 Operators & lessors of buildings, including residential
- 5553 Operators & lessors of other real property
- 5520 Real estate agents & brokers
- 5579 Real estate property managers
- 5710 Subdividers & developers, except cemeteries
- 6155 Title abstract offices

Services: Personal, Professional, & Business Services

Amusement & Recreational Services

- 9670 Bowling centers
- 9688 Motion picture & tape distribution & allied services
- 9597 Motion picture & video production
- 9639 Motion picture theaters
- 8557 Physical fitness facilities
- 9696 Professional sports & racing, including promoters & managers
- 9811 Theatrical performers, musicians, agents, producers, & related services
- 9613 Video tape rental
- 9837 Other amusement & recreational services

Automotive Services

- 8813 Automotive rental or leasing, without driver
- 8953 Automotive repairs, general & specialized
- 8839 Parking, except valet
- 8896 Other automotive services (wash, towing, etc.)

Business & Personal Services

- 7658 Accounting & bookkeeping
- 7716 Advertising, except direct mail
- 7682 Architectural services
- 6883 Authors & artists
- 8318 Barber shop (or barber)
- 8110 Beauty shop (or beautician)
- 8714 Child day care
- 7872 Computer programming, processing, data preparation, & related services
- 7922 Computer repair, maintenance, & leasing
- 7286 Consulting services
- 7799 Consumer credit reporting & collection services
- 8755 Counseling (except health practitioners)
- 7732 Employment agencies & personnel supply
- 7518 Engineering services
- 7773 Equipment rental & leasing (except computer or automotive)
- 8532 Funeral services & crematories
- 7633 Income tax preparation
- 7914 Investigative & protective services
- 7617 Legal services (or lawyer)
- 7856 Mailing, reproduction, commercial art, photography, & stenographic services
- 7245 Management services
- 8771 Ministers & chaplains
- 8334 Photographic studios
- 7260 Public relations
- 8733 Research services
- 7708 Surveying services
- 8730 Teaching or tutoring

- 7880 Other business services
- 6882 Other personal services

Hotels & Other Lodging Places

- 7237 Camps & camping parks
- 7096 Hotels, motels, & tourist homes
- 7211 Rooming & boarding houses

Laundry & Cleaning Services

- 7450 Carpet & upholstery cleaning
- 7419 Coin-operated laundries & dry cleaning
- 7435 Full-service laundry, dry cleaning, & garment service
- 7476 Janitorial & related services (building, house, & window cleaning)

Medical & Health Services

- 9274 Chiropractors
- 9233 Dentist's office or clinic
- 9217 Doctor's (M.D.) office or clinic
- 9456 Medical & dental laboratories
- 9472 Nursing & personal care facilities
- 9290 Optometrists
- 9258 Osteopathic physicians & surgeons
- 9241 Podiatrists
- 9415 Registered & practical nurses
- 9431 Offices & clinics of other health practitioners (dieticians, midwives, speech pathologists, etc.)
- 9886 Other health services

Miscellaneous Repair, Except Computers

- 9019 Audio equipment & TV repair
- 9035 Electrical & electronic equipment repair, except audio & TV
- 9050 Furniture repair & reupholstery
- 2881 Other equipment repair

Trade, Retail—Selling Goods to Individuals & Households

- 3038 Catalog or mail order
- 3046 Flea markets or shows
- 3012 Selling door to door, by telephone or party plan, or from mobile unit
- 3053 Vending machine selling

Selling From Showroom, Store, or Other Fixed Location

Apparel & Accessories

- 3921 Accessory & specialty stores & furriers for women
- 3939 Clothing, family
- 3772 Clothing, men's & boys'
- 3913 Clothing, women's
- 3756 Shoe stores
- 3954 Other apparel & accessory stores

Automotive & Service Stations

- 3558 Gasoline service stations
- 3319 New car dealers (franchised)
- 3533 Tires, accessories, & parts
- 3335 Used car dealers
- 3517 Other automotive dealers (motorcycles, recreational vehicles, etc.)

Building, Hardware, & Garden Supply

- 4416 Building materials dealers
- 4457 Hardware stores
- 4473 Nurseries & garden supply stores
- 4432 Paint, glass, & wallpaper stores

Food & Beverages

- 0612 Bakeries selling at retail
- 3086 Catering services
- 3095 Drinking places (bars, taverns, pubs, saloons, etc.)

- 3081 Eating places, fast food
- 3079 Full service restaurants
- 3210 Grocery stores (general line)
- 3251 Liquor stores
- 3236 Specialized food stores (meat, produce, candy, health food, etc.)

Furniture & General Merchandise

- 3988 Computer & software stores
- 3970 Furniture stores
- 4317 Home furnishings stores (china, floor coverings, drapes)
- 4119 Household appliance stores
- 4333 Music & record stores
- 3996 TV, audio & electronic stores
- 3715 Variety stores
- 3731 Other general merchandise stores

Miscellaneous Retail Stores

- 4812 Boat dealers
- 5017 Book stores, excluding newsstands
- 4853 Camera & photo supply stores
- 3277 Drug stores
- 5058 Fabric & needlework stores
- 4655 Florists
- 5090 Fuel dealers (except gasoline)
- 4630 Gift, novelty, & souvenir shops
- 4838 Hobby, toy, & game shops
- 4671 Jewelry stores
- 4895 Luggage & leather goods stores
- 5074 Mobile home dealers
- 4879 Optical goods stores
- 4697 Sporting goods & bicycle shops
- 5033 Stationery stores
- 4614 Used merchandise & antique stores (except motor vehicle parts)
- 5884 Other retail stores

Trade, Wholesale—Selling Goods to Other Businesses, etc.

Durable Goods, Including Machinery Equipment, Wood, Metals, etc.

- 2634 Agent or broker for other firms— more than 50% of gross sales on commission
- 2618 Selling for your own account

Nondurable Goods, Including Food, Fiber, Chemicals, etc.

- 2675 Agent or broker for other firms— more than 50% of gross sales on commission
- 2659 Selling for your own account

Transportation, Communications, Public Utilities, & Related Services

- 6619 Air transportation
- 6312 Bus & limousine transportation
- 6676 Communication services
- 6395 Courier or package delivery
- 6361 Highway passenger transportation (except chartered service)
- 6536 Public warehousing
- 6114 Taxicabs
- 6510 Trash collection without own dump
- 6635 Travel agents & tour operators
- 6338 Trucking (except trash collection)
- 6692 Utilities (dumps, snow plowing, road cleaning, etc.)
- 6551 Water transportation
- 6650 Other transportation services
- 8888 Unable to classify

C-6

Exhibit A-8 *(continued)*

Form **2848**
(Rev. December 1995)
Department of the Treasury
Internal Revenue Service

Power of Attorney
and Declaration of Representative
☐ For Paperwork Reduction and Privacy Act Notice, see the instructions.

OMB No. 1545-0150

For IRS Use Only
Received by:
Name_____
Telephone_____
Function _____
Date

Part I | **Power of Attorney** (Please type or print.)

1   Taxpayer Information (Taxpayer(s) must sign and date this form on page 2, line 9.)

Taxpayer name(s) and address	Social security number(s)	Employer identification number
	_____	
		Plan number (if applicable)
	Daytime telephone number	

hereby appoint(s) the following representative(s) as attorney(s)-in-fact:

2   Representative(s) (Representative(s) must sign and date this form on page 2, Part II.)

Name and address	CAF No. _____ Telephone No. _____ Fax No. _____ Check if new: Address ☐ Telephone No. ☐
Name and address	CAF No. _____ Telephone No. _____ Fax No. _____ Check if new: Address ☐ Telephone No. ☐
Name and address	CAF No. _____ Telephone No. _____ Fax No. _____ Check if new: Address ☐ Telephone No. ☐

to represent the taxpayer(s) before the Internal Revenue Service for the following tax matters:

3   Tax Matters

Type of Tax (Income, Employment, Excise, etc.)	Tax Form Number (1040, 941, 720, etc.)	Year(s) or Period(s)

4   Specific Use Not Recorded on Centralized Authorization File (CAF).—If the power of attorney is for a specific use not recorded on CAF, check this box. (See **Line 4 — Specific uses not recorded on CAF** on page 3.) . . . . ☐ ☐

5   Acts Authorized.—The representatives are authorized to receive and inspect confidential tax information and to perform any and all acts that I (we) can perform with respect to the tax matters described in line 3, for example, the authority to sign any agreements, consents, or other documents. The authority does not include the power to receive refund checks (see line 6 below), the power to substitute another representative unless specifically added below, or the power to sign certain returns (see **Line 5 — Acts Authorized** on page 4).
List any specific additions or deletions to the acts otherwise authorized in this power of attorney: _____
_____

Note: *In general, an unenrolled preparer of tax returns cannot sign any document for a taxpayer. See Revenue Procedure 81-38, printed as Pub. 470, for more information.*
Note: *The tax matters partner/person of a partnership or S corporation is not permitted to authorize representatives to perform certain acts. See the instructions for more information.*

6   Receipt of Refund Checks.—If you want to authorize a representative named in line 2 to receive, **BUT NOT TO ENDORSE OR CASH,** refund checks, initial here _____ and list the name of that representative below.

Name of representative to receive refund check(s) ☐

ISA

Form **2848** (Rev. 12-95)

STF FED4675F.1

Exhibit A-9   Form 2848, Power of Attorney and Declaration
of Representative, and Instructions

7   Notices and Communications.—Original notices and other written communications will be sent to you and a copy to the first representative listed in line 2 unless you check one or more of the boxes below.

  a If you also want the first representative listed on line 2 to receive the original, and yourself a copy, of such notices or communications, check this box . . . . ☐ ☐

  b If you also want the second representative listed to receive a copy of such notices and communications, check this box . . . . ☐ ☐

  c If you do not want any notices or communications sent to your representative, check this box . . . . ☐ ☐

8   Retention/Revocation of Prior Power(s) of Attorney.—The filing of this power of attorney automatically revokes all earlier power(s) of attorney on file with the Internal Revenue Service for the same tax matters and years or periods covered by this document. If you do not want to revoke a prior power of attorney, check here . . . . ☐ ☐
YOU MUST ATTACH A COPY OF ANY POWER OF ATTORNEY YOU WANT TO REMAIN IN EFFECT.

9   Signature of Taxpayer(s).—If a tax matter concerns a joint return, **both** husband and wife must sign if joint representation is requested, otherwise, see the instructions. If signed by a corporate officer, partner, guardian, tax matters partner/person, executor, receiver, administrator, or trustee on behalf of the taxpayer, I certify that I have the authority to execute this form on behalf of the taxpayer.

  ☐ **IF NOT SIGNED AND DATED, THIS POWER OF ATTORNEY WILL BE RETURNED.**

Signature	Date	Title (if applicable)
Print Name		
Signature	Date	Title (if applicable)
Print Name		

Part II	**Declaration of Representative**

Under penalties of perjury, I declare that:

  ☐ I am not currently under suspension or disbarment from practice before the Internal Revenue Service;

  ☐ I am aware of regulations contained in Treasury Department Circular No. 230 (31 CFR, Part 10), as amended, concerning the practice of attorneys, certified public accountants, enrolled agents, enrolled actuaries, and others;

  ☐ I am authorized to represent the taxpayer(s) identified in Part I for the tax matter(s) specified there; and

  ☐ I am one of the following:

    a Attorney—a member in good standing of the bar of the highest court of the jurisdiction shown below.

    b Certified Public Accountant—duly qualified to practice as a certified public accountant in the jurisdiction shown below.

    c Enrolled Agent—enrolled as an agent under the requirements of Treasury Department Circular No. 230.

    d Officer—a bona fide officer of the taxpayer's organization.

    e Full-Time Employee—a full-time employee of the taxpayer.

    f Family Member—a member of the taxpayer's immediate family (i.e., spouse, parent, child, brother, or sister).

    g Enrolled Actuary—enrolled as an actuary by the Joint Board for the Enrollment of Actuaries under 29 U.S.C. 1242 (the authority to practice before the Service is limited by section 10.3(d)(1) of Treasury Department Circular No. 230).

    h Unenrolled Return Preparer—an unenrolled return preparer under section 10.7(a)(7) of Treasury Department Circular No. 230.

☐ **IF THIS DECLARATION OF REPRESENTATIVE IS NOT SIGNED AND DATED, THE POWER OF ATTORNEY WILL BE RETURNED.**

Designation—Insert above letter **(a-h)**	Jurisdiction (state) or Enrollment Card No.	Signature	Date

STF FED4675F.2

Privacy Act and Paperwork Reduction Act Notice. —

We ask for the information on this form to carry out the Internal Revenue laws of the United States. Form 2848 is provided by the IRS for your convenience and its use is voluntary. If you choose to designate a representative to act on your behalf, under section 6109 you must disclose your social security number (SSN) or your employer identification number (EIN). The principal purpose of this disclosure is to secure proper identification of the taxpayer. We also need this information to gain access to your tax information in our files and properly respond to your request. If you do not disclose this information, the IRS may suspend processing the power of attorney and may not be able to fill your request until you provide the number.

The time needed to complete and file this form will vary depending on individual circumstances. The estimated average time is: Recordkeeping, 20 min.; Learning about the law or the form, 29 min.; Preparing the form, 29 min.; Copying, assembling, and sending the form to the IRS, 35 min.

If you have comments concerning the accuracy of these time estimates or suggestions for making this form simpler, we would be happy to hear from you. You can write to the Tax Forms Committee, Western Area Distribution Center, Rancho Cordova, CA 95743-0001. DO NOT send this form to this address. Instead, see Filing the Power of Attorney below.

General Instructions

Section references are to the Internal Revenue Code unless otherwise noted.

Purpose of form. — Use Form 2848 to grant authority to an individual to represent you before the IRS and to receive tax information. You may file this form ONLY if you want to name a person(s) to represent you and that person is a "person recognized to practice before the Service." Persons recognized to practice before the Service are listed in Part II, Declaration of Representative, items a—h. Any person not listed there is not authorized to practice before the IRS under the provisions of Treasury Department Circular No. 230 and cannot act as your representative. However, you can use Form 8821, Tax Information Authorization, to authorize any person or organization to receive and inspect confidential tax return information under the provisions of section 6103. For additional information about this or any other matter concerning practice before the IRS, get Pub. 216, Conference and Practice Requirements.

Fiduciaries. — A fiduciary (trustee, executor, administrator, receiver, or guardian) stands in the position of a taxpayer and acts as the taxpayer. Therefore, a fiduciary does not act as a representative and should not file a power of attorney. Form 56, Notice Concerning Fiduciary Relationship, should be filed to notify the IRS of the existence of a fiduciary relationship. If a fiduciary wishes to authorize an individual to represent or perform certain acts on behalf of the entity, a power of attorney must be filed and signed by the fiduciary acting in the position of the taxpayer.

Authority granted. — This power of attorney authorizes the individual(s) named to perform any

and all acts you can perform, such as signing consents extending the time to assess tax, recording the interview, or executing waivers agreeing to a tax adjustment. However, authorizing someone as your power of attorney does not relieve you of your tax obligations. Delegating authority or substituting another representative must be specifically stated on line 5. However, the authority granted to an unenrolled preparer may not exceed that allowed under Revenue Limited Practice Without Enrollment.

The power to sign tax returns can only be granted in limited situations. See Line 5-Acts authorized on page 4 for more information.

Filing the power of attorney. — File the original, photocopy, or facsimile transmission (fax) of the power of attorney with each IRS office with which you deal. If the power of attorney is filed for a matter currently pending before an office of the IRS, such as an examination, file the power of attorney with that office. Otherwise, file it with the service center where the related return was, or will be, filed. Refer to the instructions for the related tax return for the service center addresses.

Substitute Form 2848. — If you want to prepare and use a substute Form 2848, get Computer-Prepared, and Computer-Generated Tax Forms and Schedules. If your substitue Form 2848 is approved, the form approval number must be printed in the lower left margin of each substitute Form 2848 you file with the IRS.

Specific Instructions

Part I — Power of Attorney

Line 1 — Taxpayer information

Individuals. — Enter your name, SSN (and/or EIN, if applicable), and street address in the space provided. If a joint return is involved, and you and your spouse are designating the same representative(s), also enter your spouse's name and SSN, and your spouse's address if different from yours.

Corporations, partnerships, or associations. — Enter the name, EIN, and business address. If this form is being prepared for corporations filing a consolidated tax return (Form 1120), do not attach a list of subsidiaries on this form. Only the parent corporation information is required on line 1. Also, line 3 should only list Form 1120 in the Tax Form Number column. A subsidiary must file its own Form 2848 for returns that are required to be filed separately from the consolidated return, such as Form 720, Quarterly Federal Excise Tax Return, and Form 941, Employer's Quarterly Federal Tax Return.

Employee plan. — Enter the plan name, EIN of the plan sponsor, three-digit plan number, and business address of the sponsor.

Trust. — Enter the name, title, and address of the trustee, and the name and EIN of the trust.

Estate. — Enter the name, title, and address of the decedent's executor/personal representative, and the name and identification number of the estate. The identification number for an estate includes both the EIN, if the estate has one, and the decedent's SSN.

Line 2 — Representative(s). — Enter the name of your representative(s). Only individuals may be named as representatives. Use the identical name on all submissions. If you want to name more than three representatives, indicate so on this line and attach a list of additional representatives to the form.

Enter the nine-digit Centralized Authorization File (CAF) number for each representative. If a CAF number has not been assigned, enter "None," and the IRS will issue one directly to your representative. The CAF number is a unique nine-digit identification number (not the SSN, EIN, or enrollment card number) that the IRS assigns to representatives. The CAF number is not an indication of authority to practice. The representative should use the assigned CAF number on all future powers of attorney. CAF numbers will not be assigned for employee plans and exempt organizations application requests (EP/EO).

Check the appropriate box to indicate if either the address or telephone number is new since a CAF number was assigned. Enter your representative's fax telephone number, if available.

If the representative is a former employee of the Federal Government, he or she must be aware of the postemployment restrictions contained in 18 U.S.C., section 207 and in Treasury Department Circular No. 230, section 10.26. Criminal penalties are provided for violation of the statutory restrictions, and the Director of Practice is authorized to take disciplinary action against the practitioner.

Line 3 — Tax matters. — You must enter the type of tax, the tax form number, and the year(s) or period(s) in order for the power of attorney to be valid. For example, you may list "income tax, Form 1040" for calendar year "1995" and "Excise tax, Form 720" for the "1st, 2nd, 3rd, and 4th quarters of 1995." A general reference to "All years," "All periods," or "All taxes" is not acceptable. Any power of attorney with a general reference will be returned.

You may list any tax years or periods that have already ended as of the date you sign the power of attorney. However, you may include on a power of attorney only future tax periods that end no later than 3 years after the date the power of attorney is received by the IRS. You must enter the type of tax, the tax form number, and the future year(s) or period(s).

If the matter relates to estate tax, enter the date of the taxpayer's death instead of the year or period. If the type of tax, tax form number, or years or periods does not apply to the matter (i.e., representation for a penalty or filing a ruling request or determination), specifically describe on this line the matter to which the power of attorney pertains and enter "Not Applicable" in the appropriate column(s).

Line 4 — Specific uses not recorded on CAF. — Generally, the IRS records all powers of attorney on the CAF system. However, a power of attorney will not be recorded on the CAF if it does not relate to a specific tax period or it is for a specific issue. Examples of specific issues include but are not limited to the following: (a) civil penalty issues, (b) trust fund recovery penalty, (c) request for a private letter ruling, (d) application for an EIN, (e) claims filed on Form 843, Claim for

Exhibit A-9 *(continued)*

Refund and Request for Abatement, (f) corporation dissolutions, (g) a request to change accounting methods, and (h) a request to change accounting periods. Check the specific-use box on line 4 if the power of attorney is for a use that will not be listed on representative should bring a copy of the power of attorney to each meeting with the IRS. A specific-use power of attorney will not automatically revoke any prior powers of attorney.

Line 5 — Acts authorized. — If you want to modify the acts that your named representative(s) can perform, describe any specific additions or deletions in the space provided. The authority to substitute another representative or delegate authority must be specifically stated on line 5.

If you want to authorize your representative to sign an income tax return, this authorization must be specifically listed and the requirements of Regulations section 1.6012-1(a)(5) must be satisfied. In general, this regulation only permits a representative to sign your return if you are unable to make the return by reason of: (a) disease or injury, (b) continuous absence from the United States (including Puerto Rico), for a period of at least 60 days prior to the date required by law for filing the return, or (c) specific permission is requested of and granted by the district director for other good cause.

If you want to authorize a person other than a representative (an agent) to sign an income tax return, you must:

1. Complete the information on lines 1-3,
2. Check the box on line 4, and
3. Write the following on line 5:

"This power of attorney is being filed pursuant to Regulation 1.6012(a)(5), reason (a), (b), or (c), which requires a power of attorney to be attached to a return if a return is signed by an agent. No other acts on behalf of the taxpayer are authorized."

Reasons (a), (b), and (c) are defined above. The agent does not complete Part II, Declaration of Representative.

If any representative you name is an unenrolled return preparer, the acts that person can perform on your behalf are limited by Revenue Procedure 81-38 (Pub. 470). In general, an unenrolled return preparer is permitted to appear as your representative only before revenue agents and examining officers of the Examination Division and the EP/EO Division and is not permitted to represent you before other offices (i.e., Collection Division or Appeals Division) of the IRS. Also, an unenrolled return preparer is not permitted to extend the statutory period, execute waivers, delegate authority, or substitute another representative.

Tax matters partner/person. — The tax matters partner/person (TMP) (as defined in sections 6231(a)(7) and 6244) is authorized to perform various acts on behalf of the partnership or S corporation. The following are examples of acts performed by the TMP that cannot be delegated to the representative: (a) binding nonnotice partners to a settlement agreement under section 6224 and, under certain circumstances, binding all partners or shareholders to a settlement agreement under Tax Court Rule 248; (b) filing a petition for readjustment of partnership or subchapter S items in the Tax

Court, District Court, or Claims Court, under sections 6226 and 6244, based on the issuance of a notice of final partnership administrative adjustment or notice of final S corporation administrative adjustment by the IRS; (c) filing a request for administrative adjustment on behalf of the partnership or S corporation under sections 6227 and 6244; (d) filing a petition for adjustment of partnership items with respect to an administrative request in the Tax Court, District Court, or Claims Court, under sections 6228 and 6244; and (e) extending the statute of limitations on assessment of any tax attributable to partnership or subchapter S items (and affected items) under sections 6229 and 6244.

Line 6 — Receipt of refund checks. — If you want to authorize your representative to receive, but not endorse, refund checks on your behalf, you must initial and enter the name of that person in the space provided. Section 10.31 of Treasury Department Circular No. 230 prohibits an attorney, CPA, or enrolled agent, any of whom is an income tax return preparer, from endorsing or otherwise negotiating a tax refund check.

Line 7 — Notices and communications. — Original notices and other written communications will be sent to you and a copy to the first representative listed, unless you check one or more of the boxes. If you check:

1. Only box (a). The original will be sent to the first representative and a copy to you.

2. Only box (b). The original will be sent to you and copies to the first two listed representatives.

3. Both boxes (a) and (b). The original will be sent to the first representative and copies to you and the second representative listed.

4. Only box (c). The original will be sent to you. No copies will be sent to any representatives.

Line 8 — Retention/revocation of prior power(s) of attorney. — If there is any existing power(s) of attorney you do not want to revoke, check the box on this line and attach a copy of the power(s) of attorney.

If you want to revoke an existing power of attorney and do not want to name a new representative, send a copy of the previously executed power of attorney to each IRS office where the power of attorney was filed. The copy of the power of attorney must have a current signature of the taxpayer under the signature already on line 9. Write "REVOKE" across the top of the form. If you do not have a copy of the power of attorney you want to revoke, send a statement to each IRS office where you filed the power of attorney. The statement of revocation must indicate that the authority of the power of attorney is revoked and must be signed by the taxpayer. Also, the name and address of each recognized representative whose authority is revoked must be listed.

A representative can withdraw from representation by filing a statement with each office of the IRS where the power of attorney was filed. The statement must be signed by the representative and identify the name and address of the taxpayer(s) and tax matter(s) from which the representative is withdrawing. Include your CAF No. on the statement if one has been assigned to you.

The filing of a Form 2848 will not revoke any Form 8821 that is in effect.

Line 9 — Signature of taxpayer(s).

Individuals. — You must sign and date the power of attorney. If a joint return has been filed and both husband and wife will be represented by the same individual(s), both must sign the power of attorney unless one spouse authorizes the other, in writing, to sign for both. In that case, attach a copy of the authorization. However, if a joint return has been filed and husband and wife will be represented by different individuals, each taxpayer must execute his or her own power of attorney on a separate Form 2848.

Corporations or associations. — An officer having authority to bind the taxpayer must sign. However, the tax matters person may sign on behalf of an S corporation.

Partnerships. — All partners must sign unless one partner is authorized to act in the name of the partnership. A partner is authorized to act in the name of the partnership if, under state law, the partner has authority to bind the partnership. A copy of such authorization must be attached. For purposes of executing Form 2848, the tax matters partner is authorized to act in the name of the partnership. For dissolved partnerships, see Regulations section 601.503(c)(6).

Other. — If the taxpayer is a dissolved corporation, deceased, insolvent, or a person for whom or by whom a fiduciary (a trustee, guarantor, receiver, executor, or administrator) has been appointed, see Regulations section 601.503(d).

Part II — Declaration of Representative

The representative(s) you name must sign and date this declaration and enter the designation (i.e., items a — h) under which he or she is authorized to practice before the IRS. In addition, the representative(s) must list the following in the "Jurisdiction" column:

a   Attorney — Enter the two-letter abbreviation for the state (e.g., "NY" for New York) in which admitted to practice.

b   Certified Public Accountant — Enter the two-letter abbreviation for the state (e.g., "CA" for California) in which licensed to practice.

c   Enrolled Agent — Enter the enrollment card number issued by the Director of Practice.

d   Officer — Enter the title of the officer (i.e., President, Vice President, or Secretary).

e   Full-Time Employee — Enter title or position (e.g., Comptroller or Accountant).

f   Family Member — Enter the relationship to taxpayer (i.e., spouse, parent, child, brother, or sister).

g   Enrolled Actuary — Enter the enrollment card number issued by the Joint Board for the Enrollment of Actuaries.

h   Unenrolled Return Preparer — Enter the two-letter abbreviation for the state (e.g., "KY" for Kentucky) in which the return was prepared.

Note: *If the representation is outside the United States, conditions a — h do not apply.*

STF FED4675I.2

Exhibit A-9   *(continued)*

Form **870** (Rev. March 1992)	Department of the Treasury — Internal Revenue Service **Waiver of Restrictions on Assessment and Collection of Deficiency in Tax and Acceptance of Overassessment**	Date received by Internal Revenue Service

Names and address of taxpayers *(Number, street, city or town, State, ZIP code)*	Social security or employer identification number

Increase (Decrease) in Tax and Penalties

Tax year ended	Tax	Penalties			
	$	$	$	$	$
	$	$	$	$	$
	$	$	$	$	$
	$	$	$	$	$
	$	$	$	$	$
	$	$	$	$	$
	$	$	$	$	$

(For instructions, see back of form)

SAMPLE

Consent to Assessment and Collection

I consent to the immediate assessment and collection of any deficiencies *(increase in tax and penalties)* and accept any overassessment *(decrease in tax and penalties)* shown above, plus any interest provided by law. I understand that by signing this waiver, I will not be able to contest these years in the United States Tax Court, unless additional deficiencies are determined for these years.

YOUR SIGNATURE HERE		Date
SPOUSE'S SIGNATURE		Date
TAXPAYER'S REPRESENTATIVE HERE		Date
CORPORATE NAME		

CORPORATE OFFICER(S) SIGN HERE		Title	Date
		Title	Date

Form **870** (Rev. 3-92)

Exhibit A-10   Form 870, Waiver of Restrictions on Assessment
and Collection of Deficiency in Tax and Acceptance of Overassessment

Form **656**
(Rev. Sept. 1993)

Department of the Treasury—Internal Revenue Service

Offer in Compromise

☐ **See Instructions**
Page 5

(1) Name and Address of Taxpayers

For Official Use Only

Offer is *(Check applicable box)*
☐ Cash *(Paid in full)*
☐ Deferred payment

Serial Number

(Cashier's stamp)

(2) Social Security Number   **(3) Employer Identification Number**

Alpha CSED Ind. _____

To: **Commissioner of Internal Revenue Service**

Amount Paid
$

(4) **I/we** (includes all types of taxpayers) **submit this offer to compromise the tax liabilities plus any interest, penalties, additions to tax, and additional amounts required by law (tax liability)** for the tax type and period checked below: (Please mark "X" for the correct description and fill-in the correct tax period(s), adding additional periods if needed.)

☐   Income tax for the year(s) 19 ___ , 19___ , 19___ , and 19 ___

☐   Trust fund recovery penalty (formerly called the 100-percent penalty) as responsible person of _____
_____ (enter business name) for failure to pay withholding
and Federal Insurance Contributions Act taxes (Social Security taxes) for the period(s) ended _____ ,
_____ , _____ , _____ (for example - 06/30/92)

☐   Withholding and Federal Insurance Contributions Act taxes (Social Security taxes) for the period(s) ended_____ ,
_____ , _____ , _____ (for example - 06/30/92)

☐   Federal Unemployment Tax Act taxes for the year 19____ , 19____ , 19____ , and 19____

☐   Other (Be specific.)_____

(5)   **I/we offer to pay $** _____ .

If you aren't making full payment with your offer, describe below when you will make full payment (for example - within ten (10) days from the date the offer is accepted). See the instructions for Item 5.

SAMPLE

_____

_____

_____

As required by section 6621 of the Internal Revenue Code, the Internal Revenue Service (IRS) will add interest to the offered amount from the date IRS accepts the offer until the date you completely pay the amount offered. IRS compounds interest daily, as required by section 6622 of the Internal Revenue Code.

(6)   **I/we submit this offer for the reason(s) checked below:**

☐   Doubt as to collectibility ("I can't pay.") You must include a completed financial statement (Form 433-A and/or Form 433-B).

☐   Doubt as to liability ("I don't believe I owe this tax.") You must include a detailed explanation of the reason(s) why you believe you don't owe the tax.

IMPORTANT: SEE REVERSE FOR TERMS AND CONDITIONS

I accept waiver of the statutory period of limitations for the Internal Revenue Service.	Under penalties of perjury, I declare that I have examined this offer, including accompanying schedules and statements, and to the best of my knowledge and belief, it is true, correct and complete.	
Signature of authorized Internal Revenue Service Official	(8a) Signature of Taxpayer-proponent	Date
Title Date	(8b) Signature of Taxpayer-proponent	Date

Dispose of prior issues.	**Part 1 IRS Copy**	Form **656** (Rev. 9-93)
ISA		STF FED1106F.1

Exhibit A-11   Form 656, Offer in Compromise

(7) By submitting this offer, **I/we understand and agree to the following terms and conditions:**

   (a) I/we voluntarily submit all payments made on this offer.

   (b) IRS will apply payments made under the terms of this offer in the best interests of the government.

   (c) If IRS rejects the offer or I/we withdraw the offer, IRS will return any amount paid with the offer. If I/we agree in writing, IRS will apply the amount paid with the offer to the amount owed. If I/we agree to apply the payment, the date the offer is rejected or withdrawn will be considered the date of payment. I/we understand that IRS will not pay interest on any amount I/we submit with the offer.

   (d) I/we will comply with all provisions of the Internal Revenue Code relating to filing my/our returns and paying my/our required taxes for five (5) years from the date IRS accepts the offer.

   (e) I/we waive and agree to the suspension of any statutory periods of limitation (time limits provided for by law) for IRS assessment and collection of the tax liability for the tax periods checked in item (4).

   (f) IRS will keep all payments and credits made, received, or applied to the amount being compromised before this offer was submitted. IRS will also keep any payments made under the terms of an installment agreement while this offer is pending.

   (g) IRS will keep any refund, including interest, due to me/us because of overpayment of any tax or other liability, for tax periods extending through the calendar year that IRS accepts the offer. This condition doesn't apply if the offer is based only on doubt as to liability.

   (h) I/we will return to IRS any refund identified in (g) received after submitting this offer. This condition doesn't apply if the offer is based only on doubt as to liability.

   (i) The total amount IRS can collect under this offer can't be more than the full amount of the tax liability.

   (j) I//we understand that I/we remain responsible for the full amount of the tax liability unless and until IRS accepts the offer in writing and I/we have met all the terms and conditions of the offer. IRS won't remove the original amount of the tax liability from its records until I/we have met all the terms and conditions of the offer.

   (k) I/we understand that the tax I/we offer to compromise is and will remain a tax liability until I/we meet all the terms and conditions of this offer. If I/we file bankruptcy before the terms and conditions of this offer are completed, any claim the IRS files in the bankruptcy proceeding will be a tax claim.

   (l) Once IRS accepts the offer in writing, I/we have no right to contest, in court or otherwise, the amount of the tax liability.

   (m) The offer is pending starting with the date an authorized IRS official signs this form and accepts my/our waiver of the statutory periods of limitation. The offer remains pending until an authorized IRS official accepts, rejects, or withdraws the offer in writing. If I/we appeal the IRS decision on the offer, IRS will continue to treat the offer as pending until the Appeals Office accepts or rejects the offer in writing. If I/we don't file a protest within 30 days of the date IRS notifies me/us of the right to protest the decision, I/we waive the right to a hearing before the Appeals Office about this offer in compromise.

   (n) The waiver and suspension of any statutory periods of limitation for assessment and collection of the amount of the tax liability described in item (4), continues to apply:

      (i) while the offer is pending (see (m) above),

      (ii) during the time I/we haven't paid all of the amount offered,

      (iii) during the time I/we haven't completed all terms and conditions of the offer, and

      (iv) for one additional year beyond the time periods identified in (i), (ii), and (iii) above.

   (o) If I/we fail to meet any of the terms and conditions of the offer, the offer is in default, and IRS may:

      (i) immediately file suit to collect the entire unpaid balance of the offer;

      (ii) immediately file suit to collect an amount equal to the original amount of the tax liability as liquidated damages, minus any payments already received under the terms of this offer;

      (iii) disregard the amount of the offer and apply all amounts already paid under the offer against the original amount of tax liability;

      (iv) file suit or levy to collect the original amount of the tax liability, without further notice of any kind.

      IRS will continue to add interest, as required by section 6621 of the Internal Revenue Code, on the amount IRS determines is due after default. IRS will add interest from the date the offer is defaulted until I/we completely satisfy the amount owed. IRS compounds interest daily, as required by section 6622 of the Internal Revenue Code.

Part 2 IRS Copy   Form **656** (Rev. 9-93)

Exhibit A-11   *(continued)*

a Control number	22222	Void ☐	For Official Use Only ▶ OMB No. 1545-0008		

b Employer's identification number		1 Wages, tips, other compensation	2 Federal income tax withheld
c Employer's name, address, and ZIP code		3 Social security wages	4 Social security tax withheld
		5 Medicare wages and tips	6 Medicare tax withheld
		7 Social security tips	8 Allocated tips
d Employee's social security number		9 Advance EIC payment	10 Dependent care benefits
e Employee's name (first, middle initial, last)		11 Nonqualified plans	12 Benefits included in box 1
		13 See Instrs. for box 13	14 Other

	15 Statutory employee ☐	Deceased ☐	Pension plan ☐	Legal rep. ☐	Hshld. emp. ☐	Subtotal ☐	Deferred compensation ☐
f Employee's address and ZIP code							

16 State Employer's state I.D. No.	17 State wages, tips, etc.	18 State income tax	19 Locality name	20 Local wages, tips, etc.	21 Local income tax

Cat. No. 10134D

Department of the Treasury—Internal Revenue Service

Form **W-2** **Wage and Tax Statement** **1996**

For Paperwork Reduction Act Notice, see separate instructions.

Copy A For Social Security Administration

Do NOT Cut or Separate Forms on This Page

Exhibit A-12   Form W-2, Wage and Tax Statement

Form **941**

(Rev. January 1996)

Department of the Treasury
Internal Revenue Service

4141

Employer's Quarterly Federal Tax Return

▶ See separate instructions for information on completing this return.

Please type or print.

Enter state code for state in which deposits made .. ▶ (see page 3 of instructions).

Name (as distinguished from trade name)	Date quarter ended
Trade name, if any	Employer identification number
Address (number and street)	City, state, and ZIP code

OMB No. 1545-0029

T

FF

FD

FP

I

T

If address is different from prior return, check here ▶ □

IRS Use

```
1 1 1 1 1 1 1 1 1    2    3 3 3 3 3 3    4 4 4
5 5 5   6   7   8 8 8 8 8 8   9 9 9   10 10 10 10 10 10 10 10 10
```

If you do not have to file returns in the future, check here ▶ □ and enter date final wages paid ▶

If you are a seasonal employer, see **Seasonal employers** on page 1 of the instructions and check here ▶ □

1	Number of employees (except household) employed in the pay period that includes March 12th ▶	1	
2	Total wages and tips, plus other compensation	2	
3	Total income tax withheld from wages, tips, and sick pay	3	
4	Adjustment of withheld income tax for preceding quarters of calendar year	4	
5	Adjusted total of income tax withheld (line 3 as adjusted by line 4—see instructions)	5	

6a	Taxable social security wages	$	× 12.4% (.124) =	6a	
b	Taxable social security tips	$	× 12.4% (.124) =	6b	
7	Taxable Medicare wages and tips	$	× 2.9% (.029) =	7	

8	Total social security and Medicare taxes (add lines 6a, 6b, and 7). Check here if wages are not subject to social security and/or Medicare tax . . . . ▶ □	8	
9	Adjustment of social security and Medicare taxes (see instructions for required explanation) Sick Pay $_____ ± Fractions of Cents $_____ ± Other $_____ =	9	
10	Adjusted total of social security and Medicare taxes (line 8 as adjusted by line 9—see instructions)	10	
11	**Total taxes** (add lines 5 and 10).	11	
12	Advance earned income credit (EIC) payments made to employees, if any	12	
13	Net taxes (subtract line 12 from line 11). **This should equal line 17, column (d) below** (or line D of Schedule B (Form 941))	13	
14	Total deposits for quarter, including overpayment applied from a prior quarter	14	
15	**Balance due** (subtract line 14 from line 13). See instructions	15	
16	**Overpayment,** if line 14 is more than line 13, enter excess here ▶ $_____ and check if to be: □ Applied to next return **OR** □ Refunded.		

• **All filers:** If line 13 is less than $500, you need not complete line 17 or Schedule B.

• **Semiweekly schedule depositors:** Complete Schedule B and check here . . . . ▶ □

• **Monthly schedule depositors:** Complete line 17, columns (a) through (d) and check here . . . . ▶ □

17	**Monthly Summary of Federal Tax Liability.**		
(a) First month liability	**(b)** Second month liability	**(c)** Third month liability	**(d)** Total liability for quarter

Sign Here

Under penalties of perjury, I declare that I have examined this return, including accompanying schedules and statements, and to the best of my knowledge and belief, it is true, correct, and complete.

Signature ▶   Print Your Name and Title ▶   Date ▶

For Paperwork Reduction Act Notice, see page 1 of separate instructions.   ISA   Form **941** (Rev. 1-96)

STF FED1727F

Exhibit A-13   Form 941, Employer's Quarterly Federal Tax Return

<table>
<tr>
<td>

Form 4852
(Revised August 1993)

Dept. of the Treasury
Internal Revenue Service
</td>
<td>

SUBSTITUTE FOR FORM W-2, WAGE AND TAX STATEMENT OR FORM
1099R, DISTRIBUTIONS FROM PENSIONS, ANNUITIES, RETIREMENT OR
PROFIT-SHARING PLANS, IRA'S, INSURANCE CONTRACTS. ETC.

◄ **Attach to Form 1040, 1040A, 1040EZ or 1040X►**
</td>
<td>

OMB No. 1545-0458
Expires 6-30-96
</td>
</tr>
</table>

1. NAME *(First, middle, last)* | **2. SOCIAL SECURITY NUMBER**

3. ADDRESS *(Number, street, city, State, ZIP code)*

4. PLEASE FILL IN THE YEAR AT THE END OF THE STATEMENT:

I have been unable to obtain (or have received an incorrect) Form W-2, Wage and Tax Statement, or Form 1099R, Distributions From Pensions, Annuities, Retirement or Profit-Sharing Plans, IRA's, Insurance Contracts, etc., from my employer or payer named below. I have notified the Internal Revenue Service of this fact. The amounts shown below are my best estimates of all wages or payments paid to me and the Federal taxes withheld by this employer or payer during 19_____ .

5. EMPLOYER'S OR PAYER'S NAME, ADDRESS, AND ZIP CODE | **6. EMPLOYER'S OR PAYER'S IDENTIFI-CATION NUMBER** *(If known)*

7. WAGES*	_____	FEDERAL INCOME TAX WITHHELD	_____
SOCIAL SECURITY WAGES	_____	SOCIAL SECURITY TAX WITHHELD	_____
MEDICARE WAGES	_____	MEDICARE TAX WITHHELD	_____
ADVANCE EIC PAYMENTS	_____	SOCIAL SECURITY TIPS	_____

*NOTE: Include the total wages paid, (2) noncash payments, (3) tips/reported, and (4) all other compensation before deductions for taxes, insurance, etc.

8. How did you determine the amounts in item 7 above?

9. Explain your efforts to obtain Form W-2, 1099R, or W-2c, Statement of Corrected Income and Tax Amounts.

IMPORTANT NOTICE: If your employer has ceased operations or filed for bankruptcy, you may wish to send a copy of this form to the Social Security Administration office listed in your telephone directory to ensure proper social security credit.

Paperwork Reduction Notice

We ask for this information on this form to carry out the Internal Revenue laws of the United States. You are required to give us the information. We need it to ensure that you are are complying with these laws and to allow us to figure and collect the right amount of tax. The time needed to complete this form will vary depending on individual circumstances. The estimated average time is 18 minutes. If you have comments concerning the accuracy of this time estimate or suggestions for making this form more simple, we would be happy to hear from you. You can write to both the Internal Revenue Service, Attn: Reports Clearance Officer, T:FP, Washington, DC 20224 and the Office of Management and Budget, Paperwork Reduction Project (1545-0458), Washington, DC 20503. **DO NOT** send this form to either of these offices. Instead, attach it to your tax return.

Under penalties of perjury, I declare that I have examined this statement, and to the best of my knowledge and belief, it is true,correct, and complete.

10. Your signature | **11. Date**

Form **4852** (Rev. 8-93)

ISA | STF FED5318F

Exhibit A-14   Form 4852, Substitute for Form W-2 or Form 1099R

APPENDIX B

Exhibits and Tables

EXHIBIT B-1 BED AND BREAKFAST STATISTICS: REVENUE, EXPENSES, AND INCOME BY NUMBER OF ROOMS AND OVERALL

Revenues and Expenses	Number of Rooms										Overall 1994	
	1 to 4		5 to 8		9 to 12		13-20		21+			
Gross Revenues												
Room	97%	$40,427	96%	$90,216	94%	$166,928	96%	$283,077	89%	$679,096	94%	$121,785
Food	0%	$101	1%	$723	0%	$370	1%	$2,000	3%	$23,361	1%	$1,235
Beverage	0%	$0	0%	$0	0%	$267	0%	$0	0%	$3,561	0%	$163
Gift Shop	2%	$709	1%	$1,150	1%	$1,657	1%	$2,251	1%	$7,200	1%	$1,378
Specialty Food Service	0%	$0	0%	$169	0%	$350	0%	$489	0%	$0	0%	$208
Weddings	0%	$0	0%	$456	2%	$4,021	1%	$3,055	0%	$0	1%	$1,134
Meeting Room Charges	0%	$0	0%	$282	0%	$181	0%	$1,203	0%	$792	0%	$330
Service Charge	0%	$120	0%	$0	0%	$435	0%	$134	0%	$1,767	0%	$134
Rental of Equipment	0%	$0	0%	$0	0%	$0	0%	$352	2%	$16,929	0%	$564
Other	1%	$454	1%	$617	2%	$4,069	1%	$2,978	4%	$27,816	2%	$2,018
Total Revenue	100%	$41,811	100%	$93,613	100%	$178,278	100%	$295,539	100%	$760,522	100%	$128,949
Hourly Employees w/Taxes	5%	$2,084	10%	$8,945	12%	$21,596	17%	$50,537	26%	$199,678	13%	$17,284
Salaried Employees w/Taxes	2%	$639	1%	$1,361	3%	$5,914	5%	$14,522	3%	$21,967	3%	$3,548
Total Labor Expenses	7%	$2,723	11%	$10,306	15%	$27,510	22%	$65,059	29%	$221,645	16%	$20,832

Expenses

Expense	Amount	%	Amount	%	Amount	%	Amount	%	Amount	%	Amount	%
Auto Expenses	$975	2%	$1,784	2%	$2,483	1%	$2,774	1%	$4,343	1%	$1,832	1%
Bank Fees	$594	1%	$1,690	2%	$2,786	2%	$4,420	1%	$14,627	2%	$2,143	2%
Business Taxes & Fees	$2,151	5%	$4,111	4%	$6,828	4%	$8,239	3%	$16,878	2%	$4,701	4%
Commissions	$473	1%	$538	1%	$739	0%	$2,495	1%	$2,558	0%	$794	1%
Dues & Subscriptions	$948	2%	$1,095	1%	$1,753	1%	$1,864	1%	$3,927	1%	$1,298	1%
Food and Beverage	$4,555	11%	$6,384	7%	$9,634	5%	$19,287	7%	$40,756	5%	$8,491	7%
F & B Other Expenses	$859	2%	$871	1%	$1,772	1%	$2,446	1%	$3,554	0%	$1,218	1%
Gift Shop Cost of Goods Sold	$749	2%	$826	1%	$1,169	1%	$1,813	1%	$6,415	1%	$1,093	1%
Insurance	$1,240	3%	$2,381	3%	$4,162	2%	$6,996	2%	$14,954	2%	$3,097	2%
Legal & Accounting Fees	$438	1%	$909	1%	$1,580	1%	$2,487	1%	$4,272	1%	$1,118	1%
Maintenance, Repairs, and Fixtures	$3,915	9%	$5,617	6%	$10,683	6%	$12,761	4%	$21,596	3%	$6,968	5%
Marketing, Advertising & Promotion	$2,202	5%	$4,982	5%	$8,009	4%	$13,319	5%	$40,715	5%	$6,379	5%
Miscellaneous Expense	$1,487	4%	$1,745	2%	$4,007	2%	$2,355	1%	$24,120	3%	$2,613	2%
Office Supplies	$976	2%	$959	1%	$1,811	1%	$3,031	1%	$6,811	1%	$1,436	1%
Outside Services	$1,387	3%	$1,989	2%	$6,006	3%	$4,630	2%	$4,620	1%	$2,722	2%
Room and Housekeeping Supplies	$1,018	2%	$2,696	3%	$5,486	3%	$4,992	2%	$24,083	3%	$3,398	3%
Telephone Expense	$1,423	3%	$2,343	3%	$3,153	2%	$5,171	2%	$13,304	2%	$2,760	2%

EXHIBIT B-1 BED AND BREAKFAST STATISTICS: REVENUE, EXPENSES, AND INCOME BY NUMBER OF ROOMS AND OVERALL (continued)

Revenues and Expenses	Number of Rooms										Overall 1994	
	1 to 4		5 to 8		9 to 12		13-20		21+			
Towels & Linens	$947	2%	$1,466	2%	$2,000	1%	$2,040	1%	$3,366	0%	$1,510	1%
Training	$178	0%	$491	1%	$494	0%	$726	0%	$311	0%	$428	0%
Travel & Entertainment	$495	1%	$985	1%	$1,010	1%	$1,398	0%	$4,061	1%	$978	1%
Utilities Expense	$3,480	8%	$5,887	6%	$10,105	6%	$14,777	5%	$34,631	5%	$7,435	6%
Total Operating Expenses	$30,490	73%	$49,749	53%	$85,670	48%	$118,021	40%	$289,902	38%	$62,412	48%
Total Operating & Labor Expenses	$33,213	79%	$60,055	64%	$113,180	63%	$183,080	62%	$511,547	67%	$83,244	65%
Net Operating Income/Loss before Mortgage, Depreciation, Income Taxes, or Owner Draw	$8,598	21%	$33,558	36%	$65,098	37%	$112,459	38%	$248,975	33%	$45,705	35%

EXHIBIT B-2 BED AND BREAKFAST STATISTICS: REVENUE, EXPENSES, AND INCOME BY YEARS IN BUSINESS AND OVERALL

Revenues and Expenses	Years in Business						Overall					
	1 to 3		4 to 6		7+		1994		1992		1990*	
Gross Revenues												
Room	$66,616	94%	$91,827	97%	$158,386	94%	$121,785	94%	$133,863	84%	$201,807	77%
Food	$3,706	1%	$215	0%	$1,878	1%	$1,235	1%	$5,081	3%	$44,312	17%
Beverage	$200	0%	$0	0%	$282	0%	$163	0%	$1,973	1%	$7,604	3%
Gift Shop	$1,086	1%	$565	1%	$2,166	1%	$1,378	1%	$2,114	1%	$4,302	2%
Specialty Food Service	$301	0%	$255	0%	$244	0%	$208	0%	$908	0%	$947	0%
Weddings	$8,725	10%	$123	0%	$1,338	1%	$1,134	1%	$3,552	2%	na	na
Meeting Room Charges	$736	1%	$105	0%	$513	0%	$330	0%	$3,173	2%	na	na
Service Charge	$120	0%	$15	0%	$220	0%	$134	0%	$4,488	3%	na	na
Rental of Equipment	$0	0%	$0	0%	$922	1%	$564	0%	$259	0%	na	na
Other	$2,552	3%	$1,698	2%	$2,661	2%	$2,018	2%	$4,485	3%	$4,634	2%
Total Revenue	$84,042	100%	$94,803	100%	$168,610	100%	$128,949	100%	$159,896	100%	$263,606	100%
Hourly Employees w/Taxes	$6,051	7%	$8,436	9%	$26,700	16%	$17,284	13%	$33,382	21%	$35,206	13%
Salaried Employees w/Taxes	$2,334	3%	$1,928	2%	$4,850	3%	$3,548	3%	$22,430	14%	$30,094	11%
Total Labor Expenses	$8,385	10%	$10,364	11%	$31,550	19%	$20,832	16%	$55,812	35%	$65,300	25%

EXHIBIT B-2 BED AND BREAKFAST STATISTICS: REVENUE, EXPENSES, AND INCOME BY YEARS IN BUSINESS AND OVERALL (continued)

Revenues and Expenses	Years in Business						Overall					
	1 to 3		4 to 6		7+		1994		1992		1990*	
Expenses												
Auto Expenses	$1,243	1%	$1,546	2%	$2,207	1%	$1,832	1%	$2,277	1%	$2,134	1%
Bank Fees	$1,277	2%	$1,346	1%	$2,847	2%	$2,143	2%	$1,954	1%	$3,363	1%
Business Taxes & Fees	$3,563	4%	$3,236	3%	$5,777	3%	$4,701	4%	$5,520	3%	$8,439	3%
Commissions	$510	1%	$641	1%	$981	1%	$794	1%	$739	0%	$1,198	0%
Dues & Subscriptions	$1,009	1%	$1,030	1%	$1,530	1%	$1,298	1%	$1,333	1%	$1,454	1%
Food and Beverage	$6,066	7%	$6,223	7%	$10,459	6%	$8,491	7%	$8,209	5%	$28,679	11%
F & B Other Expenses	$1,157	1%	$1,222	1%	$1,235	1%	$1,218	1%	na		na	
Gift Shop Cost of Goods Sold	$398	0%	$586	1%	$1,611	1%	$1,093	1%	na		na	
Insurance	$2,162	3%	$1,932	2%	$3,972	2%	$3,097	2%	$3,820	2%	$10,617	4%
Legal & Accounting Fees	$9,314	11%	$918	1%	$1,398	1%	$1,118	1%	$1,770	1%	$3,019	1%
Maintenance, Repairs, and Fixtures	$5,175	6%	$4,640	5%	$8,713	5%	$6,968	5%	$7,905	5%	$11,823	4%
Marketing, Advertising & Promotion	$4,383	5%	$3,813	4%	$8,280	5%	$6,379	5%	$6,732	4%	$9,069	3%
Miscellaneous Expense	$1,451	2%	$937	1%	$3,799	2%	$2,613	2%	$3,238	2%	$6,746	3%
Office Supplies	$829	1%	$1,103	1%	$1,841	1%	$1,436	1%	$1,511	1%	$2,163	1%

	Amount	%	Amount	%	Amount	%	Amount	%	Amount	%	Amount	%
Outside Services	$1,873	2%	$1,658	2%	$3,519	2%	$2,722	2%	$3,633	2%	$4,781	2%
Room and Housekeeping Supplies	$1,741	2%	$3,006	3%	$4,304	3%	$3,398	3%	$4,371	3%	$6,073	2%
Telephone Expense	$2,048	2%	$2,148	2%	$3,314	2%	$2,760	2%	$2,514	2%	$3,676	1%
Towels & Linens	$1,272	2%	$1,416	1%	$1,648	1%	$1,510	1%	$1,719	1%	$2,170	1%
Training	$204	0%	$245	0%	$603	0%	$428	0%	$888	1%	na	
Travel & Entertainment	$485	1%	$652	1%	$1,331	1%	$978	1%	$1,289	1%	$1,886	1%
Utilities Expense	$5,362	6%	$6,017	6%	$8,912	5%	$7,435	6%	$7,468	5%	$11,359	4%
Total Operating Expenses	$51,522	61%	$44,315	47%	$78,281	46%	$62,412	48%	$66,890	42%	$118,649	45%
Total Operating & Labor Expenses	$59,907	71%	$54,679	58%	$109,831	65%	$83,244	65%	$122,702	77%	$183,949	70%
Net Operating Income/Loss before Mortgage, Depreciation, Income Taxes, or Owner Draw	$24,135	29%	$40,124	42%	$58,779	35%	$45,705	35%	$37,194	23%	$79,657	30%

*1990 Includes Country Inns

233

EXHIBIT B-3   BED AND BREAKFAST STATISTICS: INVESTMENT AND FINANCING BY YEARS IN BUSINESS AND OVERALL

	Years in Business			Overall (New and Existing)	Overall		
Investment and Financing	1 to 3	4-6	7+		1994	1992	1990
Year Inn Purchased	1991	1989	1986		1987	1984	1983
Total Acreage	7.08	9.52	9.48		7.58	7.39	8.59
Number of Rooms*	5.72	6.17	8.49		7.32	11	11
Square Footage of Inn	5175	5753	6528		6014	6437	6747
Owner's Living Space	871	942	917		952	854	906
% of Living Space to Total Space	17%	16%	14%		16%	13%	13%
Purchase Price	$284,154	$257,951	$376,207		$330,385	$308,979	$459,857
Preopening and Preparation Costs	$133,096	$100,062	$124,862		$120,515	$141,258	$133,169
Owner's Hours Invested	2400	1600	1600		1900	2000	1600
Outstanding Mortgage	$244,112	$184,287	$272,659		$245,997	$237,957	$350,822
Non-Mortgage Loans	$43,469	$42,471	$62,621		$52,928	$13,838	$19,537
Cost Per Room and Square Foot							
Cost per Room (Purchase Price)	$49,677	$41,807	$44,312		$45,135	$28,089	$41,805
Cost per Room (Purchase Price and Preparation)	$72,946	$58,025	$59,019		$61,598	$40,931	$53,911

	1	2	3	4	5	6
Cost per Square Foot (Purchase Price)	$55	$45	$58	$55	$48	$68
Cost per Square Foot (Purchase Price and Preparation)	$81	$62	$77	$75	$70	$88
Financing by Type Average						
Cash Equity	35%	39%	32%	34%	22%	21%
New Loan	27%	30%	29%	30%	51%	40%
Assumed Loan	18%	0%	13%	15%	3%	9%
Seller	20%	31%	26%	21%	24%	30%
	100%	100%	100%	100%	100%	100%
Number of Inns						
% Segregating Personal Property	27%	43%	50%	44%	35%	na
% Real Estate Separate from Business	19%	16%	23%	20%	na	na
% Business Separate from Land and Building	22%	22%	28%	25%	na	na

*Country Inns were included in 1990, heavily weighted to California

EXHIBIT B-4   3-, 5-, 7-, 10-, 15-, AND 20-YEAR PROPERTY

Half-Year Convention (Accelerated Method) Depreciation Rate for Recovery Period

Year	3-year	5-year	7-year	10-year	15-year	20-year
1	33.33%	20.00%	14.29%	10.00%	5.00%	3.750%
2	44.45	32.00	24.49	18.00	9.50	7.219
3	14.81	19.20	17.49	14.40	8.55	6.677
4	7.41	11.52	12.49	11.52	7.70	6.177
5		11.52	8.93	9.22	6.93	5.713
6		5.76	8.92	7.37	6.23	5.285
7			8.93	6.55	5.90	4.888
8			4.46	6.55	5.90	4.522
9				6.56	5.91	4.462
10				6.55	5.90	4.461
11				3.28	5.91	4.462
12					5.90	4.461
13					5.91	4.462
14					5.90	4.461
15					5.91	4.462
16					2.95	4.461
17						4.462
18						4.461
19						4.462
20						4.461
21						2.231

EXHIBIT B-5   STRAIGHT-LINE METHOD HALF-YEAR CONVENTION

Year	Recovery Period in Years					
	2.5	3	3.5	4	5	6
1	20.0%	16.67%	14.29%	12.5%	10.0%	8.33%
2		40.0	33.33	28.57	25.0	16.67
3		40.0	33.33	28.57	25.0	16.67
4		16.67	28.57	25.0	20.0	16.67
5				12.5	20.0	16.66
6					10.0	16.67
7						8.33

Year	6.5	7	7.5	8	8.5	9	9.5
1	7.69%	7.14%	6.67%	6.25%	5.88%	5.56%	5.26%
2	15.39	14.29	13.33	12.50	11.77	11.11	10.53
3	15.38	14.29	13.33	12.50	11.76	11.11	10.53
4	15.39	14.28	13.33	12.50	11.77	11.11	10.53
5	15.38	14.29	13.34	12.50	11.76	11.11	10.52
6	15.39	14.28	13.33	12.50	11.77	11.11	10.53
7	15.38	14.29	13.34	12.50	11.76	11.11	10.52
8		7.14	13.33	12.50	11.77	11.11	10.53
9				6.25	11.76	11.11	10.52
10						5.56	10.53

EXHIBIT B-6   NONRESIDENTIAL REAL PROPERTY

Year	Month Property Placed In Service					
	1	2	3	4	5	6
1	2.461%	2.247%	2.033%	1.819%	1.605%	1.391%
2–39	2.564	2.564	2.564	2.564	2.564	2.564
40	0.107	0.321	0.535	0.749	0.963	1.177

Year	Month Property Placed In Service					
	7	8	9	10	11	12
1	1.177%	0.963%	0.749%	0.535%	0.321%	0.107%
2–39	2.564	2.564	2.564	2.564	2.564	2.564
40	1.391	1.605	1.819	2.033	2.247	2.461

For more information on depreciation rules see Internal Revenue Service Publication 946.

EXHIBIT B-7   SAMPLE FOIA REQUEST

CERTIFIED MAIL RETURN RECEIPT REQUESTED
District Director
Internal Revenue Service
(Address)
Attention: Disclosure Officer
Re: Request for Information under the Freedom of Information Act
Dear Disclosure Officer:
Under the provisions of the Freedom of Information Act, 5 U.S.C. Section 552, I hereby request access to the following records relating to the audit of the Form 1040 filed by _____ (SSN: __ __ __) for the taxable year ending December 31, 199_.

1. The Examination Division Administrative File for the audit. The requested file includes any workpapers, notes, documents, memoranda, transmittal letters, documents

describing or recording interviews, telephone call slips, or other material prepared or accumulated relative to this examination.

2. Any files relative to this audit that may have been retained by specialist agents, either as specialty case files, desk files, or as group files, which are not otherwise included in the Administrative File. This request encompasses files retained by international examiners, economists, engineers, commodities specialists, computer audit specialists, and other specialists that may have been assigned to the case. The requested desk or group files include any workpapers, notes, documents, memoranda, transmittal letters, documents describing or recording interviews, telephone call slips, or other materials prepared or accumulated relative to this examination.

3. Any files relative to this audit that may have been prepared by independent consultants (including economists, engineers, and other independent specialists), which are not otherwise included in the Administrative File. The requested files include any workpapers, notes, documents, memoranda, transmittal letters, documents describing or recording interviews, telephone call slips, or other materials prepared or accumulated relative to this examination.

4. Any files relative to this audit that include information and documents obtained pursuant to summonses issued to third parties which are not otherwise included in the Administrative File.

I believe that the items referred to above might be located in the office of the group manager, [enter name].

In addition to the above records, please provide a list of all information relative to this audit that is maintained electronically. This list should identify the information by subject matter and format (i.e., tape, disk, etc.).

I would like the opportunity to inspect these records before any copies are made. The Internal Revenue Service is authorized to charge me for searching for the records, for reviewing the records, and for making deletions from them.

The Internal Revenue Service may incur up to $\_\_\_\_\_$ in charges without further authorization from me. If the total charges are estimated to exceed that amount, please provide me with an estimate of the charges and seek further authorization from me.

If it is determined that any requested record or portion thereof will not be disclosed, please provide me with the nonexempt records and with the nonexempt portions of the remaining records. If any requested record or portion thereof is not disclosed, please also provide me with an index and a detailed description of each record or portion thereof not disclosed and a statement describing the statutory basis for not disclosing each record or portion thereof.

My name, address, and telephone number are as follows:

_____ , _____ , ____ - _____.

Pursuant to Regs. Section 601.702(f)(3), I swear under penalties of perjury that I am a requester falling into the "Other" category of requesters, and as such, that I am not a commercial, media, educational, or noncommercial scientific institution requester.

As proof of my identity, and to establish my right to disclosure of the requested records, I have also attached a photocopy of [describe the identifier document being submitted that contains your signature; this could be a driver's license, for example].

If you have any questions concerning this request, please contact me by telephone at the number set forth above.

[Signed]

Attachments

EXHIBIT B-8 90-DAY LETTER

Internal Revenue Service
Department of Treasury
Office of International Operations

Date:
Social Security or Employer Identification Number:
Tax Year Ended and Deficiency:
Person to Contact:
Contact Telephone Number:

We have determined that you owe additional tax or other amounts, or both as shown for the tax year(s) identified above. This letter is a **NOTICE OF DEFICIENCY** as required by law. The enclosed statement shows how we figured the deficiency.

If you want to contest this determination in court before making any payment, you have 90 days from the above mailing date of this letter (150 days if addressed to you outside of the United States) to file a petition with the United States Tax Court for a redetermination of the deficiency. For a petition form, write to:

> United States Tax Court
> 400 Second Street, NW
> Washington, DC 20217

Send the completed petition form, a copy of this letter, and all relevant statements or schedules that accompanied this letter to the Tax Court at the same address. The petition must be timely filed with the court within 90 days from the above mailing date (150 days if addressed to you outside of the United States). However, if the petition is filed after the 90 day (or 150 day) period, it is considered timely filed if the postmark date falls within the prescribed period and the envelope containing the petition is properly addressed with the correct postage.

The time for filing a petition with the Court (90 or 150 days as the case may be) is set by law and cannot be extended or suspended. Thus, contacting the Service for more information or receiving other correspondence from the Service will not change the period for filing the petition with the Tax Court. The court cannot consider your case if the petition is filed late.

If this letter is addressed to both a husband and wife, and both want to petition the Tax Court, both must sign the petition or each must file a separate, signed petition. If more than one year is shown above, you only need to file one petition form showing the years you are contesting.

The Tax Court has a simplified procedure for small tax cases, when the dispute is for $10,000 or less for any one tax year. You can get information about this procedure, as well as a petition form you can use, by writing to:

> Clerk of the United States Tax Court
> 400 Second Street, NW
> Washington, DC 20217

Do this promptly if you intend to file a petition with the Tax Court.

You may represent yourself before the Tax Court, or you may be represented by anyone admitted to practice before the court.

If you decide not to file a petition with the Tax Court, please sign and return the enclosed waiver form. This will permit us to assess the deficiency quickly and can help limit the accumulation of interest. The enclosed envelope is for your convenience.

If you decide not to sign and return the statement and you do not file a petition with the Tax Court within the time limit, the law requires us to assess and bill you for the deficiency after 90 days from the above mailing date of this letter (150 days if this letter is addressed to you outside the United States).

If you have any questions, please write to the person whose name and address are shown on this letter. If you write, please attach this letter to help identify your account. Keep the copy for your records. Also, please include your telephone number and the most convenient time to call, so we can contact you if we need additional information.

If you prefer, you may call the IRS contact person at the telephone number shown above. If this number is outside your local calling area, there will be a long distance charge to you. You may call the IRS telephone number listed in your directory. An IRS employee there may be able to help you, but the contact person at the address shown on this letter is most familiar with your case. Thank you for your cooperation.

Sincerely,

Commissioner

By

Enclosures:
Copy of this letter
Waiver

Envelope:
 Director of International Operations
 1325 K St. NW, Washington, DC 20225

Letter 892(10)(Rev. 11-80)

APPENDIX C

Court Cases, IRC, Treasury Regulations, Revenue Rulings, and Revenue Procedures

IRC SEC. 61 INCOME

(a) General Definition
Except as otherwise provided in this subtitle, gross income means all income from whatever source derived, including (but not limited to) the following items:
   (1) Compensation for services, including fees, commissions, fringe benefits, and similar items;
   (2) Gross income derived from business;
   (3) Gains derived from dealings in property;
   (4) Interest;
   (5) Rents;
   (6) Royalties;
   (7) Dividends;
   (8) Alimony and separate maintenance payments;
   (9) Annuities;
   (10) Income from life insurance and endowment contracts;
   (11) Pensions;
   (12) Income from discharge of indebtedness;
   (13) Distributive share of partnership gross income;
   (14) Income in respect of a decedent; and
   (15) Income from an interest in an estate or trust.

SEC. 119. MEALS OR LODGING FURNISHED FOR THE CONVENIENCE OF THE EMPLOYER

(a) Meals And Lodging Furnished To Employee, His Spouse, And His Dependents Pursuant To Employment

There shall be excluded from gross income of an employee the value of any meals or lodging furnished to him, his spouse, or any of his dependents by or on behalf of his employer for the convenience of the employer, but only if—

> *(1) in the case of meals, the meals are furnished on the business premises of the employer, or*
>
> *(2) in the case of lodging, the employee is required to accept such lodging on the business premises of his employer as a condition of his employment.*

(b) Special Rules

For purposes of subsection (a)—

> *(1) Provisions Of Employment Contract Or State Statute Not To Be Determinative*
>
> *In determining whether meals or lodging are furnished for the convenience of the employer, the provisions of an employment contract or of a State statute fixing terms of employment shall not be determinative of whether the meals or lodging are intended as compensation.*
>
> *(2) Certain Factors Not Taken Into Account With Respect To Meals*
>
> *In determining whether meals are furnished for the convenience of the employer, the fact that a charge is made for such meals, and the fact that the employee may accept or decline such meals, shall not be taken into account.*
>
> *(3) Certain Fixed Charges For Meals*
>
> > *(A) In General*
> >
> > > *If—*
> > >
> > > > *(i) an employee is required to pay on a periodic basis a fixed charge for his meals, and*
> > > >
> > > > *(ii) such meals are furnished by the employer for the convenience of the employer, there shall be excluded from the employee's gross income an amount equal to such fixed charge.*
> >
> > *(B) Application Of Subparagraph(a)*
> >
> > *Subparagraph (A) shall apply—*
> >
> > > *(i) whether the employee pays the fixed charge out of his stated compensation or out of his own funds, and*
> > >
> > > *(ii) only if the employee is required to make the payment whether he accepts or declines the meals.*

(c) Employees Living In Certain Camps

> *(1) In General*
>
> *In the case of an individual who is furnished lodging in a camp located in a foreign country by or on behalf of his employer, such camp shall be considered to be part of the business premises of the employer.*
>
> *(2) Camp*
>
> *For purposes of this section, a camp constitutes lodging which is—*
>
> > *(A) provided by or on behalf of the employer for the convenience of the employer because the place at which such individual renders services is in a remote area where satisfactory housing is not available on the open market,*

       (B) located, as near as practicable, in the vicinity of the place at which such individual renders services, and

       (C) furnished in a common area (or enclave) which is not available to the public and which normally accommodates 10 or more employees.

(d) Lodging Furnished By Certain Educational Institutions To Employees

    (1) In General

    In the case of an employee of an educational institution, gross income shall not include the value of qualified campus lodging furnished to such employee during the taxable year.

    (2) Exception In Cases Of Inadequate Rent

    Paragraph (1) shall not apply to the extent of the excess of—

    (A) the lesser of—

       (i) 5 percent of the appraised value of the qualified campus lodging, or

       (ii) the average of the rentals paid by individuals (other than employees or students of the educational institution) during such calendar year for lodging provided by the educational institution which is comparable to the qualified campus lodging provided to the employee, over

    (B) the rent paid by the employee for the qualified campus lodging during such calendar year. The appraised value under subparagraph (A)(i) shall be determined as of the close of the calendar year in which the taxable year begins, or, in the case of a rental period not greater than 1 year, at any time during the calendar year in which such period begins.

    (3) Qualified Campus Lodging

    For purposes of this subsection, the term "qualified campus lodging" means lodging to which subsection (a) does not apply and which is—

    (A) located on, or in the proximity of, a campus of the educational institution, and

    (B) furnished to the employee, his spouse, and any of his dependents by or on behalf of such institution for use as a residence.

    (4) Educational Institution

    For purposes of this paragraph, the term "educational institution" means an institution described in section 170(b)(1)(A)(ii).

SEC. 121. ONE-TIME EXCLUSION OF GAIN FROM SALE OF PRINCIPAL RESIDENCE BY INDIVIDUAL WHO HAS ATTAINED AGE 55

121(a) General Rule

At the election of the taxpayer, gross income does not include gain from the sale or exchange of property if—

    121(a)(1) the taxpayer has attained the age of 55 before the date of such sale or exchange, and

121(a)(2) during the 5-year period ending on the date of the sale or exchange, such property has been owned and used by the taxpayer as his principal residence for periods aggregating 3 years or more.

121(b) Limitations

121(b)(1) Dollar Limitation

The amount of the gain excluded from gross income under subsection (a) shall not exceed $125,000 ($62,500 in the case of a separate return by a married individual).

121(b)(2) Application To Only 1 Sale Or Exchange

Subsection (a) shall not apply to any sale or exchange by the taxpayer if an election by the taxpayer or his spouse under subsection (a) with respect to any other sale or exchange is in effect.

121(b)(3) Additional Election If Prior Sale Was Made On Or Before July 26, 1978

In the case of any sale or exchange after July 26, 1978, this section shall be applied by not taking into account any election made with respect to a sale or exchange on or before such date.

121(c) Election

An election under subsection (a) may be made or revoked at any time before the expiration of the period for making a claim for credit or refund of the tax imposed by this chapter for the taxable year in which the sale or exchange occurred, and shall be made or evoked in such manner as the Secretary shall by regulations prescribe. In the case of a taxpayer who is married, an election under subsection (a) or a revocation thereof may be made only if his spouse joins in such election or revocation.

SEC. 179. ELECTION TO EXPENSE CERTAIN DEPRECIABLE BUSINESS ASSETS

(a) Treatment As Expenses

A taxpayer may elect to treat the cost of any section 179 property as an expense which is not chargeable to capital account. Any cost so treated shall be allowed as a deduction for the taxable year in which the section 179 property is placed in service.

179(b) Limitations

179(b)(1) Dollar Limitation

The aggregate cost which may be taken into account under subsection (a) for any taxable year shall not exceed $17,500.

179(b)(2) Reduction In Limitation

The limitation under paragraph (1) for any taxable year shall be reduced (but not below zero) by the amount by which the cost of section 179 property placed in service during such taxable year exceeds $200,000.

179(b)(3) Limitation Based On Income From Trade Or Business

179(b)(3)(A) In General

The amount allowed as a deduction under subsection (a) for any taxable year (determined after the application of paragraphs (1) and (2)) shall not exceed the aggregate amount of taxable income of the tax-payer for such taxable year which is derived from the active conduct by the taxpayer of any trade or business during such taxable year.

179(b)(3)(B) Carryover Of Disallowed Deduction

The amount allowable as a deduction under subsection (a) for any taxable year shall be increased by the lesser of—

179(b)(3)(B)(i) the aggregate amount disallowed under subpara-graph (A) for all prior taxable years (to the extent not previously allowed as a deduction by reason of this subparagraph), or

179(b)(3)(B)(ii) the excess (if any) of—

179(b)(3)(B)(ii)(I) the limitation of paragraphs (I) and (2) (or if lesser, the aggregate amount of taxable income referred to in subparagraph (A)), over

179(b)(3)(B)(ii)(II) the amount allowable as a deduction under subsection (a) for such taxable year without regard to this subparagraph.

179(b)(3)(C) Computation Of Taxable Income

For purposes of this paragraph, taxable income derived from the conduct of a trade or business shall be computed without regard to the deduction allowable under this section.

179(b)(4) Married Individuals Filing Separately

In the case of a husband and wife filing separate returns for the taxable year—

179(b)(4)(A) such individuals shall be treated as 1 taxpayer for purposes of paragraphs (I) and (2), and

179(b)(4)(B) unless such individuals elect otherwise, 50 percent of the cost which may be taken into account under subsection (a) for such tax-able year (before application of paragraph (3)) shall be allocated to each such individual.

179(c) Election

179(c)(1) In General

An election under this section for any taxable year shall—

179(c)(1)(A) specify the items of section 179 property to which the elec-tion applies and the portion of the cost of each of such items which is to be taken into account under subsection (a), and

179(c)(1)(B) be made on the taxpayer's return of the tax imposed by this chapter for the taxable year. Such election shall be made in such man-ner as the Secretary may by regulations prescribe.

179(c)(2) Election Irrevocable

Any election made under this section, and any specification contained in any such election, may not be revoked except with the consent of the Secretary.

179(d) Definitions And Special Rules

179(d)(1) Section 179 Property

For purposes of this section, the term "section 179 property" means any tangible property (to which section 168 applies) which is section 1245 (as defined in section 1245(a)(3)) property and which is acquired by purchase for use in the active conduct of in [sic] a trade or business.

179(d)(2) Purchase Defined

For purposes of paragraph (1), the term "purchase" means any acquisition of property, but only if—

179(d)(2)(A) the property is not acquired from a person whose relationship to the person acquiring it would result in the disallowance of losses under section 267 or 707(b) (but, in applying section 267(b) and (c) for purposes of this section, paragraph (4) of section 267(c) shall be treated as providing that the family of an individual shall include only his spouse, ancestors, and lineal descendants),

179(d)(2)(B) the property is not acquired by one component member of a controlled group from another component member of the same controlled group, and

179(d)(2)(C) the basis of the property in the hands of the person acquiring it is not determined—

179(d)(2)(C)(i) in whole or in part by reference to the adjusted basis of such property in the hands of the person from whom acquired, or

179(d)(2)(C)(ii) under section 1014(a) (relating to property acquired from a decedent).

179(d)(3) Cost

For purposes of this section, the cost of property does not include so much of the basis of such property as is determined by reference to the basis of other property held at any time by the person acquiring such property.

179(d)(4) Section Not To Apply To Estates And Trusts

This section shall not apply to estates and trusts.

SEC. 183. ACTIVITIES NOT ENGAGED IN FOR PROFIT

183(a) General Rule

In the case of an activity engaged in by an individual or an S corporation, if such activity is not engaged in for profit, no deduction attributable to such activity shall be allowed under this chapter except as provided in this IRC Section.

183(b) Deductions Allowable

In the case of an activity not engaged in for profit to which subsection (a) applies, there shall be allowed—

183(b)(1) the deductions which would be allowable under this chapter for the taxable year without regard to whether or not such activity is engaged in for profit, and

183(b)(2) a deduction equal to the amount of the deductions which would be allowable under this chapter for the taxable year only if such activity were engaged in for profit, but only to the extent that the gross income derived from such activity for the taxable year exceeds the deductions allowable by reason of paragraph (1).

183(c) Activity Not Engaged In For Profit Defined

For purposes of this section, the term "activity not engaged in for profit" means any activity other than one with respect to which deductions are allowable for the taxable year under IRC Section 162 or under paragraph (1) or (2) of IRC Section 212.

183(d) Presumption

If the gross income derived from an activity for 3 or more of the taxable years in the period of 5 consecutive taxable years which ends with the taxable year exceeds the deductions attributable to such activity (determined without regard to whether or not such activity is engaged in for profit), then, unless the Secretary establishes to the contrary, such activity shall be presumed for purposes of this chapter for such taxable year to be an activity engaged in for profit. In the case of an activity which consists in major part of the breeding, training, showing, or racing of horses, the preceding sentence shall be applied by substituting "2" for "3" and "7" for "5."

SEC. 195. START-UP EXPENDITURES

195(a) Capitalization Of Expenditures

Except as otherwise provided in this section, no deduction shall be allowed for start-up expenditures.

195(b) Election To Amortize

195(b)(1) In General

Start-up expenditures may, at the election of the taxpayer, be treated as deferred expenses. Such deferred expenses shall be allowed as a deduction prorated equally over such period of not less than 60 months as may be selected by the taxpayer (beginning with the month in which the active trade or business begins).

195(b)(2) Dispositions Before Close Of Amortization Period

In any case in which a trade or business is completely disposed of by the taxpayer before the end of the period to which paragraph (1) applies, any deferred expenses attributable to such trade or business which were not allowed as a deduction by reason of this section may be deducted to the extent allowable under section 165.

195(c) Definitions

For purposes of this section—

195(c)(1) Start-up Expenditures

The term "start-up expenditure" means any amount—

195(c)(1)(A) paid or incurred in connection with—

195(c)(1)(A)(i) investigating the creation or acquisition of an active trade or business, or

195(c)(1)(A)(ii) *creating an active trade or business, or*

195(c)(1)(A)(iii) *any activity engaged in for profit and for the production of income before the day on which the active trade or business begins, in anticipation of such activity becoming an active trade or business, and*

195(c)(1)(B) *which, if paid or incurred in connection with the operation of an existing active trade or business (in the same field as the trade or business referred to in subparagraph (A)), would be allowable as a deduction for the taxable year in which paid or incurred. The term "start–up expenditure" does not include any amount with respect to which a deduction is allowable under section 163(a), 164, or 174.*

195(c)(2) *Beginning Of Trade Or Business*

195(c)(2)(A) *In General*

Except as provided in subparagraph (B), the determination of when an active trade or business begins shall be made in accordance with such regulations as the Secretary may prescribe.

195(c)(2)(B) *Acquired Trade Or Business*

An acquired active trade or business shall be treated as beginning when the taxpayer acquires it.

195(d) *Election*

195(d)(1) *Time For Making Election*

An election under subsection (b) shall be made not later than the time prescribed by law for filing the return for the taxable year in which the trade or business begins (including extensions thereof).

195(d)(2) *Scope Of Election*

The period selected under subsection (b) shall be adhered to in computing taxable income for the taxable year for which the election is made and all subsequent taxable years.

(Added Pub. L. 96–605, title I, 102(a), Dec. 28, 1980, 94 Stat. 3522, and amended Pub. L. 98–369, div. A, title I, 94(a), July 18, 1984, 98 Stat. 614.)

SEC. 280A. DISALLOWANCE OF CERTAIN EXPENSES IN CONNECTION WITH BUSINESS USE OF HOME, RENTAL OF VACATION HOMES, ETC.

280A(a) *General Rule*

Except as otherwise provided in this section, in the case of a taxpayer who is an individual or an S corporation, no deduction otherwise allowable under this chapter shall be allowed with respect to the use of a dwelling unit which is used by the taxpayer during the taxable year as a residence.

§280A(b) *Exception For Interest, Taxes, Casualty Losses, Etc.*

Subsection (a) shall not apply to any deduction allowable to the taxpayer without regard to its connection with his trade or business (or with his income-producing activity).

§*280A(c) Exceptions For Certain Business Or Rental Use; Limitation On Deductions For Such Use*

280A(c)(1) Certain Business Use

Subsection (a) shall not apply to any item to the extent such item is allocable to a portion of the dwelling unit which is exclusively used on a regular basis—

280A(c)(1)(A) the principal place of business for any trade or business of the taxpayer.

280A(c)(1)(B) as a place of business which is used by patients, clients, or customers in meeting or dealing with the taxpayer in the normal course of his trade or business, or

280A(c)(1)(C) in the case of a separate structure which is not attached to the dwelling unit, in connection with the taxpayer's trade or business. In the case of an employee, the preceding sentence shall apply only if the exclusive use referred to in the preceding sentence is for the convenience of his employer.

280A(c)(2) Certain Storage Use

Subsection (a) shall not apply to any item to the extent such item is allocable to space within the dwelling unit which is used on a regular basis as a storage unit for the inventory of the taxpayer held for use in the taxpayer's trade or business of selling products at retail or wholesale, but only if the dwelling unit is the sole fixed location of such trade or business.

280A(c)(4)(C) Allocation Formula

If a portion of the taxpayer's dwelling unit used for the purposes described in subparagraph (A) is not used exclusively for those purposes, the amount of the expenses attributable to that portion shall not exceed an amount which bears the same ratio to the total amount of the items allocable to such portion as the number of hours the portion is used for such purposes bears to the number of hours the portion is available for use.

280A(c)(5) Limitation On Deductions

In the case of a use described in paragraph (1), (2), or (4), and in the case of a use described in paragraph (3) where the dwelling unit is used by the taxpayer during the taxable year as a residence, the deductions allowed under this chapter for the taxable year by reason of being attributed to such use shall not exceed the excess of—

280A(c)(5)(A) the gross income derived from such use for the taxable year, over

280A(c)(5)(B) the sum of—

280A(c)(5)(B)(i) the deductions allocable to such use which are allowable under this chapter for the taxable year whether or not such unit (or portion thereof) was so used, and

280A(c)(5)(B)(ii) the deductions allocable to the trade or business (or rental activity) in which such use occurs (but which are not allocable to such use) for such taxable year. Any amount not allowable as a deduction under this chapter by reason of the preceding sentence shall be taken into account as a deduction (allocable to such use) under this chapter for the succeeding taxable year. Any amount taken into account for any taxable year under the preceding sentence shall be subject to the limitation of the 1st sentence of this paragraph whether or not the dwelling unit is used as a residence during such taxable year.

280A(c)(6) Treatment Of Rental To Employer

Paragraphs (1) and (3) shall not apply to any item which is attributable to the rental of the dwelling unit (or any portion thereof) by the taxpayer to his employer during any period in which the taxpayer uses the dwelling unit (or portion) in performing services as an employee of the employer.

280A(d) Use As Residence

280A(d)(1) In General

For purposes of this section, a taxpayer uses a dwelling unit during the taxable year as a residence if he uses such unit (or portion thereof) for personal purposes for a number of days which exceeds the greater of—

280A(d)(1)(A) 14 days, or

280A(d)(1)(B) 10 percent of the number of days during such year for which such unit is rented as a fair rental. For purposes of subparagraph (B), a unit shall not be treated as rented at a fair rental for any day for which it is used for personal purposes.

280A(d)(2) Personal Use Of Unit

For purposes of this section, the taxpayer shall be deemed to have used a dwelling unit for personal purposes for a day if, for any part of such day, the unit is used—

280A(d)(2)(A) for personal purposes by the taxpayer or any other person who has an interest in such unit, or by any member of the family (as defined in section 267(c)(4)) of the taxpayer or such other person;

280A(d)(2)(B) by any individual who uses the unit under an arrangement which enables the taxpayer to use some other dwelling unit (whether or not a rental is charged for the use of such other unit); or

280A(d)(2)(C) by any individual (other than an employee with respect to whose use section 119 applies), unless for such day the dwelling unit is rented for a rental which, under the facts and circumstances, is fair rental. The Secretary shall prescribe regulations with respect to the circumstances under which use of the unit for repairs and annual maintenance will not constitute personal use under this paragraph, except that if the taxpayer is engaged in repair and maintenance on a substantially full time basis for any day, such authority shall not allow the Secretary to treat a dwelling unit as being used for personal use by the taxpayer on such day merely because other individuals who are on the premises on such day are not so engaged.

280A(d)(3) Rental To Family Member, Etc., For Use As Principal Residence

280A(d)(3)(A) In General

A taxpayer shall not be treated as using a dwelling unit for personal purposes by reason of a rental arrangement for any period if for such period such dwelling unit is rented, at a fair rental, to any person for use as such person's principal residence.

280A(d)(3)(B) Special Rules For Rental To Person Having Interest In Unit

280A(d)(3)(B)(i) Rental Must Be Pursuant To Shared Equity Financing Agreement

Subparagraph (A) shall apply to a rental to a person who has an interest in the dwelling unit only if such rental is pursuant to a shared equity financing agreement.

280A(d)(3)(B)(ii) Determination Of Fair Rental

In the case of a rental pursuant to a shared equity financing agreement, fair rental shall be determined as of the time the agreement is entered into and by taking into account the occupant's qualified ownership interest.

280A(d)(3)(C) Shared Equity Financing Agreement

For purposes of this paragraph, the term "shared equity financing agreement" means an agreement under which—

280A(d)(3)(C)(i) 2 or more persons acquire qualified ownership interests in a dwelling unit, and

280A(d)(3)(C)(ii) the person (or persons) holding 1 or more of such interests—

280A(d)(3)(C)(ii)(I) is entitled to occupy the dwelling unit for use as a principal residence, and

280A(d)(3)(C)(ii)(II) is required to pay rent to 1 or more other persons holding qualified ownership interests in the dwelling unit.

280A(d)(3)(D) Qualified Ownership Interest

For purposes of this paragraph, the term "qualified ownership interest" means an undivided interest for more than 50 years in the entire dwelling unit and appurtenant land being acquired in the transaction to which the shared equity financing agreement relates.

280A(d)(4) Rental Of Principal Residence

280A(d)(4)(A) In General

For purposes of applying subsection (c)(5) to deductions allocable to a qualified rental period, a taxpayer shall not be considered to have used a dwelling unit for personal purposes for any day during the taxable year which occurs before or after a qualified rental period described in subparagraph (B)(i), or before a qualified rental period described in subparagraph (B)(ii), if with respect to such day such unit constitutes the principal residence (within the meaning of section 1034) of the taxpayer.

280A(d)(4)(B) Qualified Rental Period

For purposes of subparagraph (A), the term "qualified rental period" means a consecutive period of—

280A(d)(4)(B)(i) 12 or more months which begins or ends in such taxable year, or

280A(d)(4)(B)(ii) less than 12 months which begins in such taxable year and at the end of which such dwelling unit is sold or exchanged, and for which such unit is rented, or is held for rental, at a fair rental.

280A(e) Expenses Attributable To Rental

280A(e)(1) In General

In any case where a taxpayer who is an individual or an S corporation uses a dwelling unit for personal purposes on any day during the taxable year (whether or not he is treated under this section as using such unit as a residence), the amount deductible under this chapter with respect to expenses attributable to the rental of the unit (or portion thereof) for the taxable year shall not exceed an amount which bears the same relationship to such expenses as the number of days during each year that the unit (or portion thereof) is rented at a fair rental bears to the total number of days during such year that the unit (or portion thereof) is used.

280A(e)(2) Exception For Deductions Otherwise Allowable

This subsection shall not apply with respect to deductions which would be allowable under this chapter for the taxable year whether or not such unit (or portion thereof) was rented.

280A(f) Definitions And Special Rules

280A(f)(1) Dwelling Unit Defined

For purposes of this section—

280A(f)(1)(A) In General

The term "dwelling unit" includes a house, apartment, condominium, mobile home, boat, or similar property, and all structures or other property appurtenant to such dwelling unit.

280A(f)(1)(B) Exception

The term "dwelling unit" does not include that portion of a unit which is used exclusively as a hotel, motel, inn, or similar establishment.

280A(f)(2) Personal Use By Shareholders Of S Corporation

In the case of an S corporation, subparagraphs (A) and (B) of subsection (d)(2) shall be applied by substituting "any shareholder of the S corporation" for "the taxpayer" each place it appears.

280A(f)(3) Coordination With Section 183

If subsection (a) applies with respect to any dwelling unit (or portion thereof) for the taxable year—

280A(f)(3)(A) section 183 (relating to activities not engaged in for profit) shall not apply to such unit (or portion thereof) for such year, but

280A(f)(3)(B) such year shall be taken into account as a taxable year for purposes of applying subsection (d) of section 183 (relating to 5–year presumption).

280A(f)(4) Coordination With Section 162(a)(2)

Nothing in this section shall be construed to disallow any deduction allowable under section 162(a)(2) (or any deduction which meets the tests of section 162(a)(2) but is allowable under another provision of this title) by reason of the taxpayer's being away from home in the pursuit of a trade or business (other than the trade or business of renting dwelling units).

280A(g) Special Rule For Certain Rental Use

Notwithstanding any other provision of this section or section 183, if a dwelling unit is used during the taxable year by the taxpayer as a residence and such dwelling unit is actually rented for less than 15 days during the taxable year, then—

280A(g)(1) no deduction otherwise allowable under this chapter because of the rental use of such dwelling unit shall be allowed, and

280A(g)(2) the income derived from such use for the taxable year shall not be included in the gross income of such taxpayer under section 61.

SEC. 351. TRANSFER TO CORPORATION CONTROLLED BY TRANSFEROR

351(a) General Rule

No gain or loss shall be recognized if property is transferred to a corporation by one or more persons solely in exchange for stock in such corporation and immediately after the exchange such person or persons are in control (as defined in section 368(c)) of the corporation.

351(b) Receipt Of Property

If subsection (a) would apply to an exchange but for the fact that there is received, in addition to the stock permitted to be received under subsection (a), other property or money, then—

351(b)(1) gain (if any) to such recipient shall be recognized, but not in excess of—

351(b)(1)(A) the amount of money received, plus

351(b)(1)(B) the fair market value of such other property received;

and

351(b)(2) no loss to such recipient shall be recognized.

351(c) Special Rule

In determining control, for purposes of this section, the fact that any corporate transferor distributes part or all of the stock which it receives in the exchange to its shareholders shall not be taken into account.

351(d) Services, Certain Indebtedness, And Accrued Interest Not Treated As Property

For purposes of this section, stock issued for—

351(d)(1) services,

351(d)(2) indebtedness of the transferee corporation which is not evidenced by a security, or

351(d)(3) interest on indebtedness of the transferee corporation which accrued on or after the beginning of the transferor's holding period for the debt, shall not be considered as issued in return for property.

SEC. 1034. ROLLOVER OF GAIN ON SALE OF PRINCIPAL RESIDENCE

(a) Nonrecognition Of Gain

If property (in this section called "old residence") used by the taxpayer as his principal residence is sold by him and, within a period beginning 2 years before the date of such sale and ending 2 years after such date, property (in this section called "new residence") is purchased and used by the taxpayer as his principal residence, gain (if any) from such sale shall be recognized only to the extent that the taxpayer's adjusted sales price (as defined in subsection (b)) of the old residence exceeds the taxpayer's cost of purchasing the new residence.

(b) Adjusted Sales Price Defined

(1) In General

For purposes of this section, the term "adjusted sales price" means the amount realized, reduced by the aggregate of the expenses for work performed on the old residence in order to assist in its sale.

(2) Limitations

The reduction provided in paragraph (1) applies only to expenses—

(A) for work performed during the 90-day period ending on the day on which the contract to sell the old residence is entered into;

(B) which are paid on or before the 30th day after the date of the sale of the old residence; and

(C) which are—

(i) not allowable as deductions in computing taxable income under IRC Section 63 (defining taxable income), and

(ii) not taken into account in computing the amount realized from the sale of the old residence.

(c) Rules For Application Of Section

For purposes of this section:

(1) An exchange by the taxpayer of his residence for other property shall be treated as a sale of such residence, and the acquisition of a residence on the exchange of property shall be treated as a purchase of such residence.

(2) A residence, any part of which was constructed or reconstructed by the taxpayer, shall be treated as purchased by the taxpayer. In determining the taxpayer's cost of purchasing a residence, there shall be included only so much of his cost as is attributable to the acquisition, construction, reconstruction, and improvements made which are properly chargeable to capital account, during the period specified in subsection (a).

(3) If a residence is purchased by the taxpayer before the date of his sale of the old residence, the purchased residence shall not be treated as his new residence if sold or otherwise disposed of by him before the date of the sale of the old residence.

(4) If the taxpayer, during the period described in subsection (a), purchases more than one residence which is used by him as his principal residence at some time within 2 years after the date of the sale of the old residence, only the last of such residences so used by him after the date of such sale shall constitute the new residence. If a principal residence is sold in a sale to which subsection (d)(2) applies within 2 years after the sale of the old residence, for purposes of applying the preceding sentence with respect to the old residence, the principal residence so sold shall be treated as the last residence used during such 2-year period.

(d) Limitation

(1) In General

Subsection (a) shall not apply with respect to the sale of the taxpayer's residence if within 2 years before the date of such sale the taxpayer sold at a gain other property used by him as his principal residence, and any part of such gain was not recognized by reason of subsection (a).

(2) Subsequent Sale Connected With Commencing Work At New Place

Paragraph (1) shall not apply with respect to the sale of the taxpayer's residence if—

(A) such sale was in connection with the commencement of work by the taxpayer as an employee or as a self-employed individual at a new principal place of work, and

(B) if the residence so sold is treated as the former residence for purposes of IRC Section 217 (relating to moving expenses), the taxpayer would satisfy the conditions of subsection (c) of section 217 (as modified by the other subsections of such section).

(e) Basis Of New Residence

Where the purchase of a new residence results, under subsection (a) or under section 112 (n) of the Internal Revenue Code of 1939, in the nonrecognition of gain on the sale of an old residence, in determining the adjusted basis of the new residence as of any time following the sale of the old residence, the adjustments to basis shall include a reduction by an amount equal to the amount of the gain not so recognized on the sale of the old residence. For this purpose, the amount of the gain not so recognized on the sale of the old residence includes only so much of such gain as is not recognized by reason of the cost, up to such time, of purchasing the new residence.

(f) Tenant-stockholder In A Cooperative Housing Corporation

For purposes of this section, section 1016 (relating to adjustments to basis), and section 1223 (relating to holding period), references to property used by the taxpayer as his principal residence, and references to the residence of a taxpayer, shall include stock held by a tenant-stockholder (as defined in section 216, relating to deduction for amounts representing taxes and interest paid to a cooperative housing corporation) in a cooperative housing corporation (as defined in such section) if—

(1) in the case of stock sold, the house or apartment which the taxpayer was entitled to occupy as such stockholder was used by him as his principal residence, and

(2) in the case of stock purchased, the taxpayer used as his principal residence the house or apartment which he was entitled to occupy as such stockholder.

(g) *Husband And Wife*

If the taxpayer and his spouse, in accordance with regulations which shall be prescribed by the Secretary pursuant to this subsection, consent to the application of paragraph (2) of this subsection, then—

(1) for purposes of this section—

(A) the taxpayer's adjusted sales price of the old residence is the adjusted sales price (of the taxpayer, or of the taxpayer and his spouse) of the old residence, and

(B) the taxpayer's cost of purchasing the new residence is the cost (to the taxpayer, his spouse, or both) of purchasing the new residence (whether held by the taxpayer, his spouse, or the taxpayer and his spouse); and

(2) so much of the gain on the sale of the old residence as is not recognized solely by reason of this subsection, and so much of the adjustment under subsection (e) to the basis of the new residence as results solely from this subsection shall be allocated between the taxpayer and his spouse as provided in such regulations. This subsection shall apply only if the old residence and the new residence are each used by the taxpayer and his spouse as their principal residence. In case the taxpayer and his spouse do not consent to the application of paragraph (2) of this subsection then the recognition of gain on the sale of the old residence shall be determined under this section without regard to the rules provided in this subsection. For purposes of this subsection, except to the extent provided in regulations, in the case of an individual who dies after the date of the sale of the old residence and is married on the date of death, consent to the application of paragraph (2) by such individual's spouse and use of the new residence as the principal residence of such spouse shall be treated as consent and use by such individual.

SEC. 1239. GAIN FROM SALE OF DEPRECIABLE PROPERTY BETWEEN CERTAIN RELATED TAXPAYERS

(a) *Treatment Of Gain As Ordinary Income*

In the case of a sale or exchange of property, directly or indirectly, between related persons, any gain recognized to the transferor shall be treated as ordinary income if such property is, in the hands of the transferee, of a character which is subject to the allowance for depreciation provided in section 167.

(b) *Related Persons*

For purposes of subsection (a), the term "related persons" means—

(1) a person and all entities which are controlled entities with respect to such person,

(2) a taxpayer and any trust in which such taxpayer (or his spouse) is a beneficiary, unless such beneficiary's interest in the trust is a remote contingent interest (within the meaning of section 318(a)(3)(B)(i)).

(c) Controlled Entity Defined

(1) General Rule

For purposes of this section, the term "controlled entity" means, with respect to any person—

(A) a corporation more than 50 percent of the value of the outstanding stock of which is owned (directly or indirectly) by or for such person,

(B) a partnership more than 50 percent of the capital interest or profits interest in which is owned (directly or indirectly) by or for such person, and

(C) any entity which is a related person to such person under paragraph (3), (10), (11), or (12) of section 267(b).

(2) Constructive Ownership

For purposes of this section, ownership shall be determined in accordance with rules similar to the rules under section 267(c) (other than paragraph (3) thereof).

(d) Employer And Related Employee Association

For purposes of subsection (a), the term "related person" also includes—

(1) an employer and any person related to the employer (within the meaning of subsection (b)), and

(2) a welfare benefit fund (within the meaning of section 419(e)) which is controlled directly or indirectly by persons referred to in paragraph (1).

SEC. 1372. PARTNERSHIP RULES TO APPLY FOR FRINGE BENEFIT PURPOSES

1372(a) General Rule

For purposes of applying the provisions of this subtitle which relate to employee fringe benefits—

1372(a)(1) the S corporation shall be treated as a partnership, and

1372(a)(2) any 2–percent shareholder of the S corporation shall be treated as a partner of such partnership.

SEC. 3509. DETERMINATION OF EMPLOYER'S LIABILITY FOR CERTAIN EMPLOYMENT TAXES

3509(a) In General

If any employer fails to deduct and withhold any tax under chapter 24 or subchapter A of chapter 21 with respect to any employee by reason of treating such employee as not being an employee for purposes of such chapter or subchapter, the amount of the employer's liability for—

3509(a)(1) Withholding Taxes

Tax under chapter 24 for such year with respect to such employee shall be determined as if the amount required to be deducted and withheld were equal to 1.5 percent of the wages (as defined in section 3401) paid to such employee.

3509(a)(2) Employee Social Security Tax

Taxes under subchapter A of chapter 21 with respect to such employee shall be determined as if the taxes imposed under such subchapter were 20 percent of the amount imposed under such subchapter without regard to this subparagraph.

3509(b) Employer's Liability Increased Where Employer Disregards Reporting Requirements

3509(b)(1) In General

In the case of an employer who fails to meet the applicable requirements of section 6041(a), 6041A, or 6051 with respect to any employee, unless such failure is due to reasonable cause and not willful neglect, subsection (a) shall be applied with respect to such employee—

3509(b)(1)(A) by substituting "3 percent" for "1.5 percent" in paragraph (1); and

3509(b)(1)(B) by substituting "40 percent" for "20 percent" in paragraph (2).

3509(b)(2) Applicable Requirements

For purposes of paragraph (1), the term "applicable requirements" means the requirements described in paragraph (1) which would be applicable consistent with the employer's treatment of the employee as not being an employee for purposes of chapter 24 or subchapter A of chapter 21.

GLOSSARY

ACCRUAL METHOD. A method of accounting that reflects expenses incurred and income earned for any one tax year.

ADJUSTED BASIS. The original cost of property, plus certain additions and improvements, minus certain deductions such as depreciation allowed or allowable and casualty losses.

ALLOCATION. Apportioning costs or expenses among several assets or use categories.

AMORTIZATION. The allocation (and charge to expense) of the cost or other basis of an intangible asset over the asset's estimated useful life.

APPELLATE DIVISION. Part of the Internal Revenue Service that handles appeals of audit determinations and issues.

ARM'S LENGTH TRANSACTION. A transaction entered into by unrelated parties, each acting in their own best interest.

AUDIT. The examination of a taxpayer's return or other taxable transactions by the Internal Revenue Service in order to determine the correct tax liability.

AUDIT NOTICE. Notification to taxpayer that a tax return will require further documentation.

BASIS. The starting point in determining the gain or loss from the sale or other disposition of an asset, or the depreciation (or depletion or amortization) on an asset.

BED AND BREAKFAST. Form of rental where guests stay for short periods in a home where they receive both lodging and a daily breakfast.

BURDEN OF PROOF. The weight of evidence in a legal case or in a tax proceeding.

BUSINESS ENTITY. Type of business structure; determines rights of owners regarding the business, methods of operation and tax rules that will effect the business; can be sole proprietorship, partnership, LLC, or corporation.

BUSINESS PURPOSE. A justifiable business reason for carrying out a transaction. It has long been established that mere tax avoidance is not an acceptable business purpose.

BUY-SELL AGREEMENT. An arrangement, particularly appropriate in the case of a closely held corporation or a partnership, whereby the surviving owner(s) (shareholders or partners) of the entity agrees to purchase the interest of a withdrawing owner. The buy-sell agreement provides for an orderly disposition of an interest in a business and may aid in setting the value of the interest for death tax purposes.

CID. *See* **Criminal Investigation Division.**

C CORPORATION. A so-called regular corporation that is a separate tax-paying entity and subject to the tax rules contained in Subchapter C of the Internal Revenue Code (as opposed to an S corporation that is subject to the tax rules of Subchapter S of the Code).

C SCHEDULE. Form for determining the profit or loss of a sole proprietorship; submitted with the personal F-1040.

CAPITAL EXPENDITURE. Any amount paid for new buildings or for permanent improvements; any expenditures which add to the value or prolong the life of property or adapt the property to a new or different use. Capital expenditures should be added to the basis of the property improved.

CAPITALIZED. When the costs of an asset are totaled and depreciated or written off over time, as opposed to expensed in the current period.

CARRYOVER BASIS.   When an asset is contributed to a business, it will continue to have the same basis (base for depreciation or determining a gain) as the person who contributed it.

CASH BASIS.   Method of conducting a business and keeping the books; most of the expenses and earnings are reported at the time the cash is paid or received (as compared to accrual method).

CIVIL FRAUD.   Intentional distortion of the truth or facts in order to gain an advantage. (*See also* **Criminal Matter**)

CIVIL MATTER.   Legal issue between parties or agencies where the worst that can happen is imposition of fines and penalties.

CLASSIFIER.   An Internal Revenue Service employee who screens tax returns prior to assignment to audit.

CLASS LIFE/LIVES.   A number of years that establishes the property class and recovery period for most types of property under the General Depreciation System (GDS) and Alternative.

COMMON AREAS.   Portion of the property or home shared by the owner and the guests; may not be included in the calculation of expenses or depreciation on the premises.

COMMUNITY PROPERTY.   Form of ownership of property by husbands and wives in the eleven states that are called community property states; all assets, with some exceptions, acquired during the marriage are considered to be community property.

CONTROLLED CORPORATION.   Corporation where one person owns or has control of more than 50 percent of the outstanding stock, as defined by IRC Section 1239.

CORPORATION.   Form of business entity created by filing in the state where business is located; separates ownership and management functions; amount of loss by owners limited to amount invested; has perpetual existence and ability to transfer shares in the business.

COST BASIS.   The actual cost of the asset, assuming it was purchased at fair market value.

COST RECOVERY ALLOWANCE.   The portion of the cost of an asset written off under ACRS, which replaced the depreciation system as a method for writing off the cost of an asset for most assets placed in service after 1980.

CRIMINAL INVESTIGATION DIVISION. Division within the Internal Revenue Service responsible for investigation of serious legal violations and criminal activities like tax fraud.

CRIMINAL MATTER. Behavior which violates criminal statutes and can subject the person to arrest, prosecution, and incarceration.

DIF. *See* Discriminate Function Program.

DIF SELECTION SCORE. Part of the general program audits by the IRS in which tax returns are rated on their deviation from category norms; high scores lead to selection of returns for scrutiny and audit.

DOL. Department of Labor; federal agency that administers labor laws governing such areas as wages and hours and employment of minors.

DORA. *See* District Office Research Analysis.

DEDUCTIONS. Costs that can be subtracted from income to determine amount of profit.

DEED. Written document by which title to real estate is conveyed.

DEFERRAL OF GAIN. Same as rollover gain; governed by IRC Section 1034, which permits taxes on the profits from the sale of a residence to be deferred if a new residence is purchased.

DEPRECIATION. The deduction of the cost or other basis of a tangible asset over the asset's estimated useful life. (*See also* Cost recovery allowance)

DISCRIMINATE FUNCTION (DIF) PROGRAM. Program of the Internal Revenue Service that screens tax returns against statistical norms for that category of returns; is being phased out.

DIRECT EXPENSE. Costs incurred solely for the use of the customer; can be expensed 100 percent.

DISTRICT OFFICE RESEARCH ANALYSIS (DORA). A new Internal Revenue Service program to analyze tax data and other statistical data available for the purpose of revealing trends.

DOCUMENTARY EVIDENCE. Written records that establish certain facts.

DOCUMENTATION. Evidence provided regarding claims of income or expense and showing written corroboration thereof.

DUE ON SALE CLAUSE. Provision in a mortgage that the entire principal balance will immediately become due if the property is sold or conveyed.

DWELLING UNIT. Residential property; for purposes of the Internal Revenue Code, is defined as having cooking facilities as well as living quarters.

EIN. *See* Employer Identification Number.

EMPLOYER IDENTIFICATION NUMBER. Number used by business to provide information related to employer contributions of FICA; required of all businesses with employees.

ENTITY. An organization or being that possesses separate existence for tax purposes. Examples are corporations, partnerships, estates, and trusts.

EXCLUSIVE USE TEST. Defined by IRC Reg. § 1.280A-2(g); To meet the exclusive use test, the portion of the residence used for business must be used solely for the purpose of carrying on a trade or business. This test will not be satisfied where there is a mixed use (i.e., both business and personal) of the portion in question.

EXPENSE. Those costs incurred in the generation of income that can be currently deducted from earnings.

EXPENSED. A cost that is deducted from earnings at the time it is incurred, as contrasted to being capitalized, when the cost is depreciated over time.

FICA. Federal Insurance Contribution Act; also known as the social security contribution withheld from employee pay.

FOIA REQUEST. *See* Freedom of Information Act request.

FTD. Federal Tax Deposit; form used by employers to submit tax payments to the Internal Revenue Service.

F-1040. *See* Form 1040.

F-1099. *See* Form 1099.

FAIR MARKET VALUE. The amount at which property would change hands between a willing buyer and a willing seller, neither being under any compulsion to buy or sell and both having reasonable knowledge of the relevant facts.

FAIR RENTAL VALUE. The amount that a property could be rented for on the open market.

FIELD AUDIT DIVISION. Division within the Internal Revenue Service that examines business returns.

FIFTH AMENDMENT TO THE CONSTITUTION. Guarantees against self-incrimination in criminal matters; a person cannot be compelled to give testimony against himself or herself.

FORM 1040. Form used by individual taxpayers to calculate, report, and pay personal income taxes.

FORM 1099. Form provided to independent contractors showing miscellaneous income.

FREEDOM OF INFORMATION ACT REQUEST. Method of securing access to government documents that would otherwise be unavailable.

GENERAL PROGRAM AUDITS. Routine audits of tax returns performed by the Internal Revenue Service; can include office audits or field audits.

GOODWILL. An intangible property such as the advantage or benefit received in property beyond its mere value. It is not confined to a name but can also be attached to a particular area where business is transacted, to a list of customers, or to other elements of value in business as a going concern.

HOBBY LOSS. A nondeductible loss arising from a personal hobby as contrasted with an activity engaged in for profit. Generally, the law provides a refutable presumption that an activity is engaged in for profit if profits are earned during any three or more years during a five-year period.

I-9. Form required by the Immigration Service by employers of alien workers.

ICE. *See* Informant's Claim Examiner.

IRC. *See* Internal Revenue Code.

IRS. *See* Internal Revenue Service.

INDEPENDENT CONTRACTOR. A self-employed person who provides services for another; distinguished from an employee by IRC Section 530.

INDIRECT COSTS. Costs which do not qualify as direct costs but are of some benefit to the business or customers; amount to be expensed is determined by the proportion of the premises used solely by the guests.

INFORMANTS. People who provide information on taxpayers to the IRS with the hope that there will be a reward for them.

INFORMANT'S CLAIM EXAMINER. Monitors the cases generated by informants and arranges for rewards when appropriate.

INTEREST. Money paid for the use of money; rate to determine amount to pay for use of money; usually deductible as an expense.

INTERNAL REVENUE CODE. The regulations that are administered by the Internal Revenue Service and govern the calculation and collection of income taxes.

INTERNAL REVENUE SERVICE. Federal agency responsible for administering the tax code, collecting taxes, and enforcing tax regulations.

JOINT TENANCY. Property held by two or more owners, where each has an undivided interest in the property. Joint tenancy includes the right of survivorship, which means that upon the death of an owner, his or her share passes to the surviving owner(s).

LLC. *See* Limited Liability Company.

LEASE. Written document by which possession of land and/or improvements are given by the owner to another for a fixed period of time at a specified rent.

LEGAL RIGHTS. Term used to refer to Miranda warnings, where a person who is being charged with a criminal offense is told of the right to remain silent and avoid self-incrimination and the right to have an attorney; usually signals to the person that there are criminal charges pending.

LIMITED LIABILITY COMPANY.   Form of business entity permitted in some states; permits owners to limit financial risks; treated as a partnership for tax purposes.

LIMITED PARTNERSHIP.   A partnership formed by two or more persons having as members one or more general partners and one or more limited partners with limited liability.

LISTED PROPERTY.   Property that includes passenger automobiles; other transportation vehicles; property of a type used for entertainment, recreation, or amusement; computers and their peripheral equipment (except if used exclusively at a regular business establishment); and cellular telephones or similar telecommunications equipment.

LOSS.   Occurs when a business's expenses exceed income.

LOSS LIMITATION RULES.   Restrictions on the type and amounts that a business can expense against the earnings of the business if the hobby loss rules or the vacation home rules apply.

MACS.   *See* Midwest Automated Compliance System.

MSSP.   *See* Market Segment Specialization Program.

MARKET SEGMENT SPECIALIZATION PROGRAM.   New Internal Revenue Service program to target types of businesses and train auditors to know an industry in depth before performing audits; 40 industries have been selected.

MIDWEST AUTOMATED COMPLIANCE SYSTEM.   Software program developed by the Internal Revenue Service to search and locate specific tax returns on a wide range of criteria.

NET PROFIT.   Revenue less all expenses (also called net income). Other elements involved in computing net profit include extraordinary items (net of tax) and cumulative effect of a change in accounting principle (net of tax).

NINETY-DAY LETTER (90-DAY LETTER).   Also called Statutory Notice of Deficiency; sent to taxpayer when the IRS and the taxpayer cannot reach an agreement.

NONRESIDENTIAL REAL PROPERTY.   Most real property other than residential rental property.

NONTAXABLE EXCHANGE.   An exchange of property in which any gain or loss realized is not recognized (included in or deducted from income) for tax purposes. This usually involves exchanges of like-kind property.

OMBUDSMAN.   Person with a government agency who serves as a liaison for citizens working with that agency.

ONE-TIME EXCLUSION.   As established by IRC Section 121 for homeowners over 55 to write off up to $125,000 of deferred gains on their residence.

OFFICE AUDIT DIVISION.   Division within the Internal Revenue Service that examines the tax returns of individuals.

PARTNERSHIP.   A partnership is treated as a conduit and is not subject to taxation. Various items of partnership income, expenses, gains, and losses flow through to the individual partners and are reported on each partner's personal income tax return.

PARTNERSHIP AGREEMENT.   Agreement among partners, usually written, defining their ownership, rights, and operation of the business.

PASSIVE ACTIVITY LOSS.   Any loss from (1) activities in which the taxpayer does not materially participate, (2) rental activities, or (3) tax shelter activities.

PLACED IN SERVICE.   The time that property is ready and available for a specified use whether in business, an activity to produce income, a tax-exempt activity, or a personal activity.

PERSONAL PROPERTY.   Generally, all property other than real estate. Personal property can also refer to property not used in a taxpayer's trade or business or held for the production or collection of income.

PERSONAL RESIDENCE.   The sale of a personal residence generally results in the recognition of capital gain (but not loss). However, the gain may be deferred if the adjusted sales price of the old residence is reinvested in the purchase of a new residence within certain prescribed time periods.

PERSONAL USE DAYS.   As defined by IRC Section 280A, a day when a room is used by someone other than a guest.

PERSONAL USE TEST.   Test established by IRC Section 280A to determine if property will be affected by loss limitation rules.

POWER OF ATTORNEY.   Specifically with regard to the Internal Revenue Service, an authorization to permit the IRS to communicate an individual's designated representative regarding the taxpayer's tax matters; Form 2848.

PRINCIPAL RESIDENCE.   Home for most of the year; in a Bed and Breakfast, the portion of the structure that the operator occupies.

PROFIT.   The amount of earnings left after business expenses are subtracted from receipts.

PROPERTY CLASS.   A category for property under MACRS. It generally determines the depreciation method, recovery period, and convention.

REAL PROPERTY.   Real estate and all improvements to it.

REASONABLE BUSINESSMAN TEST.   Court test to determine the reasonableness or appropriateness of a decision by comparing it to what a hypothetical businessman would do in similar circumstances; used to determine if certain acts were consistent with good business practice.

RECAPTURE.   When a depreciated asset is sold for more than the amount of its depreciated value/basis, the difference must be recaptured and treated as taxable gain.

RECOVERY PERIOD.   The number of years over which the basis (cost) of an item of property is recovered.

RENTED DAY.   As defined by IRC Section 280A, a day in which a dwelling unit was rented for fair rental value.

REPETITIVE AUDITS.   Provide relief when the taxpayer has been audited more than two years in a row for the same issue.

REPRESENTATIVE.   Person chosen to represent a taxpayer in dealings with the Internal Revenue Service; designated with their power of attorney; need not be an attorney or CPA.

RESIDENTIAL RENTAL PROPERTY.   Real property, generally buildings or structures, if 80 percent or more of its annual gross rental income is from dwelling units.

REVENUE AGENT.   Employee of the Internal Revenue Service who conducts field audits and works with business returns.

ROLL-OVER GAINS.   Deferral of profit from the sale of a residence; if another residence is purchased for more money, no tax will be paid on the profit.

SSN.   *See* Social Security number.

S CORPORATION.   An elective provision permitting certain small business corporations (IRC Section 1361) and their shareholder elect (IRC Section 1362) to be treated for income tax purposes in accordance with the operating rules of IRC Sections 1363–1379. Of major significance are the facts that S status avoids the corporate income tax and corporate losses can be claimed by the shareholders.

SCHEDULE C.   Form used by self-employed persons (sole proprietorships) to calculate the earnings and expenses of the business; treated as a portion of.

SCHEDULE SE.   Form used by self-employed individuals to calculate their FICA contribution plus the employer contribution.

SECTION 179 PROPERTY.   Assets that may be fully expensed during the year acquired, rather than capitalized and depreciated over the useful life of the asset. Section 179 is subject to a maximum $17,500 in 1995.

SELF-EMPLOYMENT TAX.   Based on the net profits from a business; includes FICA plus employer's portion; reported on Form SE.

SELF-INCRIMINATION.   Protected against by the Fifth Amendment to the Constitution; no citizen can be compelled to give evidence against himself or herself.

SOCIAL SECURITY NUMBER.   Identification number to contribute and receive FICA contributions; also the ID of a sole proprietorship unless it has employees.

SOLE-PROPRIETORSHIP.   A business that is owned and managed for a profit by one person.

STANDARD MILEAGE RATE.   The established amount for optional use in determining a tax deduction for automobiles instead of deducting depreciation and actual operating expenses.

START-UP COSTS. One-time costs incurred in the beginning phase of a business; may be for both tangible and intangible assets; most must be capitalized and amortized over time.

STATUTE OF LIMITATIONS. Provisions of the law that specify the maximum period of time in which action may be taken on a past event. IRC Sections 6501–6504 contain the limitation periods applicable to the IRS for additional assessments, and IRC Sections 6511–6515 relate to refund claims by taxpayers.

STATUTORY NOTICE OF DEFICIENCY. Commonly referred to as a 90-day letter, this notice is sent to a taxpayer upon request, upon the expiration of the 30-day letter, or upon exhaustion by the taxpayer of his or her administrative remedies before the IRS. The notice gives the taxpayer 90 days in which to file a petition with the U.S. Tax Court. If such a petition is not filed, the IRS will issue a demand for payment of the assessed deficiency.

STRAIGHT-LINE DEPRECIATION. Form of calculating depreciation which is equal each year over the useful life of the asset.

STRAIGHT-LINE METHOD. A way to figure depreciation for property that ratably deducts the same amount for each year in the recovery period. The rate (in percentage terms) is determined by dividing 1.0 by the number of years in the recovery period.

STRUCTURAL COMPONENTS. Parts that together form an entire structure, such as a building. The term includes such parts of a building as walls, partitions, floors, and ceilings, as well as any permanent coverings such as paneling or tiling, windows and doors, and all components of a central air-conditioning or heating system including motors, compressors, pipes, and ducts. It also includes plumbing fixtures such as sinks, bathtubs, electrical wiring and lighting fixtures, and other parts that form the structure.

TCMP. *See* Taxpayer Compliance Measurement Program.

TAXABLE EXCHANGE. An exchange of property in which the gain or loss is recognized (included in or deducted from income) for tax purposes.

TAX COURT. Federal Court available to taxpayers to appeal Internal Revenue Service rulings and assessments.

TAXPAYER'S BILL OF RIGHTS. Statement of policy to protect the rights of taxpayers before the Internal Revenue Service.

TAXPAYER COMPLIANCE MEASUREMENT PROGRAM. Internal Revenue Service program where tax returns are randomly selected and every income source and all deductions require documentation; program is being phased out.

TENANCY IN COMMON. A form of co-ownership that permits any number of co-owners, with any interests, and without the right of survivorship.

THIRTY-DAY LETTER (30-DAY LETTER). Provided to taxpayer after an audit to inform him or her what they must do or pay within 30 days to prevent a notice of deficiency being filed.

TIPS. Gratuities provided for services; must be reported like other income.

UNADJUSTED DEPRECIABLE BASIS. The basis of an item of property for purposes of figuring gain on a sale without taking into account any depreciation taken in earlier years but with adjustments for amortization, the Section 179 deduction, any deduction claimed for clean-fuel vehicles or clean-fuel vehicle refueling property, and any electric vehicle credit.

USEFUL LIFE. An estimate of how long an item of property can be expected to be usable in trade or business or to produce income. Under MACRS, you recover the cost of property over a set recovery period. The recovery period is based on the property class to which your property is assigned. The class your property is assigned to is generally determined by its class life.

VACATION HOME. The IRC places restrictions upon taxpayers who rent their residences or vacation homes for part of the tax year. The restrictions may result in a scaling down of expense deductions for such taxpayers.

W-2. Form used to report wages and taxes for an employee.

W-4. Form used to determine the number of dependents and amount of tax to be withheld from paychecks.

W-9. Form used to request an Employer Identification Number (EIN), necessary when a business has employees.

WILL. Document used to convey a person's real and personal property after they die.

INDEX

Personal property, 31, 32
PIA, *see* Principal industry activity
Place of business, 94
Power of attorney, 97, 98
Practice before the IRS, 98
Pretrial settlements, 105
Principal industry activity (PIA), 91
Professional Association of
    Innkeepers International (PAII),
    8, 15, 19, 55, 112
Profit motive, 10, 36

R

Record keeping, 12, 18, 20, 25, 40,
    58
Records, 3, 22, 25, 42, 46, 48, 49, 73,
    94, 95, 96, 97, 98, 100, 101, 108
    accounting records, 42
    alternative records, 98
    documentation, 25, 42, 89, 93, 96,
        98, 100, 101, 105
    lost or destroyed, 98
    marginal documentation, 100
    missing documents, 98
Recovery period, 28, 29, 31, 32, 35
Regulatory agencies, 8, 9, 12
Representation, 93, 95
Representative, 3, 7, 69, 97, 98, 101,
    104
Residential property, 28
Revenue
    by number of rooms and overall,
        228–230
    by years in business and overall,
        231–233
Revenue agent, 92, 94, 96
Reward, 92, 109
Rights of taxpayers, *see* Taxpayer's
    Bill of Rights
Rights to privacy, 96
Roll-over gains, 39

S

S corporation, 39, 68, 74, 76, 78,
    83, 84, 85, 87

S election, 59, 83
Schedule C, 9, 32, 43
Schedule SE, 44, 45
Section 179, 32, 33, 34, 35
Self-employment tax, 44
Self-incrimination, 88, 95
SIC, *see* Standard Industry Activity
    Codes
Sole proprietorship, 24, 39, 40, 41,
    70, 74, 76
SS-4, 54
Standard Industry Activity Codes
    (SIC), 91
Statutory Notice of Deficiency
    (Ninety-Day Letter), 104, 105
    example of, 241–243
Subcontractors, 47

T

Tax court petition, 105
Tax preparers, 6, 92
Taxpayer Compliance
    Measurement Program
    (TCMP), 2, 89, 90, 91
Taxpayer's Bill of Rights, 88
Taxpayer's rights, 205–208
TCMP, *see* Taxpayer Compliance
    Measurement Program
Thirty-Day Letter, 103, 104
Trade associations, 110
Transfer of ownership, 40, 76
Transient, 28, 61

U

Useful life, 28, 31, 32, 33

V

Vacation home rules, 56, 60, 62

W

W-4, 54
Waiver of restrictions on
    assessment, 103

INDEX OF IRS FORMS

INDEX OF INTERNAL REVENUE CODE